Boys over Flowers
Hana Yori Dango
Vol. #15
Shôjo Edition

Story and Art by
Yoko Kamio

English Adaptation/Gerard Jones
Translation/JN Productions
Touch-up Art & Lettering/Stephen Dutro
Cover & Interior Design/Yuki Ameda
Editor/Ian Robertson

Managing Editor/Annette Roman
Director of Production/Noboru Watanabe
Vice President of Publishing/Alvin Lu
Sr. Director of Acquisitions/Rika Inouye
Vice President of Sales & Marketing/Liza Coppola
Publisher/Hyoe Narita

Printed in Canada

Published by VIZ Media, LLC
P.O. Box 77010
San Francisco, CA 94107

10 9 8 7 6 5 4 3 2 1
First printing, November 2005

RATED T FOR TEEN
PARENTAL ADVISORY
BOYS OVER FLOWERS is rated T for Teen and is recommended for ages 13 and up. May contain sexual themes.

Story thus far

It's the start of a new year, and Tsukushi befriends a boy named Junpei Oribe, who comes from a middle-class background much like her own. But Junpei has a secret job as a model. By a twist of fate, Tsukushi lands on the cover of a magazine posing with Junpei—which, of course, makes Tsukasa blow his top.

Then, one morning, Tsukushi finds a "red slip" in her locker for the second time! Once again, she is targeted for bullying by the students of Eitoku, and the viciousness only escalates. As Tsukushi is being beaten up by a boy, Junpei arrives to save her...

BOYS over FLOWERS

Hana Yori Dango

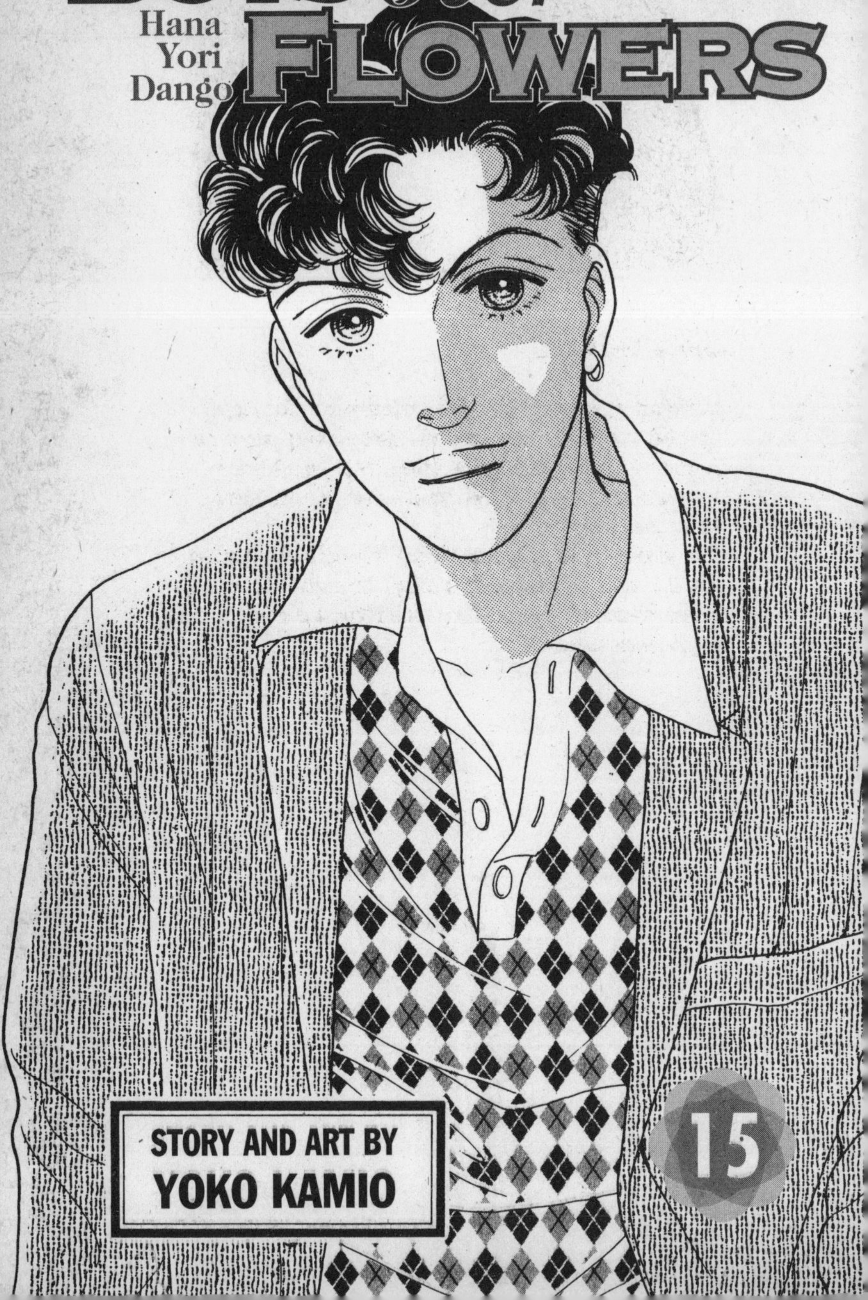

15

STORY AND ART BY
YOKO KAMIO

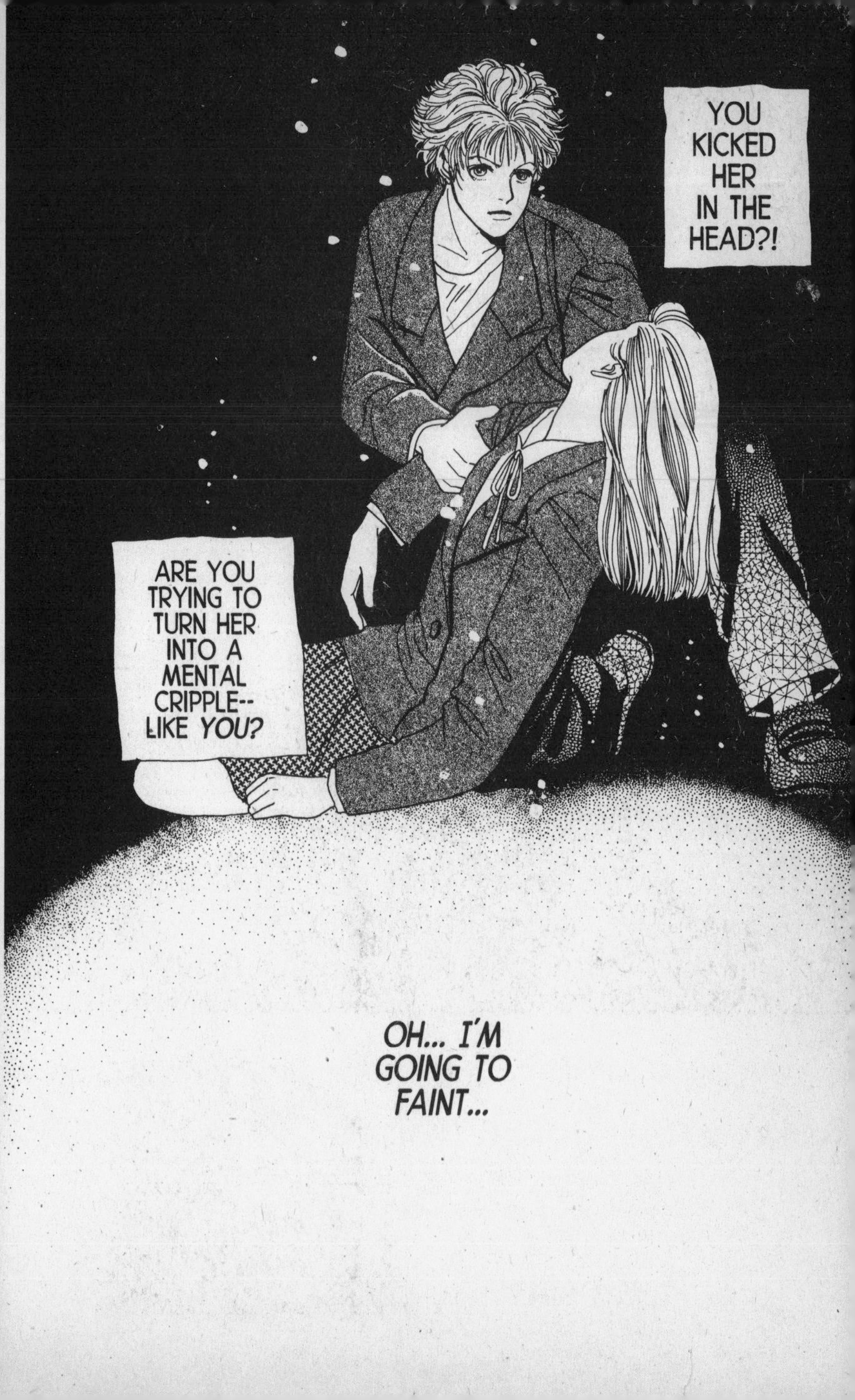
YOU KICKED HER IN THE HEAD?!
ARE YOU TRYING TO TURN HER INTO A MENTAL CRIPPLE-- LIKE *YOU?*
OH... I'M GOING TO FAINT...

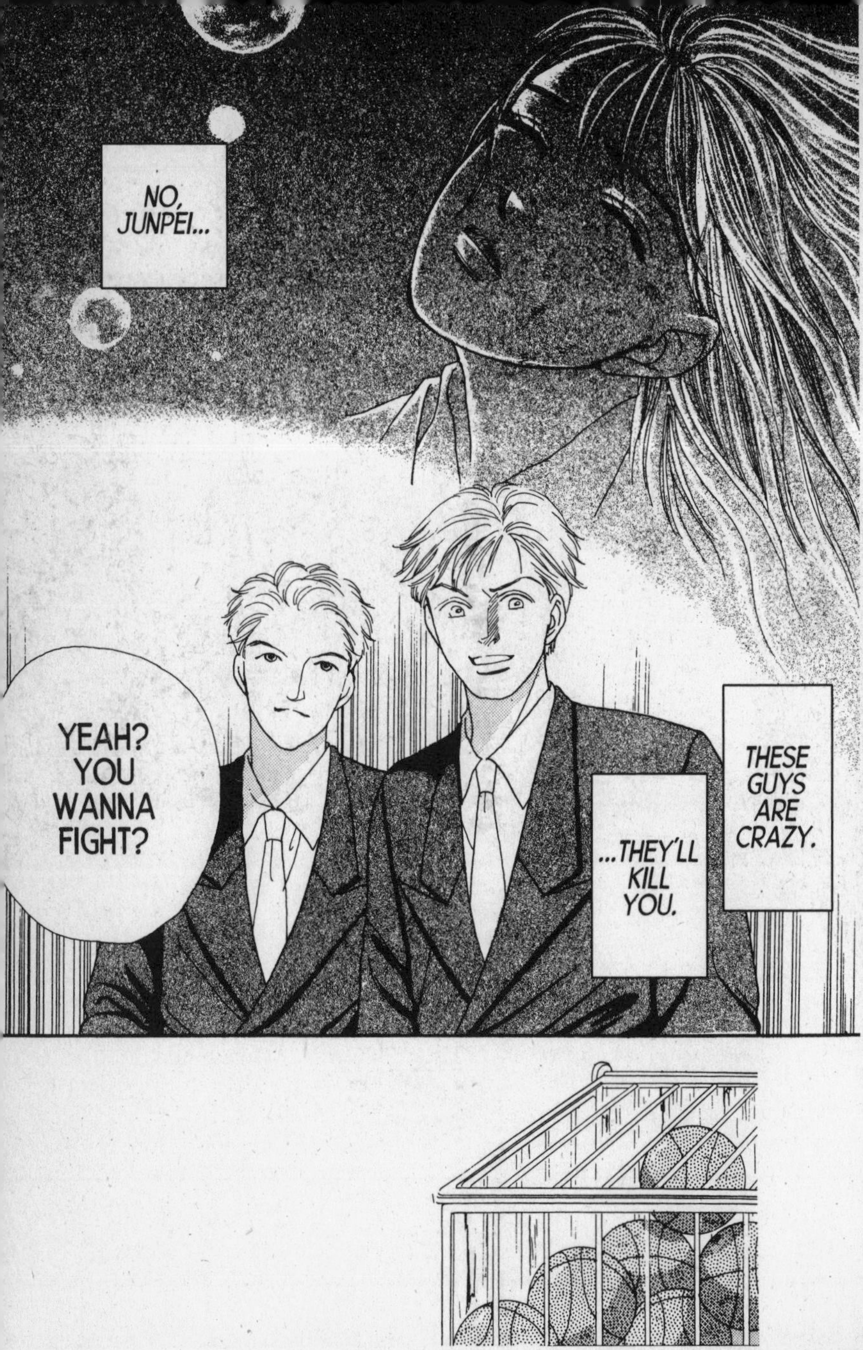
NO, JUNPEI...
THESE GUYS ARE CRAZY.
...THEY'LL KILL YOU.
YEAH? YOU WANNA FIGHT?

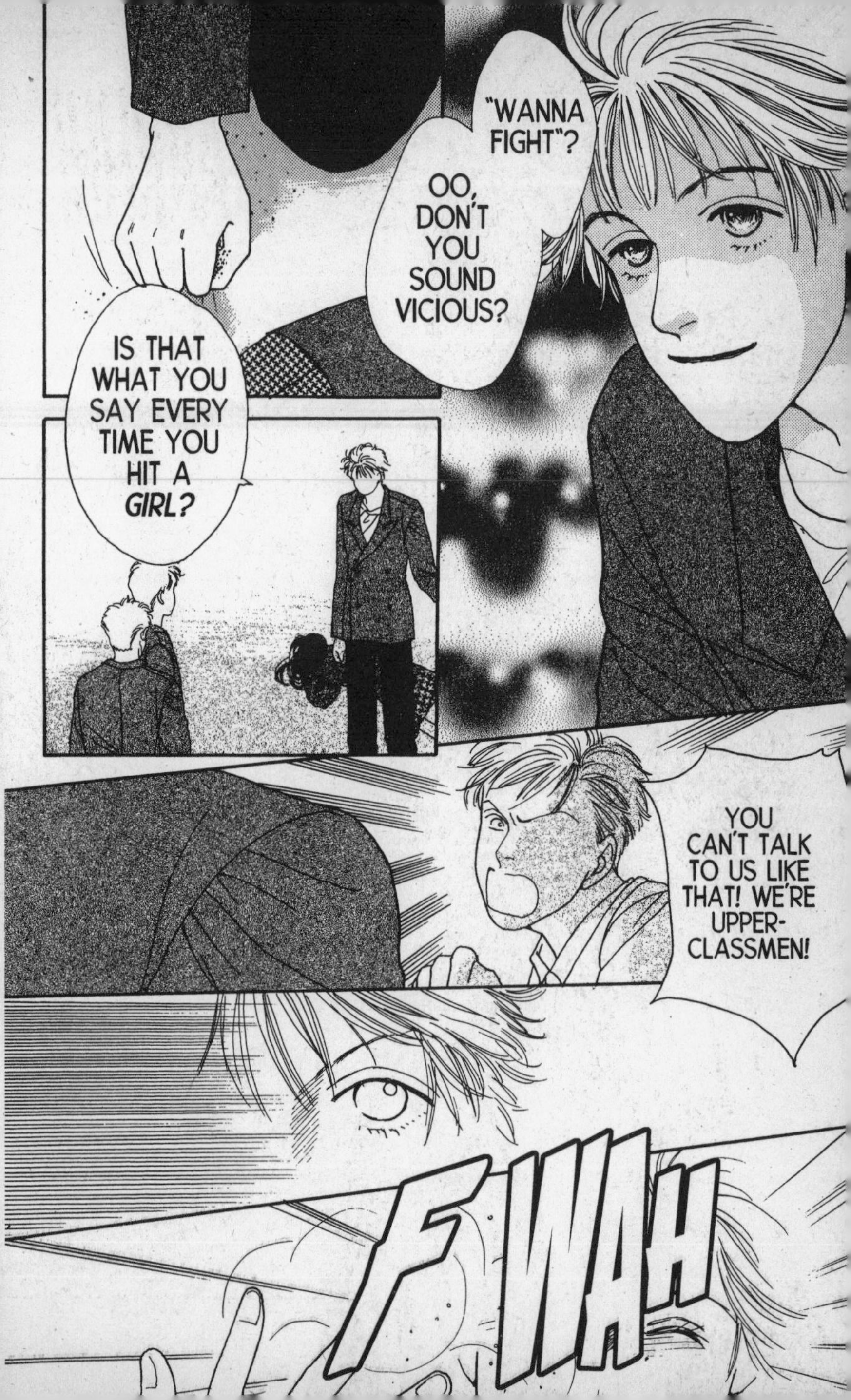
"WANNA FIGHT"?
OO, DON'T YOU SOUND VICIOUS?
IS THAT WHAT YOU SAY EVERY TIME YOU HIT A *GIRL?*
YOU CAN'T TALK TO US LIKE THAT! WE'RE UPPER-CLASSMEN!
FWAH

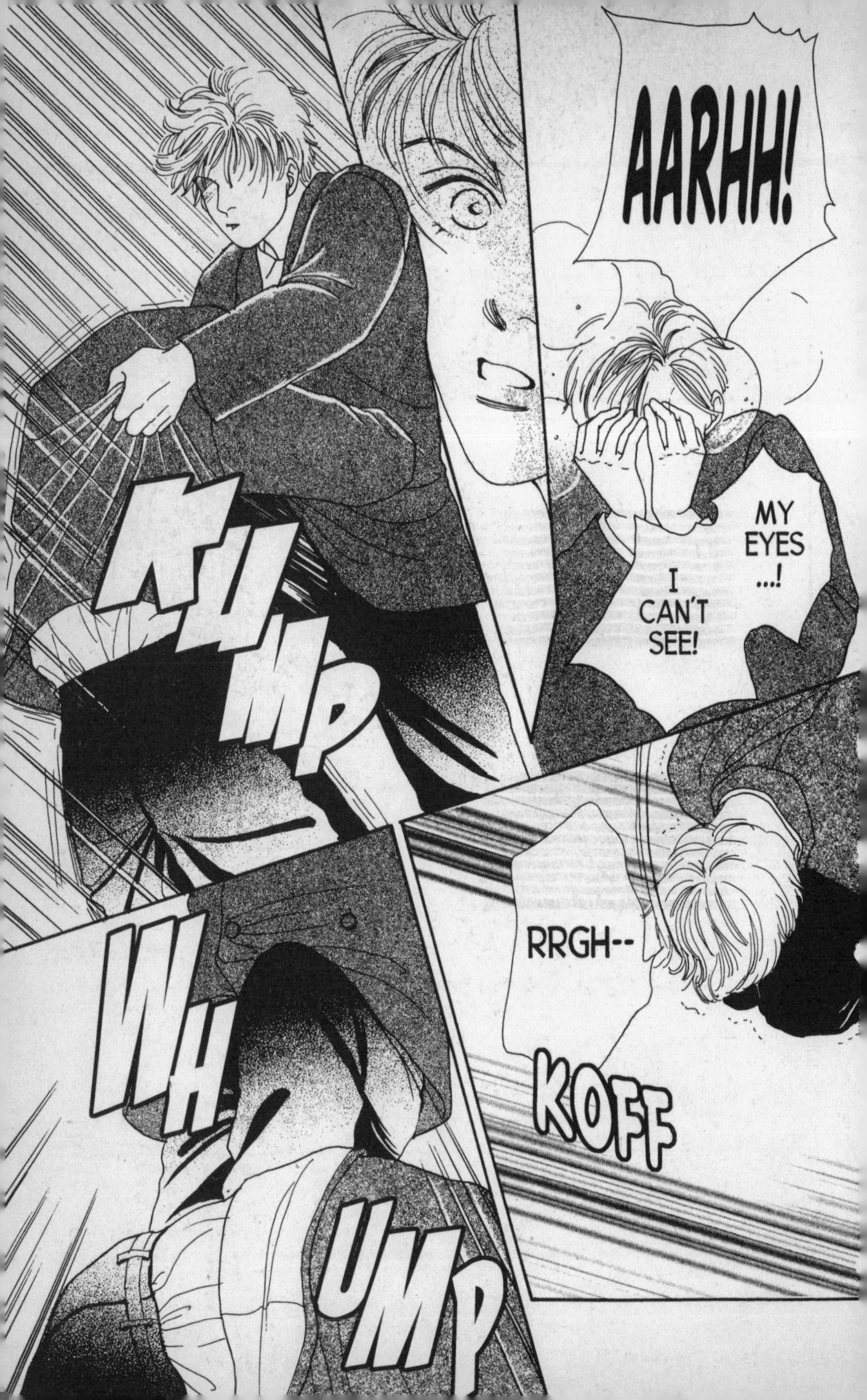
AARHH!
MY EYES ...!
I CAN'T SEE!
RRGH--
KOFF
WHUMP

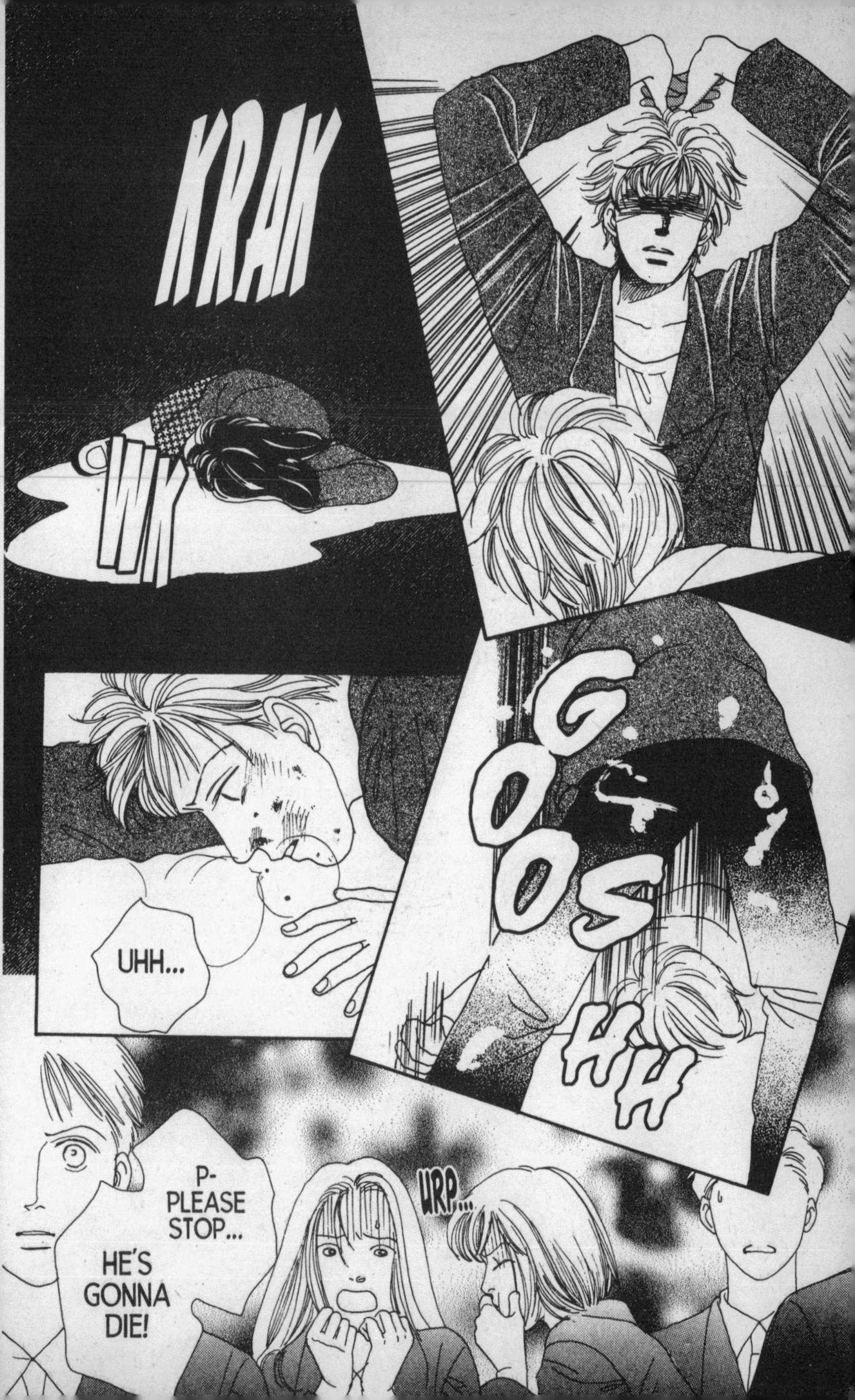
KRAK
UHH...
URP...
P-PLEASE STOP...
HE'S GONNA DIE!

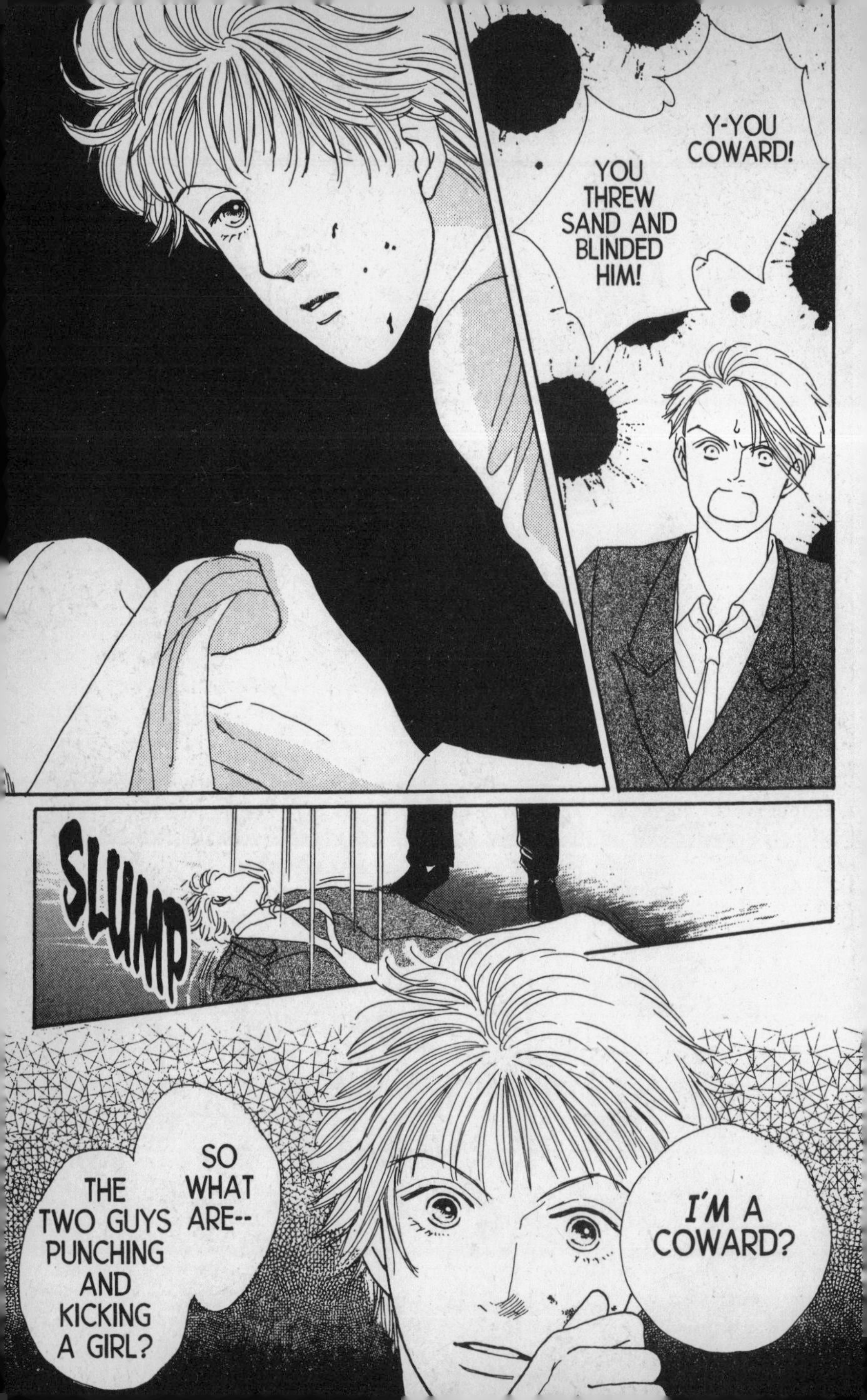
Y-YOU COWARD!
YOU THREW SAND AND BLINDED HIM!
SLUMP
I'M A COWARD?
SO WHAT ARE-- THE TWO GUYS PUNCHING AND KICKING A GIRL?

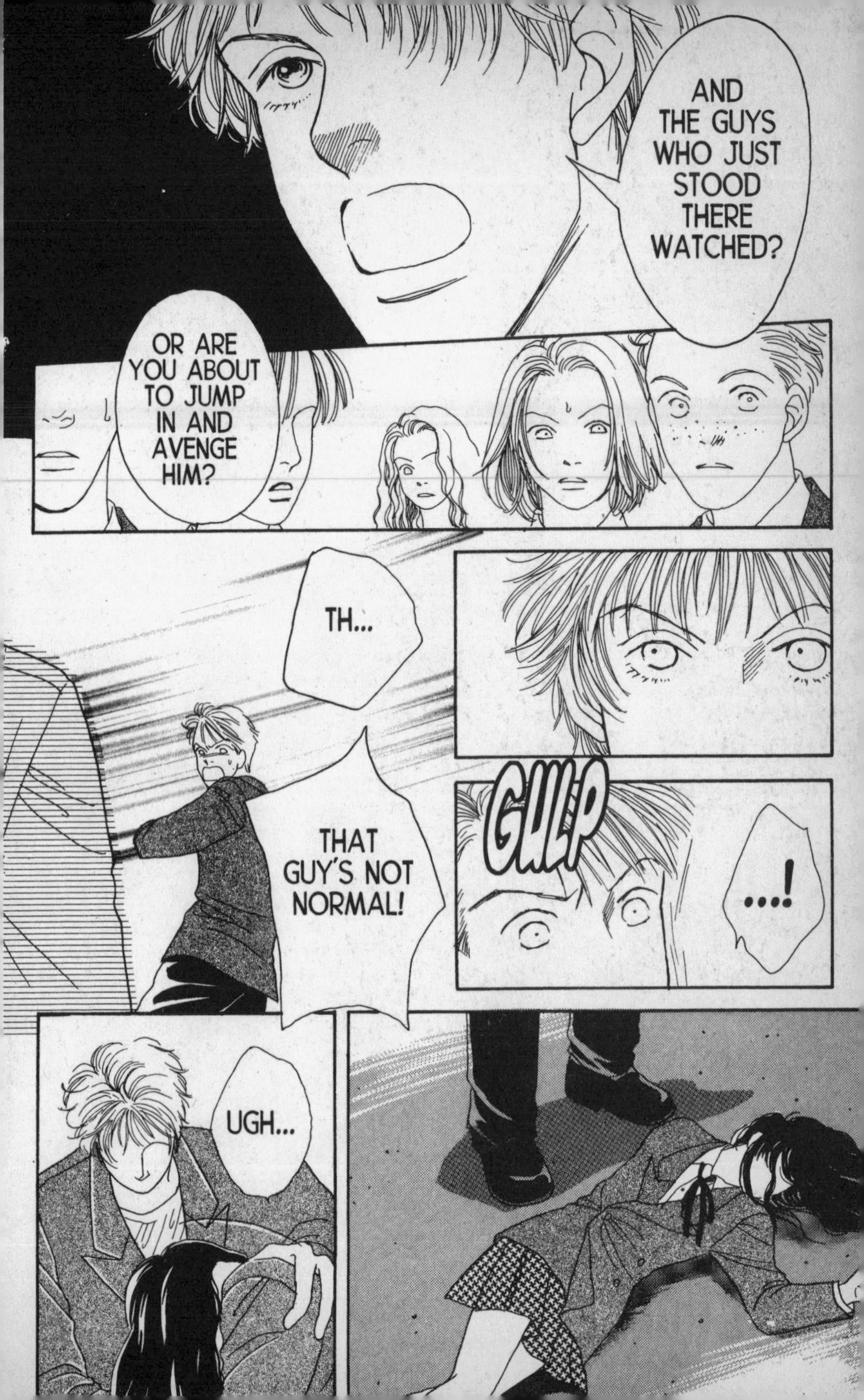
AND THE GUYS WHO JUST STOOD THERE WATCHED?
OR ARE YOU ABOUT TO JUMP IN AND AVENGE HIM?
GULP
...!
TH...
THAT GUY'S NOT NORMAL!
UGH...

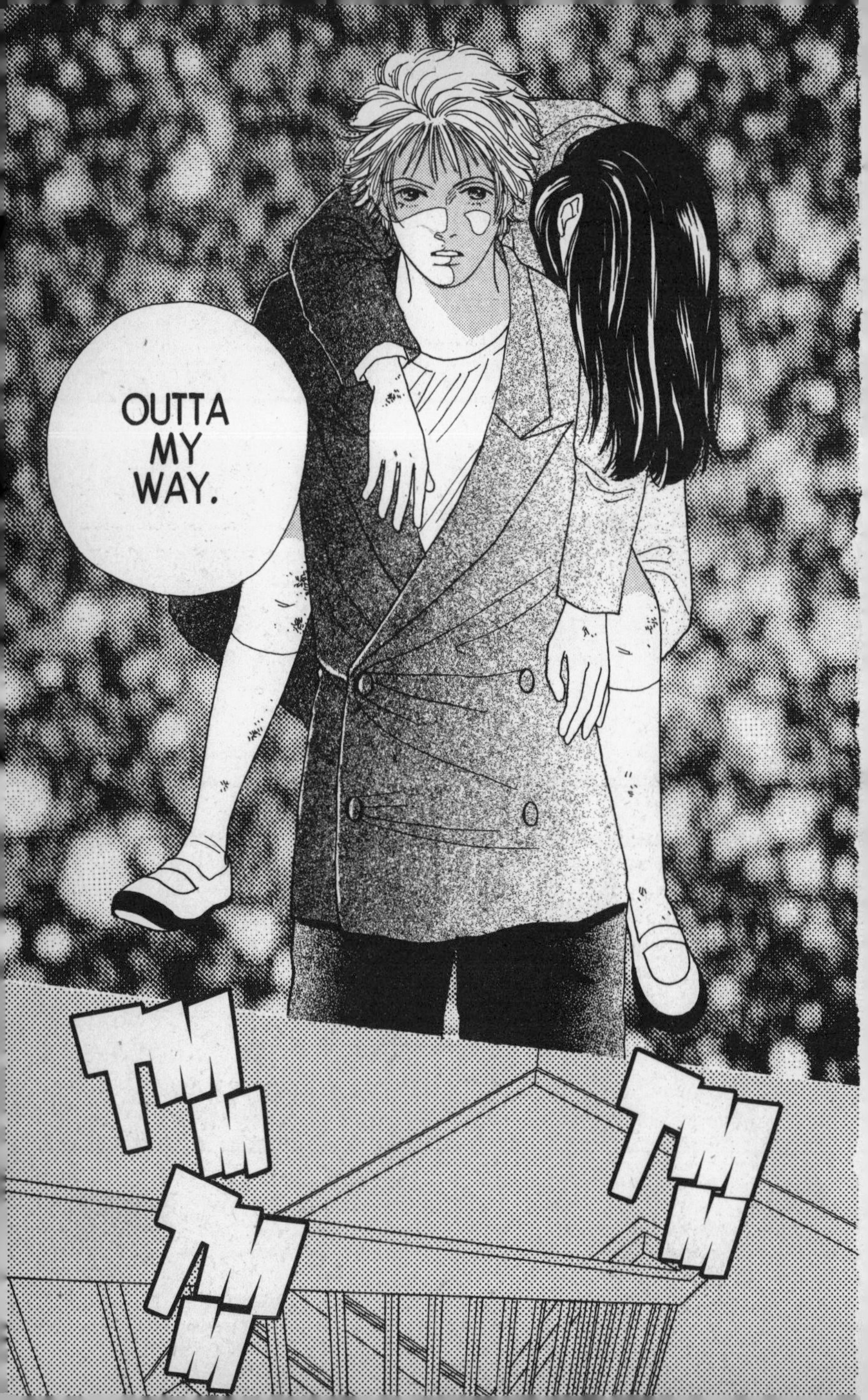
OUTTA MY WAY.
TMM
TMM
TMM

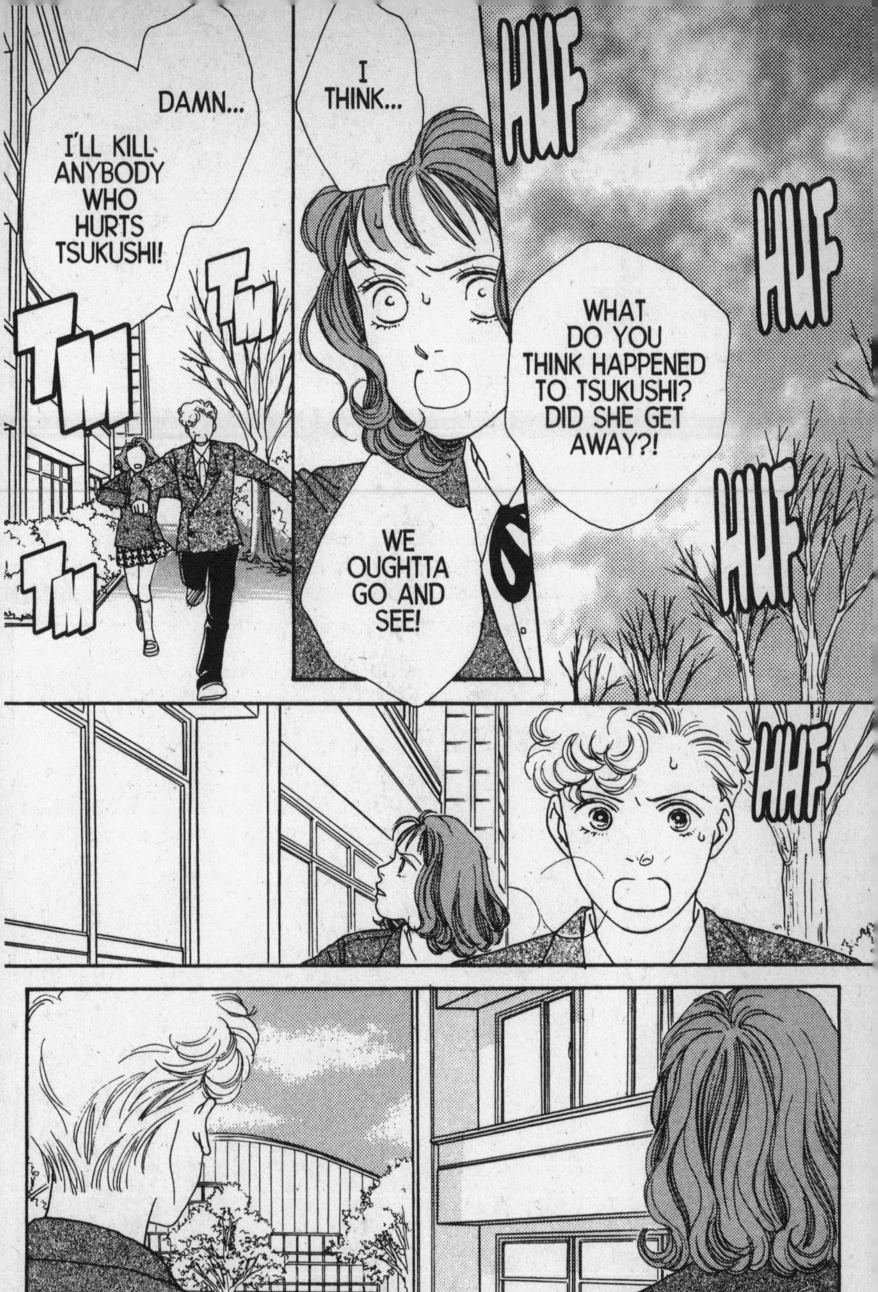
HUF
HUF
WHAT DO YOU THINK HAPPENED TO TSUKUSHI? DID SHE GET AWAY?!
HUF
I THINK...
WE OUGHTTA GO AND SEE!
DAMN...
I'LL KILL ANYBODY WHO HURTS TSUKUSHI!
TM
TM
TM
HUF

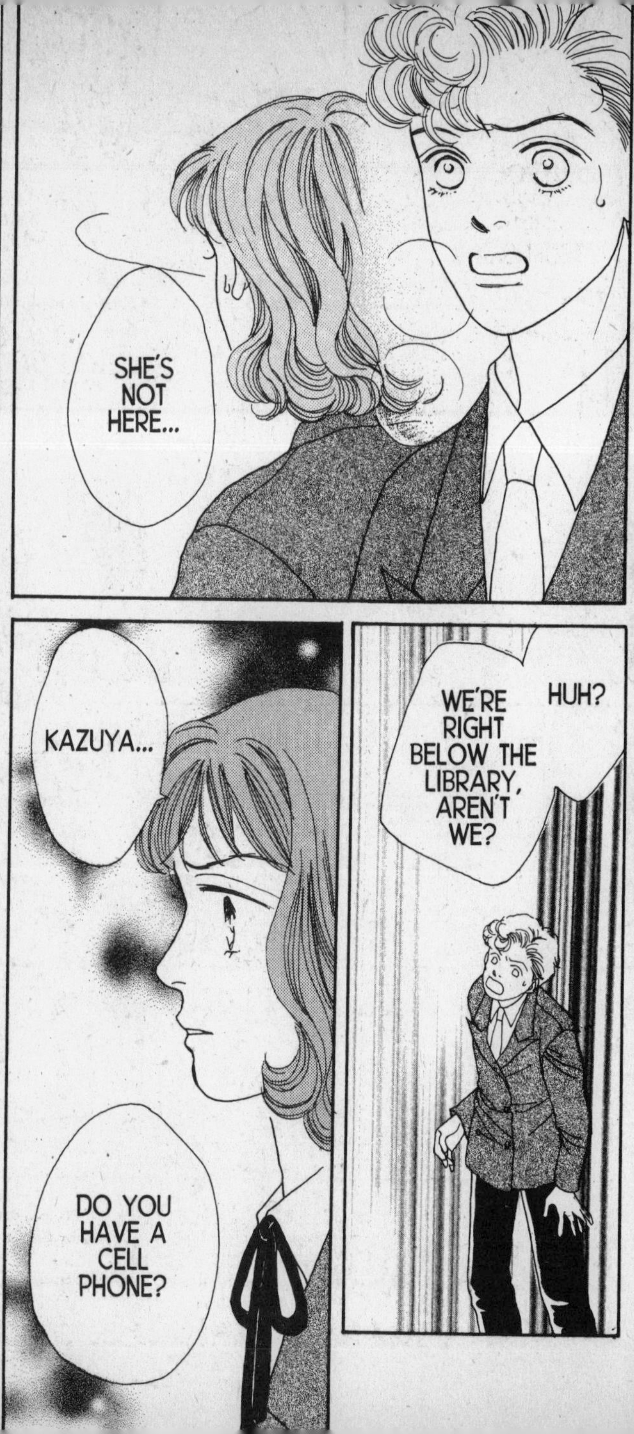
SHE'S NOT HERE...
HUH?
WE'RE RIGHT BELOW THE LIBRARY, AREN'T WE?
KAZUYA...
DO YOU HAVE A CELL PHONE?

Hello!

It's Volume 15, already!

I recently celebrated my 100th installment. Whew! 100! I've been at this for 4-1/2 years, so I guess it's to be expected...but when you see the number written, it's kind of amazing!

I've been able to continue so long because of all your support. Thank you so much for all your letters!!

I even get letters from abroad. They make me so happy!

It's not likely I'll reach 200 installments...but I'll keep drawing as long as I can!

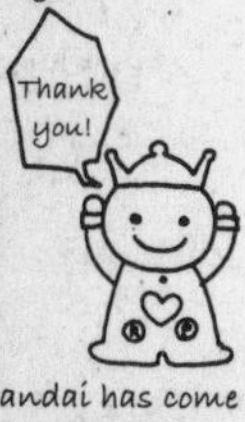
Thank you!

Bandai has come out with Boys over Flowers merchandise. I especially like this "VoiCell."

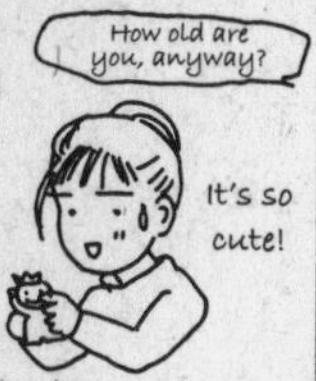
How old are you, anyway?
It's so cute!

And convenient... I can leave messages!

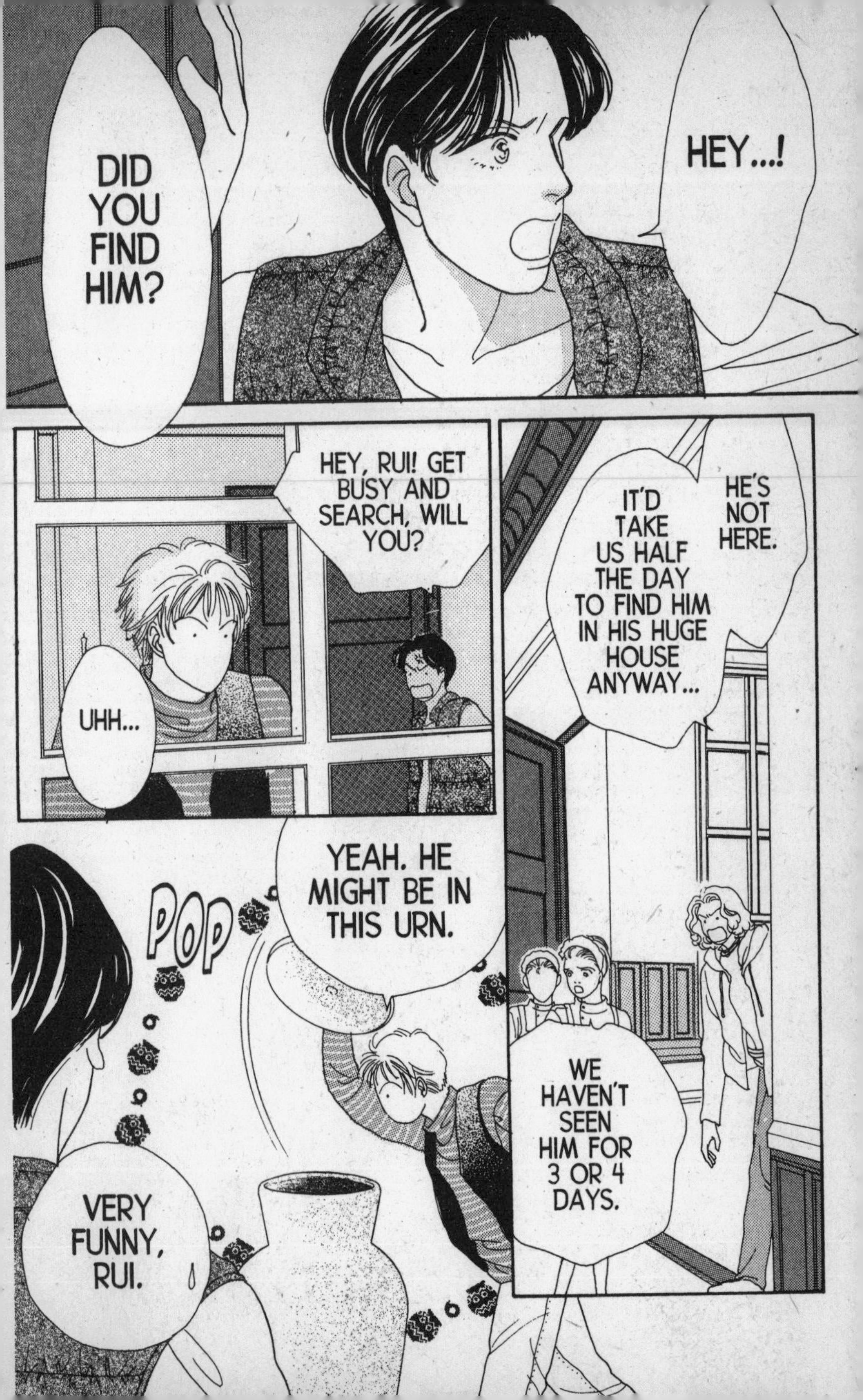
HEY...!
DID YOU FIND HIM?
HE'S NOT HERE.
IT'D TAKE US HALF THE DAY TO FIND HIM IN HIS HUGE HOUSE ANYWAY...
WE HAVEN'T SEEN HIM FOR 3 OR 4 DAYS.
HEY, RUI! GET BUSY AND SEARCH, WILL YOU?
UHH...
YEAH. HE MIGHT BE IN THIS URN.
POP
VERY FUNNY, RUI.

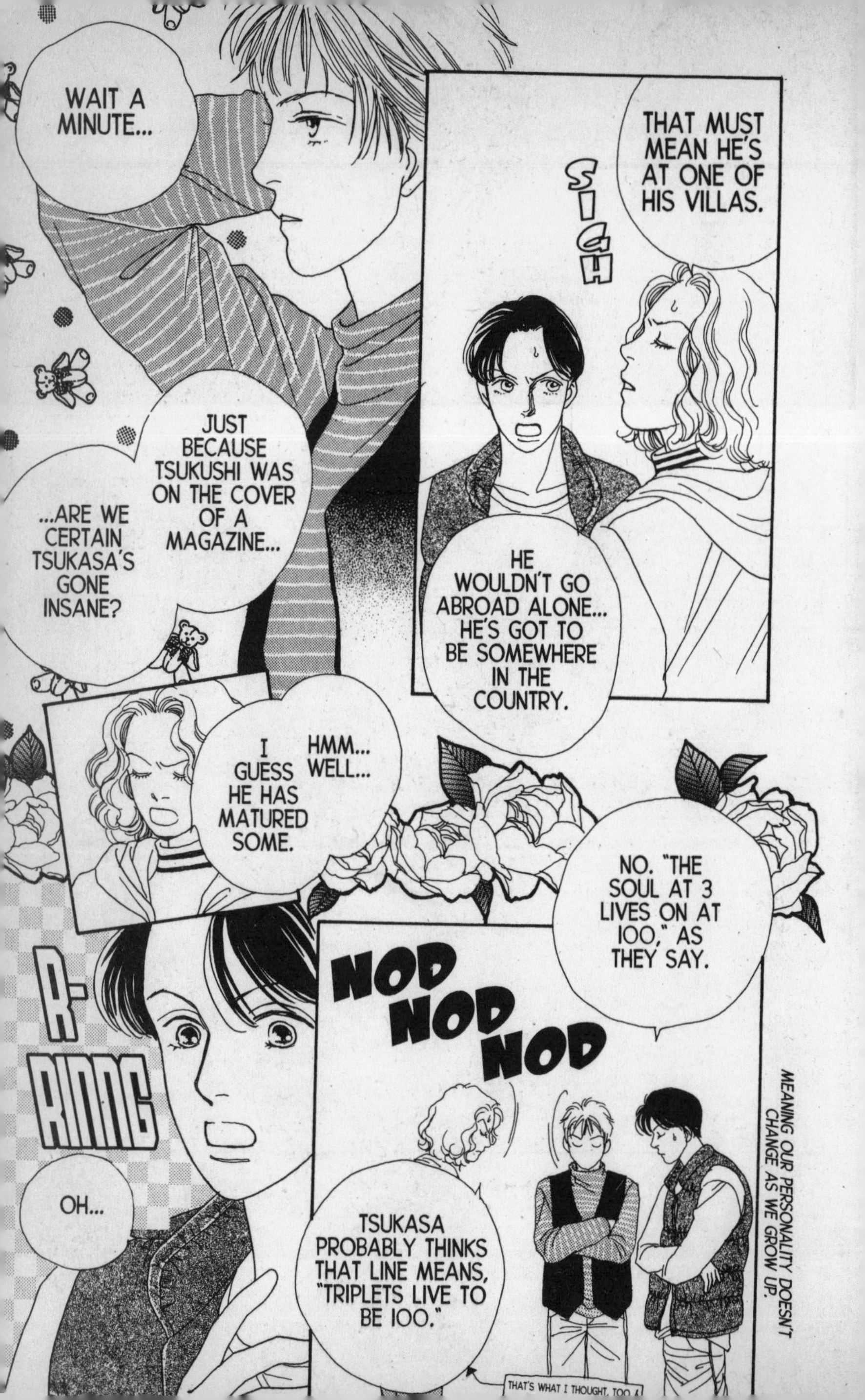
THAT MUST MEAN HE'S AT ONE OF HIS VILLAS.
SIGH
HE WOULDN'T GO ABROAD ALONE... HE'S GOT TO BE SOMEWHERE IN THE COUNTRY.
WAIT A MINUTE...
JUST BECAUSE TSUKUSHI WAS ON THE COVER OF A MAGAZINE...
...ARE WE CERTAIN TSUKASA'S GONE INSANE?
HMM... WELL...
I GUESS HE HAS MATURED SOME.
NO. "THE SOUL AT 3 LIVES ON AT 100," AS THEY SAY.
NOD NOD NOD
MEANING OUR PERSONALITY DOESN'T CHANGE AS WE GROW UP.
TSUKASA PROBABLY THINKS THAT LINE MEANS, "TRIPLETS LIVE TO BE 100."
THAT'S WHAT I THOUGHT, TOO
R-RING
OH...

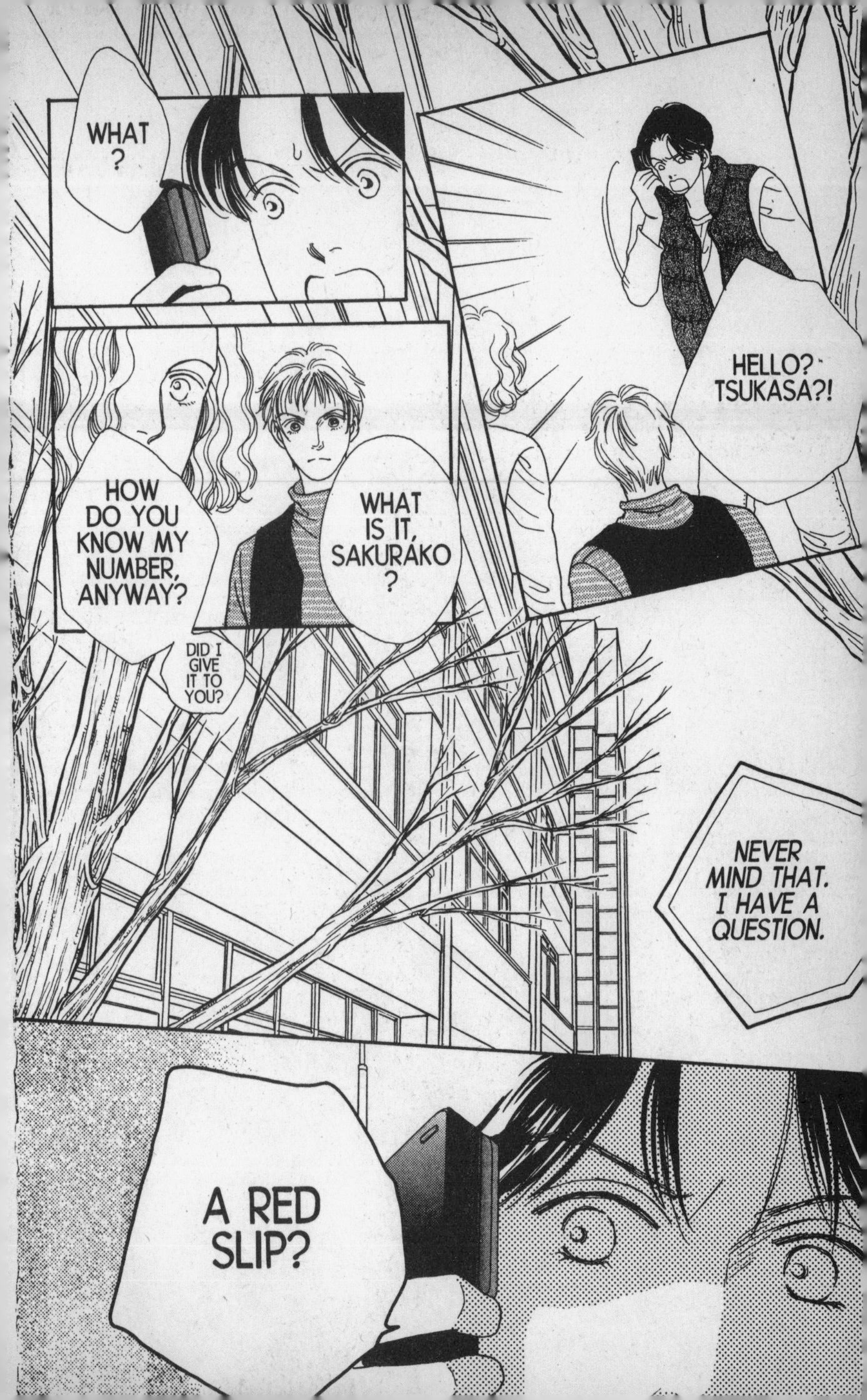
HELLO? TSUKASA?!
WHAT ?
WHAT IS IT, SAKURAKO ?
HOW DO YOU KNOW MY NUMBER, ANYWAY?
DID I GIVE IT TO YOU?
NEVER MIND THAT. I HAVE A QUESTION.
A RED SLIP?

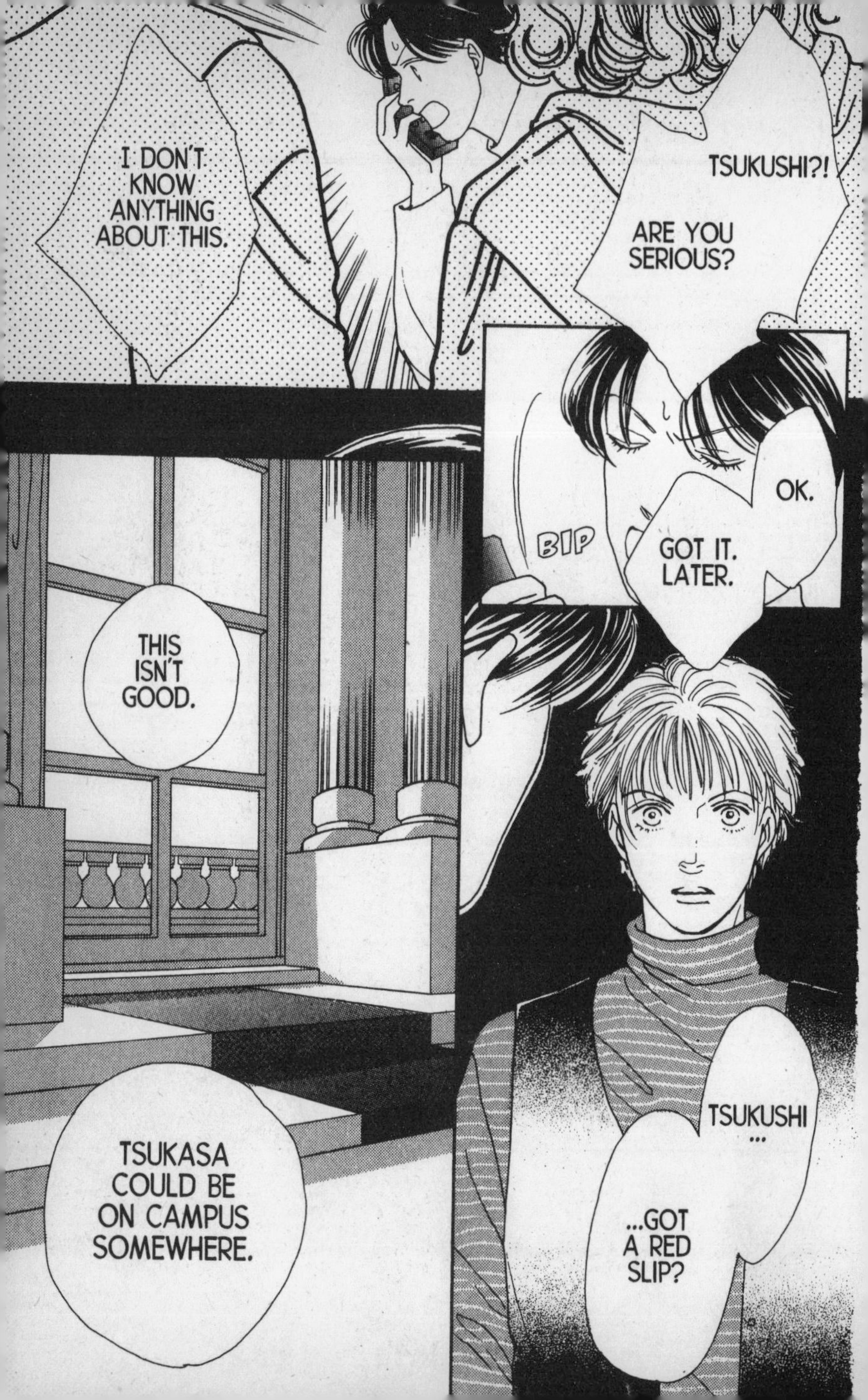
TSUKUSHI?!
ARE YOU SERIOUS?
I DON'T KNOW ANYTHING ABOUT THIS.
OK.
GOT IT. LATER.
BIP
TSUKUSHI ...
...GOT A RED SLIP?
THIS ISN'T GOOD.
TSUKASA COULD BE ON CAMPUS SOMEWHERE.

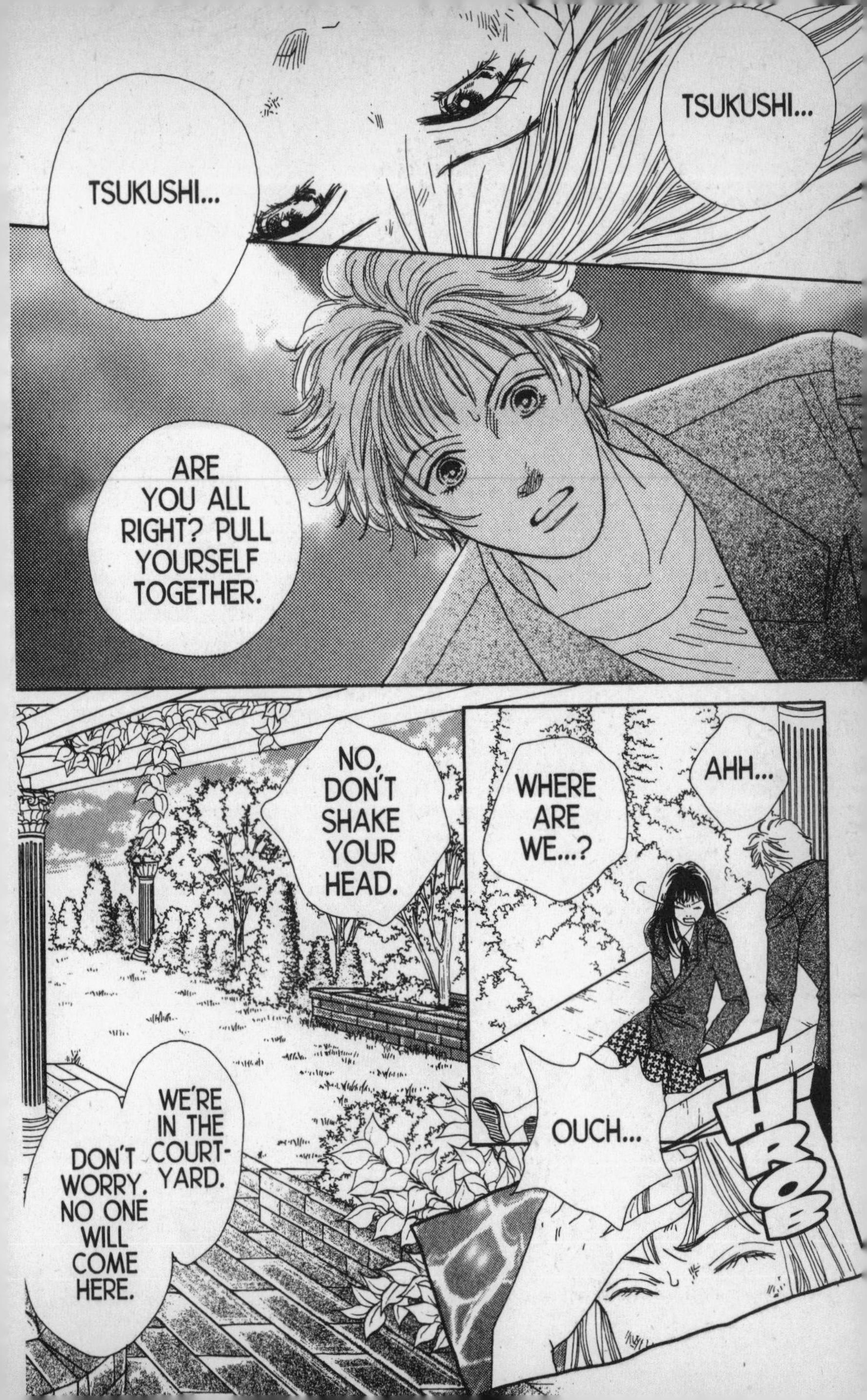
TSUKUSHI...
TSUKUSHI...
ARE YOU ALL RIGHT? PULL YOURSELF TOGETHER.
AHH...
WHERE ARE WE...?
OUCH...
THROB
NO, DON'T SHAKE YOUR HEAD.
WE'RE IN THE COURTYARD.
DON'T WORRY. NO ONE WILL COME HERE.

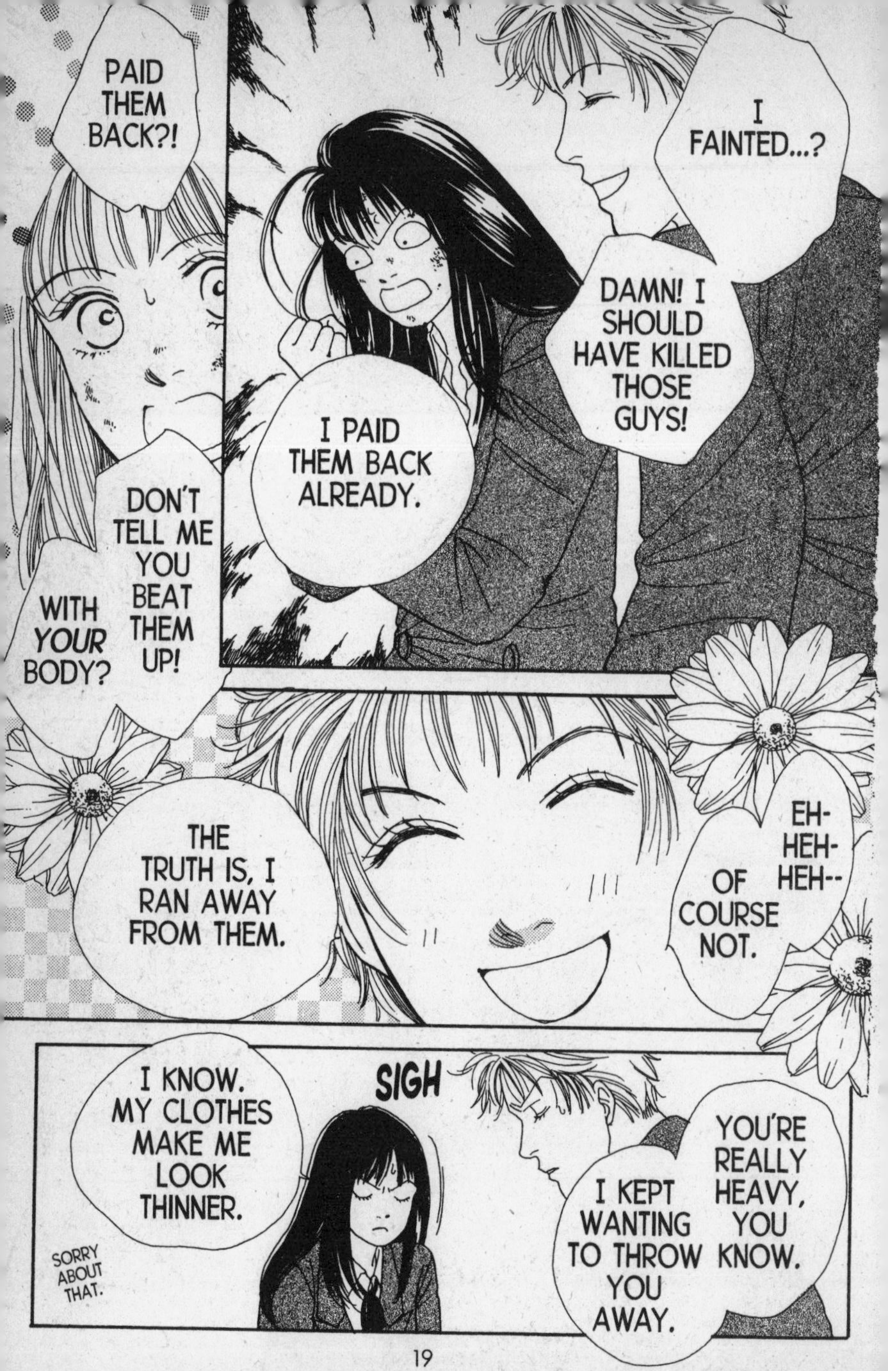
I FAINTED...?
DAMN! I SHOULD HAVE KILLED THOSE GUYS!
I PAID THEM BACK ALREADY.
PAID THEM BACK?!
DON'T TELL ME YOU BEAT THEM UP!
WITH *YOUR* BODY?
EH-HEH-HEH--
OF COURSE NOT.
THE TRUTH IS, I RAN AWAY FROM THEM.
YOU'RE REALLY HEAVY, YOU KNOW.
I KEPT WANTING TO THROW YOU AWAY.
SIGH
I KNOW. MY CLOTHES MAKE ME LOOK THINNER.
SORRY ABOUT THAT.

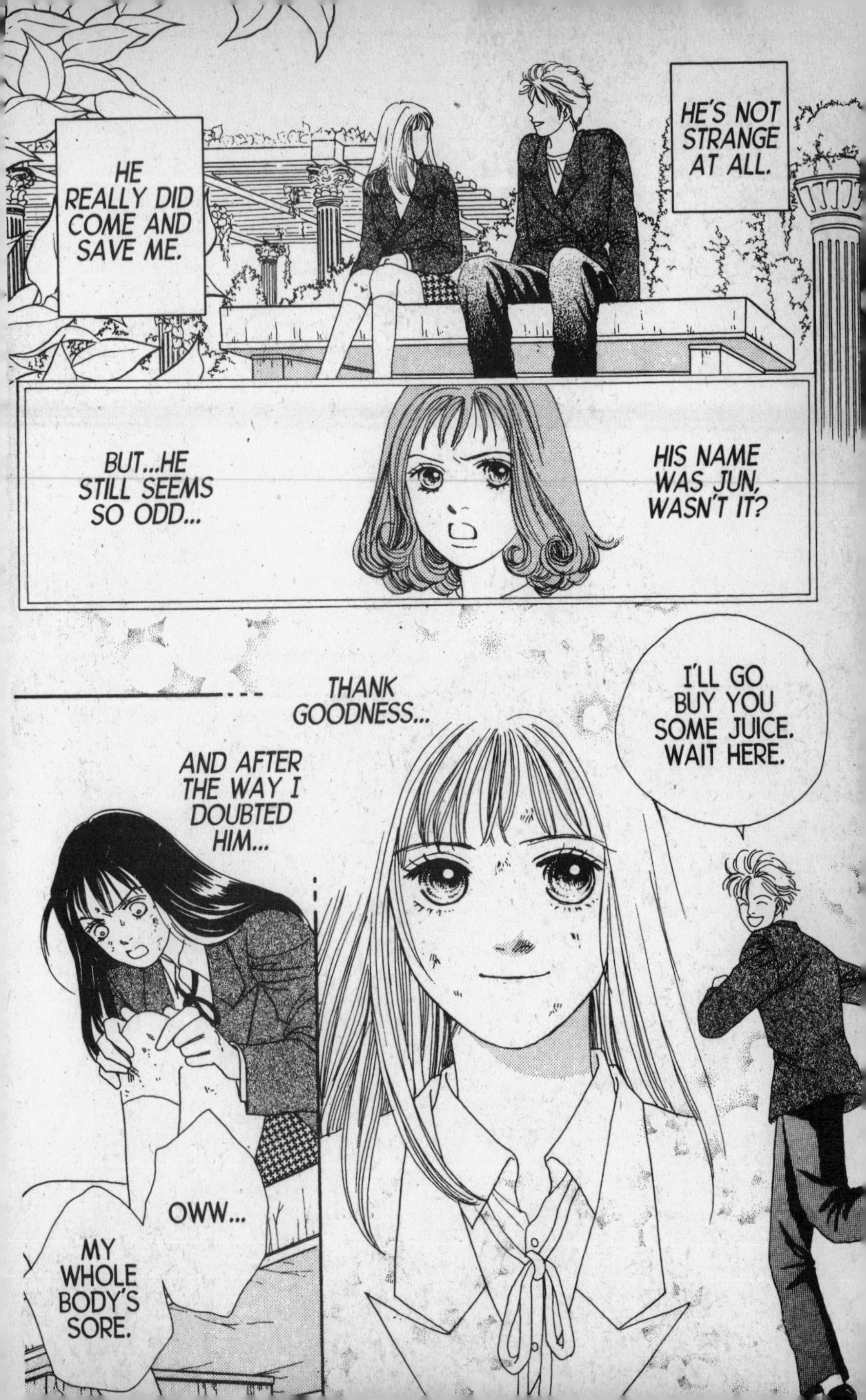
HE'S NOT STRANGE AT ALL.
HE REALLY DID COME AND SAVE ME.
HIS NAME WAS JUN, WASN'T IT?
BUT...HE STILL SEEMS SO ODD...
I'LL GO BUY YOU SOME JUICE. WAIT HERE.
THANK GOODNESS...
AND AFTER THE WAY I DOUBTED HIM...
OWW...
MY WHOLE BODY'S SORE.

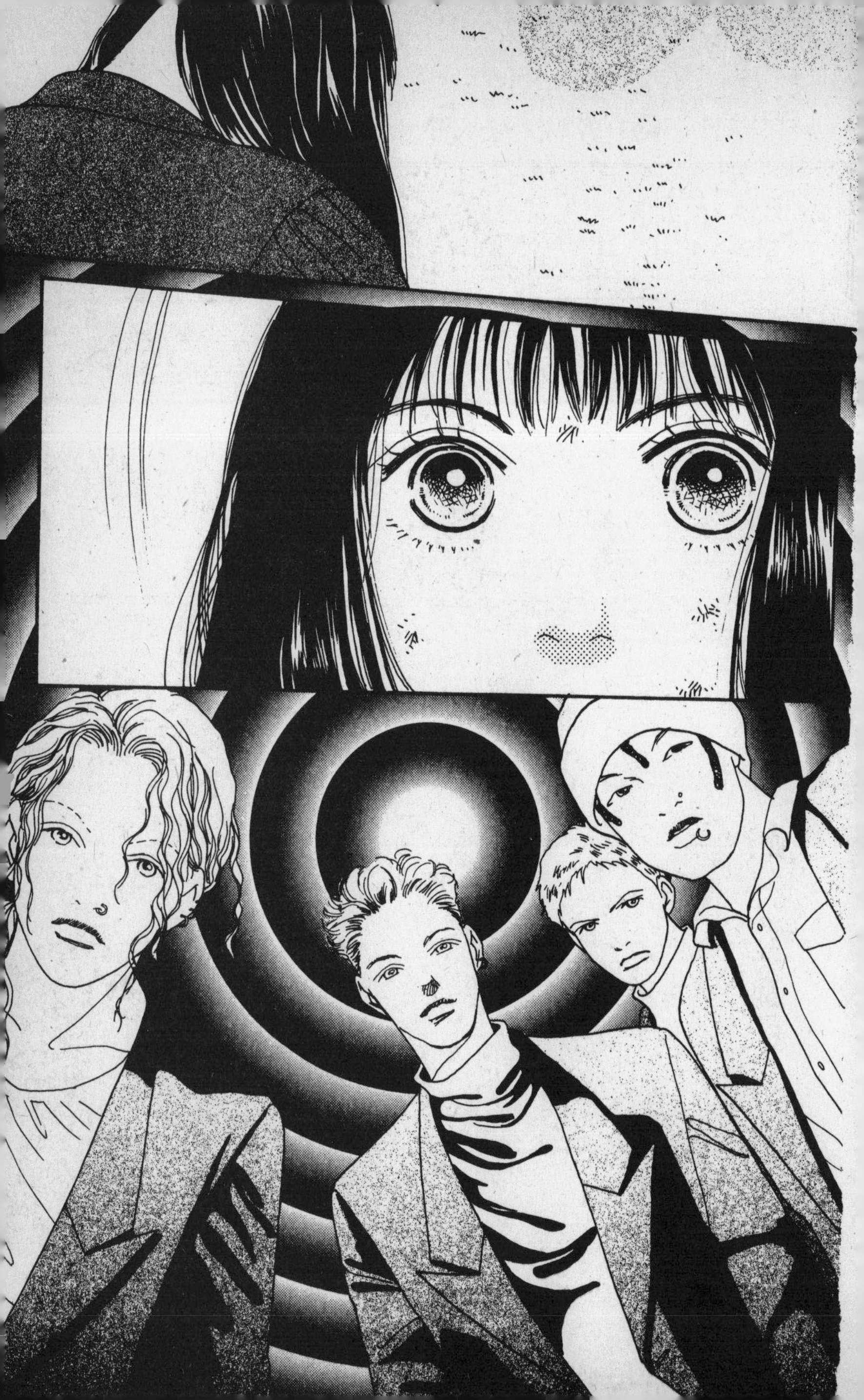

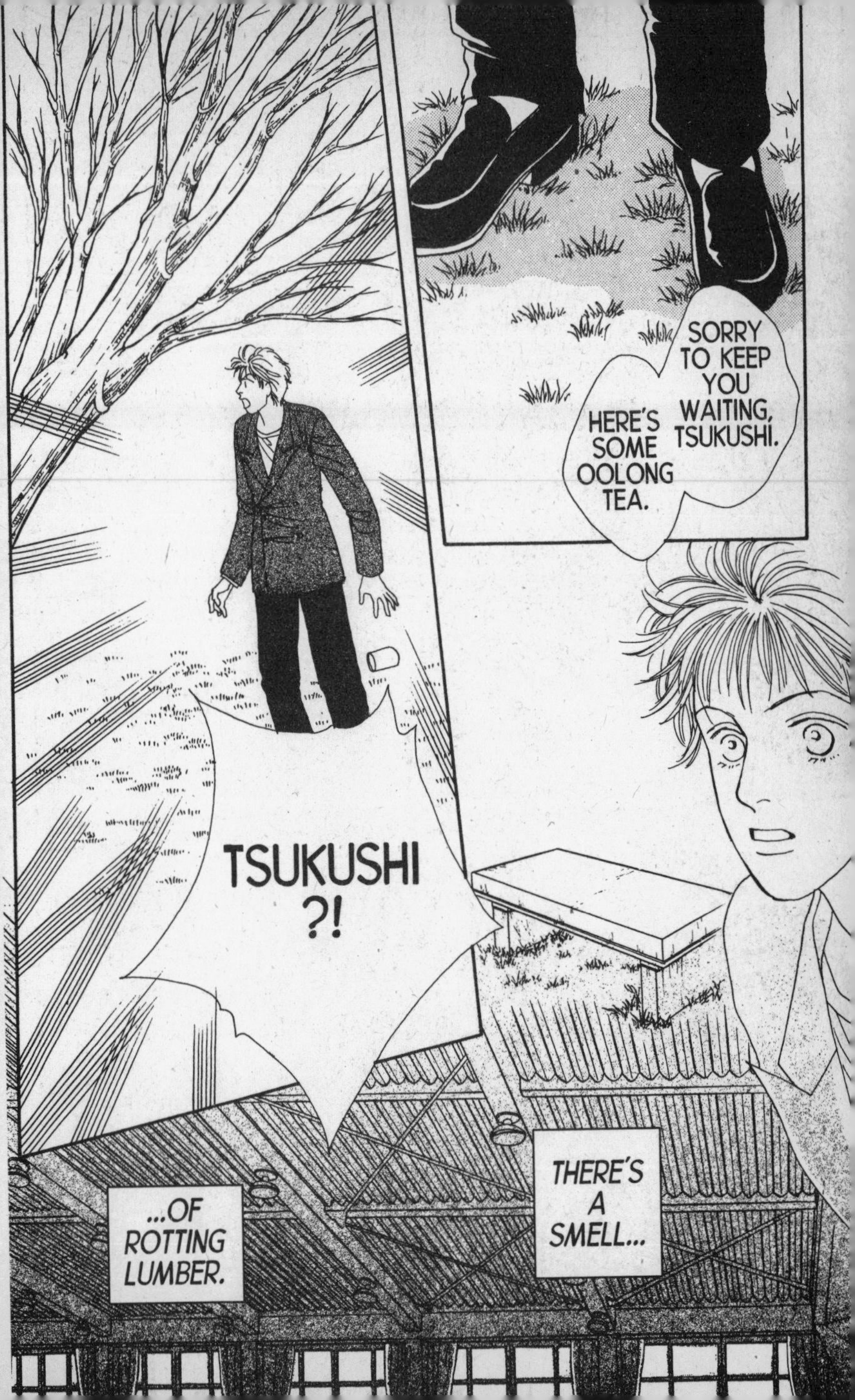
SORRY TO KEEP YOU WAITING, TSUKUSHI.
HERE'S SOME OOLONG TEA.
TSUKUSHI ?!
THERE'S A SMELL...
...OF ROTTING LUMBER.

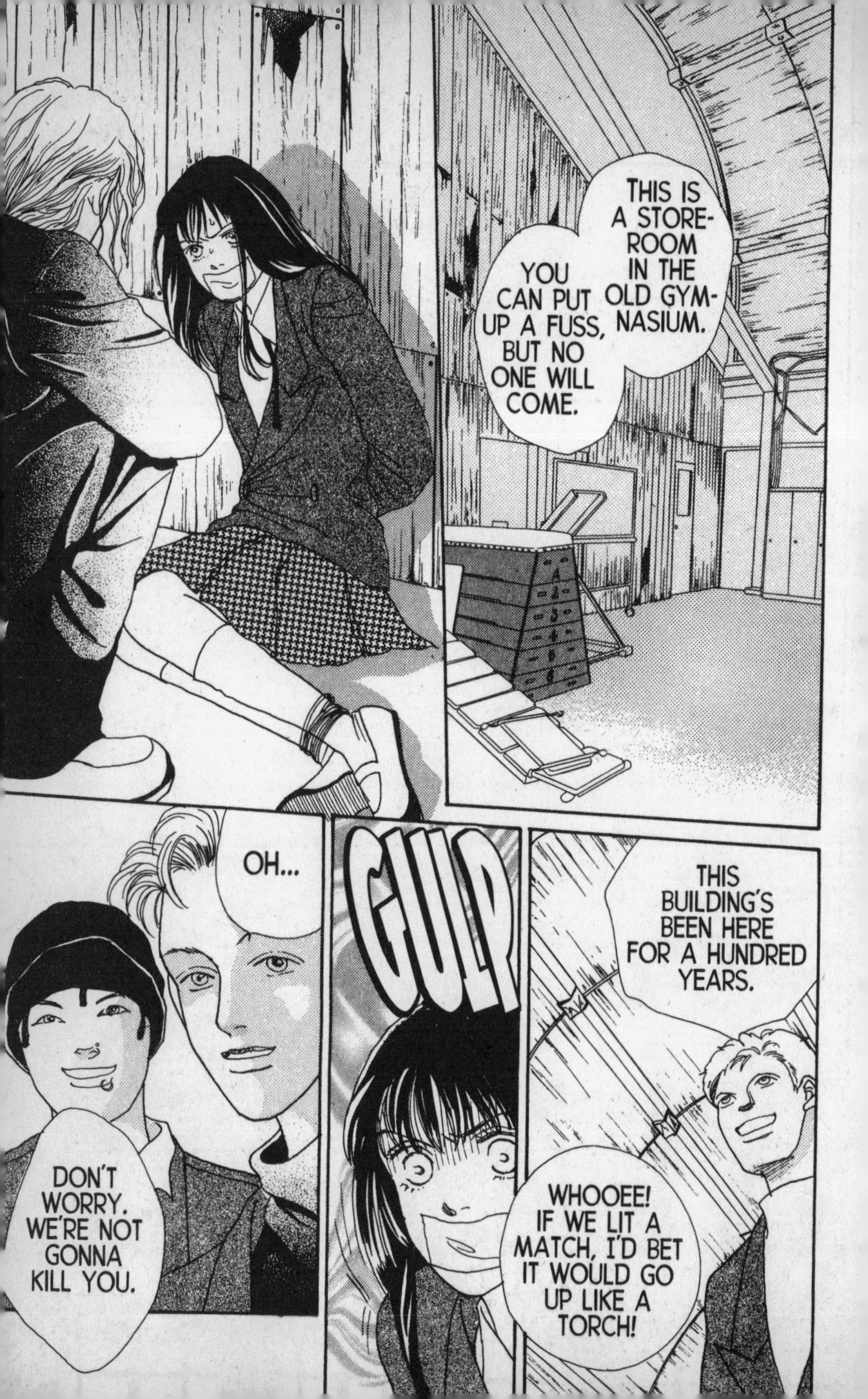
THIS IS A STOREROOM IN THE OLD GYMNASIUM.
YOU CAN PUT UP A FUSS, BUT NO ONE WILL COME.
THIS BUILDING'S BEEN HERE FOR A HUNDRED YEARS.
WHOOEE! IF WE LIT A MATCH, I'D BET IT WOULD GO UP LIKE A TORCH!
GULP
OH...
DON'T WORRY. WE'RE NOT GONNA KILL YOU.

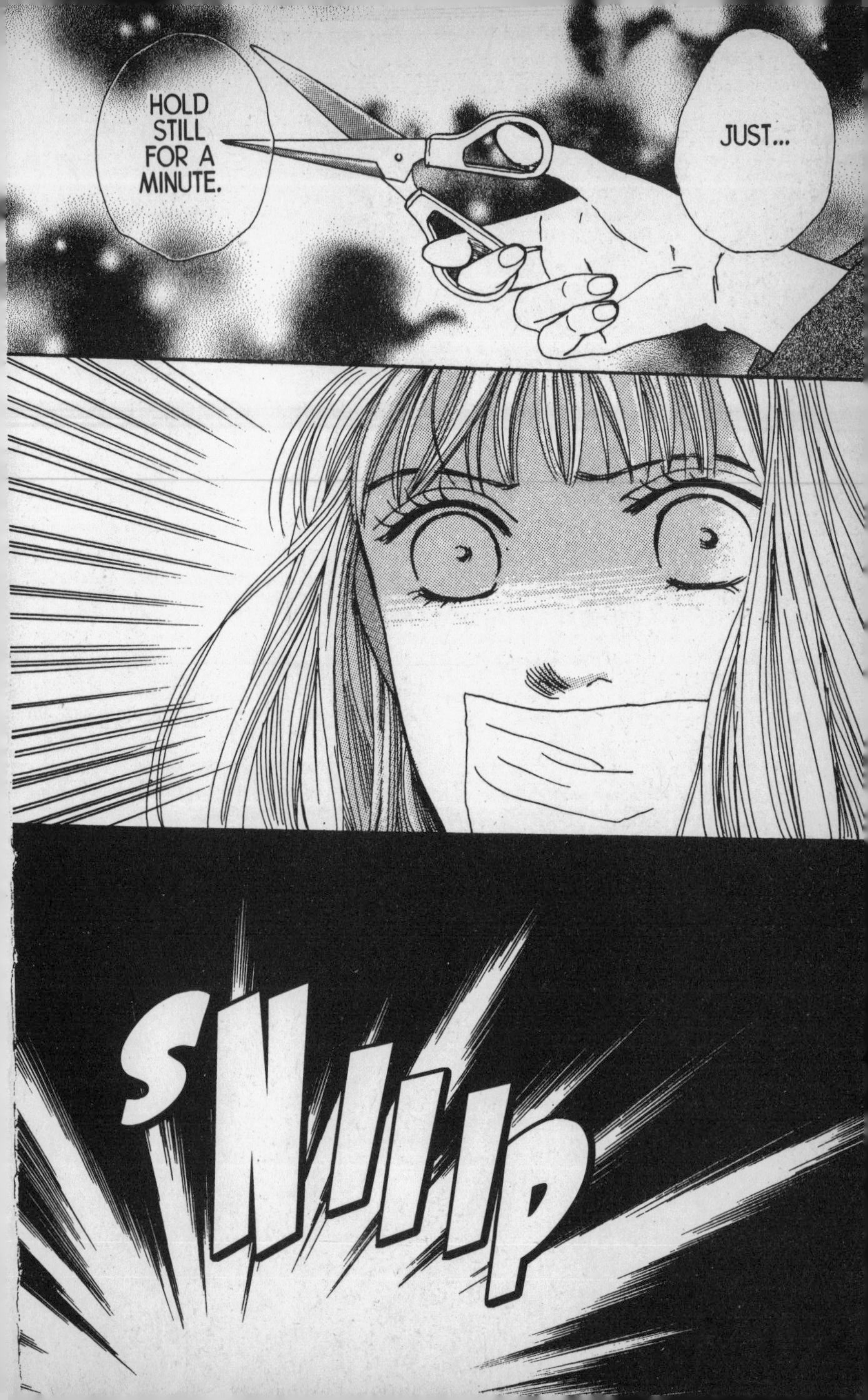
JUST...
HOLD STILL FOR A MINUTE.
SNIIIP

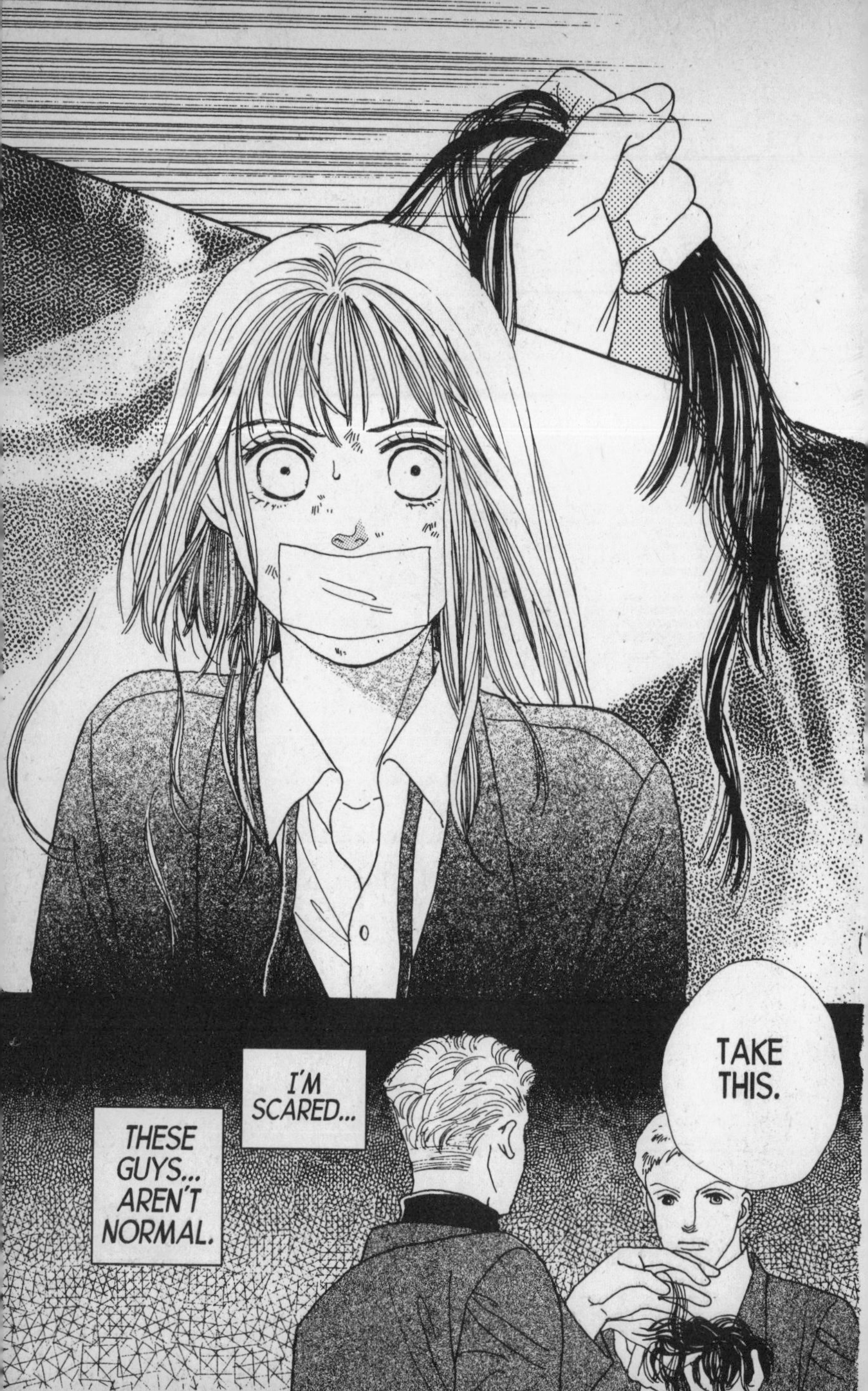
TAKE THIS.
I'M SCARED...
THESE GUYS... AREN'T NORMAL.

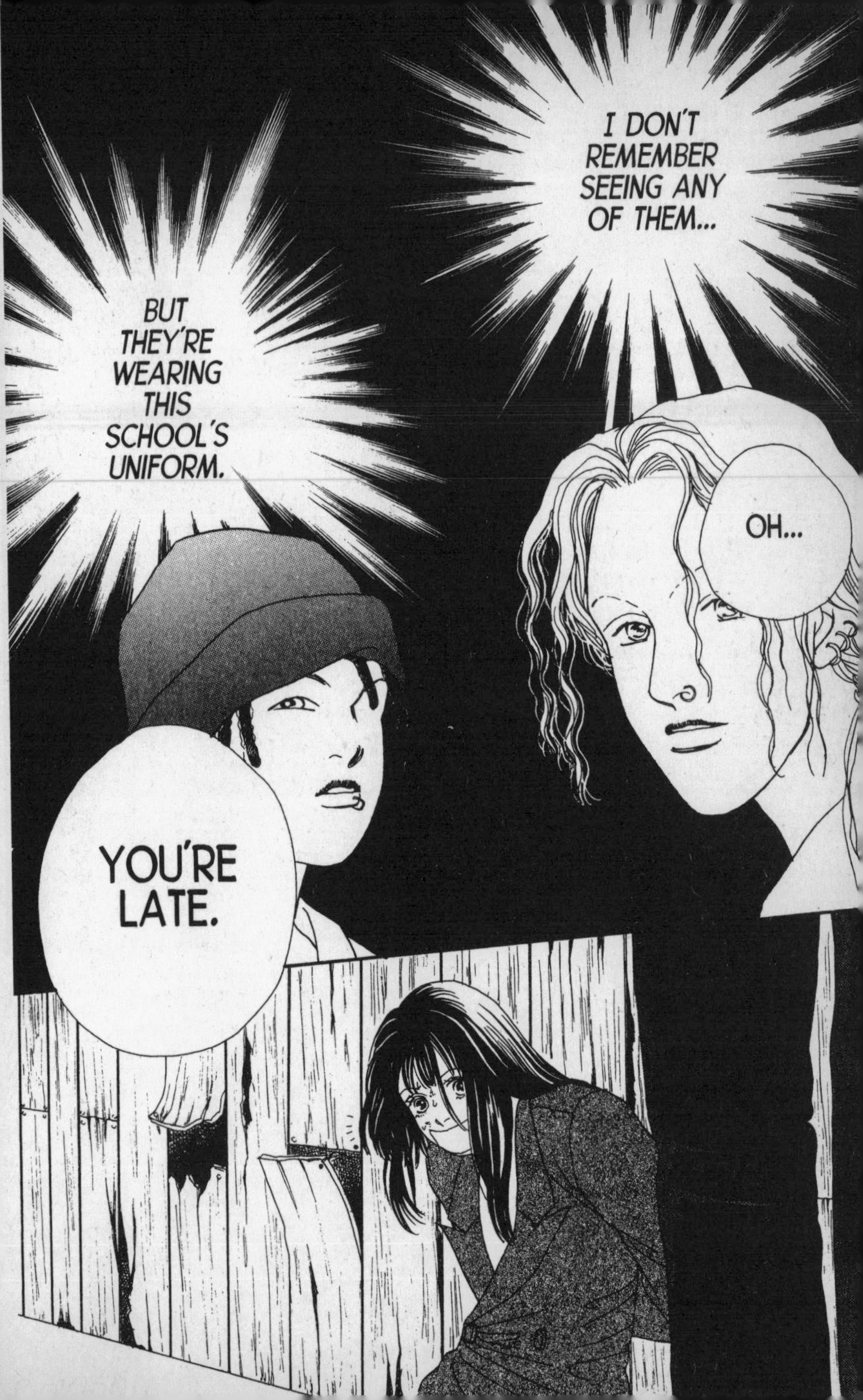
I DON'T REMEMBER SEEING ANY OF THEM...
BUT THEY'RE WEARING THIS SCHOOL'S UNIFORM.
OH...
YOU'RE LATE.

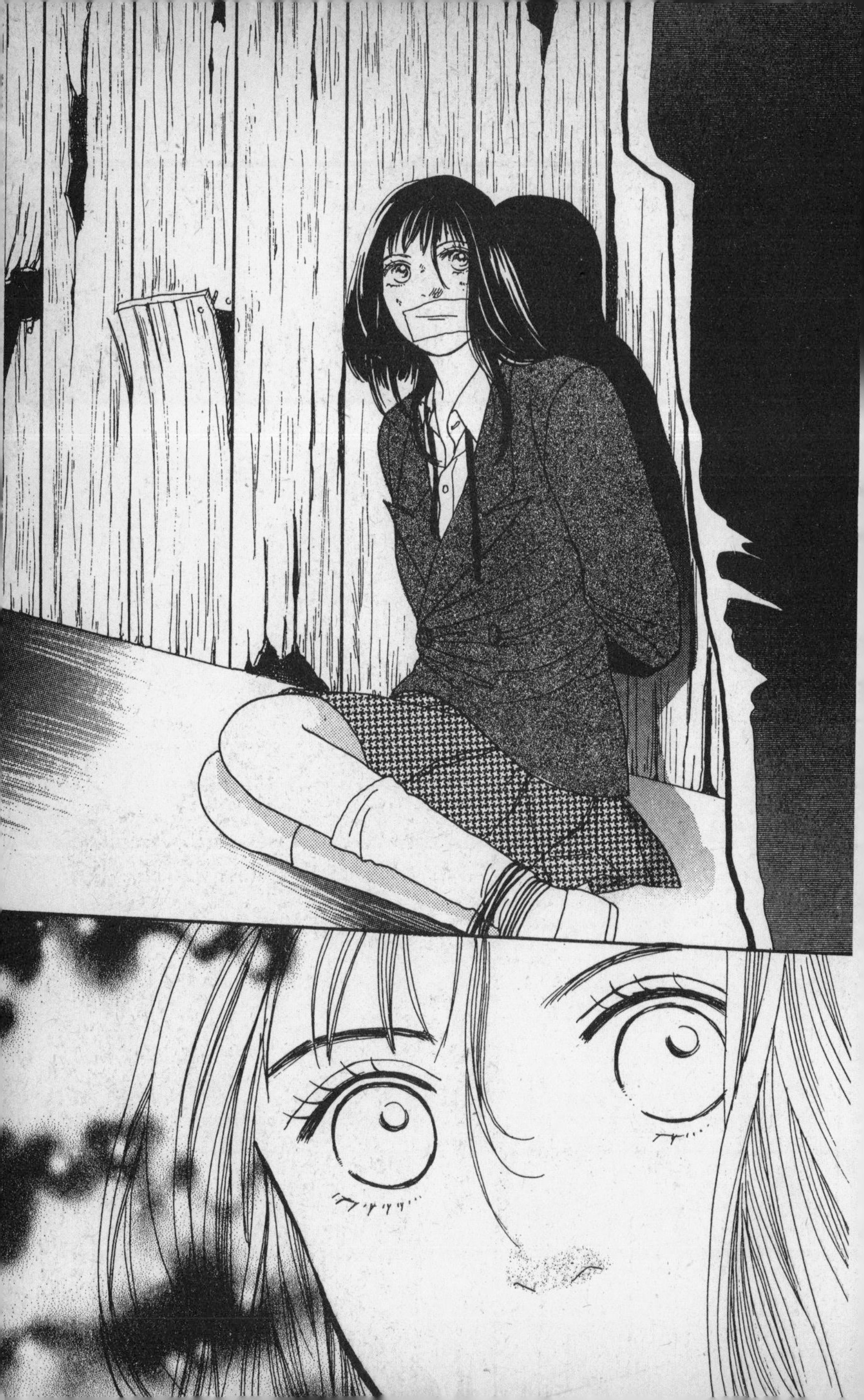

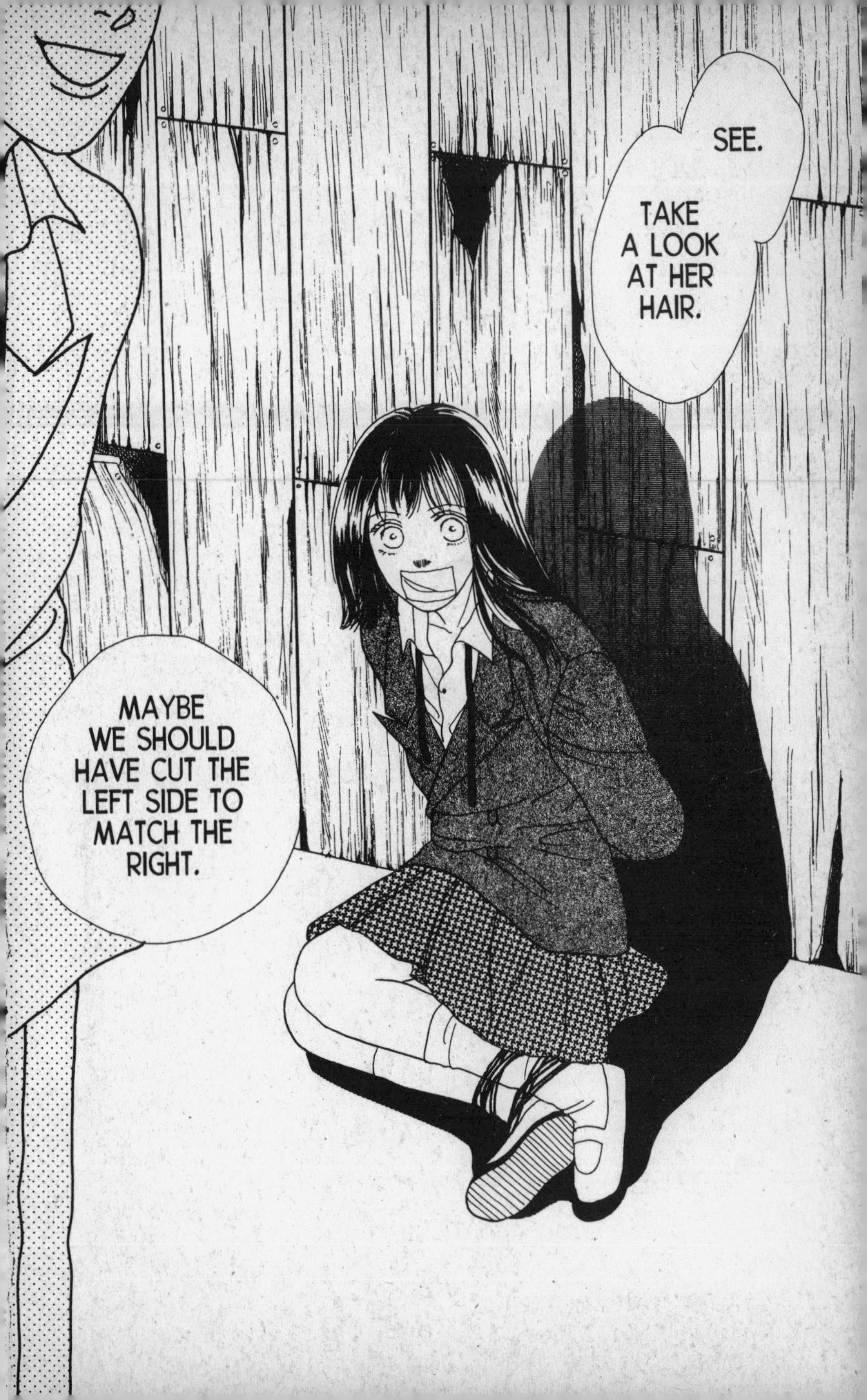
SEE. TAKE A LOOK AT HER HAIR.
MAYBE WE SHOULD HAVE CUT THE LEFT SIDE TO MATCH THE RIGHT.

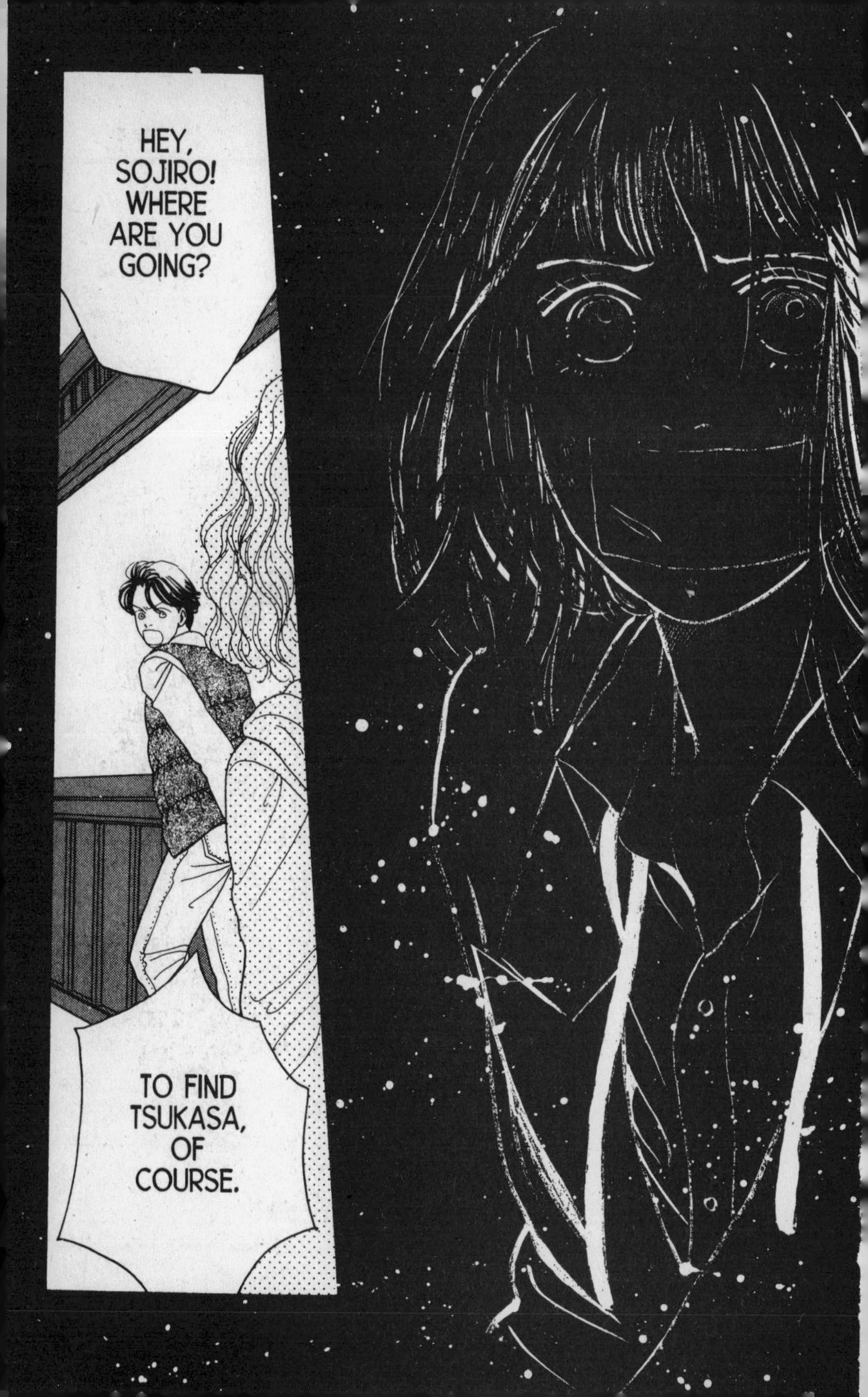
HEY, SOJIRO! WHERE ARE YOU GOING?
TO FIND TSUKASA, OF COURSE.

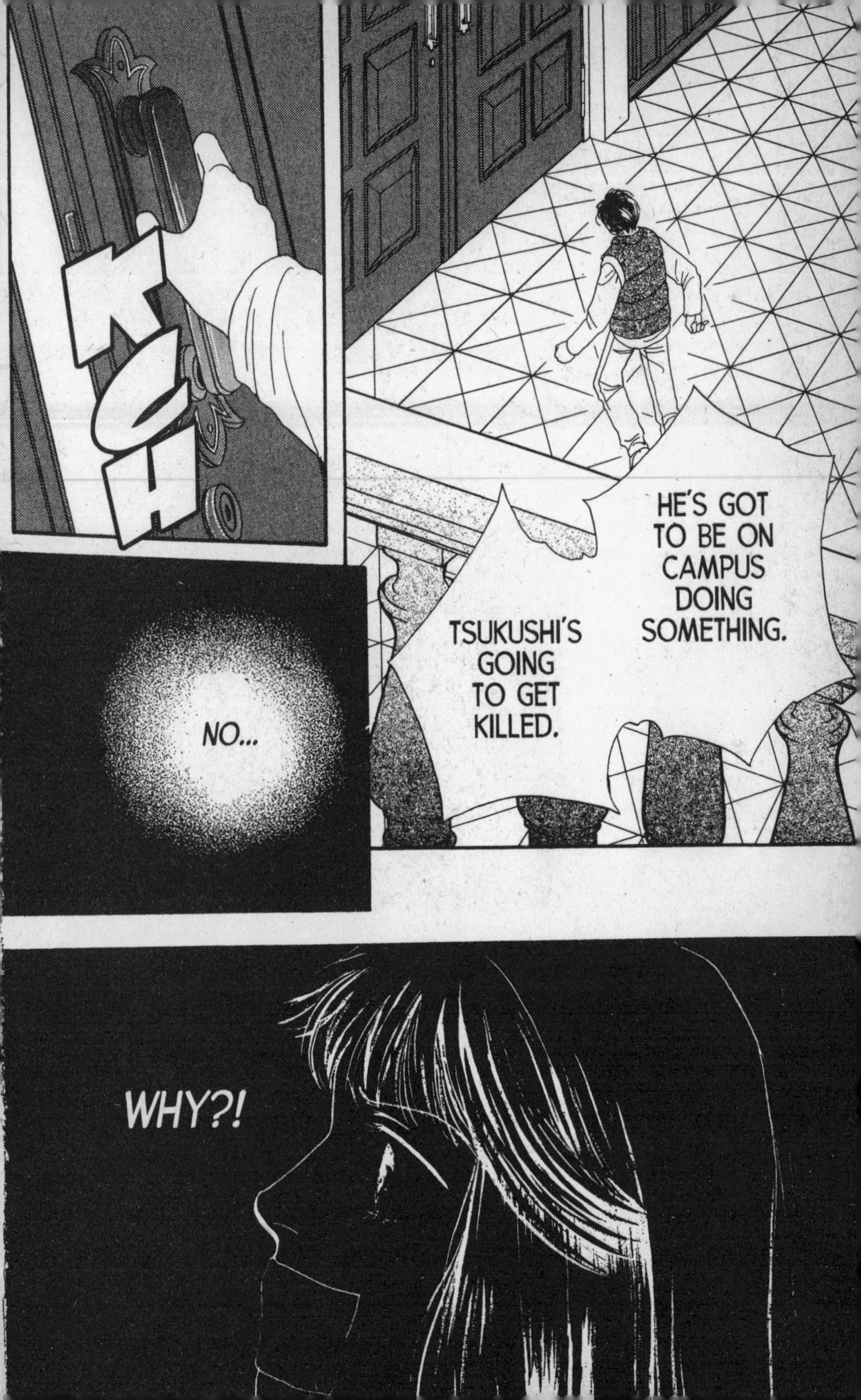
HE'S GOT TO BE ON CAMPUS DOING SOMETHING.
TSUKUSHI'S GOING TO GET KILLED.
KCH
NO...
WHY?!

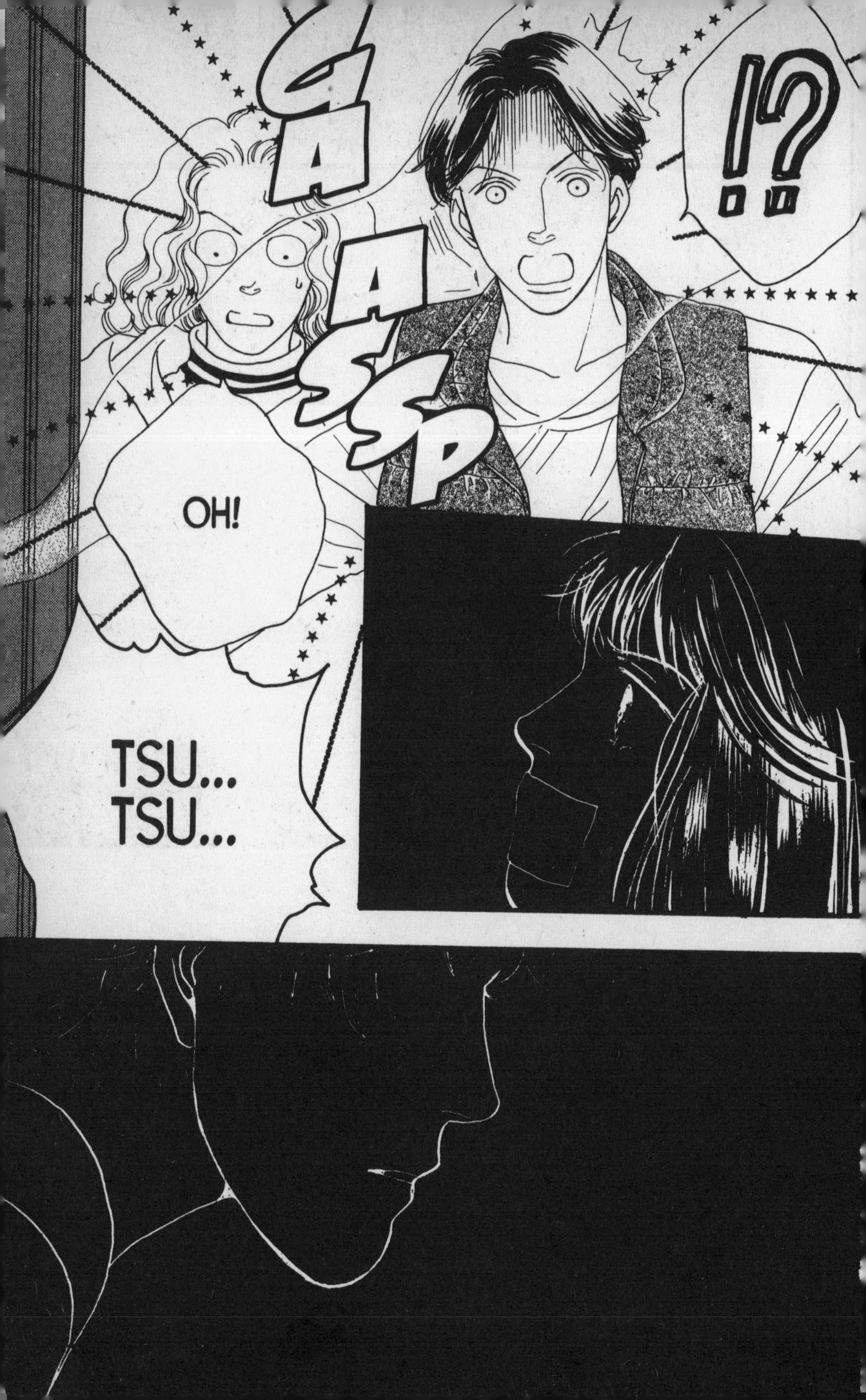
!?
GASP
OH!
TSU... TSU...

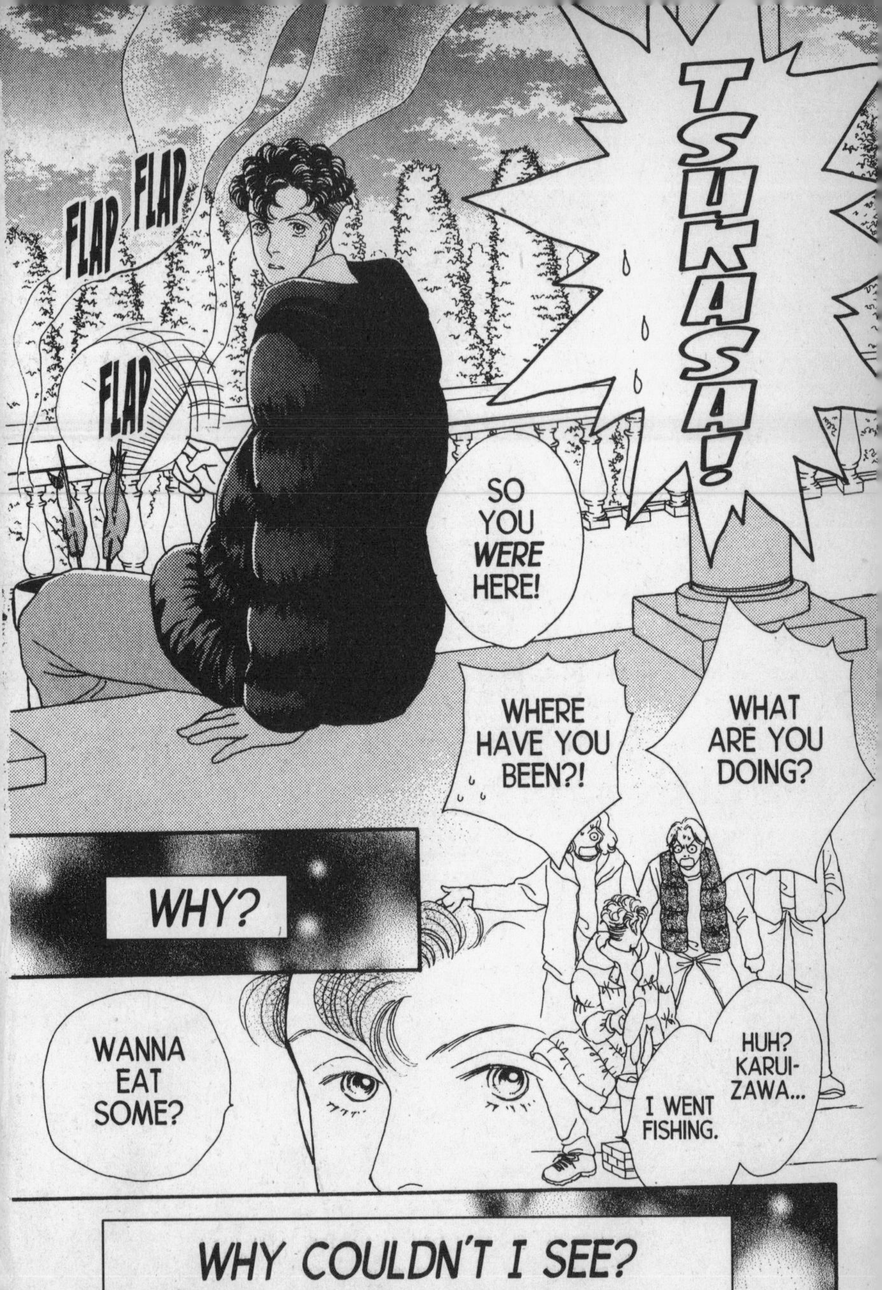
TSUKASA!
SO YOU WERE HERE!
FLAP FLAP
FLAP
WHAT ARE YOU DOING?
WHERE HAVE YOU BEEN?!
WHY?
HUH? KARUI-ZAWA...
I WENT FISHING.
WANNA EAT SOME?
WHY COULDN'T I SEE?

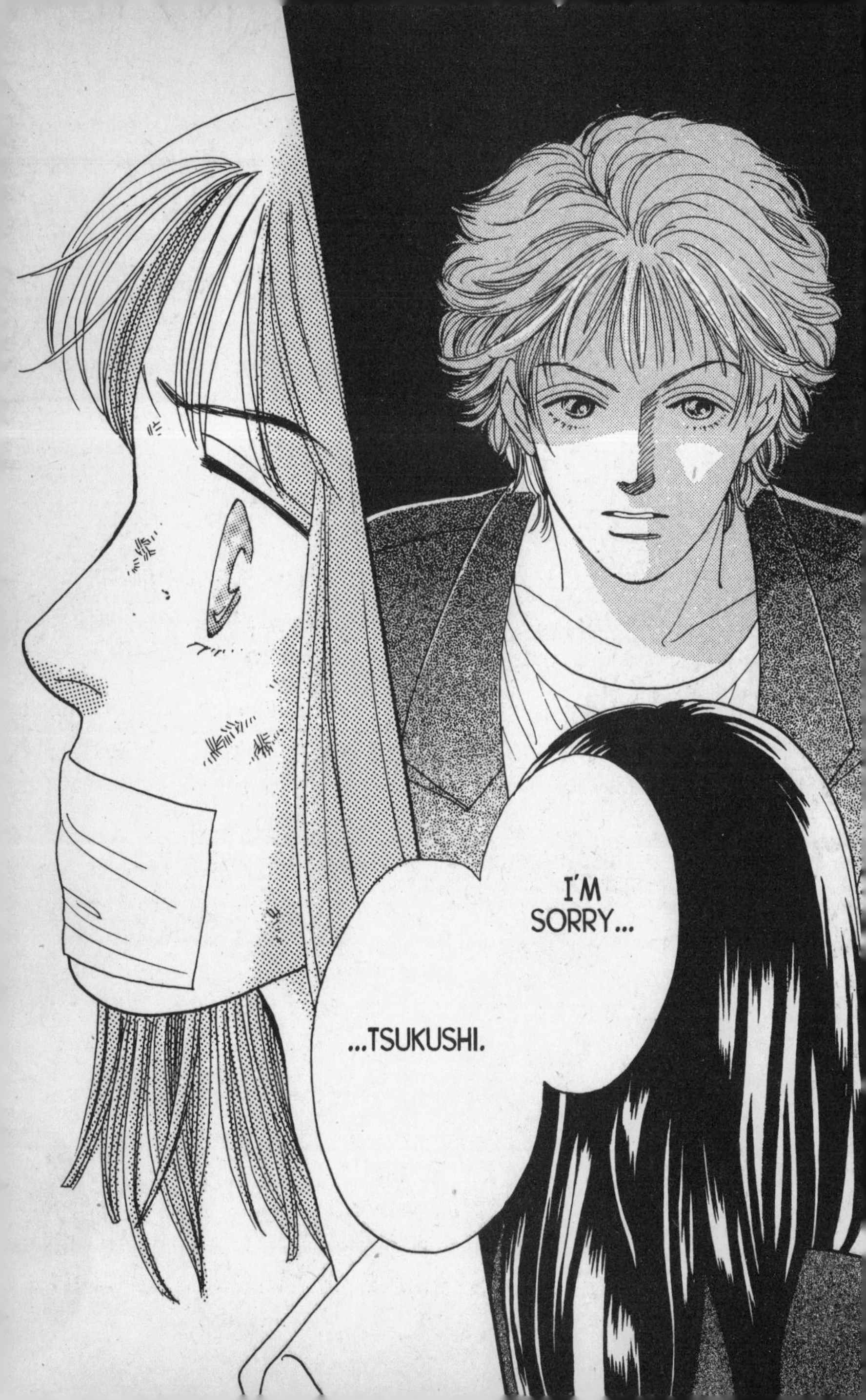
I'M SORRY...
...TSUKUSHI.

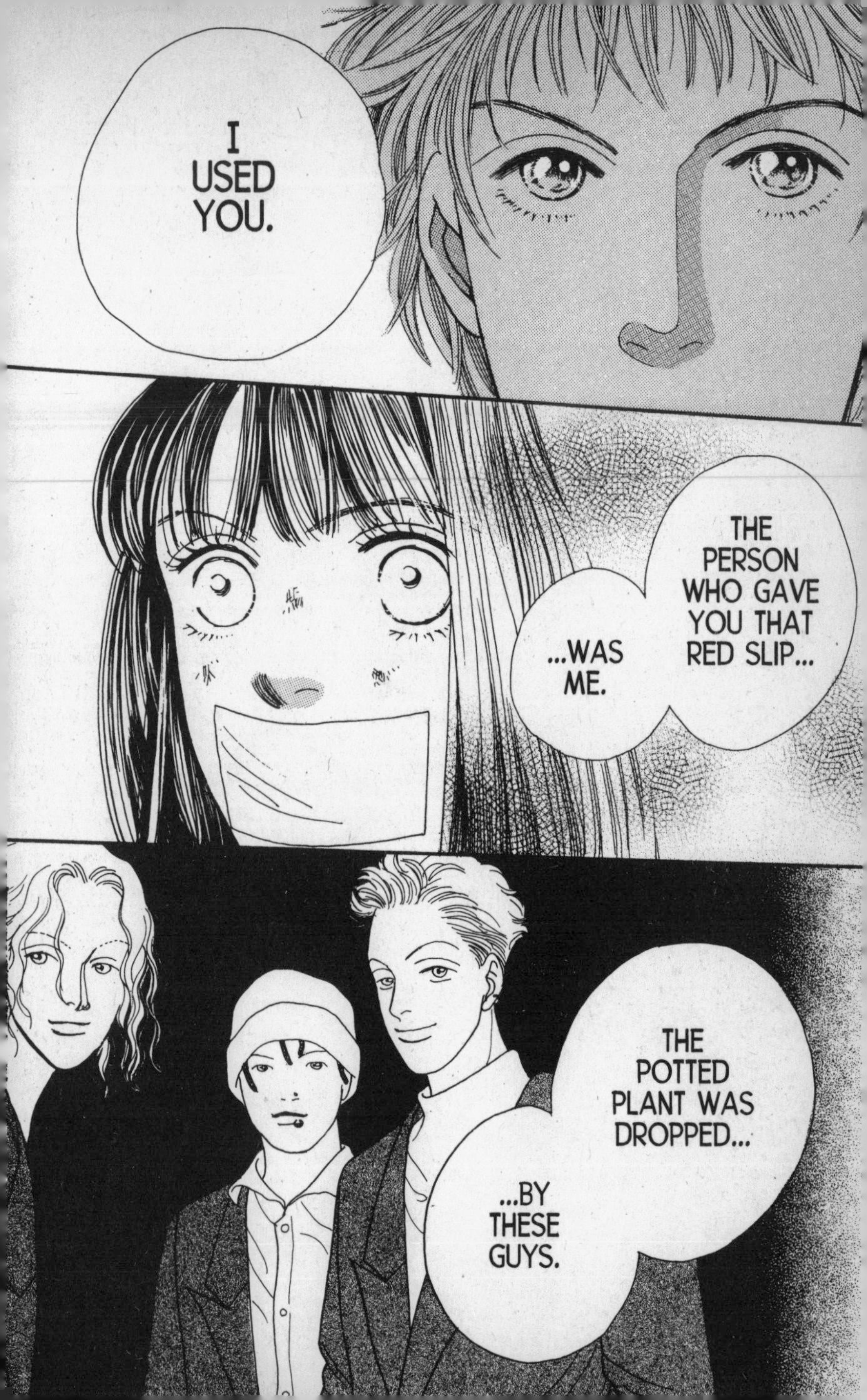
I USED YOU.
THE PERSON WHO GAVE YOU THAT RED SLIP...
...WAS ME.
THE POTTED PLANT WAS DROPPED...
...BY THESE GUYS.

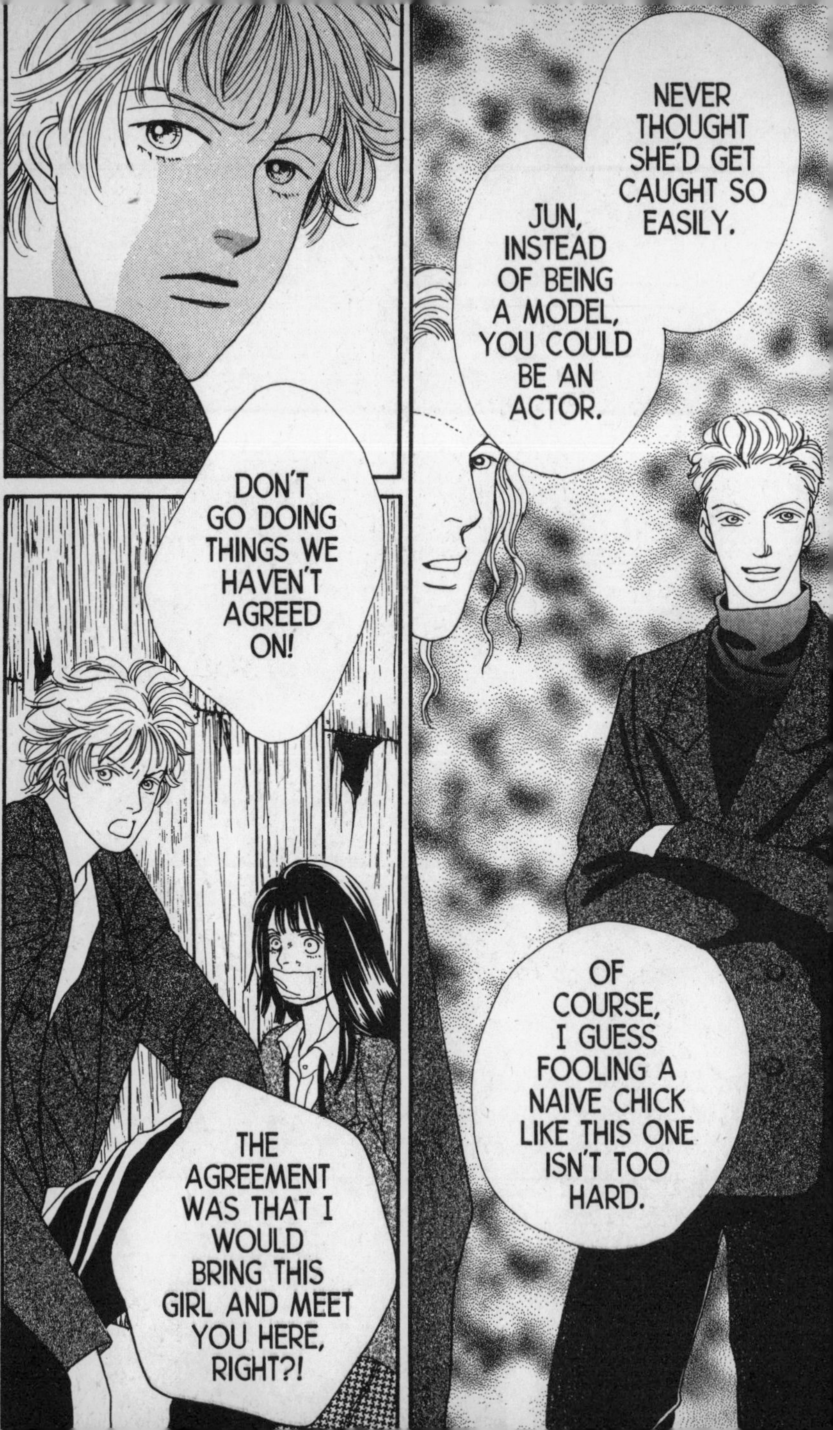
NEVER THOUGHT SHE'D GET CAUGHT SO EASILY.
JUN, INSTEAD OF BEING A MODEL, YOU COULD BE AN ACTOR.
OF COURSE, I GUESS FOOLING A NAIVE CHICK LIKE THIS ONE ISN'T TOO HARD.
DON'T GO DOING THINGS WE HAVEN'T AGREED ON!
THE AGREEMENT WAS THAT I WOULD BRING THIS GIRL AND MEET YOU HERE, RIGHT?!

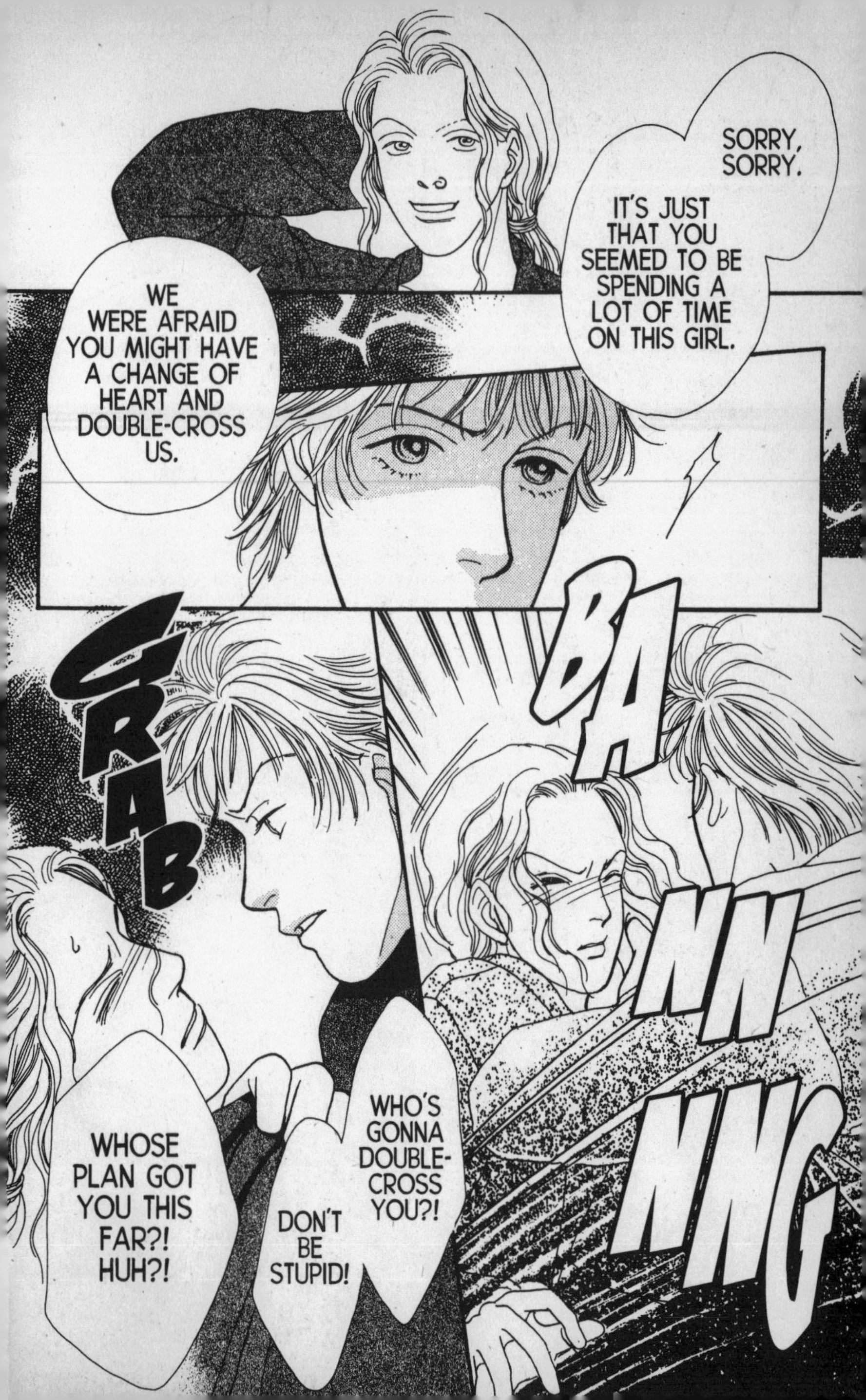
SORRY, SORRY.
IT'S JUST THAT YOU SEEMED TO BE SPENDING A LOT OF TIME ON THIS GIRL.
WE WERE AFRAID YOU MIGHT HAVE A CHANGE OF HEART AND DOUBLE-CROSS US.
BANNNNG
GRAB
WHO'S GONNA DOUBLE-CROSS YOU?!
DON'T BE STUPID!
WHOSE PLAN GOT YOU THIS FAR?! HUH?!

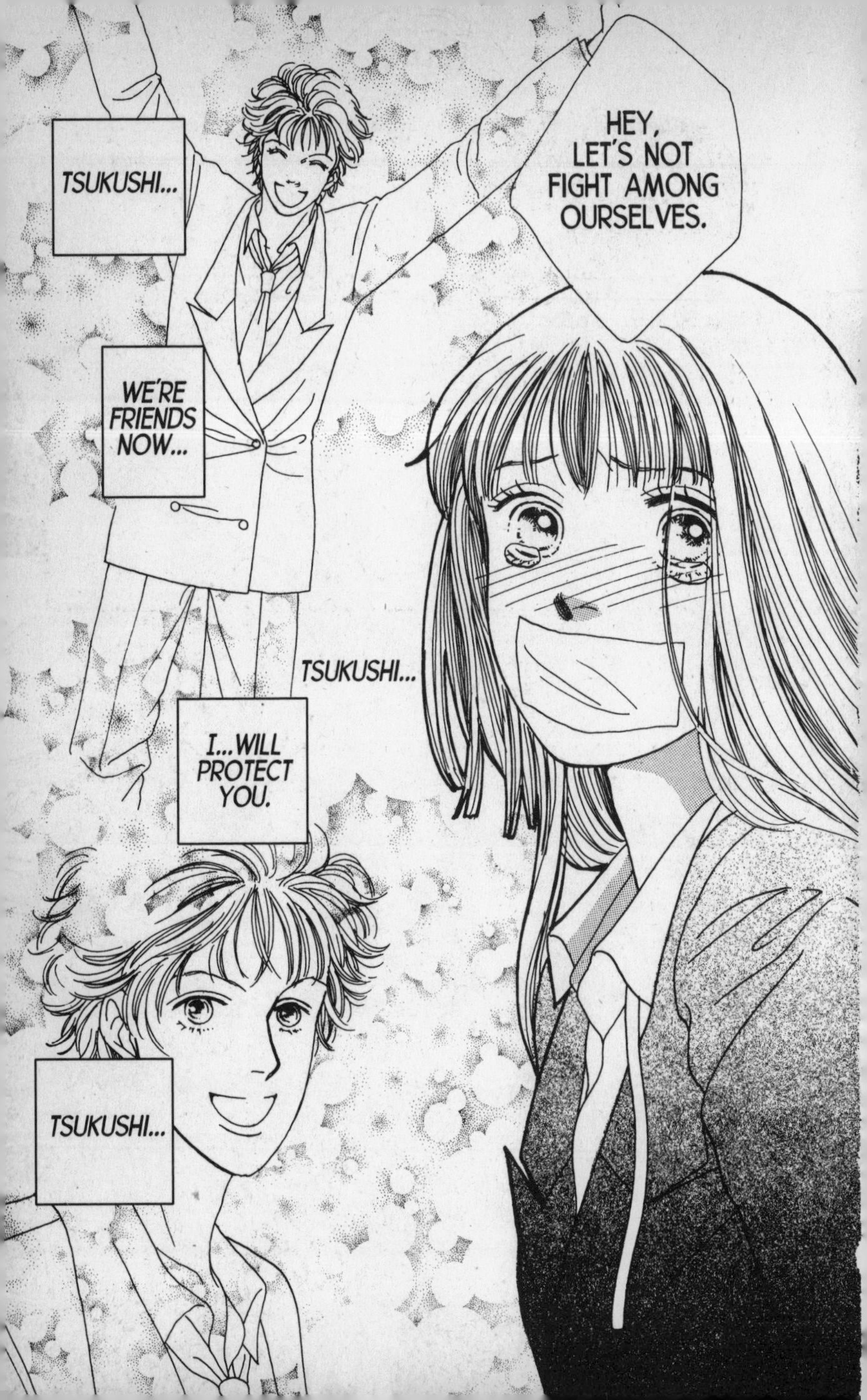
HEY, LET'S NOT FIGHT AMONG OURSELVES.
TSUKUSHI...
TSUKUSHI...
WE'RE FRIENDS NOW...
I...WILL PROTECT YOU.
TSUKUSHI...

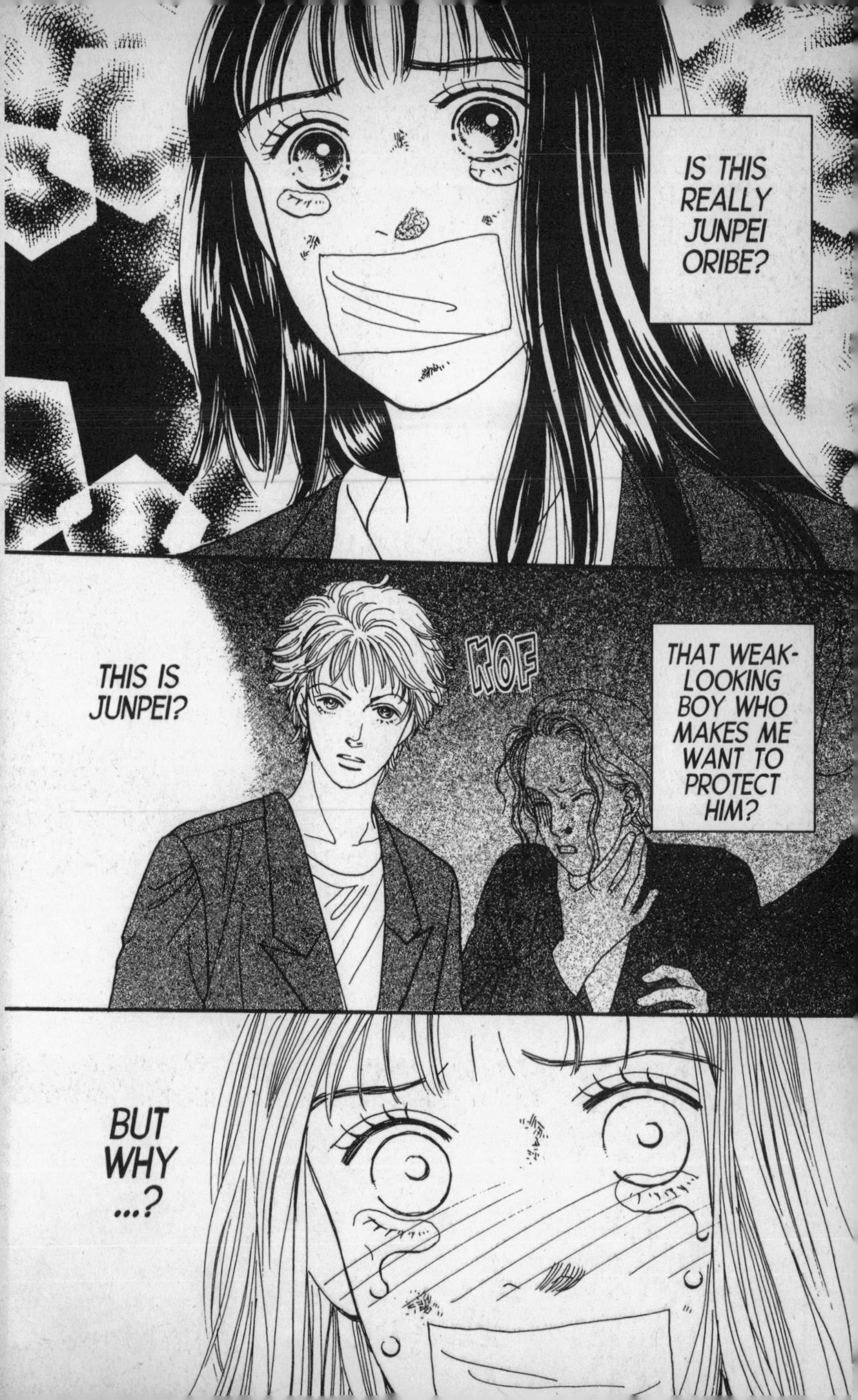
IS THIS REALLY JUNPEI ORIBE?
THAT WEAK-LOOKING BOY WHO MAKES ME WANT TO PROTECT HIM?
KOF
THIS IS JUNPEI?
BUT WHY ...?

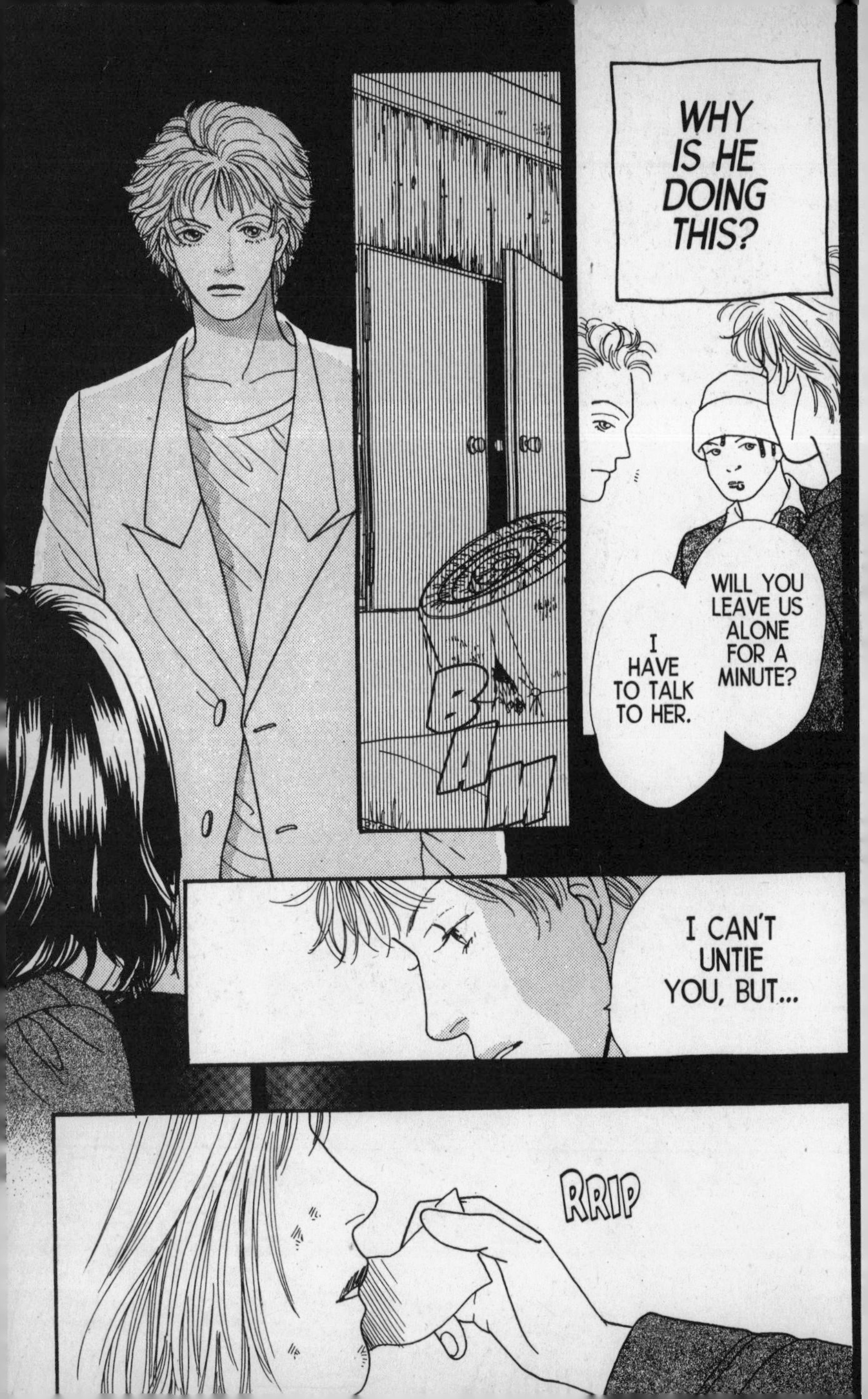
WHY IS HE DOING THIS?
WILL YOU LEAVE US ALONE FOR A MINUTE?
I HAVE TO TALK TO HER.
I CAN'T UNTIE YOU, BUT...
RRIP

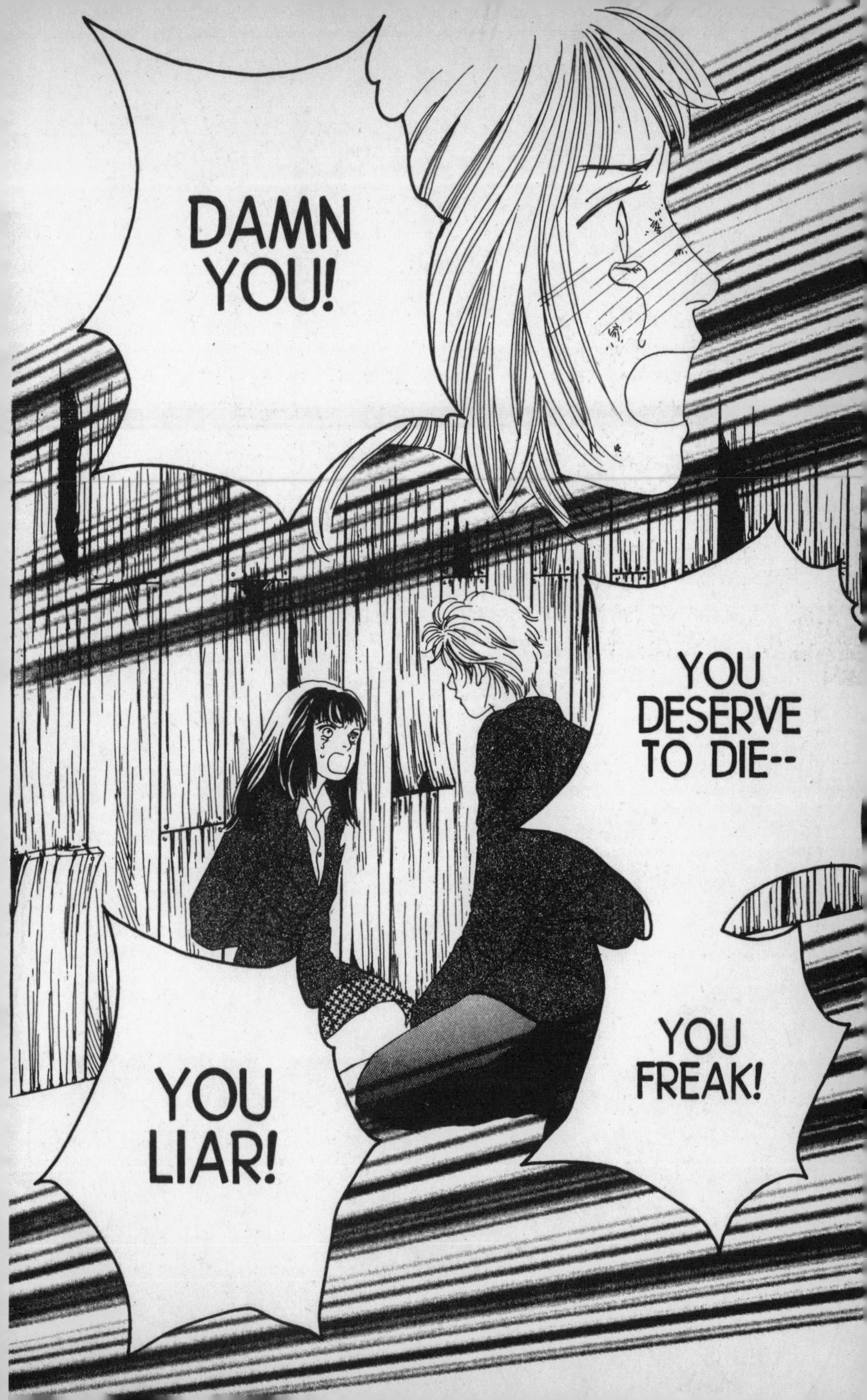
DAMN YOU!
YOU DESERVE TO DIE--
YOU FREAK!
YOU LIAR!

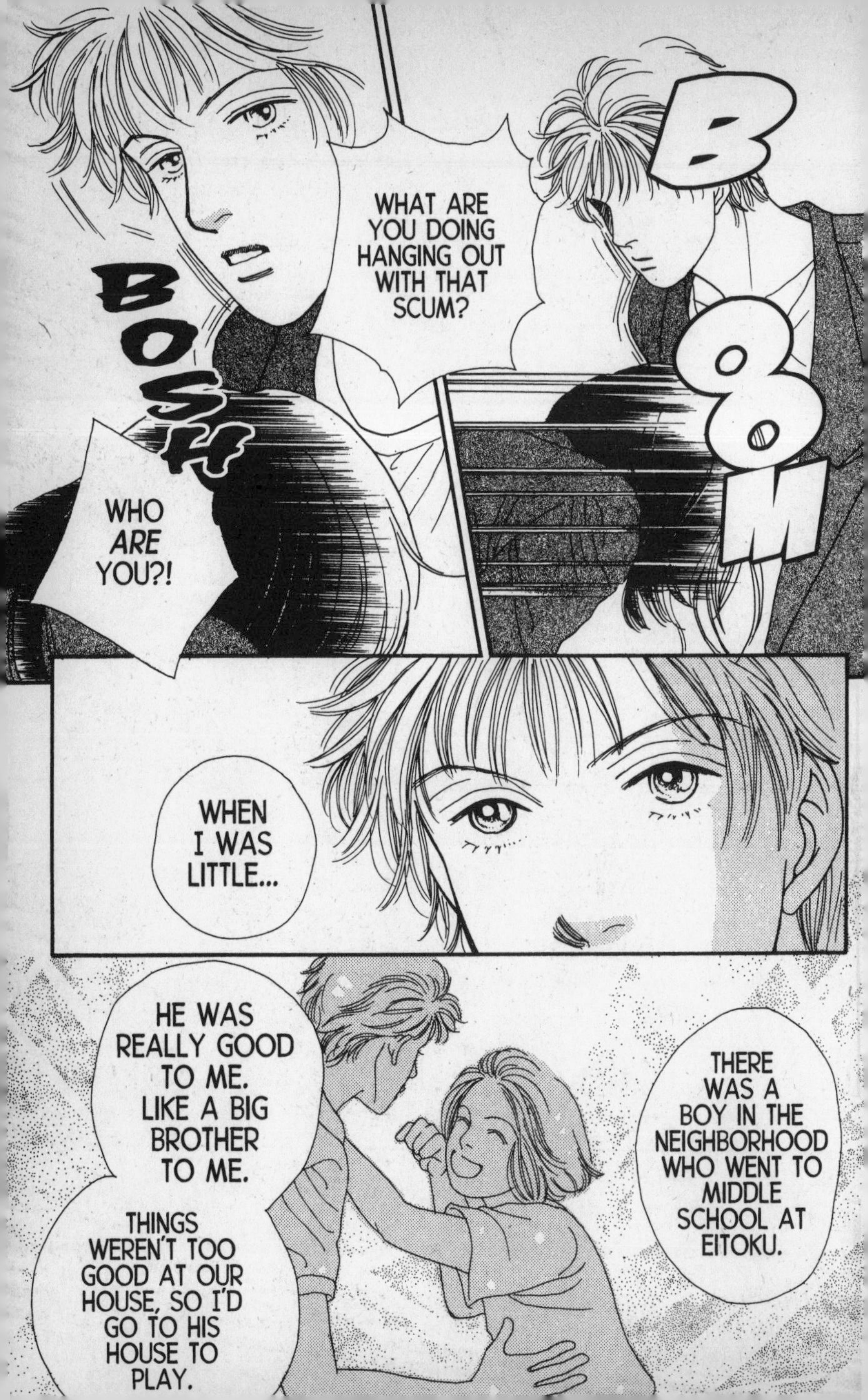
WHAT ARE YOU DOING HANGING OUT WITH THAT SCUM?
BOOM
BOSH
WHO *ARE* YOU?!
WHEN I WAS LITTLE...
THERE WAS A BOY IN THE NEIGHBORHOOD WHO WENT TO MIDDLE SCHOOL AT EITOKU.
HE WAS REALLY GOOD TO ME. LIKE A BIG BROTHER TO ME.
THINGS WEREN'T TOO GOOD AT OUR HOUSE, SO I'D GO TO HIS HOUSE TO PLAY.

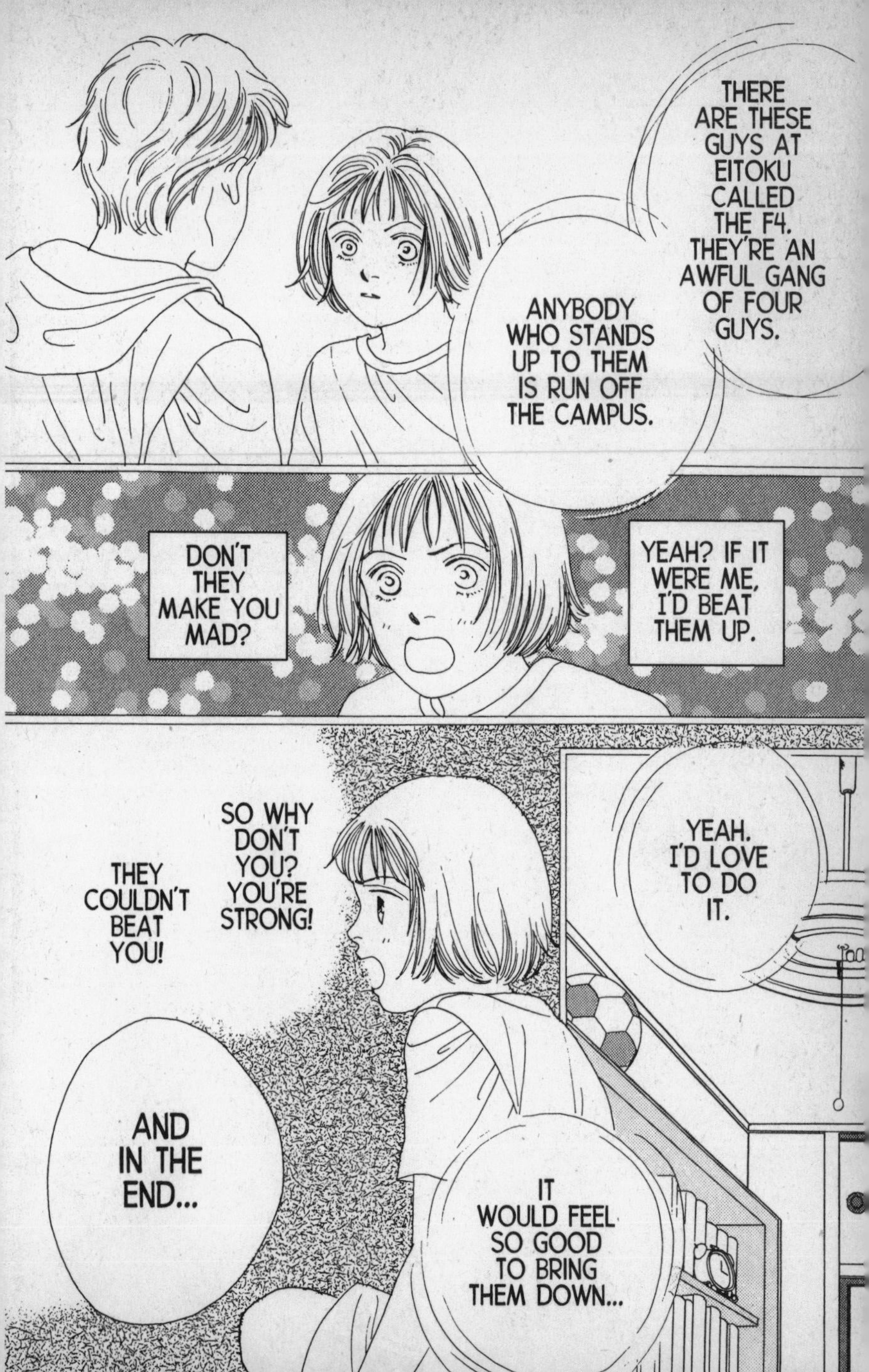
THERE ARE THESE GUYS AT EITOKU CALLED THE F4. THEY'RE AN AWFUL GANG OF FOUR GUYS.
ANYBODY WHO STANDS UP TO THEM IS RUN OFF THE CAMPUS.
YEAH? IF IT WERE ME, I'D BEAT THEM UP.
DON'T THEY MAKE YOU MAD?
YEAH. I'D LOVE TO DO IT.
SO WHY DON'T YOU? YOU'RE STRONG!
THEY COULDN'T BEAT YOU!
IT WOULD FEEL SO GOOD TO BRING THEM DOWN...
AND IN THE END...

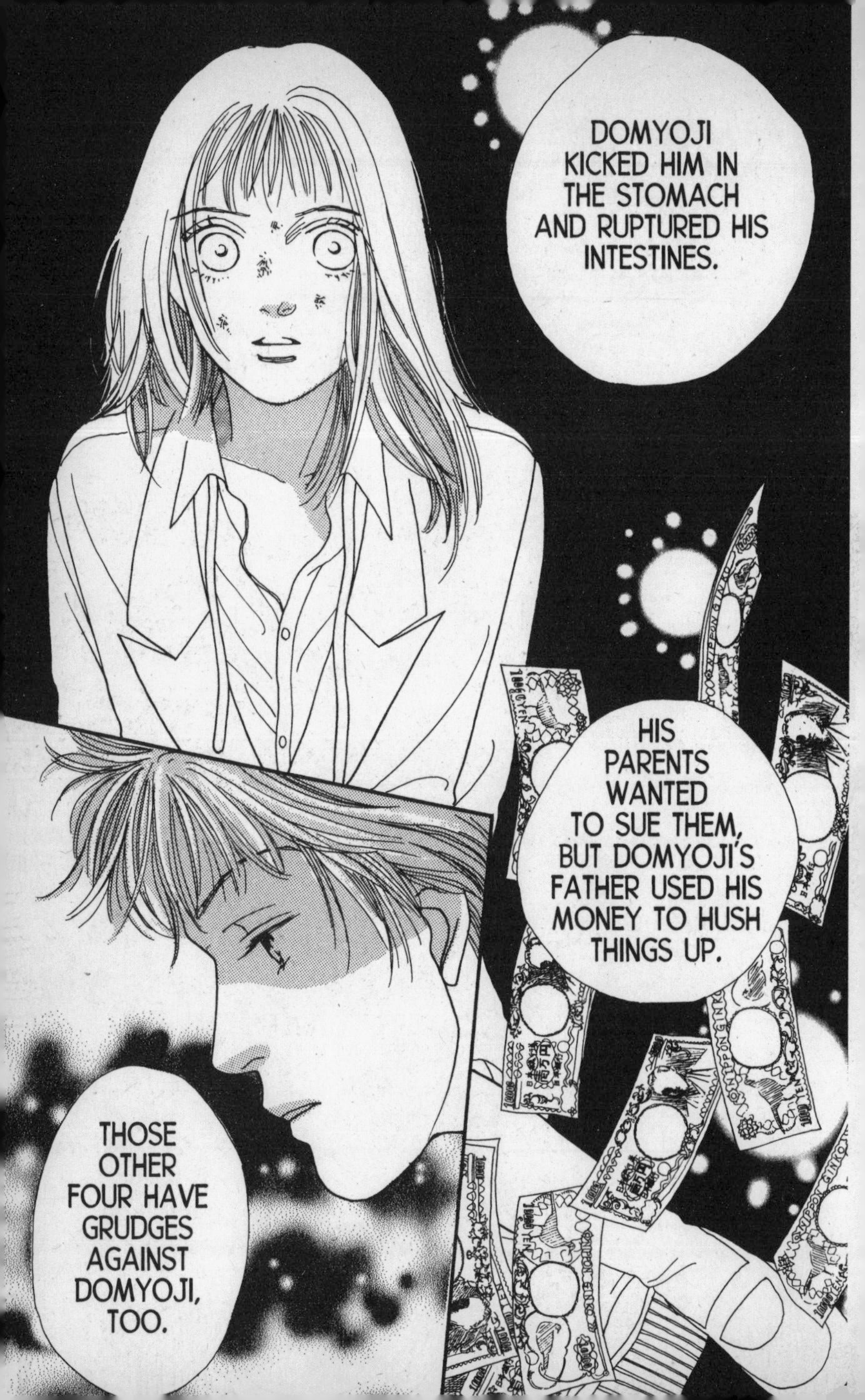
DOMYOJI KICKED HIM IN THE STOMACH AND RUPTURED HIS INTESTINES.
HIS PARENTS WANTED TO SUE THEM, BUT DOMYOJI'S FATHER USED HIS MONEY TO HUSH THINGS UP.
THOSE OTHER FOUR HAVE GRUDGES AGAINST DOMYOJI, TOO.

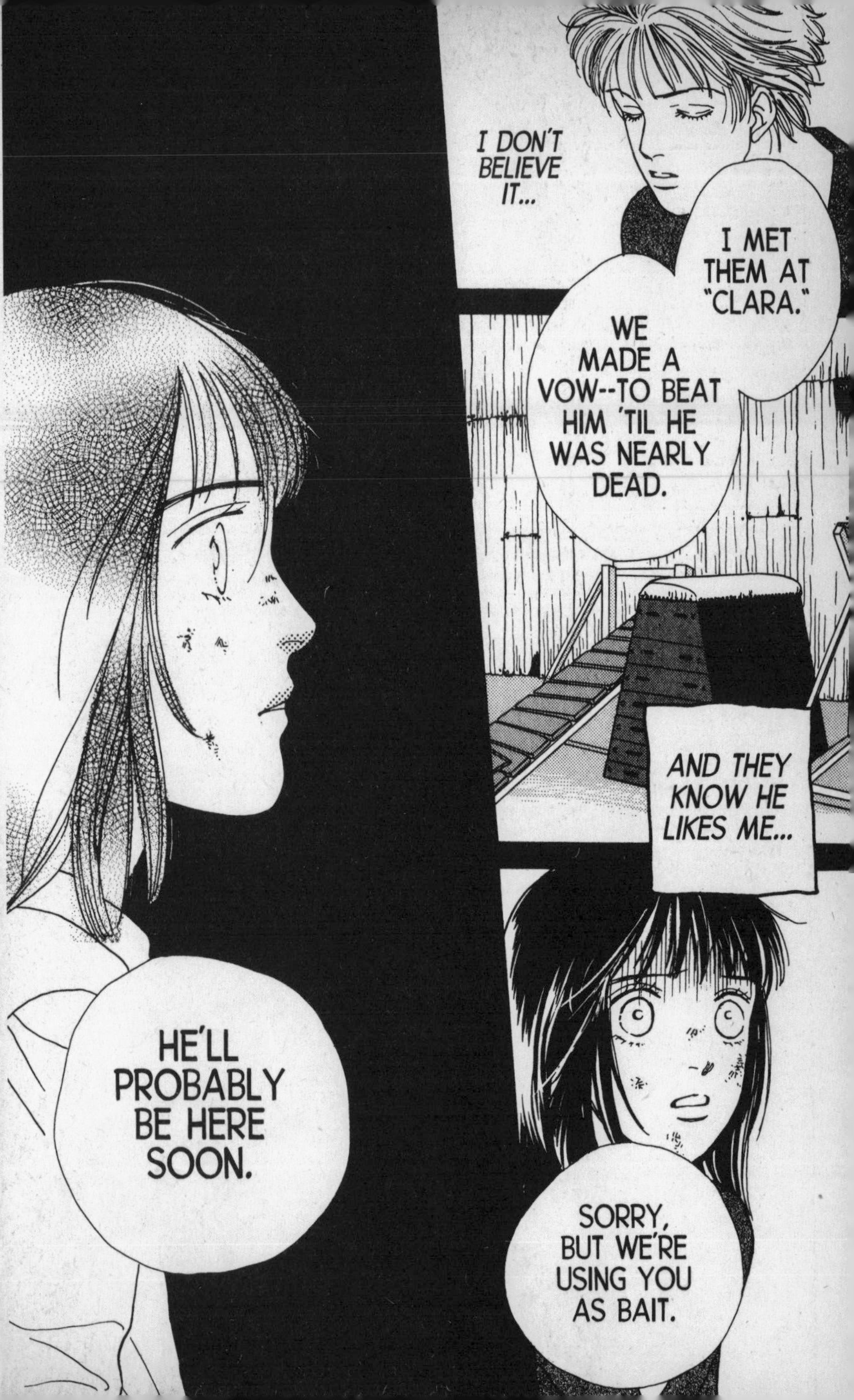
I DON'T BELIEVE IT...
I MET THEM AT "CLARA."
WE MADE A VOW--TO BEAT HIM 'TIL HE WAS NEARLY DEAD.
AND THEY KNOW HE LIKES ME...
SORRY, BUT WE'RE USING YOU AS BAIT.
HE'LL PROBABLY BE HERE SOON.

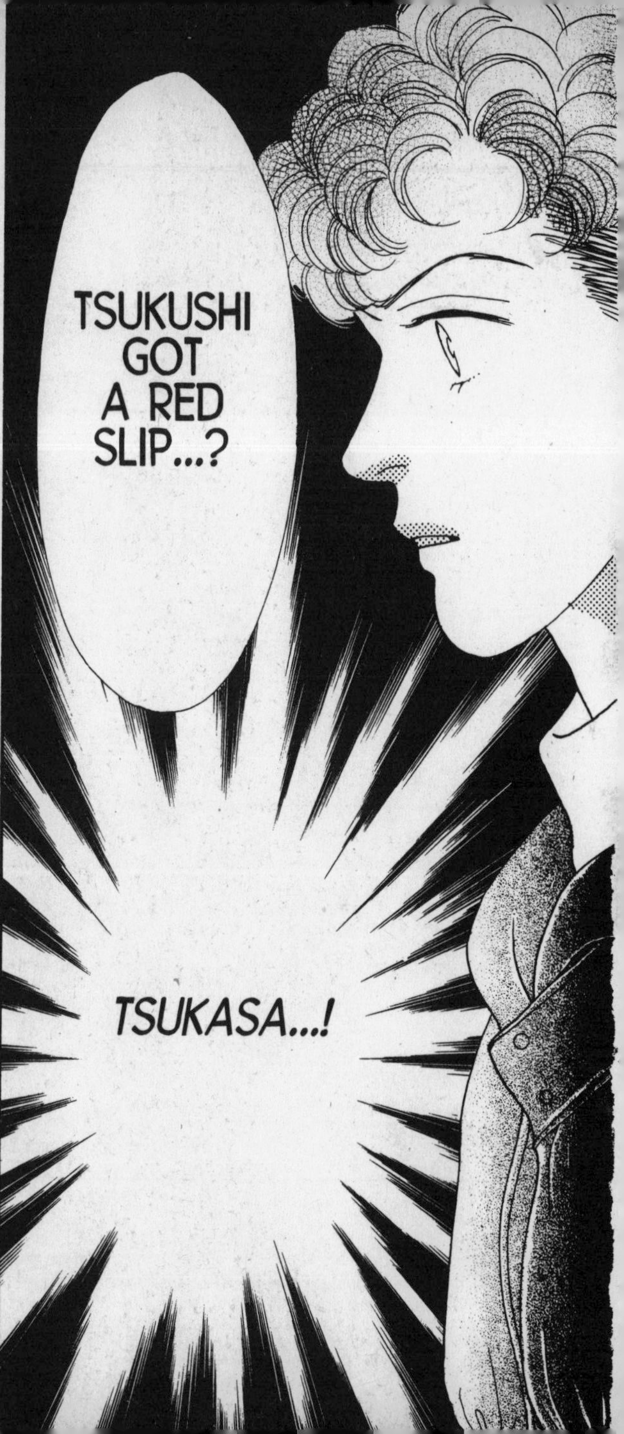
TSUKUSHI GOT A RED SLIP...?
TSUKASA...!

Here's the question I've been getting most frequently:

"Is Tsukasa 17? Or 18?"

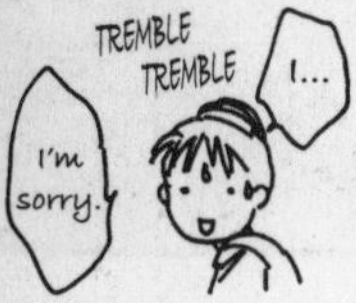
TREMBLE TREMBLE
I...
I'm sorry.

I wrote that he was 18 once, but that was a mistake. Tsukasa was born on December 31, so he's turning 18 in this volume.

And in Volume 3, I gave you the address for fan letters, but it's changed since. (Your letters are still reaching me, though.)

Editor's note:
Don't worry the address is the same for the English version!

Boys over Flowers
Viz LLC
P.O. Box 77010
San Francisco, CA
94107

Please keep writing!!

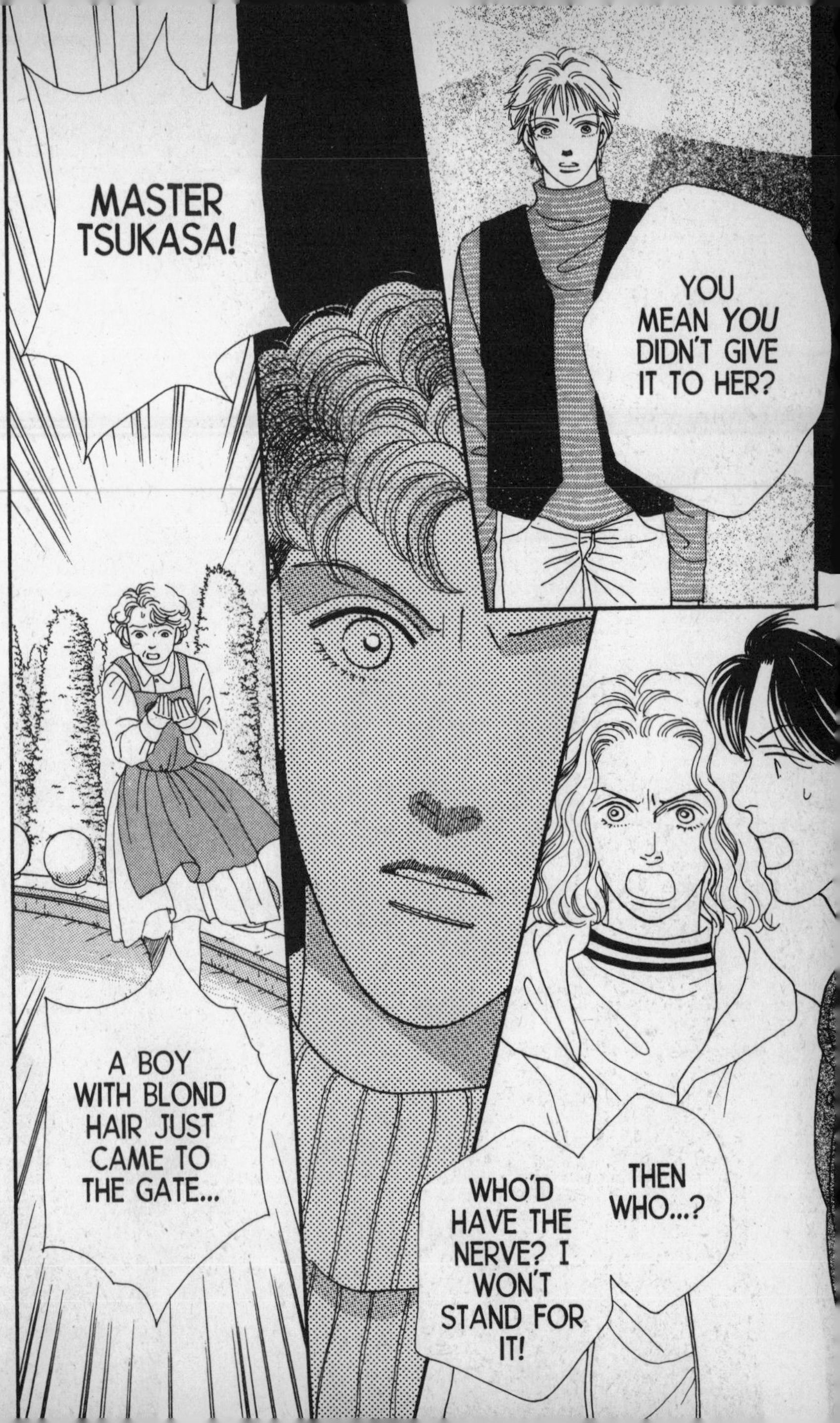
YOU MEAN *YOU* DIDN'T GIVE IT TO HER?
THEN WHO...?
WHO'D HAVE THE NERVE? I WON'T STAND FOR IT!
MASTER TSUKASA!
A BOY WITH BLOND HAIR JUST CAME TO THE GATE...

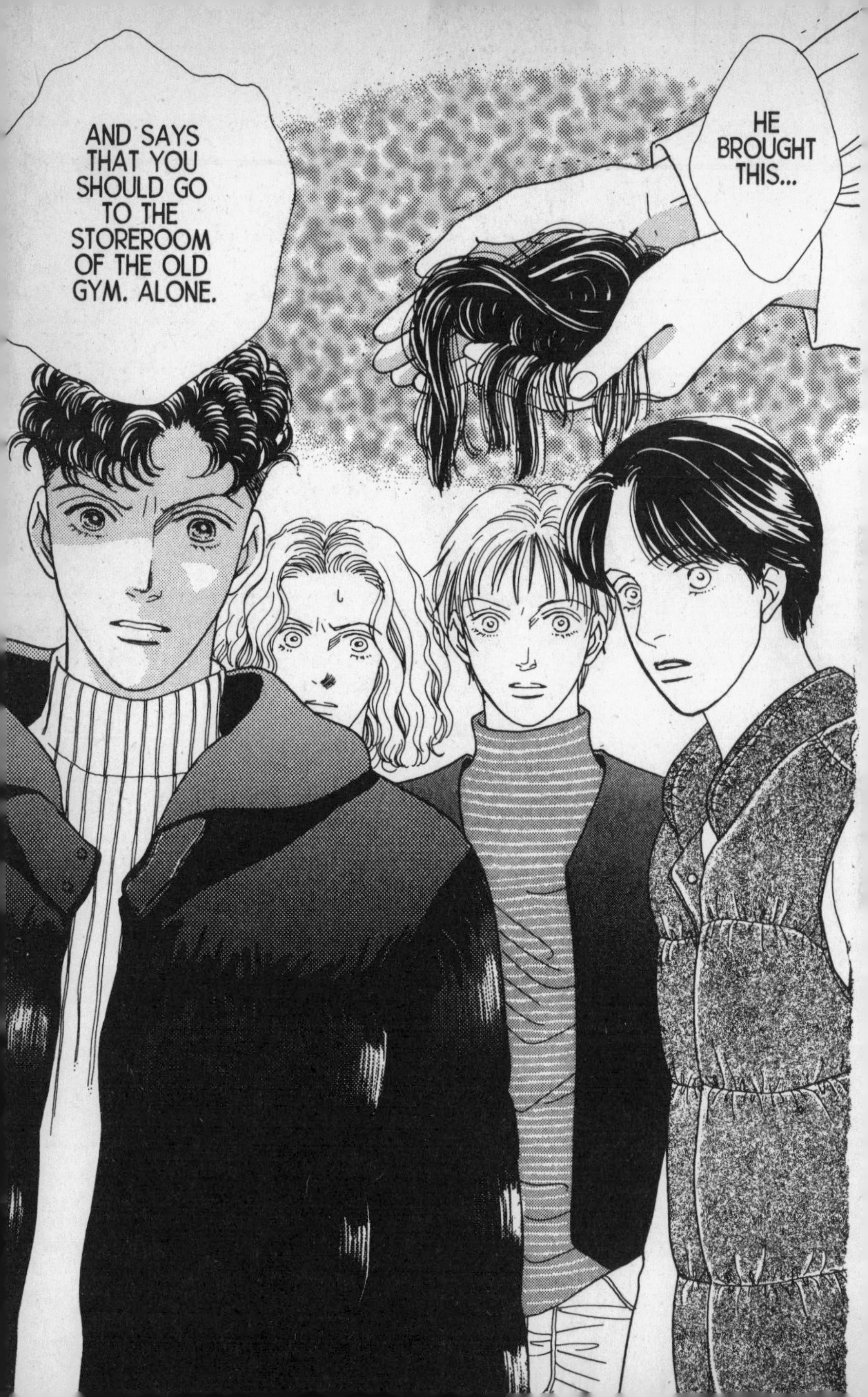
HE BROUGHT THIS...
AND SAYS THAT YOU SHOULD GO TO THE STOREROOM OF THE OLD GYM. ALONE.

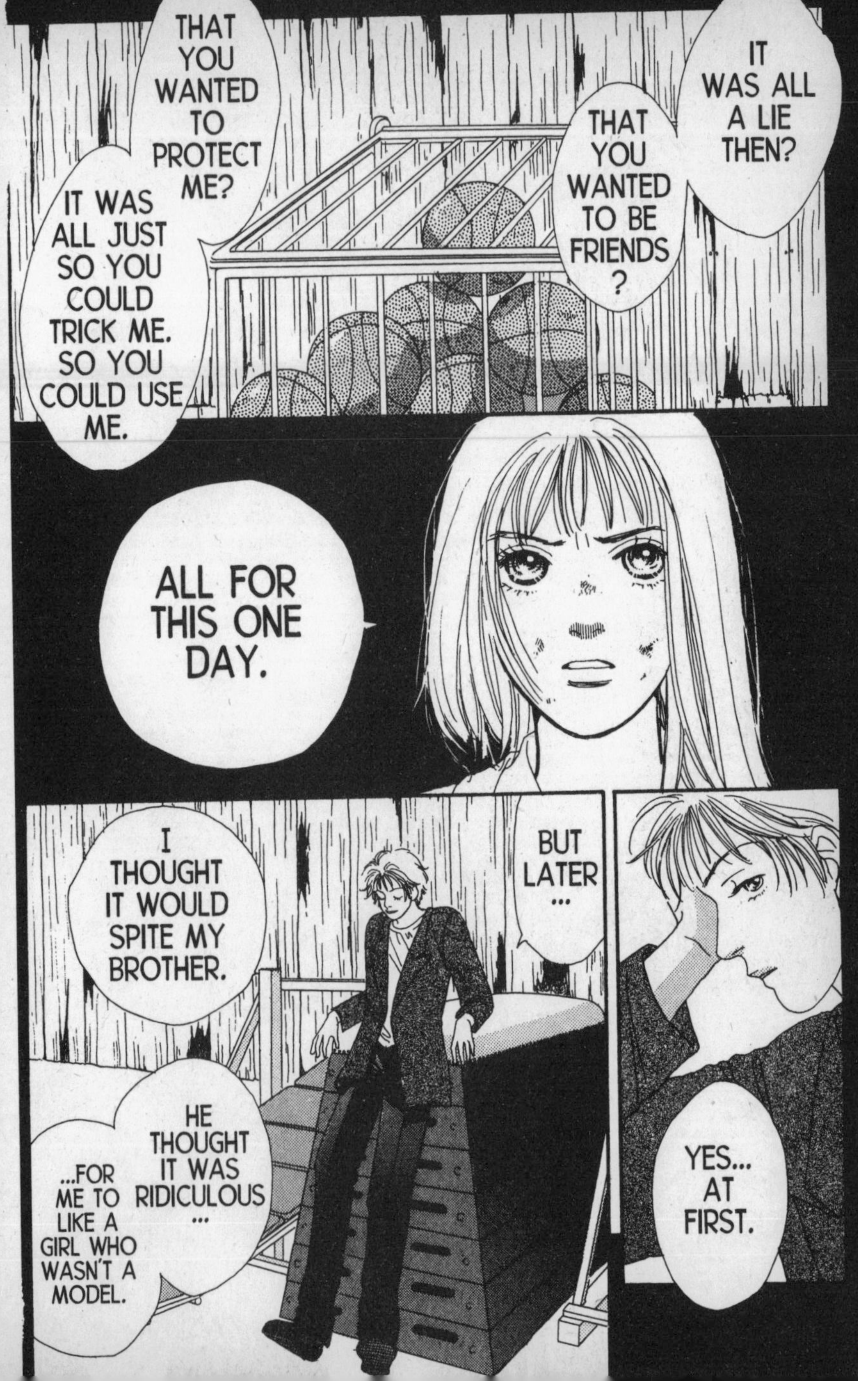
IT WAS ALL A LIE THEN?
THAT YOU WANTED TO BE FRIENDS?
THAT YOU WANTED TO PROTECT ME?
IT WAS ALL JUST SO YOU COULD TRICK ME. SO YOU COULD USE ME.
ALL FOR THIS ONE DAY.
YES... AT FIRST.
BUT LATER...
I THOUGHT IT WOULD SPITE MY BROTHER.
HE THOUGHT IT WAS RIDICULOUS...
...FOR ME TO LIKE A GIRL WHO WASN'T A MODEL.

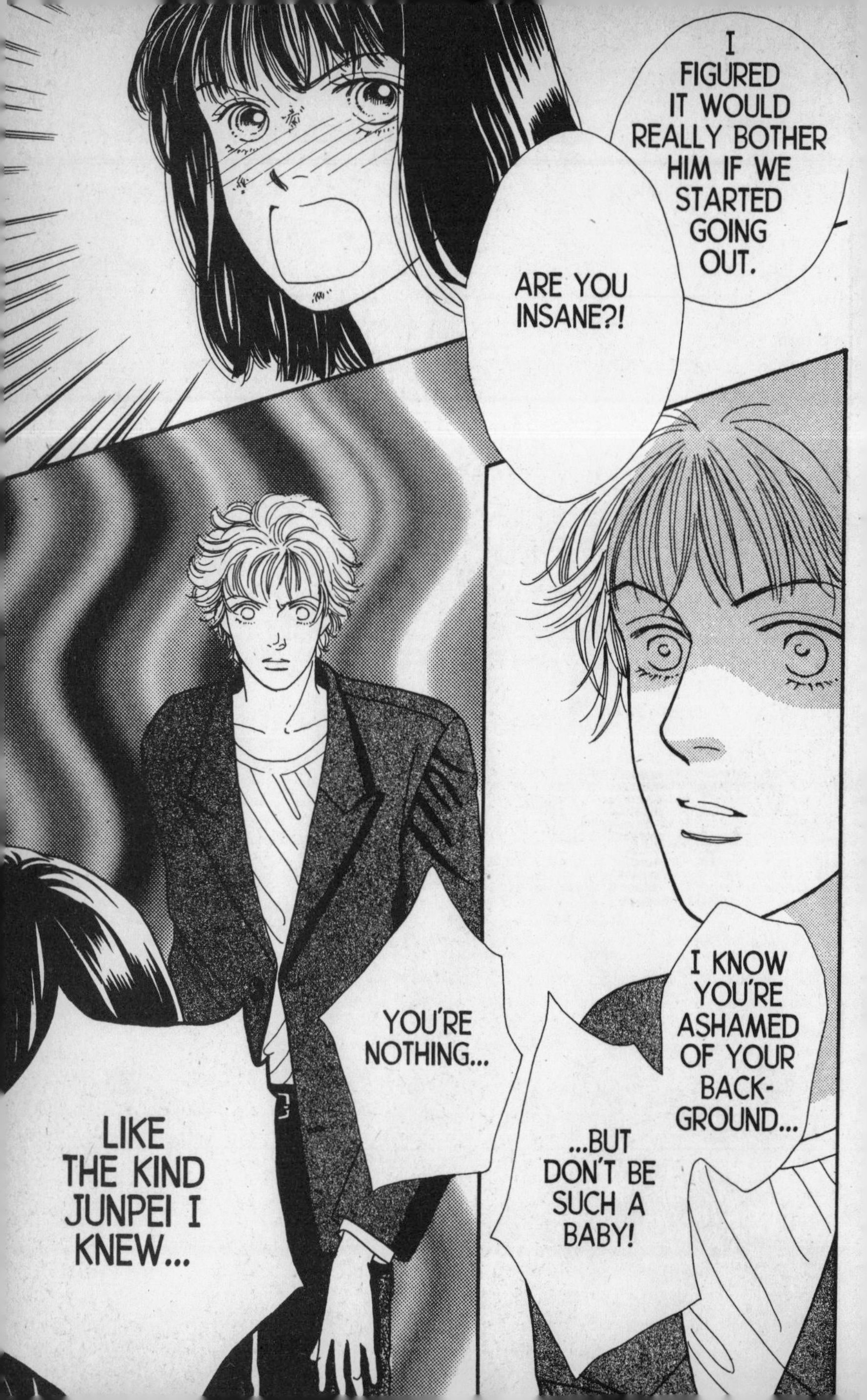
I FIGURED IT WOULD REALLY BOTHER HIM IF WE STARTED GOING OUT.
ARE YOU INSANE?!
I KNOW YOU'RE ASHAMED OF YOUR BACK-GROUND...
...BUT DON'T BE SUCH A BABY!
YOU'RE NOTHING...
LIKE THE KIND JUNPEI I KNEW...

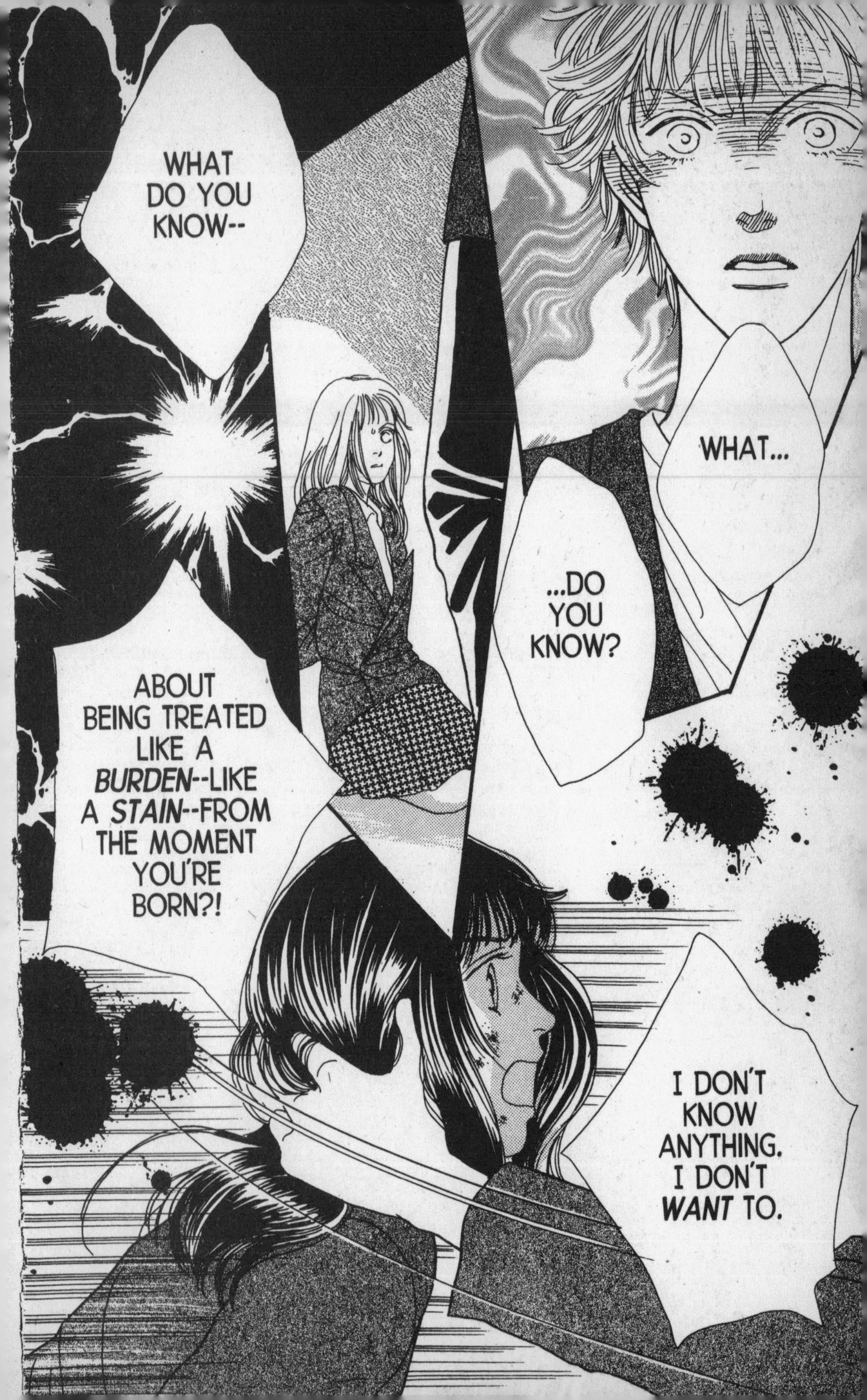
WHAT...
...DO YOU KNOW?
WHAT DO YOU KNOW--
ABOUT BEING TREATED LIKE A *BURDEN*--LIKE A *STAIN*--FROM THE MOMENT YOU'RE BORN?!
I DON'T KNOW ANYTHING. I DON'T *WANT* TO.

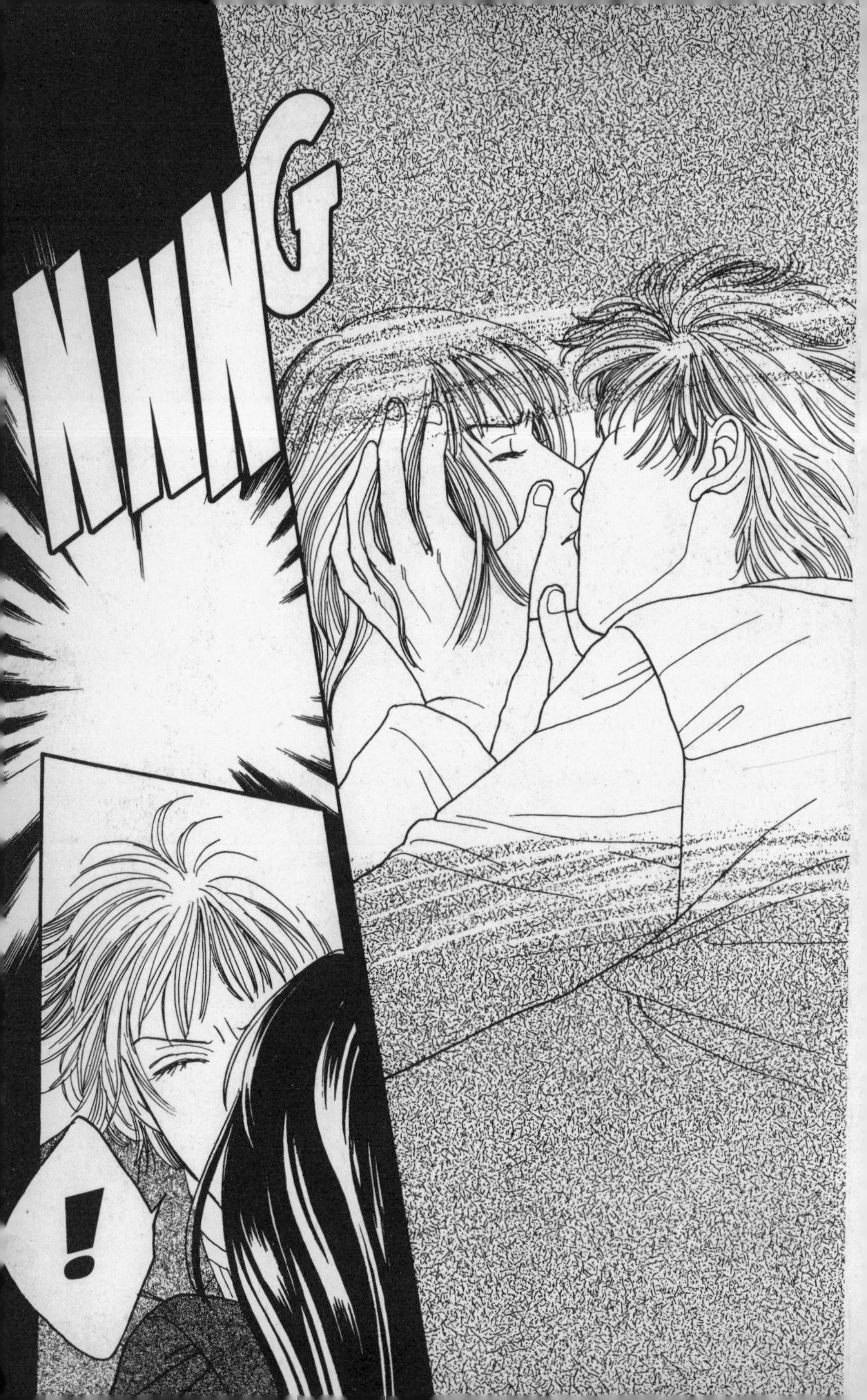
MMMMG
!

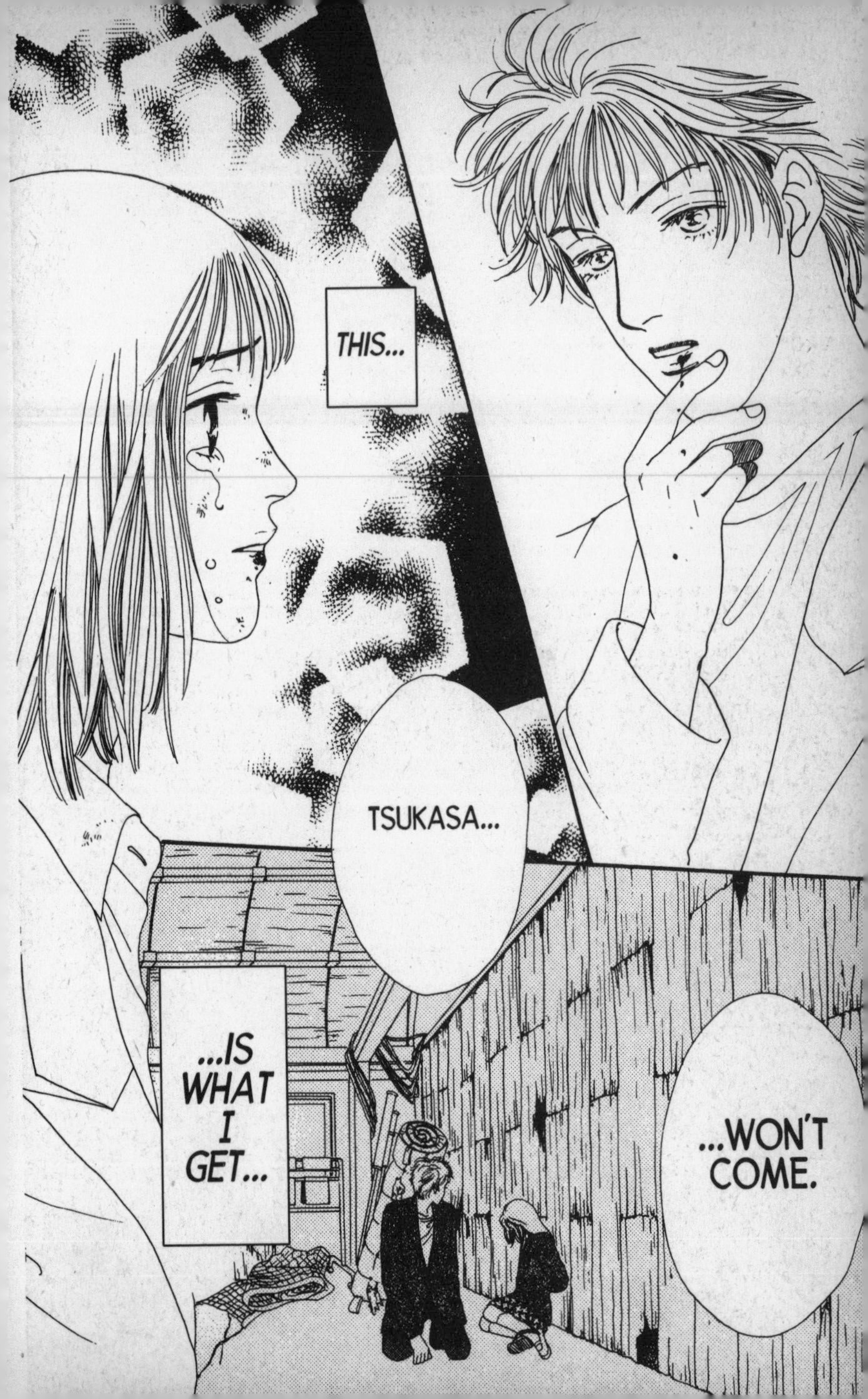
TSUKASA...
...WON'T COME.
THIS...
...IS WHAT I GET...

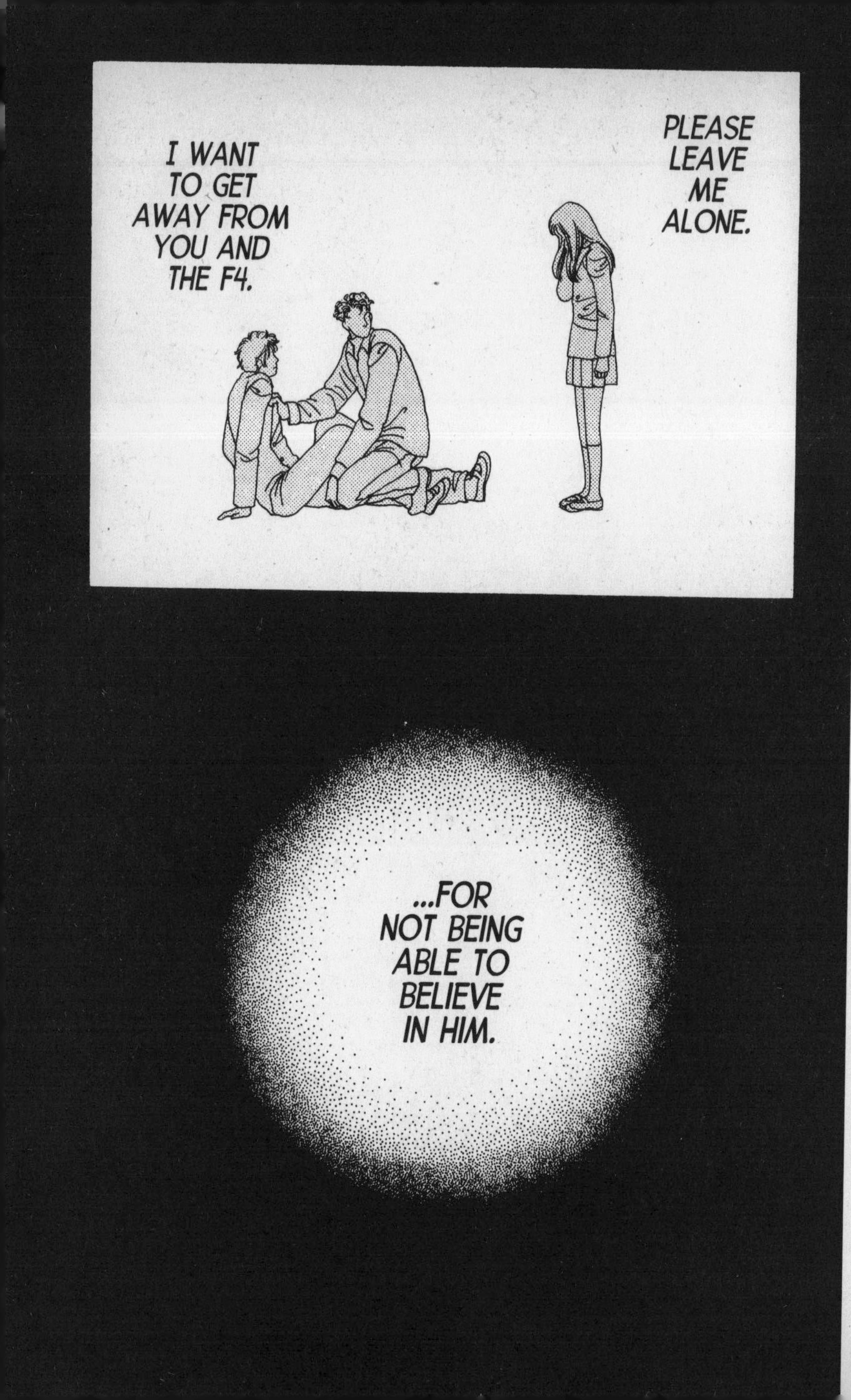
PLEASE LEAVE ME ALONE.
I WANT TO GET AWAY FROM YOU AND THE F4.
...FOR NOT BEING ABLE TO BELIEVE IN HIM.

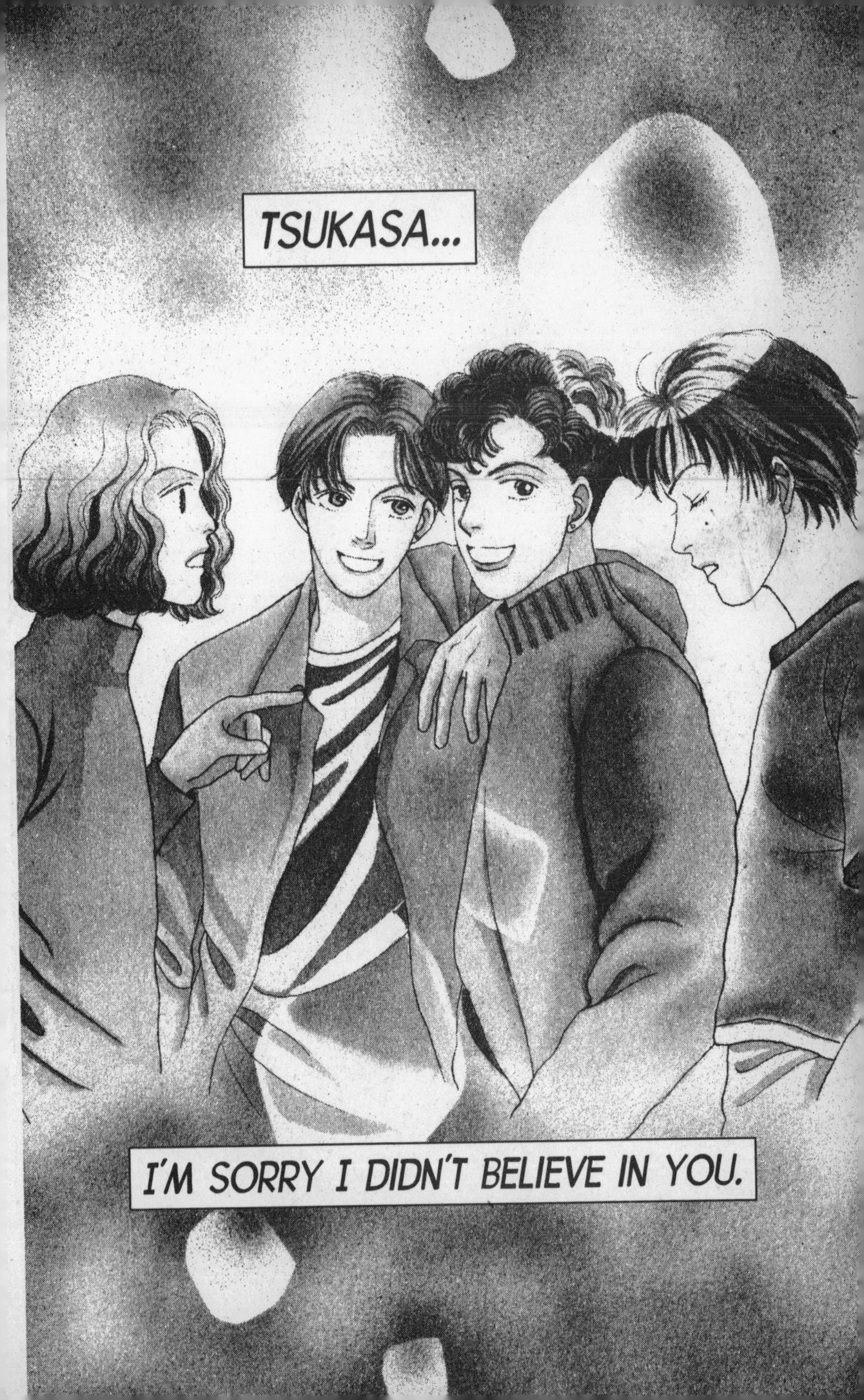
TSUKASA...
I'M SORRY I DIDN'T BELIEVE IN YOU.

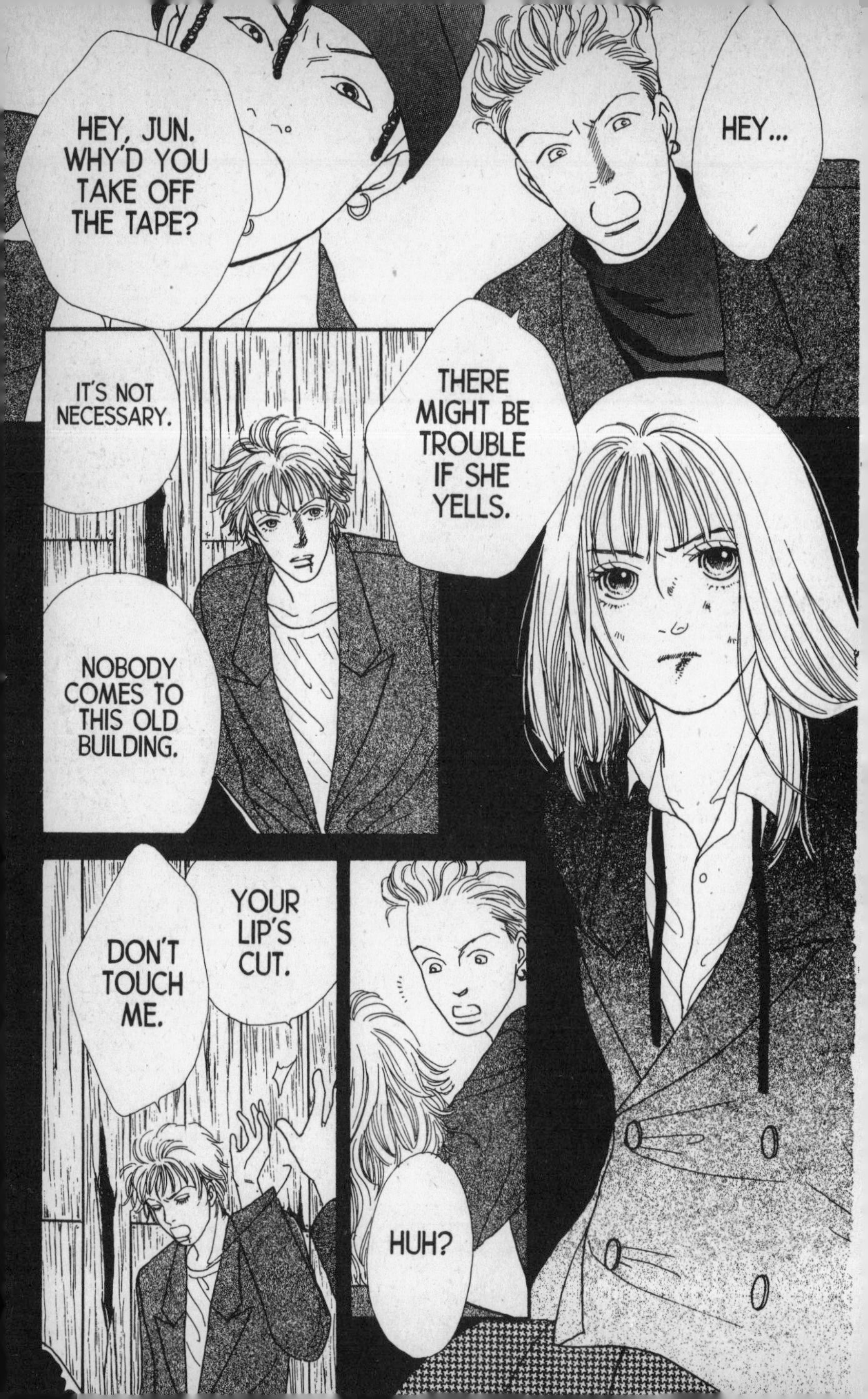
HEY...
HEY, JUN. WHY'D YOU TAKE OFF THE TAPE?
THERE MIGHT BE TROUBLE IF SHE YELLS.
IT'S NOT NECESSARY.
NOBODY COMES TO THIS OLD BUILDING.
YOUR LIP'S CUT.
DON'T TOUCH ME.
HUH?

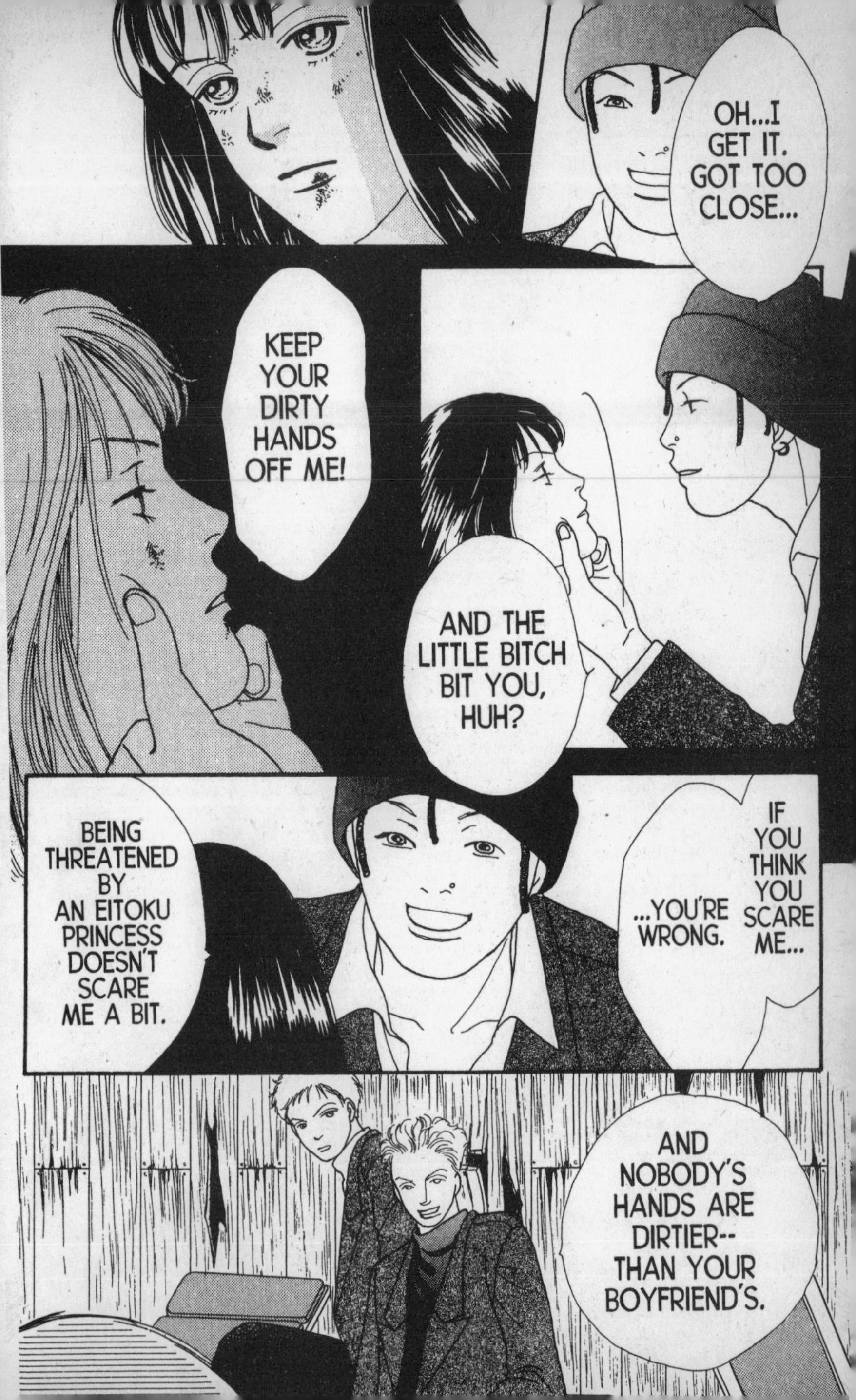
OH...I GET IT. GOT TOO CLOSE...
AND THE LITTLE BITCH BIT YOU, HUH?
KEEP YOUR DIRTY HANDS OFF ME!
IF YOU THINK YOU SCARE ME...
...YOU'RE WRONG.
BEING THREATENED BY AN EITOKU PRINCESS DOESN'T SCARE ME A BIT.
AND NOBODY'S HANDS ARE DIRTIER-- THAN YOUR BOYFRIEND'S.

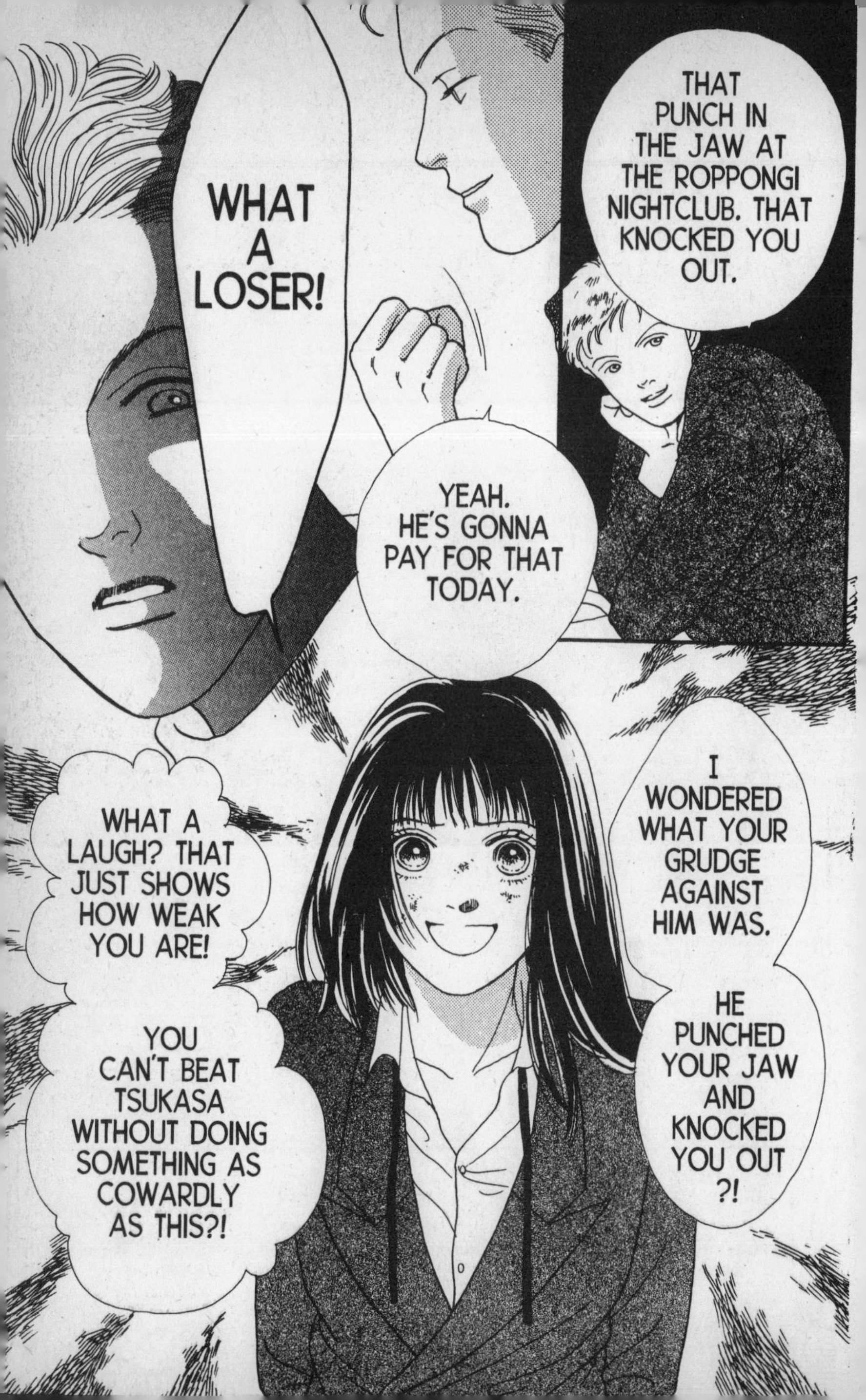
THAT PUNCH IN THE JAW AT THE ROPPONGI NIGHTCLUB. THAT KNOCKED YOU OUT.
WHAT A LOSER!
YEAH. HE'S GONNA PAY FOR THAT TODAY.
I WONDERED WHAT YOUR GRUDGE AGAINST HIM WAS.
HE PUNCHED YOUR JAW AND KNOCKED YOU OUT ?!
WHAT A LAUGH? THAT JUST SHOWS HOW WEAK YOU ARE!
YOU CAN'T BEAT TSUKASA WITHOUT DOING SOMETHING AS COWARDLY AS THIS?!

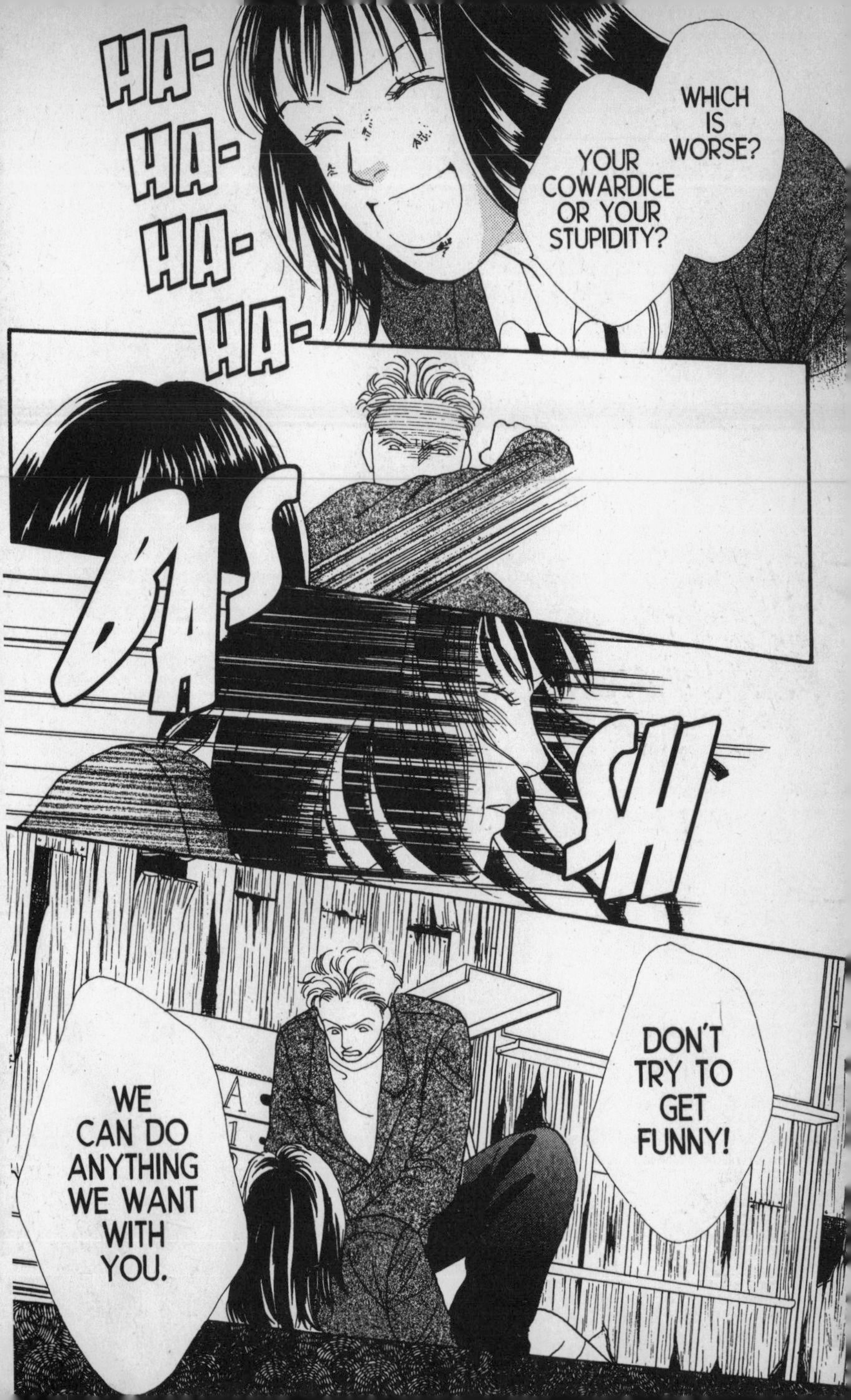
WHICH IS WORSE? YOUR COWARDICE OR YOUR STUPIDITY?
HA-HA-HA-HA-
BASH
DON'T TRY TO GET FUNNY!
WE CAN DO ANYTHING WE WANT WITH YOU.

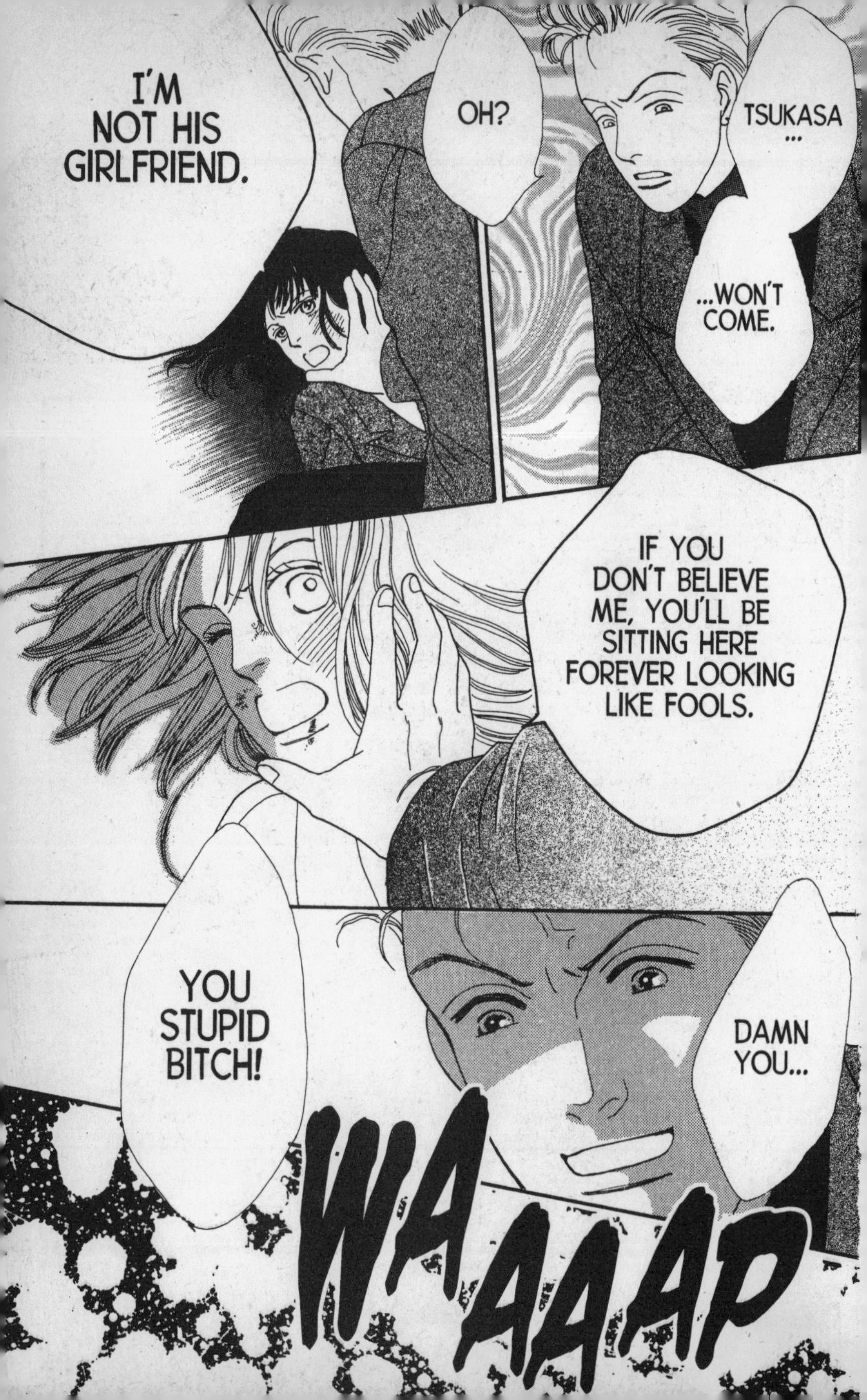
TSUKASA ...
...WON'T COME.
OH?
I'M NOT HIS GIRLFRIEND.
IF YOU DON'T BELIEVE ME, YOU'LL BE SITTING HERE FOREVER LOOKING LIKE FOOLS.
DAMN YOU...
YOU STUPID BITCH!
WAAAAP

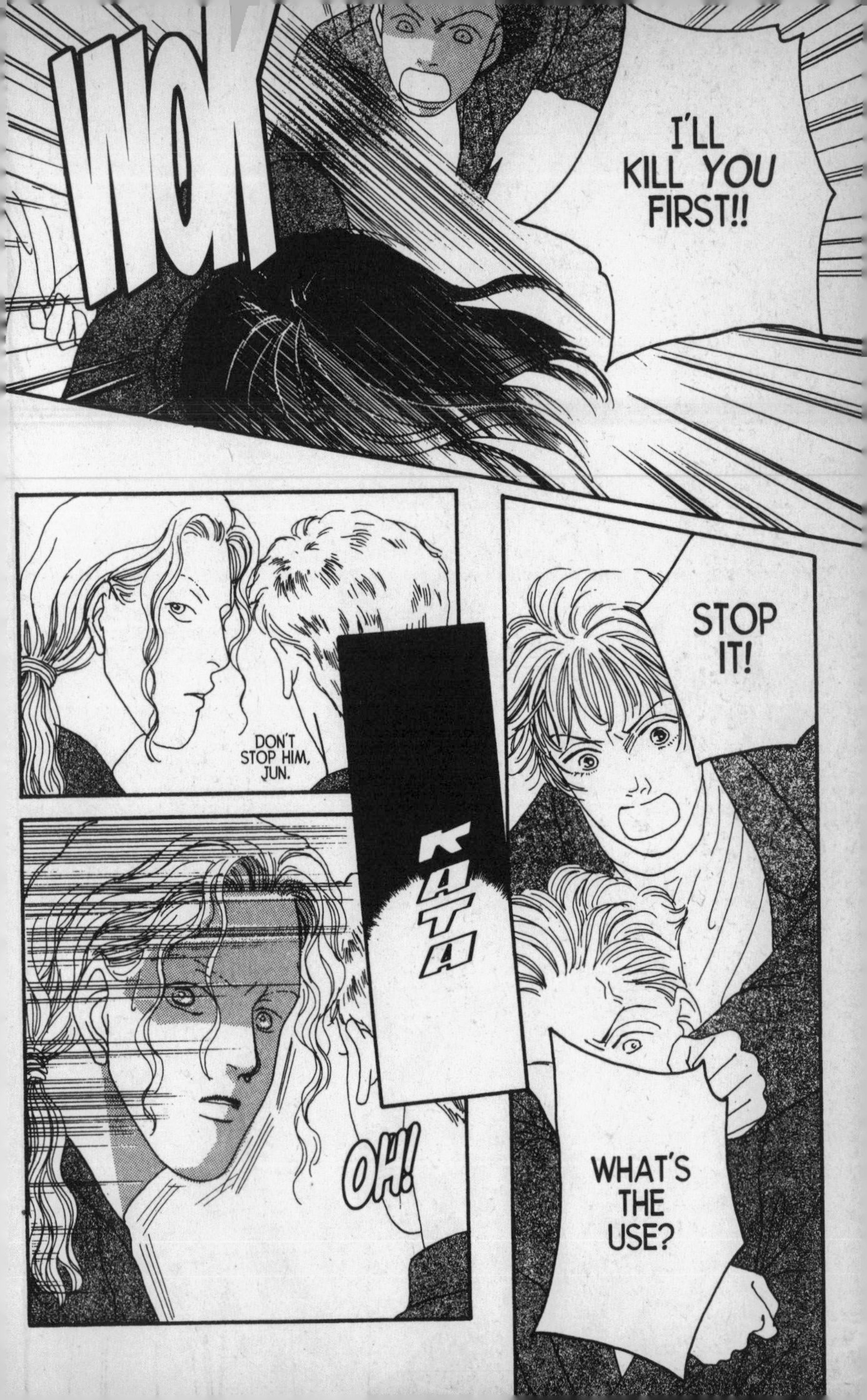
I'LL KILL *YOU* FIRST!!
WOK
STOP IT!
WHAT'S THE USE?
KATA
DON'T STOP HIM, JUN.
OH!

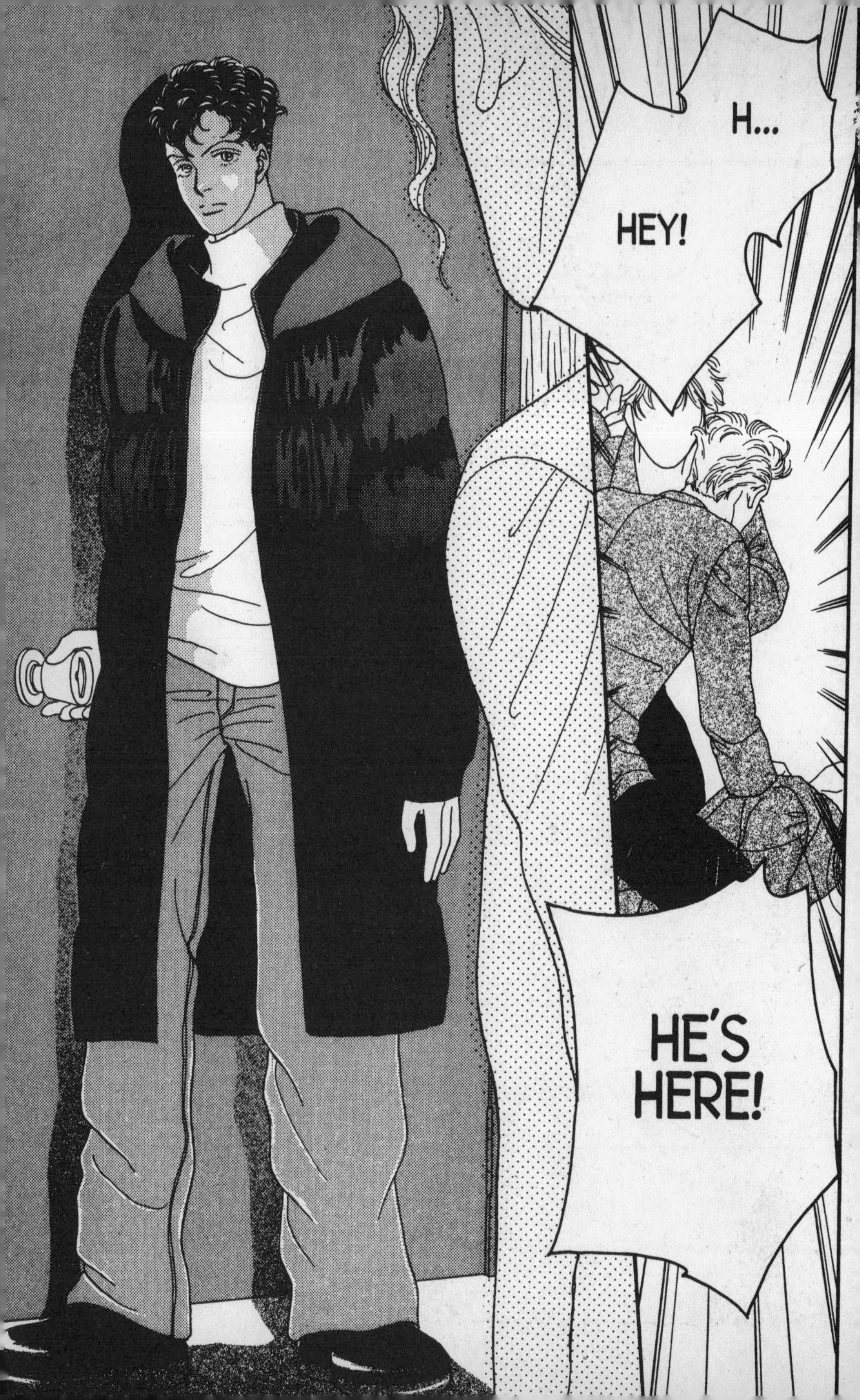
H...
HEY!
HE'S HERE!

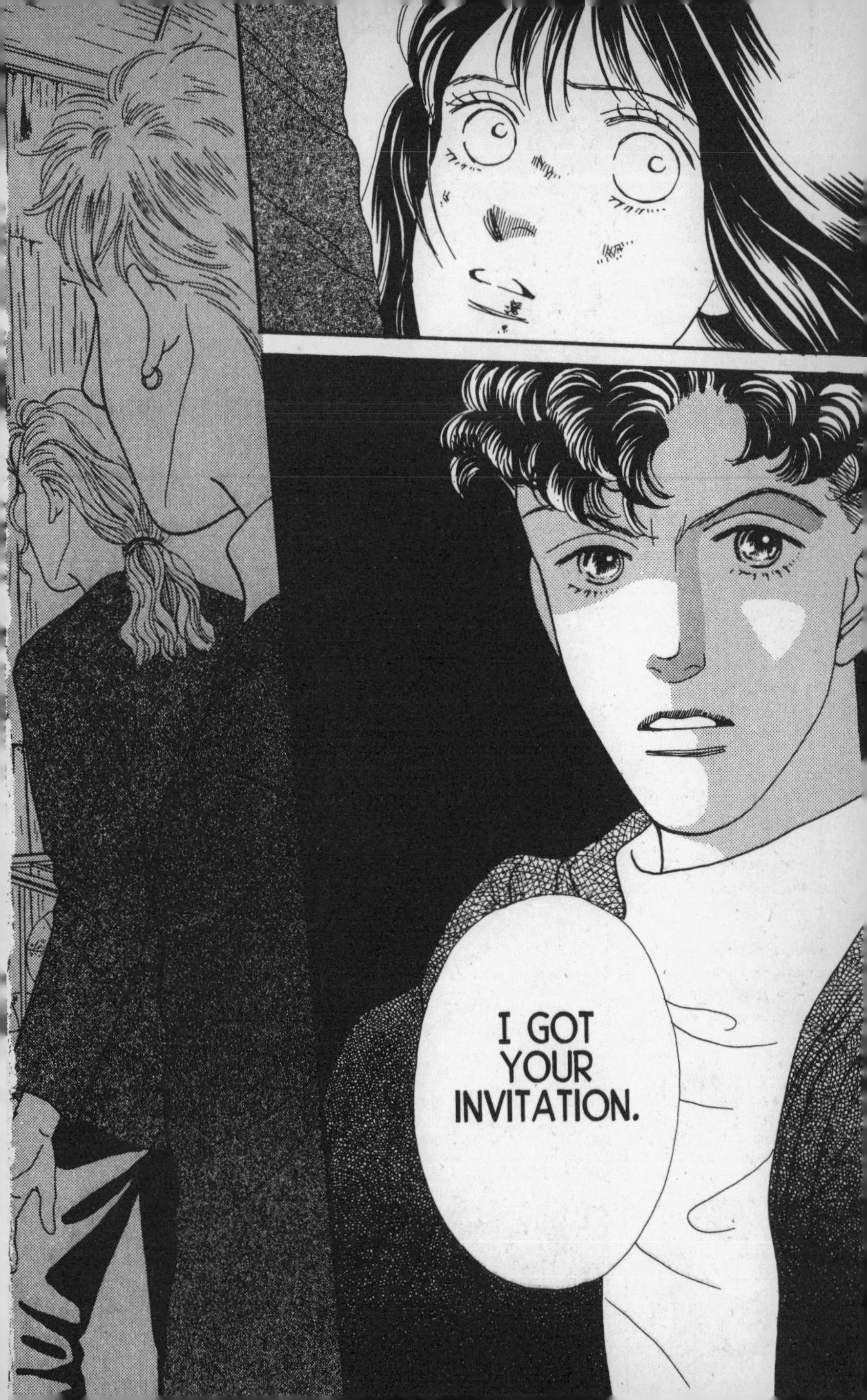
I GOT YOUR INVITATION.

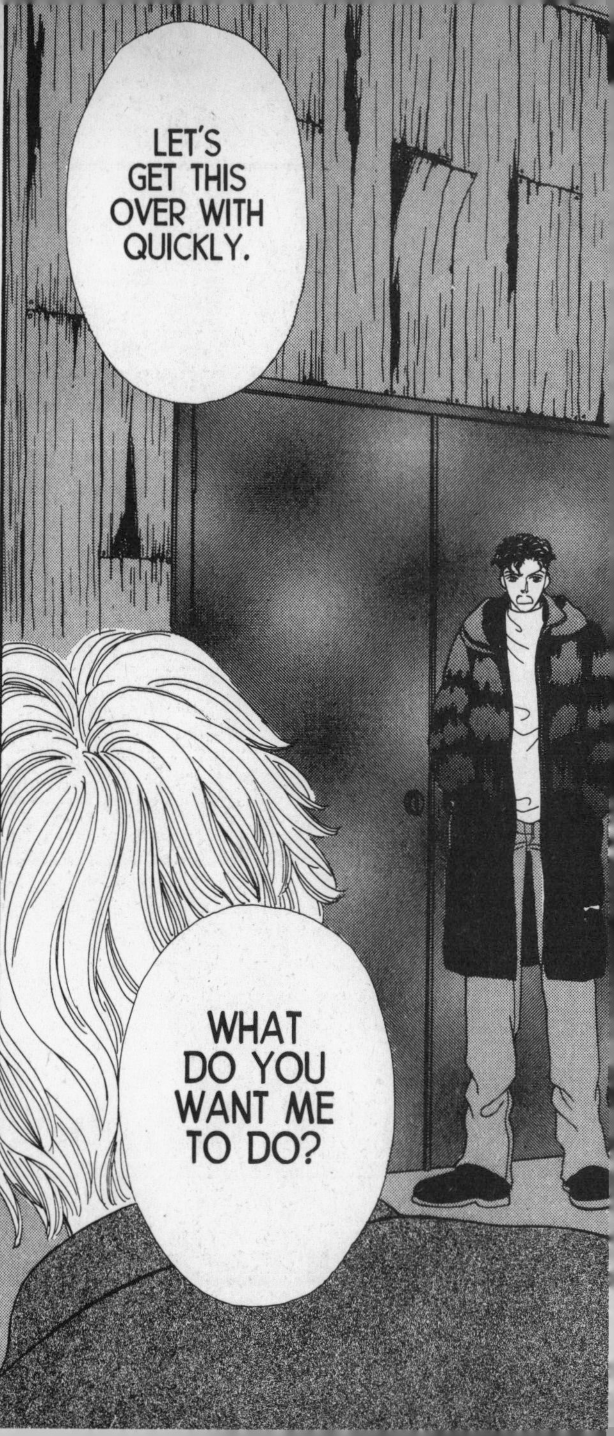
LET'S GET THIS OVER WITH QUICKLY.
WHAT DO YOU WANT ME TO DO?

I'm still working nights, as usual, but I've been getting up early on Sundays.

Why?

I watch the anime. Yes, *this* anime! Do you all watch it?

I don't usually go back and reread my own work, but as I'm watching the anime I think, "Oh, is that what I drew...?" I feel like one of my readers, and it's fun. The artwork on the backgrounds is very pretty. It makes me feel I've got to try harder.

It's fantastic to think that life is being breathed into this work by the animators, the voice actors, and many other people.

I always used to think how wonderful it would be to have music to go with my comics. It's all very exciting.

Akira's voice is really cool. When I met Mochizuki Yuta, the actor who played Akira...

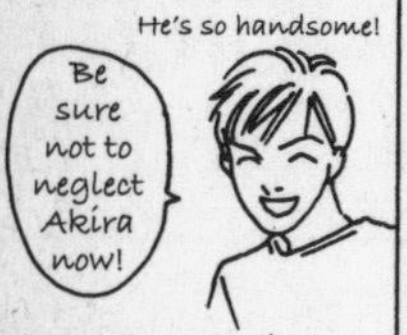
He's so handsome!
Be sure not to neglect Akira now!

That's what he said to me. (In that voice!) It made me want to make him the main character... Well, not really...

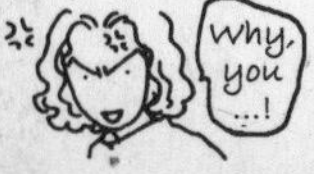
Why, you ...!

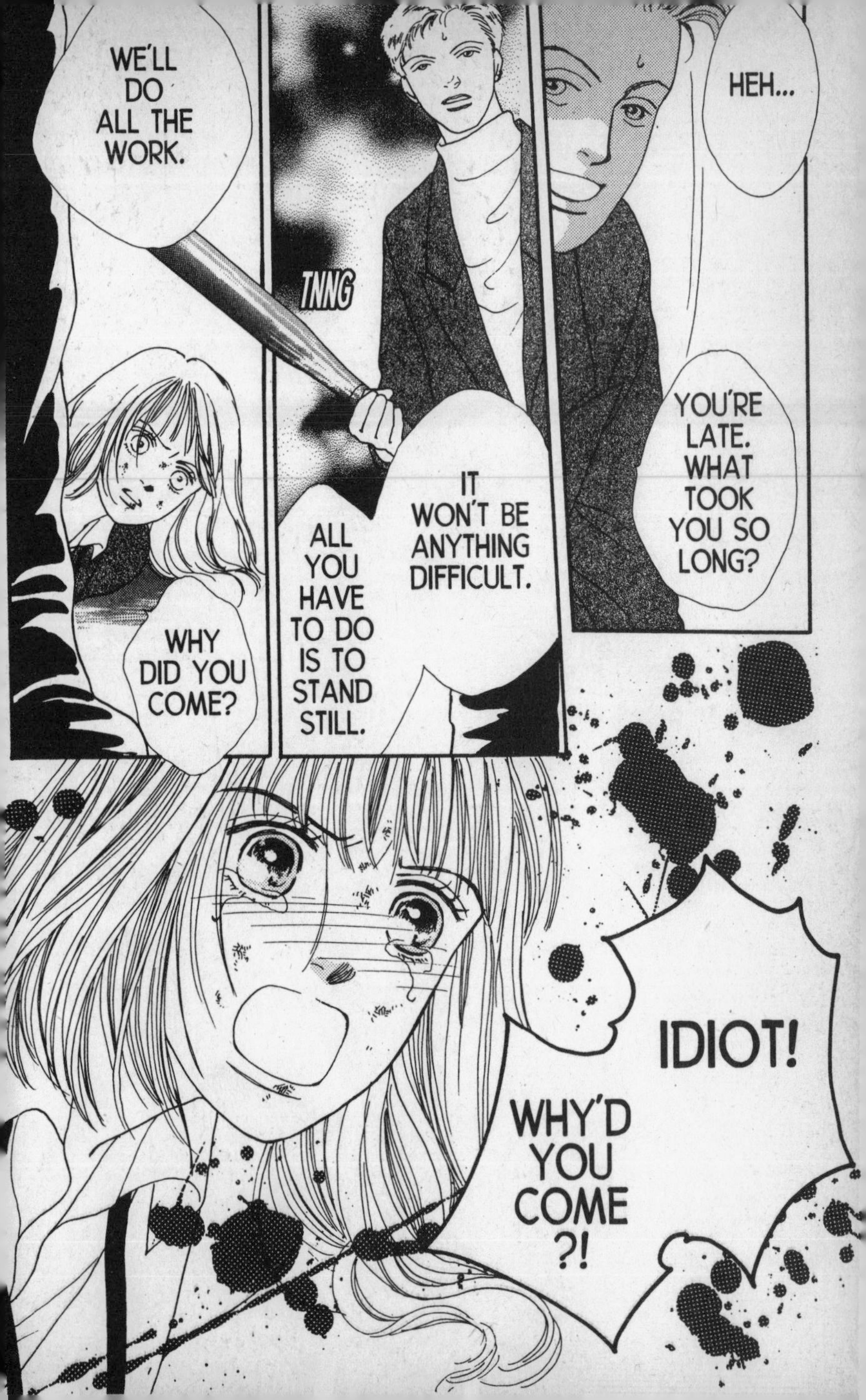
HEH...
YOU'RE LATE. WHAT TOOK YOU SO LONG?
TNNG
IT WON'T BE ANYTHING DIFFICULT.
ALL YOU HAVE TO DO IS TO STAND STILL.
WE'LL DO ALL THE WORK.
WHY DID YOU COME?
IDIOT!
WHY'D YOU COME?!

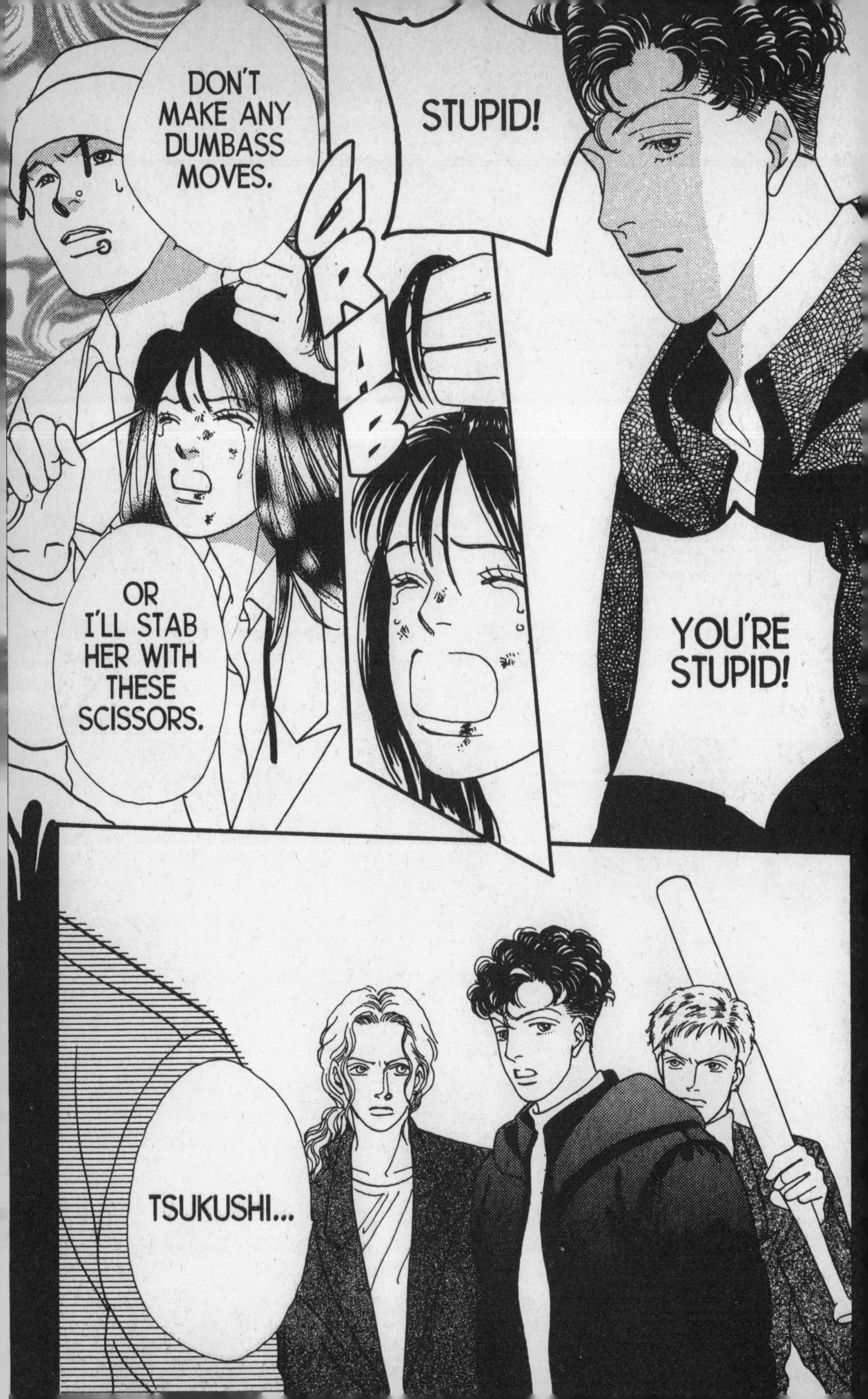
STUPID!
YOU'RE STUPID!
GRAB
DON'T MAKE ANY DUMBASS MOVES.
OR I'LL STAB HER WITH THESE SCISSORS.
TSUKUSHI...

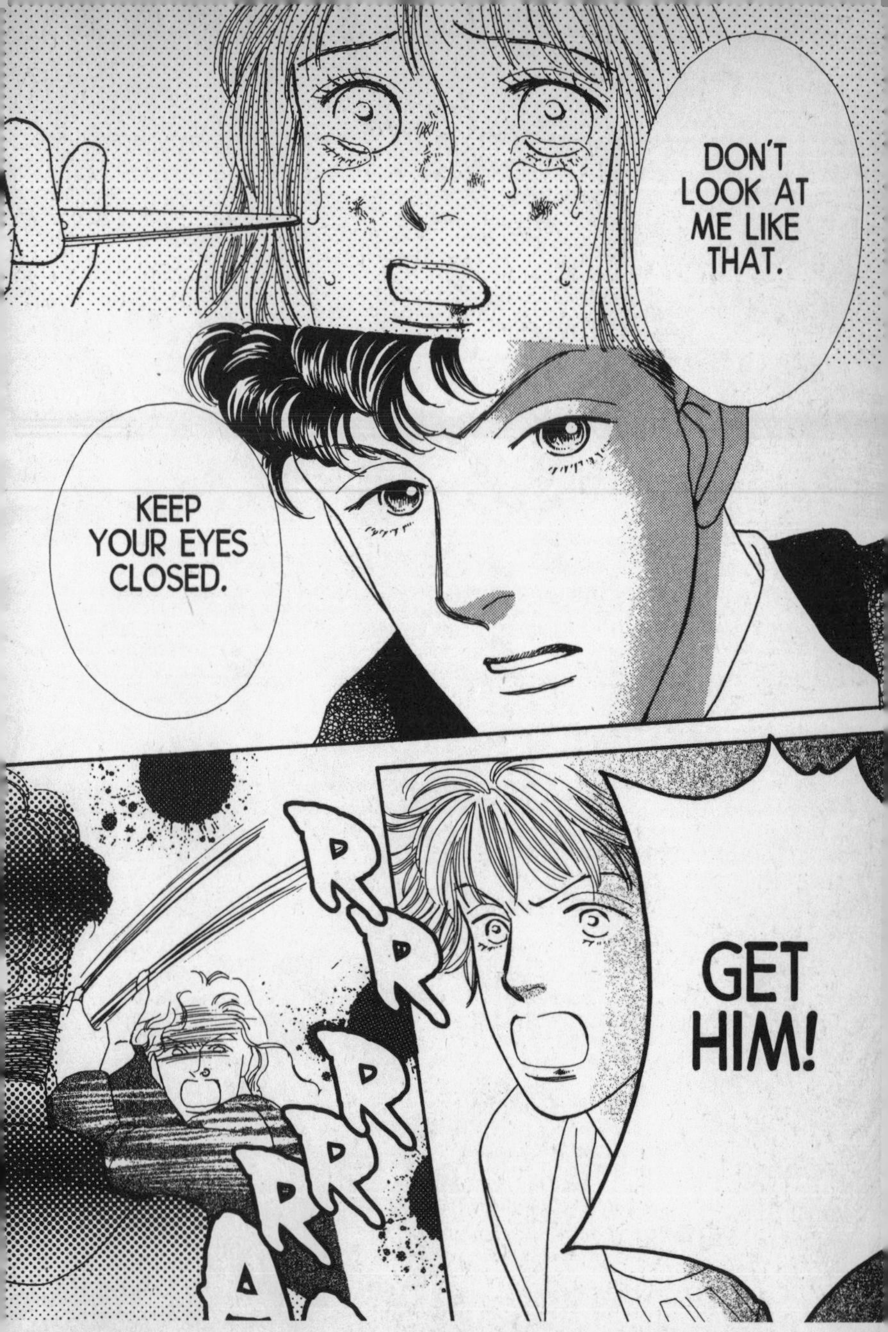
DON'T LOOK AT ME LIKE THAT.
KEEP YOUR EYES CLOSED.
GET HIM!
RRRRRA

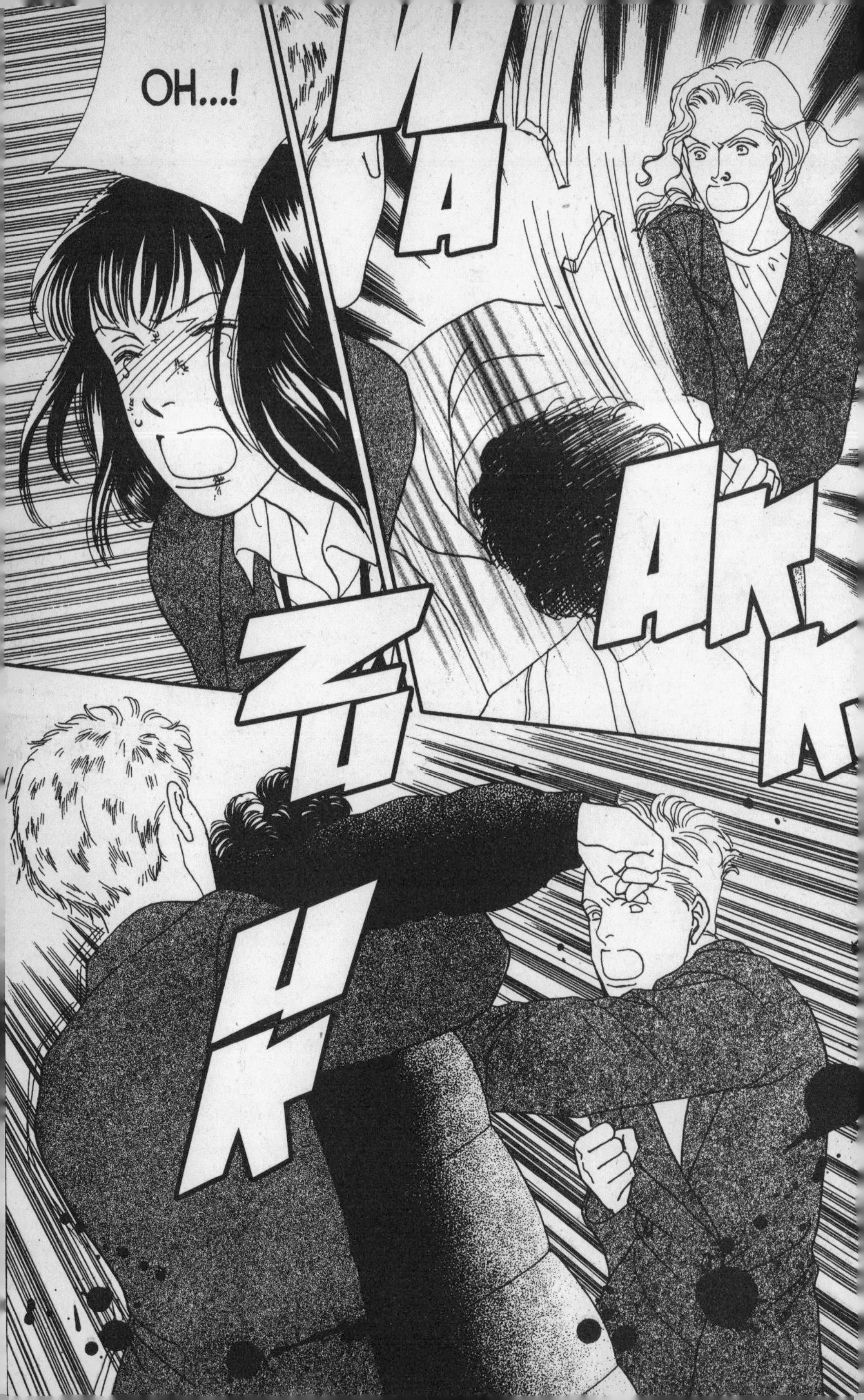
OH...!
WA
AKK
ZUUK

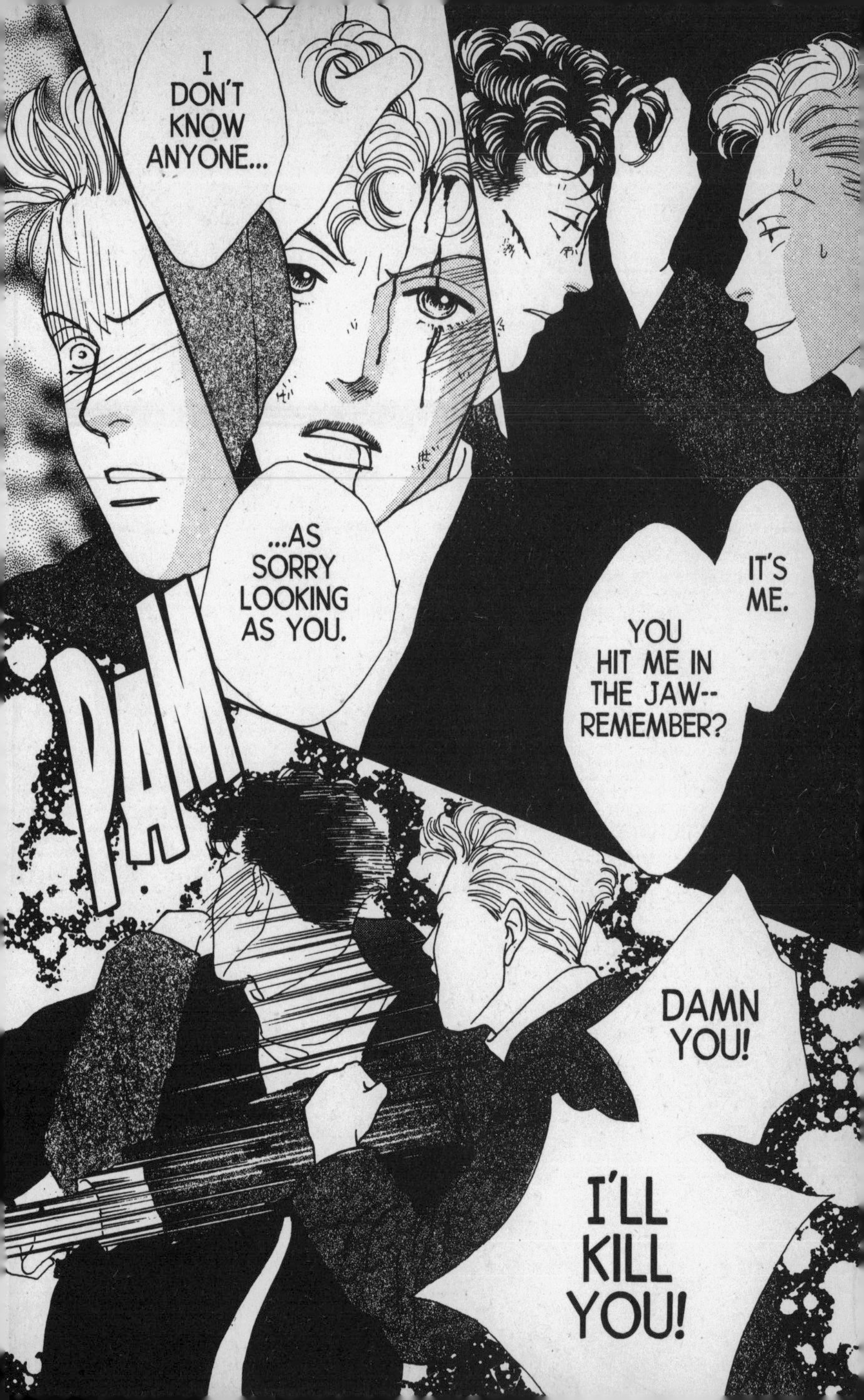
IT'S ME.
YOU HIT ME IN THE JAW-- REMEMBER?
I DON'T KNOW ANYONE...
...AS SORRY LOOKING AS YOU.
DAMN YOU!
I'LL KILL YOU!
PAM

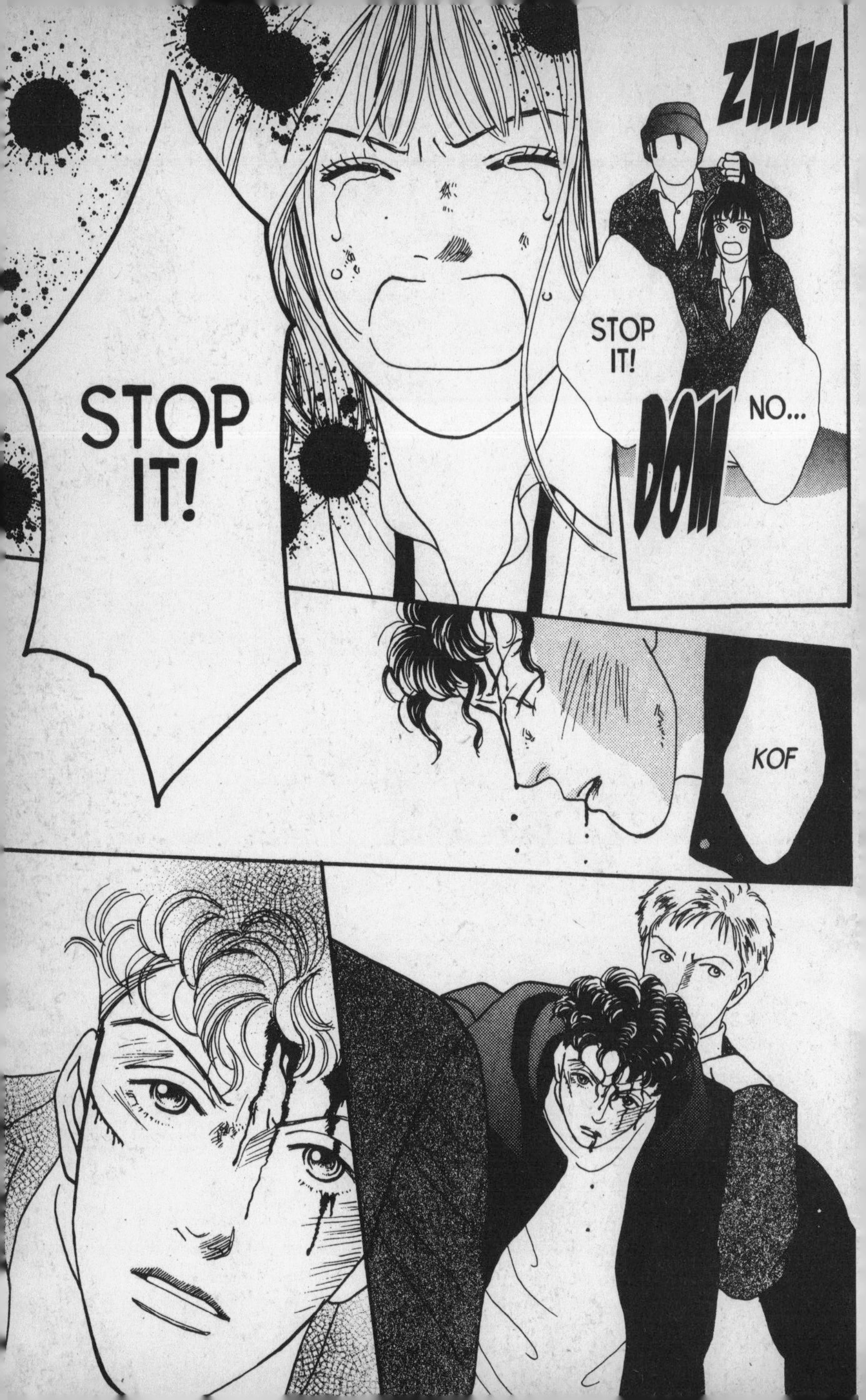
ZMM
STOP IT!
NO...
DOM
STOP IT!
KOF

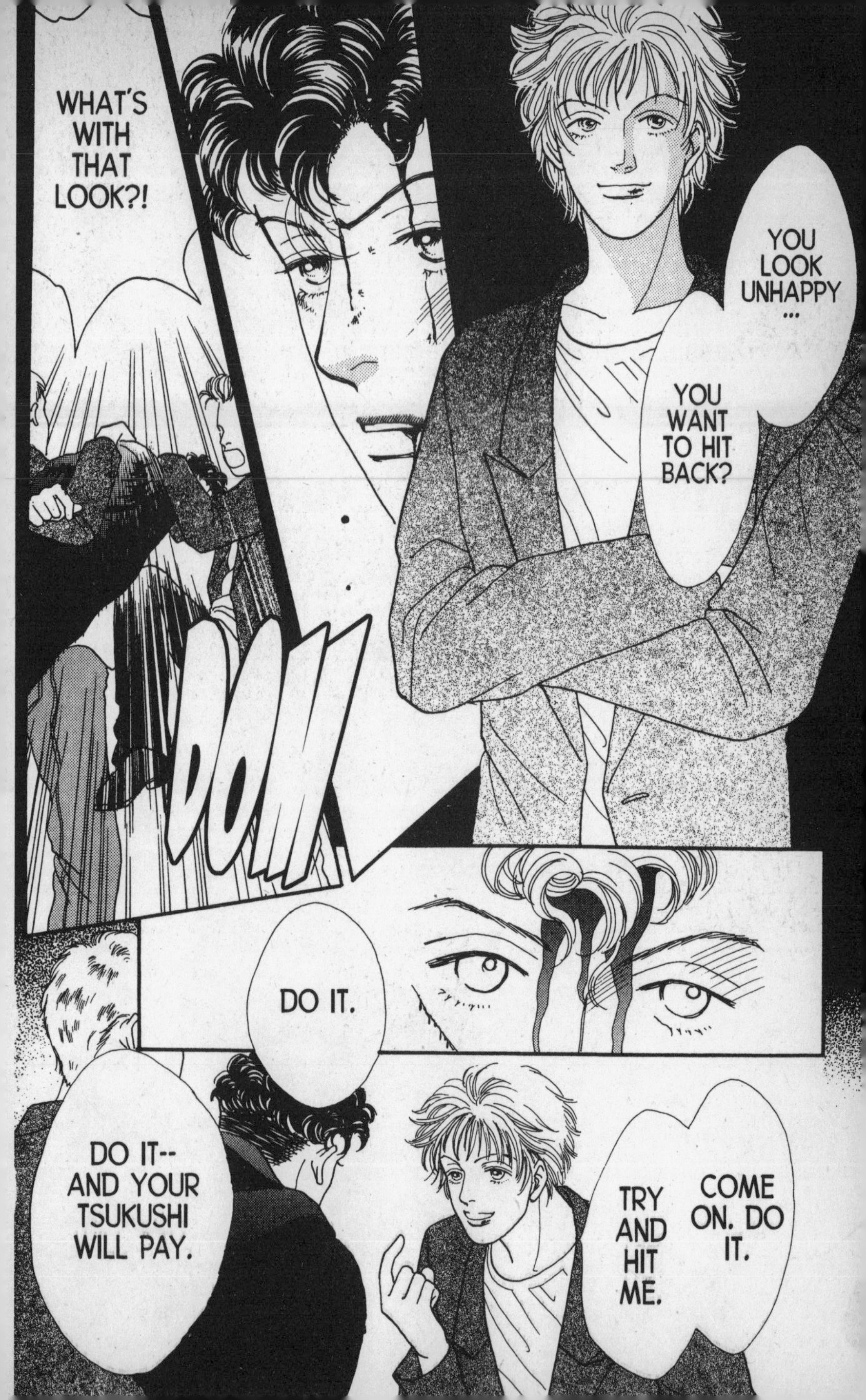
YOU LOOK UNHAPPY ...
YOU WANT TO HIT BACK?
WHAT'S WITH THAT LOOK?!
DOM
DO IT.
COME ON. DO IT.
TRY AND HIT ME.
DO IT-- AND YOUR TSUKUSHI WILL PAY.

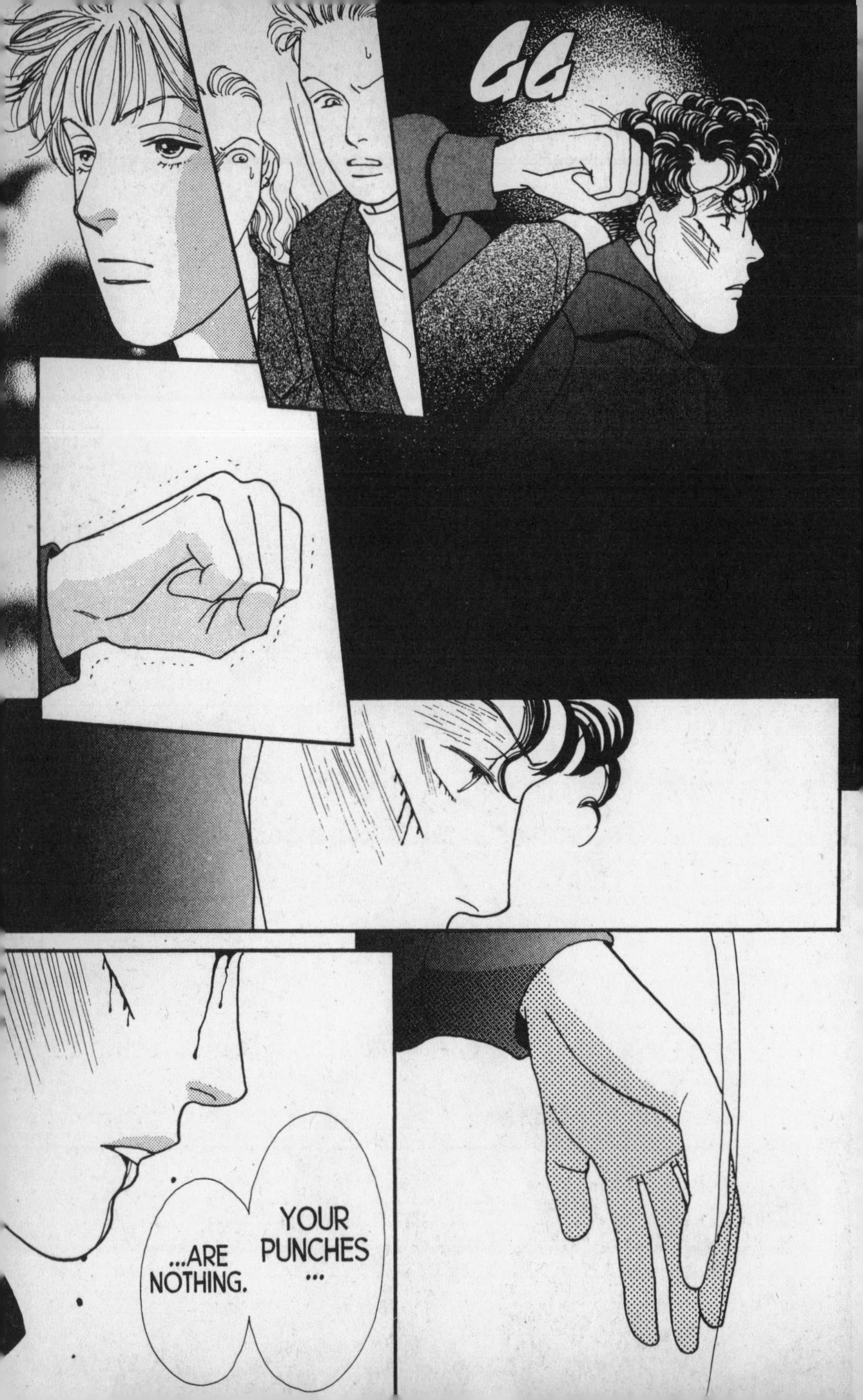
GG
YOUR PUNCHES ...
...ARE NOTHING.

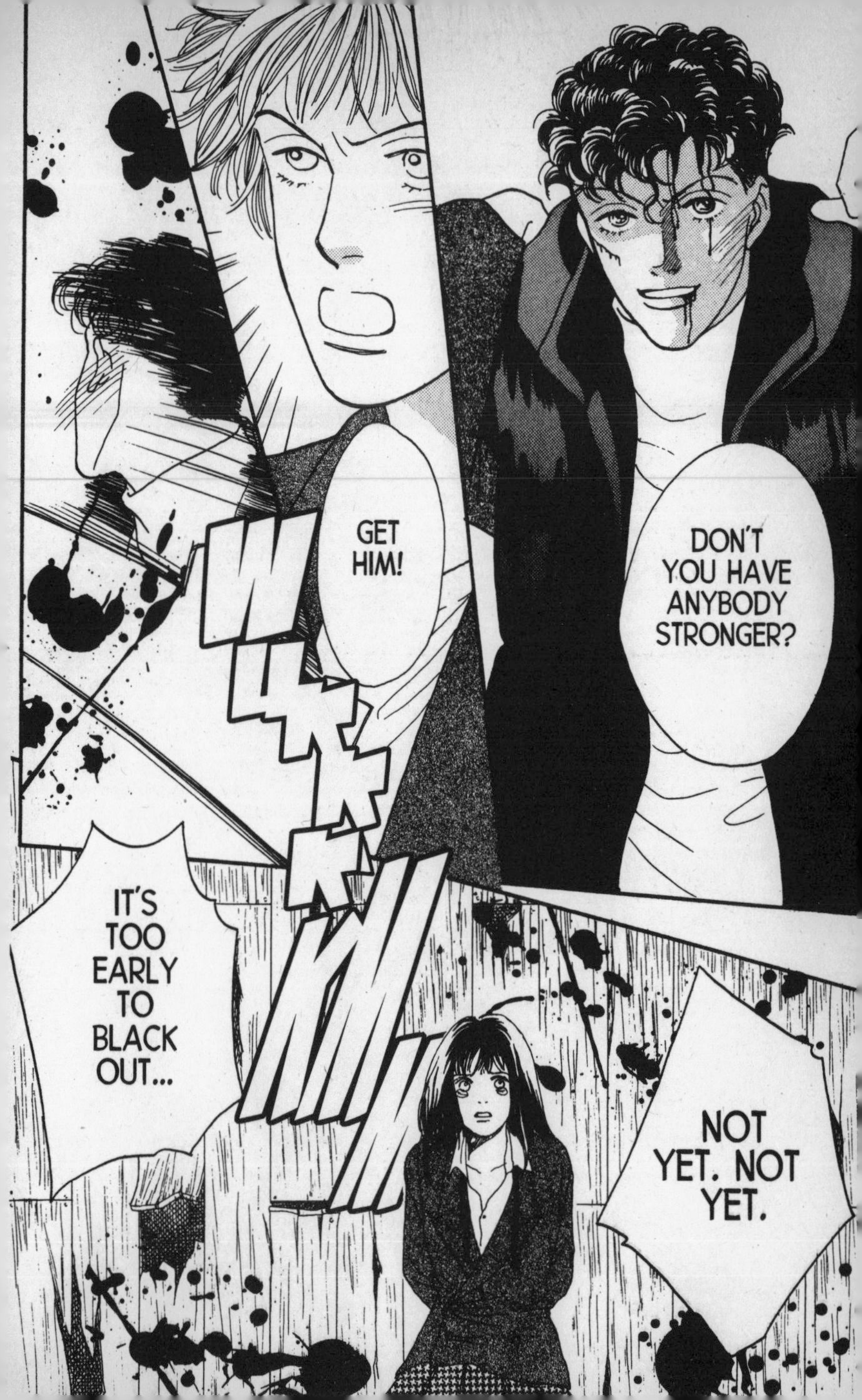
DON'T YOU HAVE ANYBODY STRONGER?
GET HIM!
NOT YET. NOT YET.
IT'S TOO EARLY TO BLACK OUT...

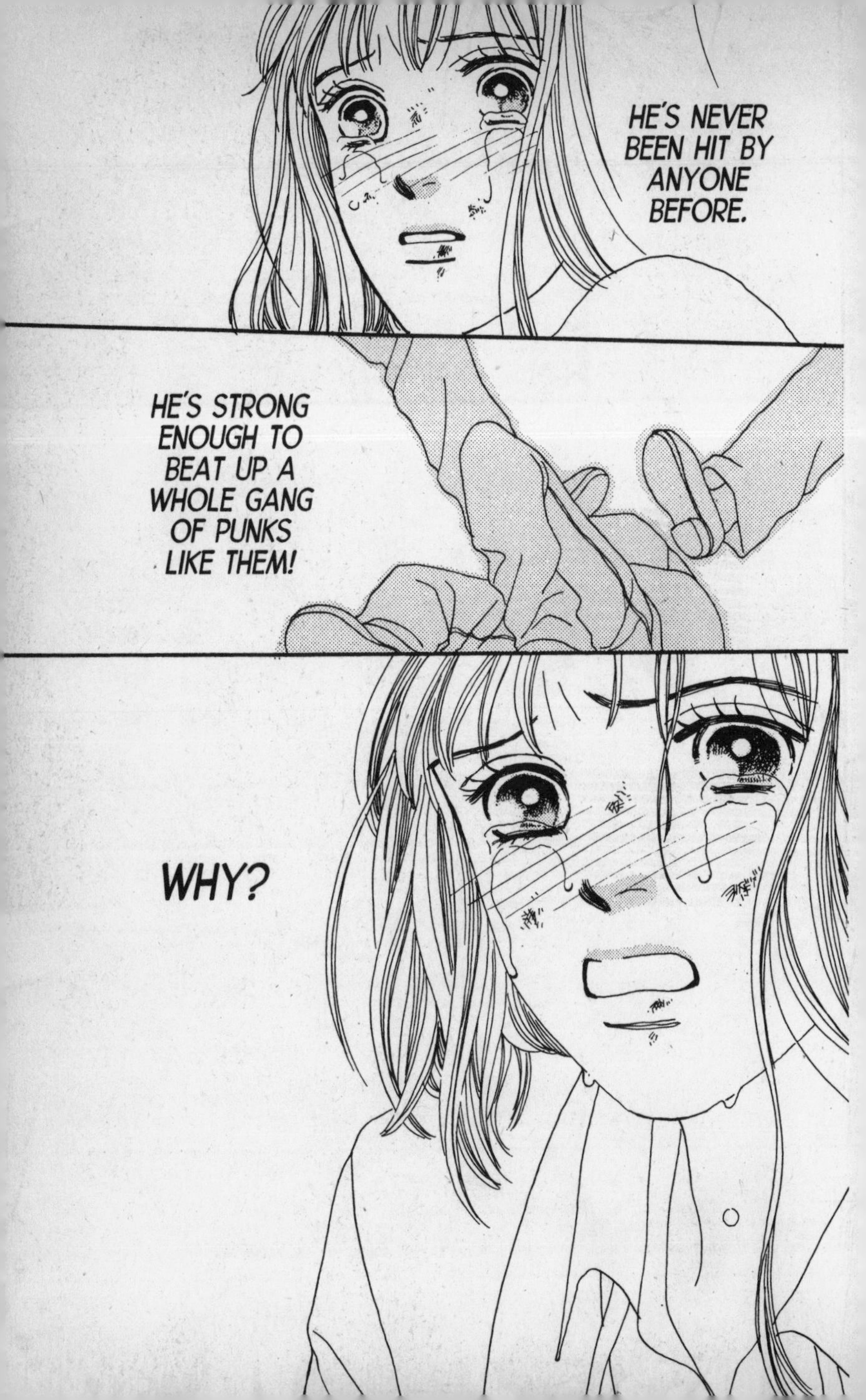
HE'S NEVER BEEN HIT BY ANYONE BEFORE.
HE'S STRONG ENOUGH TO BEAT UP A WHOLE GANG OF PUNKS LIKE THEM!
WHY?

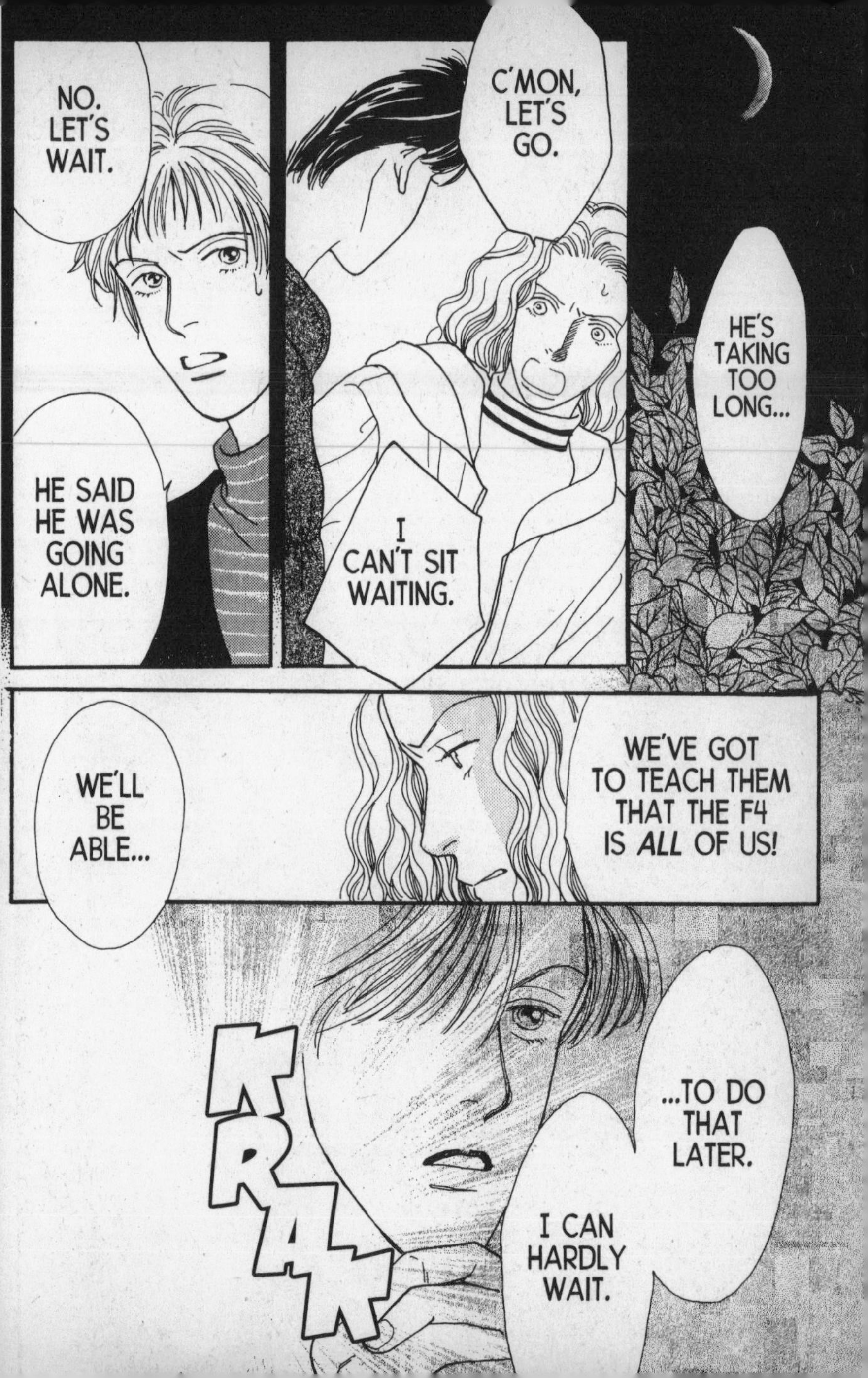
HE'S TAKING TOO LONG...
C'MON, LET'S GO.
I CAN'T SIT WAITING.
NO. LET'S WAIT.
HE SAID HE WAS GOING ALONE.
WE'VE GOT TO TEACH THEM THAT THE F4 IS *ALL* OF US!
WE'LL BE ABLE...
...TO DO THAT LATER.
I CAN HARDLY WAIT.
KRAK

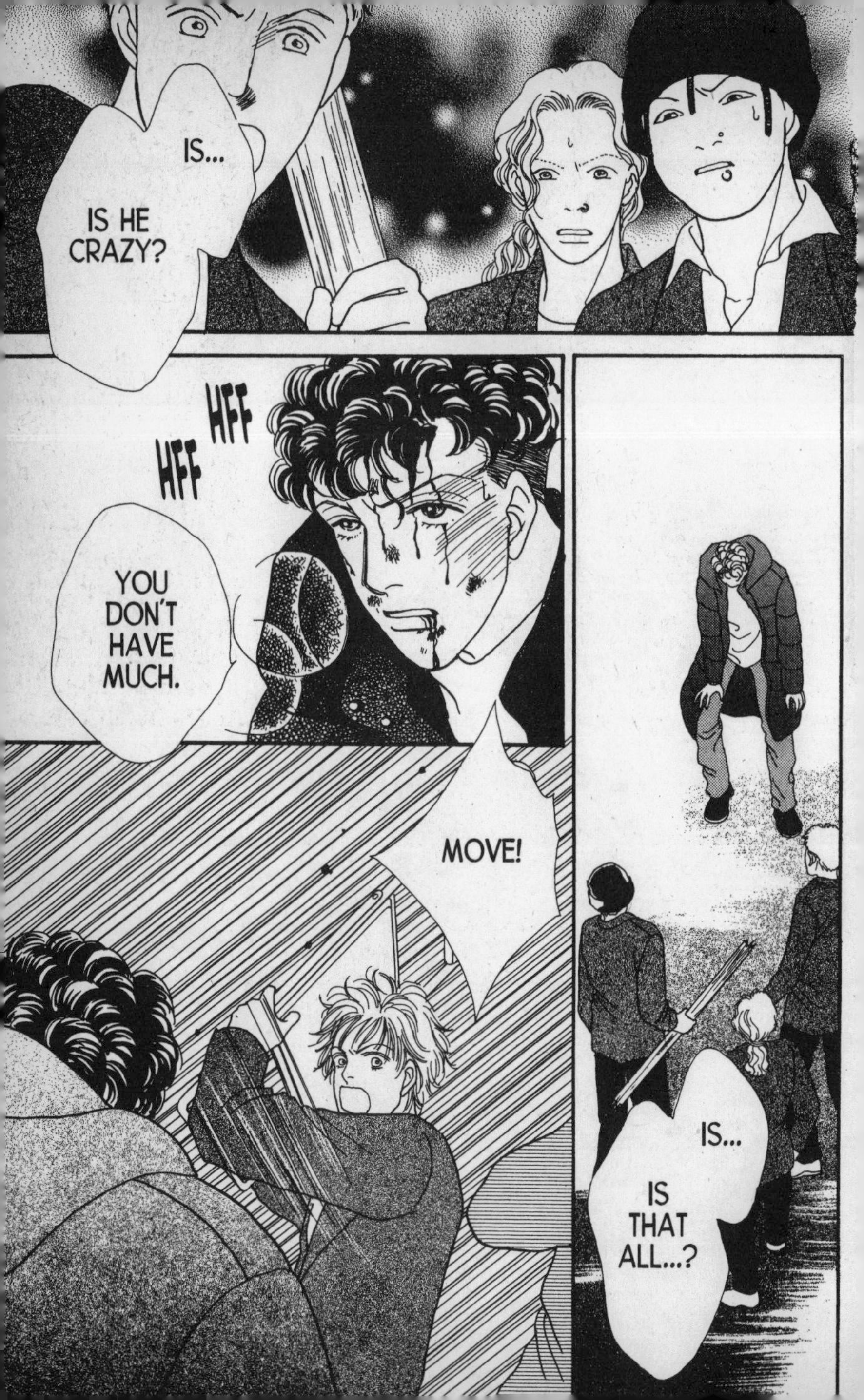
IS...
IS HE CRAZY?
IS...
IS THAT ALL...?
HFF HFF
YOU DON'T HAVE MUCH.
MOVE!

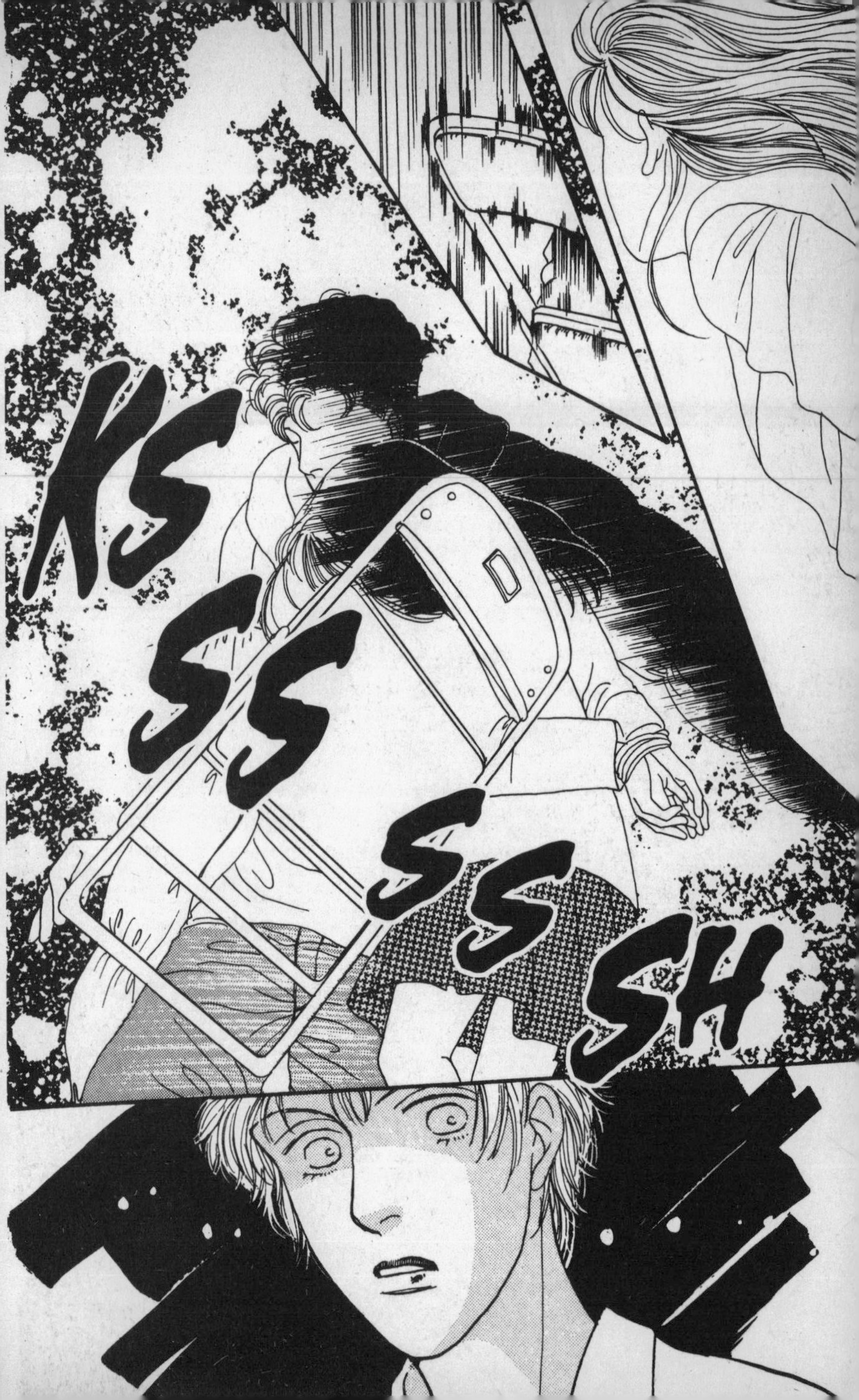
KSSSSSSH

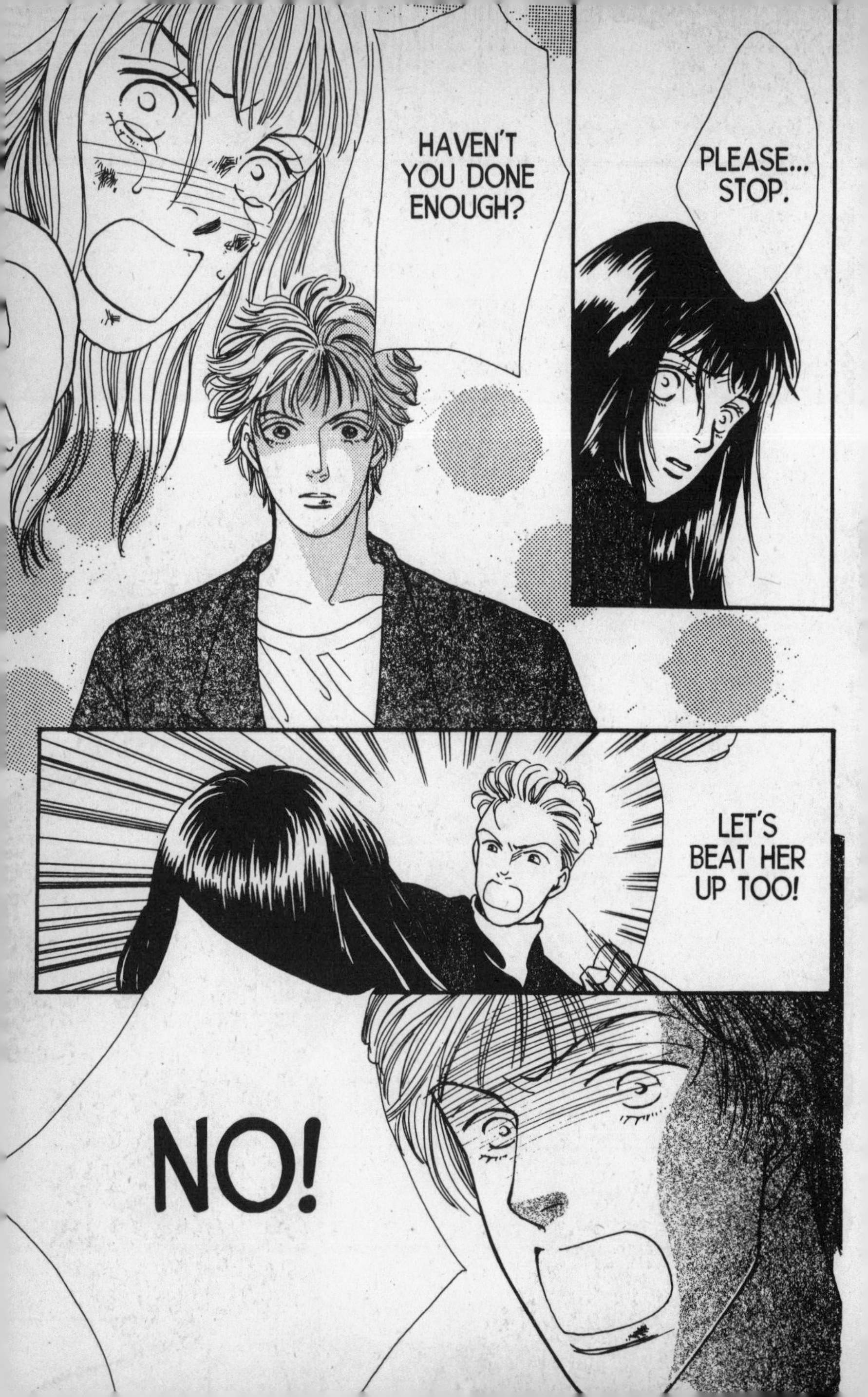
PLEASE... STOP.
HAVEN'T YOU DONE ENOUGH?
LET'S BEAT HER UP TOO!
NO!

JUN?!
HUH!
THIS'LL TEACH YOU NOT TO STRUT YOUR STUFF!
B-BAM!
REMEMBER THIS!
THAT'S ENOUGH.
LET'S GO.

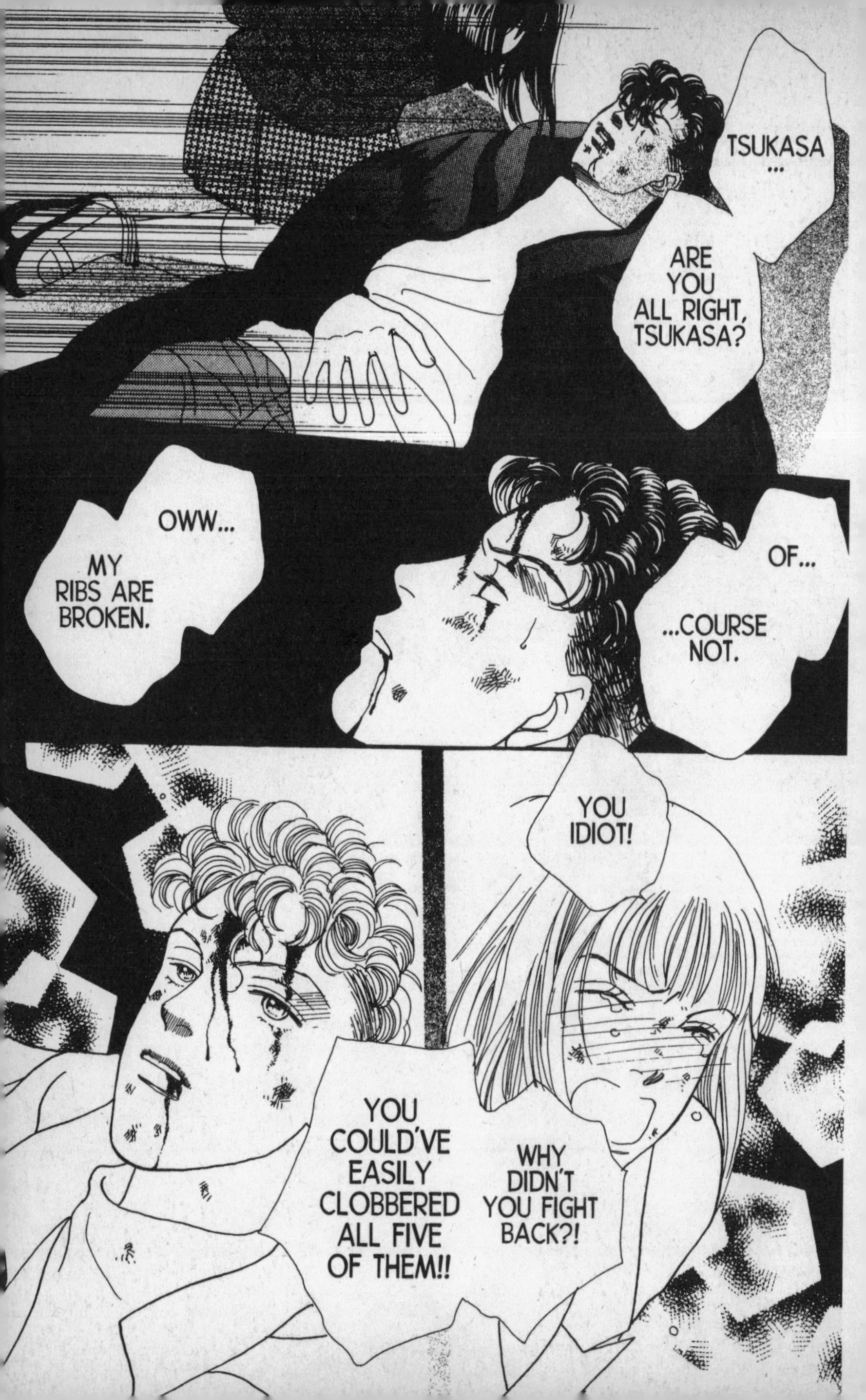
TSUKASA ...
ARE YOU ALL RIGHT, TSUKASA?
OF...
...COURSE NOT.
OWW...
MY RIBS ARE BROKEN.
YOU IDIOT!
WHY DIDN'T YOU FIGHT BACK?!
YOU COULD'VE EASILY CLOBBERED ALL FIVE OF THEM!!

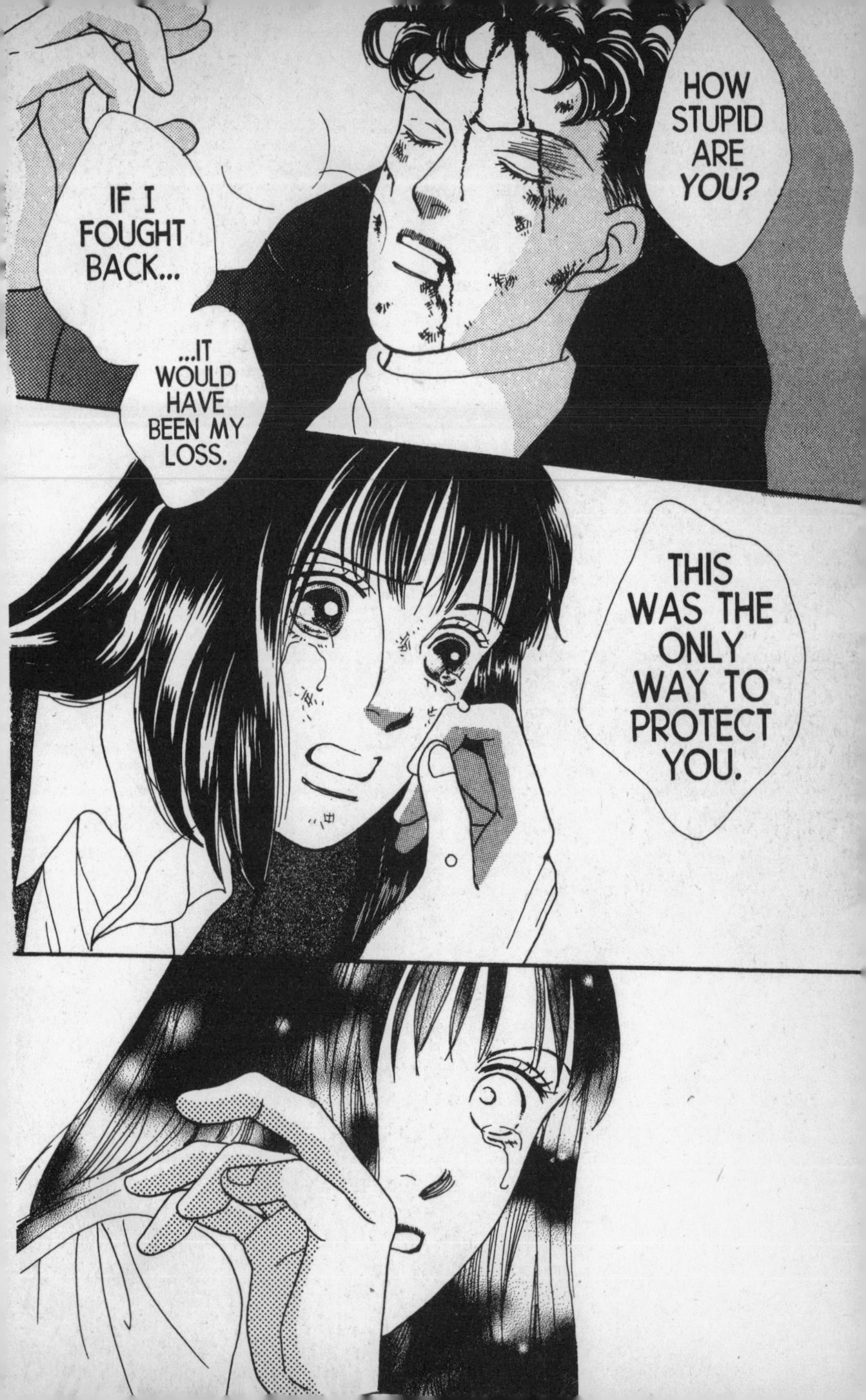
HOW STUPID ARE *YOU?*
IF I FOUGHT BACK...
...IT WOULD HAVE BEEN MY LOSS.
THIS WAS THE ONLY WAY TO PROTECT YOU.

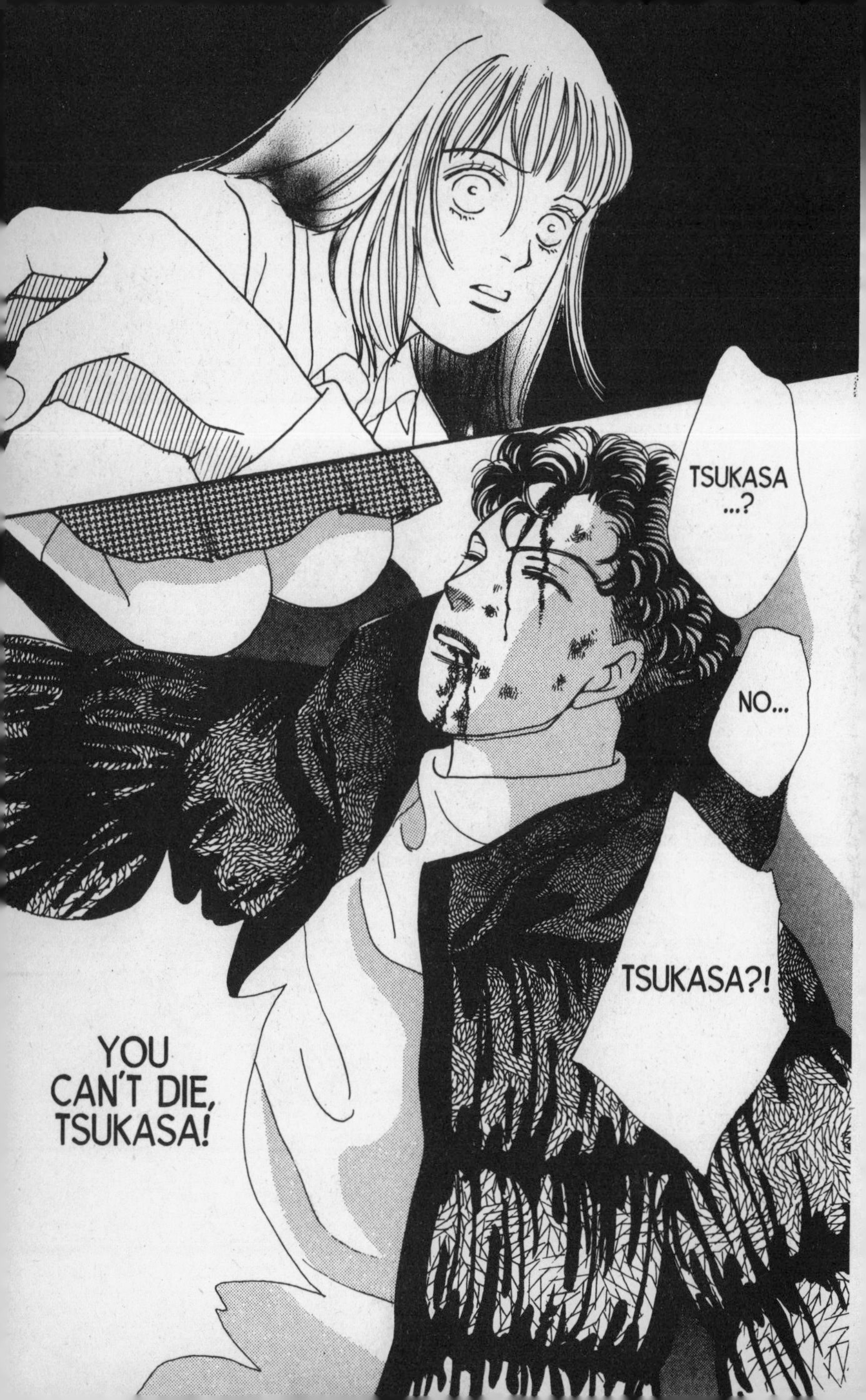
TSUKASA ...?
NO...
TSUKASA?!
YOU CAN'T DIE, TSUKASA!

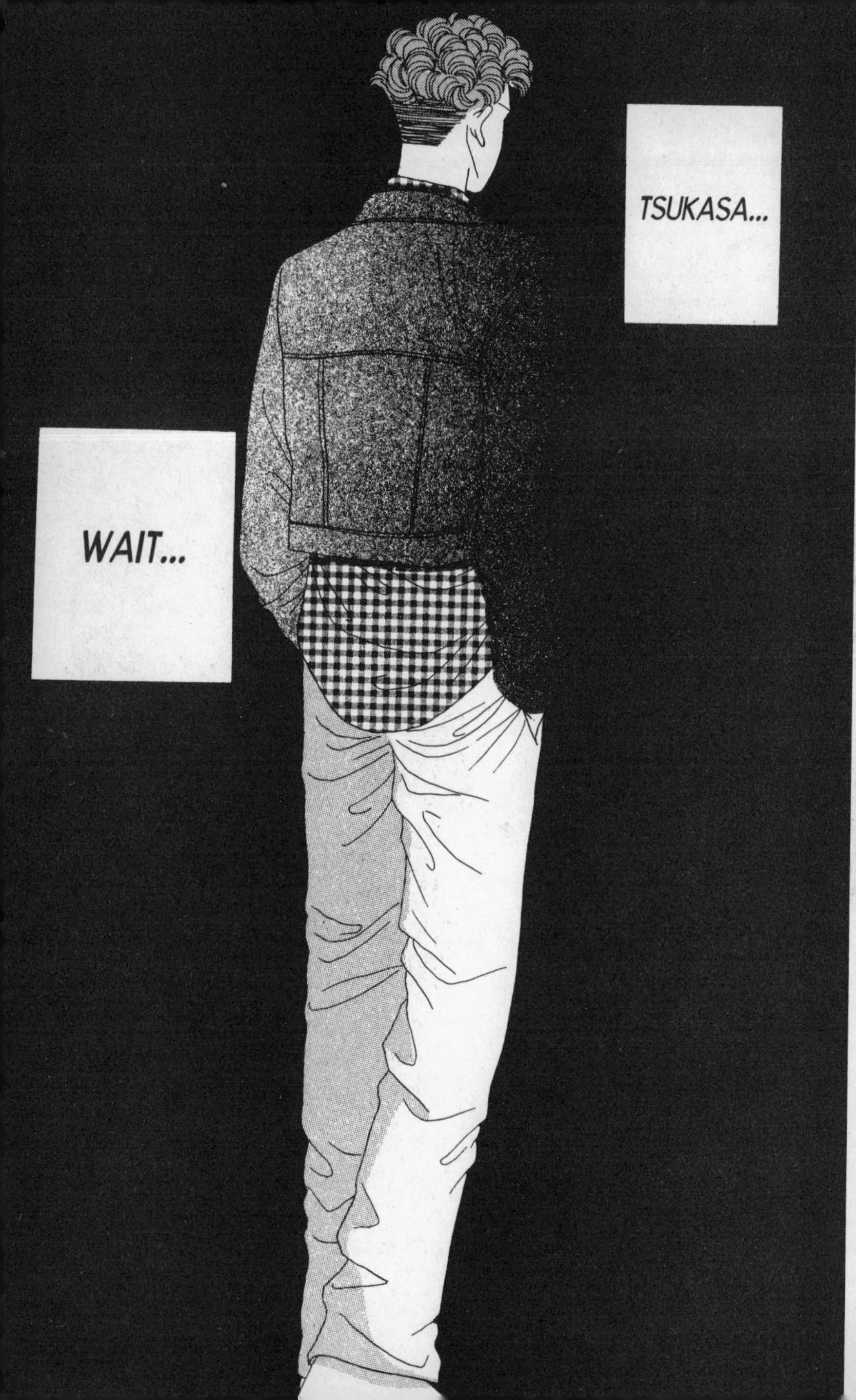
TSUKASA...
WAIT...

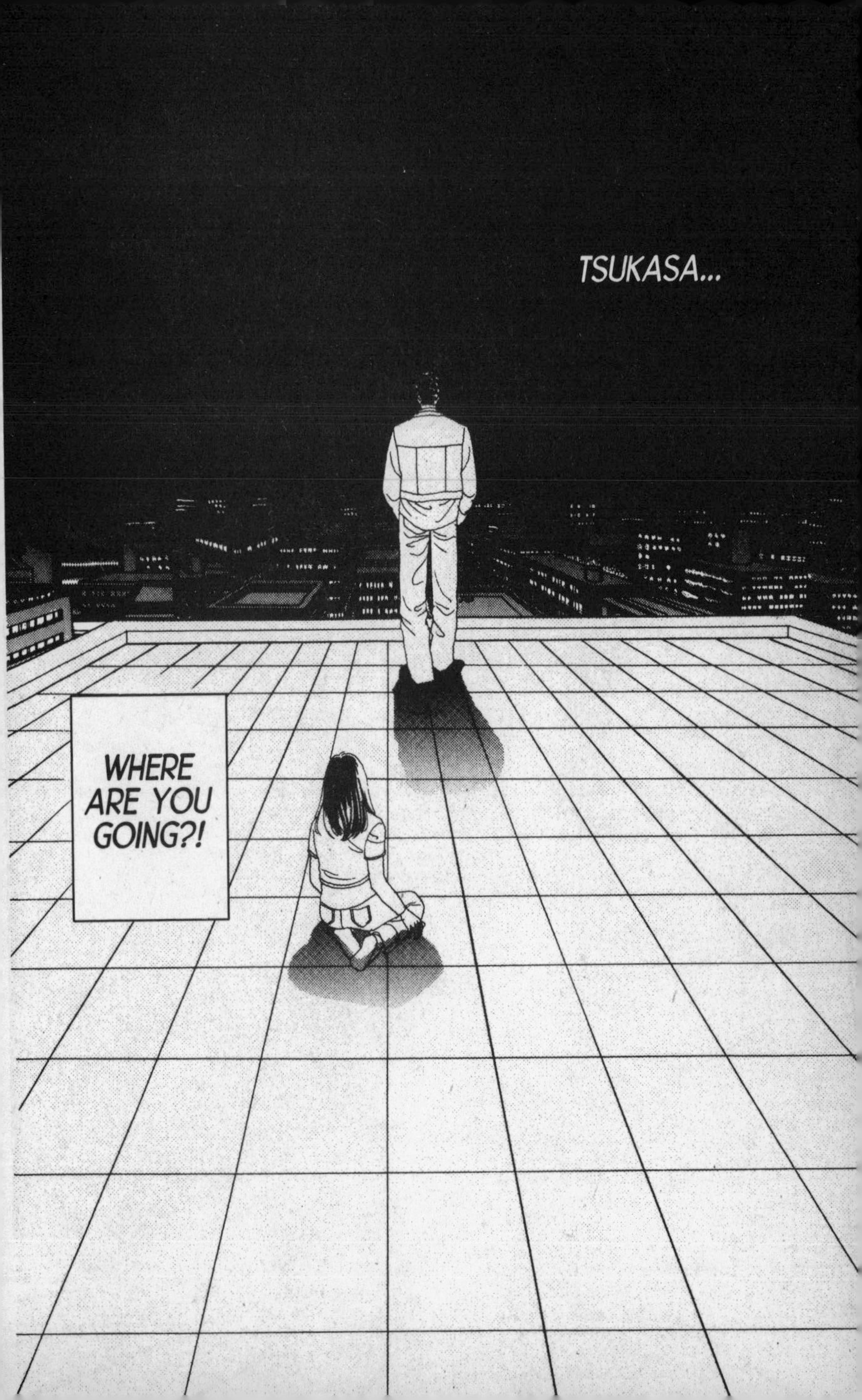
TSUKASA...
WHERE ARE YOU GOING?!

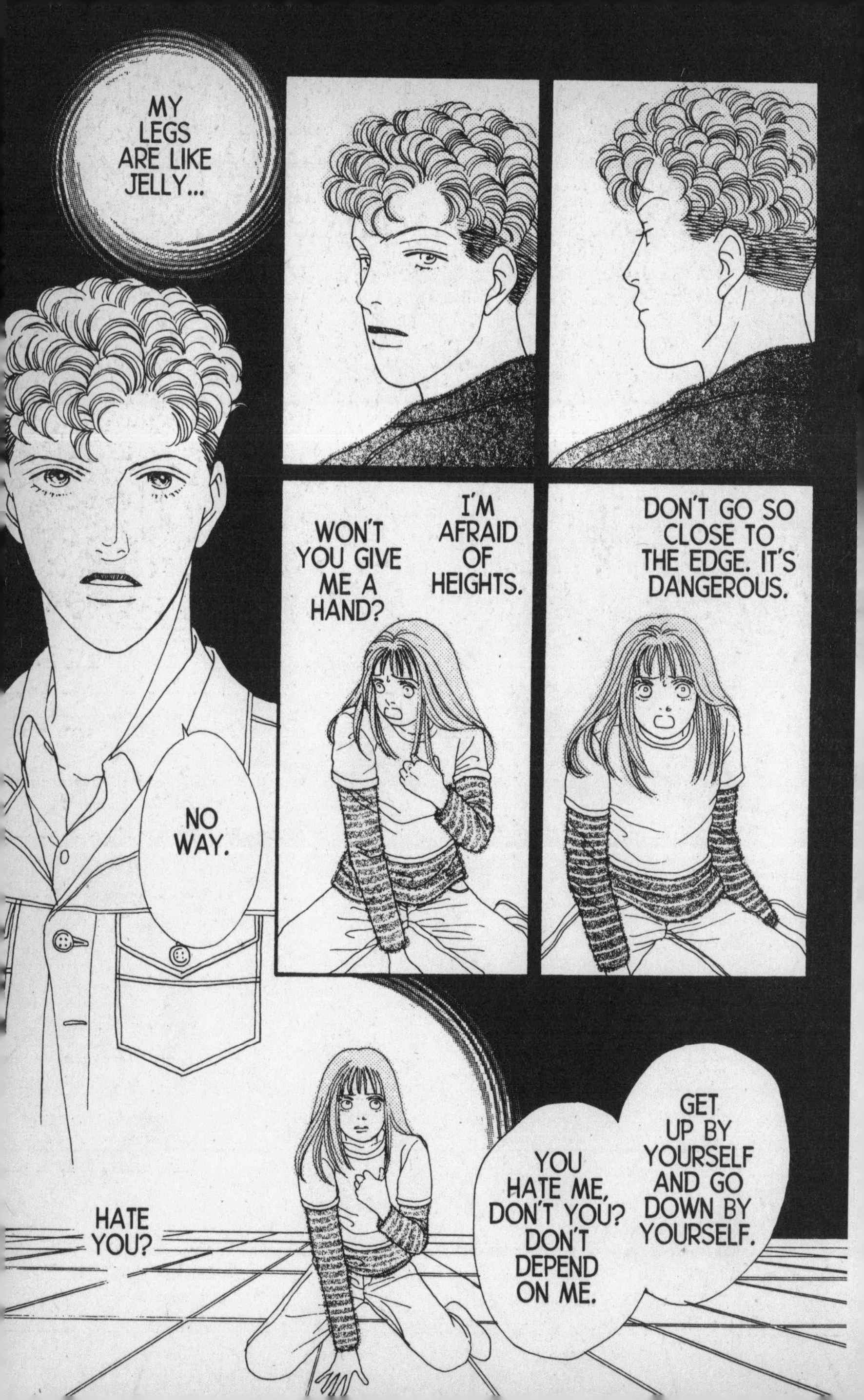
DON'T GO SO CLOSE TO THE EDGE. IT'S DANGEROUS.
I'M AFRAID OF HEIGHTS.
WON'T YOU GIVE ME A HAND?
MY LEGS ARE LIKE JELLY...
NO WAY.
GET UP BY YOURSELF AND GO DOWN BY YOURSELF.
YOU HATE ME, DON'T YOU? DON'T DEPEND ON ME.
HATE YOU?

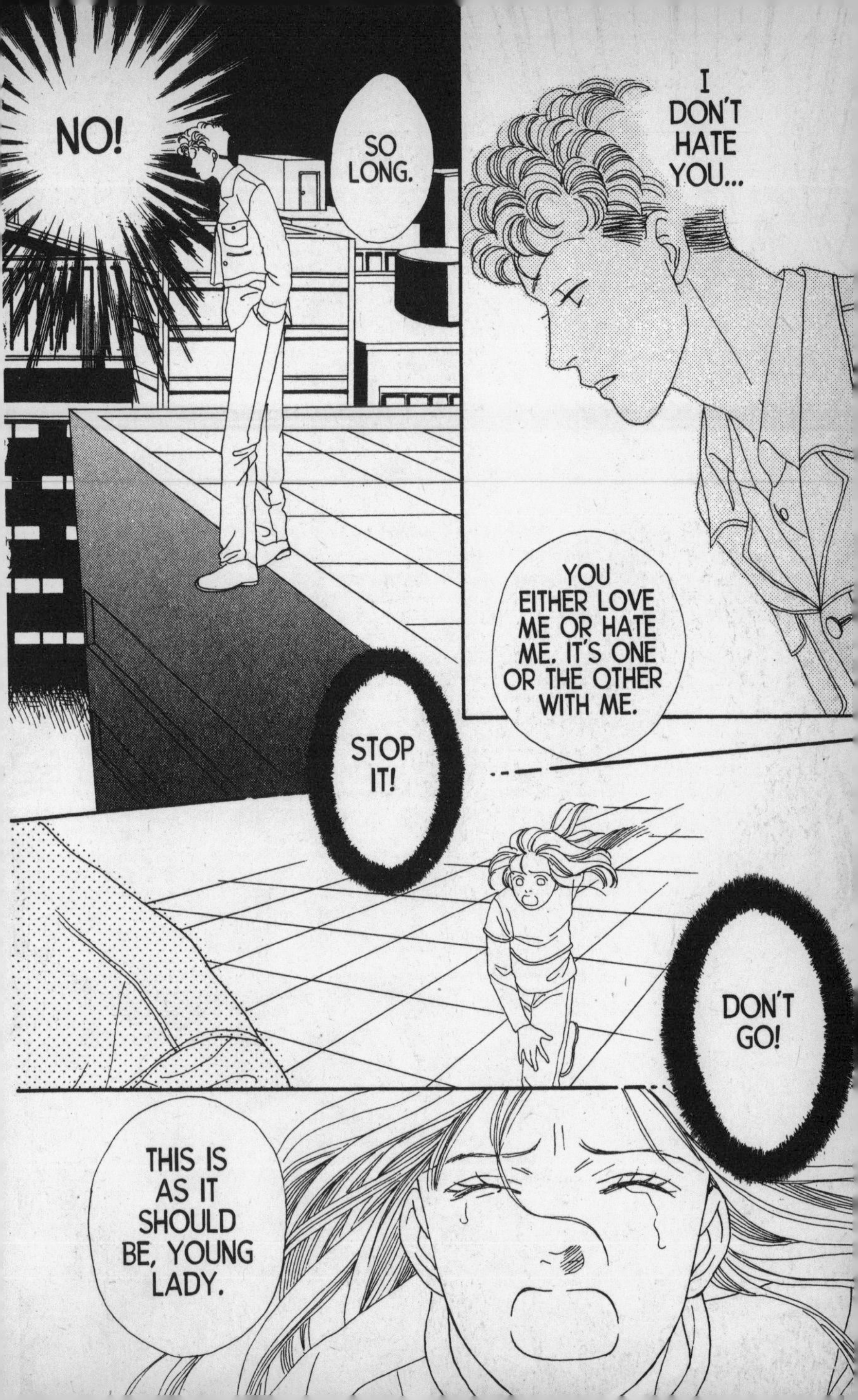
I DON'T HATE YOU...
YOU EITHER LOVE ME OR HATE ME. IT'S ONE OR THE OTHER WITH ME.
SO LONG.
NO!
STOP IT!
DON'T GO!
THIS IS AS IT SHOULD BE, YOUNG LADY.

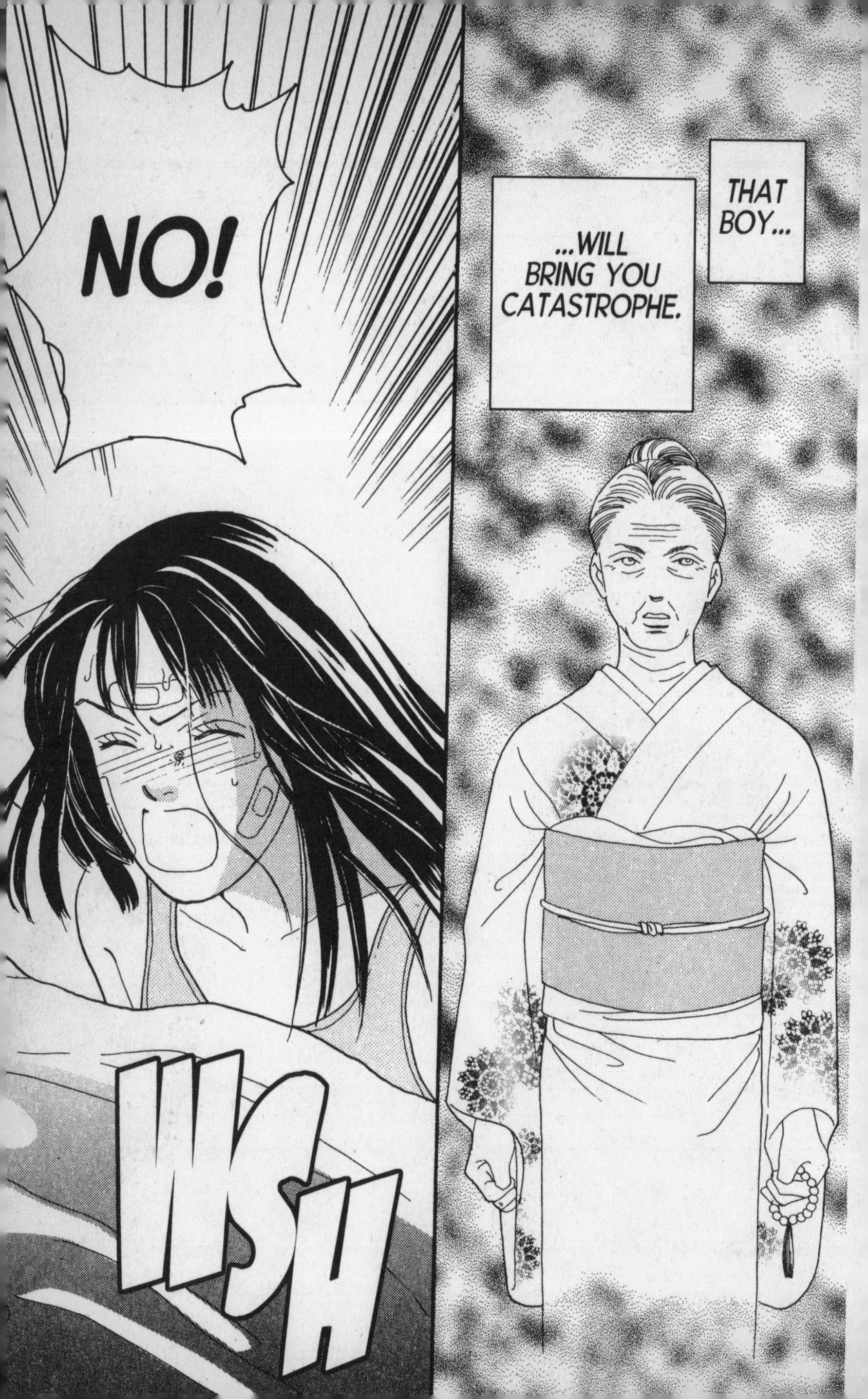
THAT BOY...
...WILL BRING YOU CATASTROPHE.
NO!
WHSH

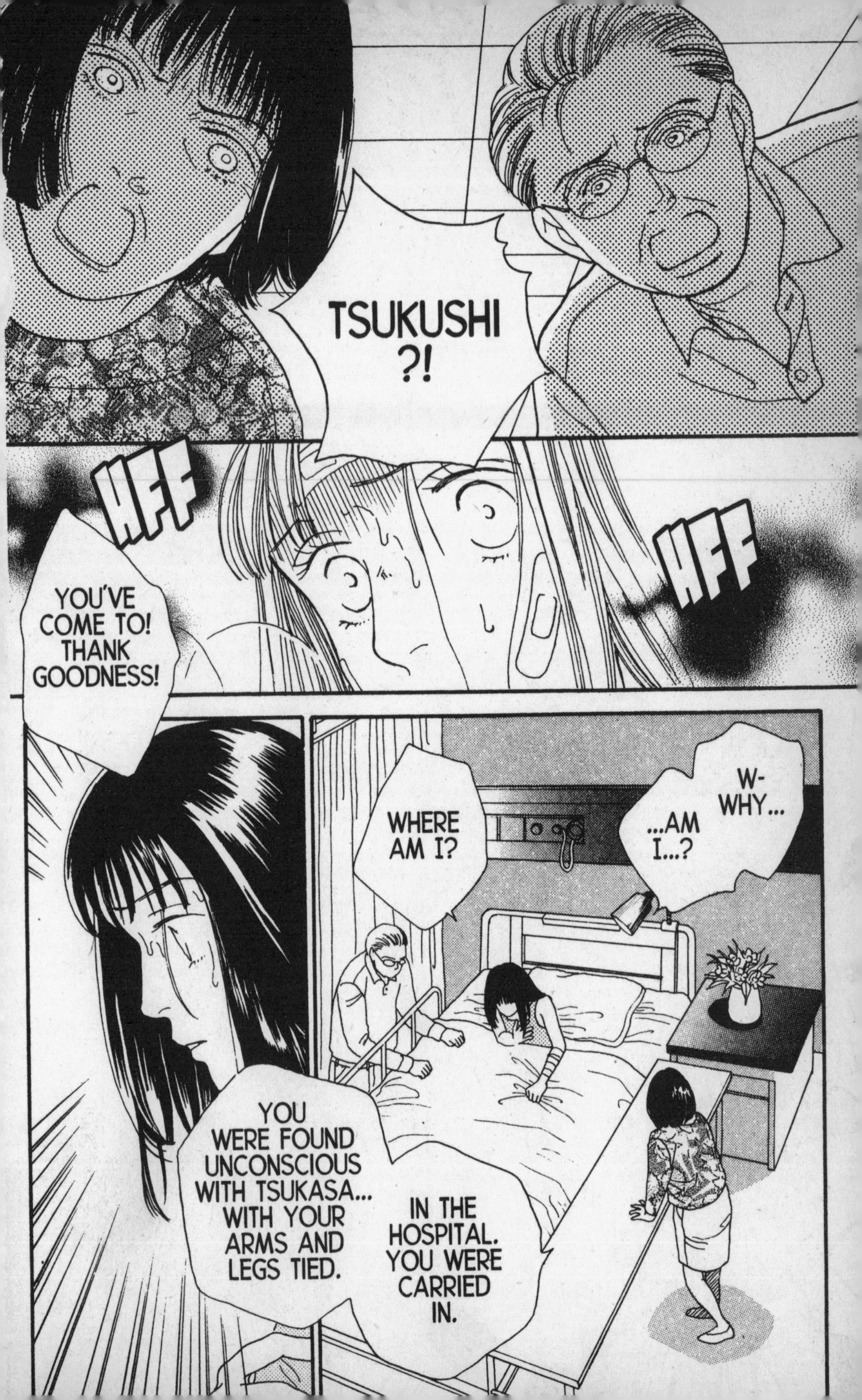
TSUKUSHI ?!
HFF
HFF
YOU'VE COME TO! THANK GOODNESS!
W- WHY...
...AM I...?
WHERE AM I?
IN THE HOSPITAL. YOU WERE CARRIED IN.
YOU WERE FOUND UNCONSCIOUS WITH TSUKASA... WITH YOUR ARMS AND LEGS TIED.

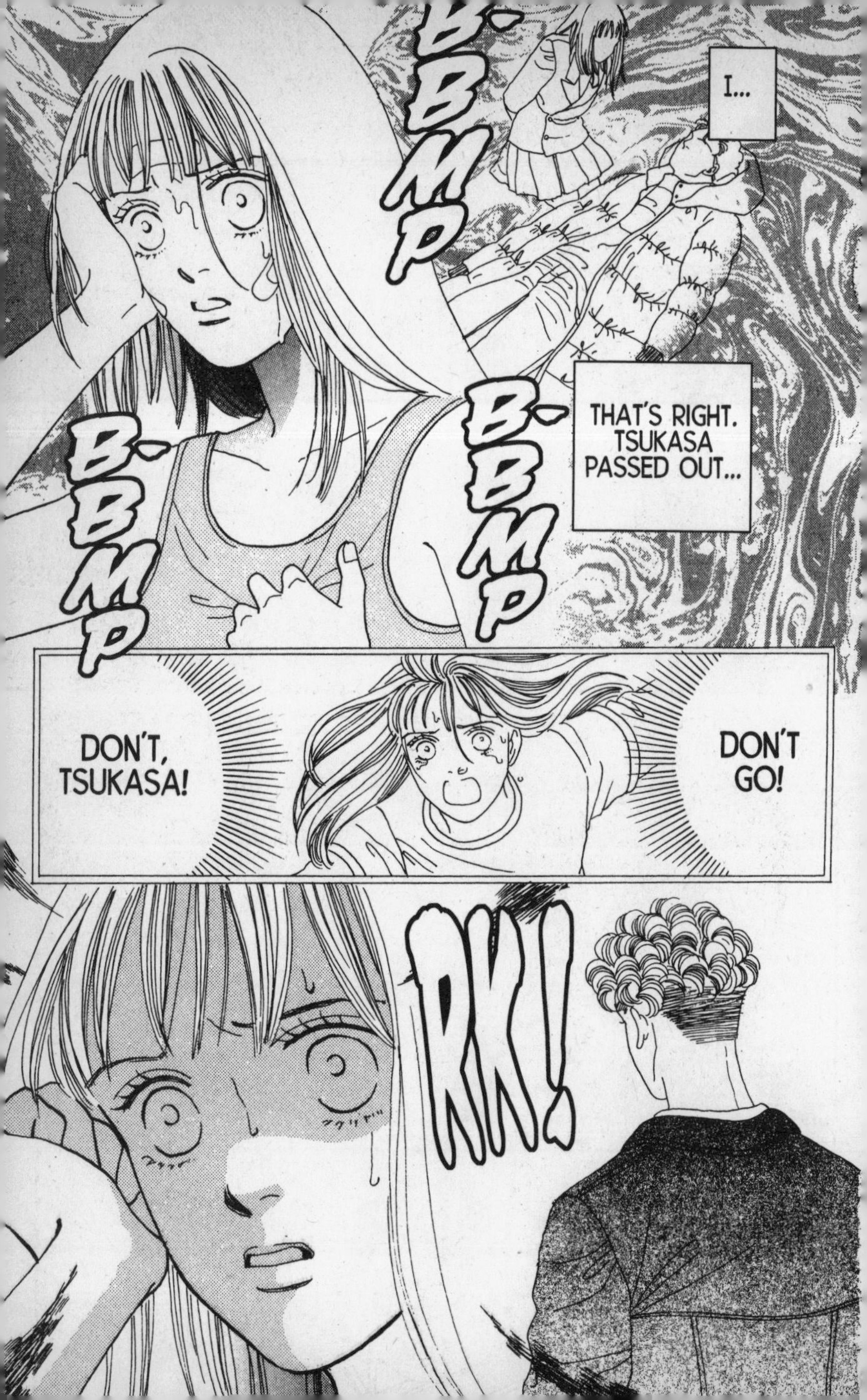
I...
B-BBMP
THAT'S RIGHT. TSUKASA PASSED OUT...
B-BBMP
B-BBMP
DON'T GO!
DON'T, TSUKASA!
RK!

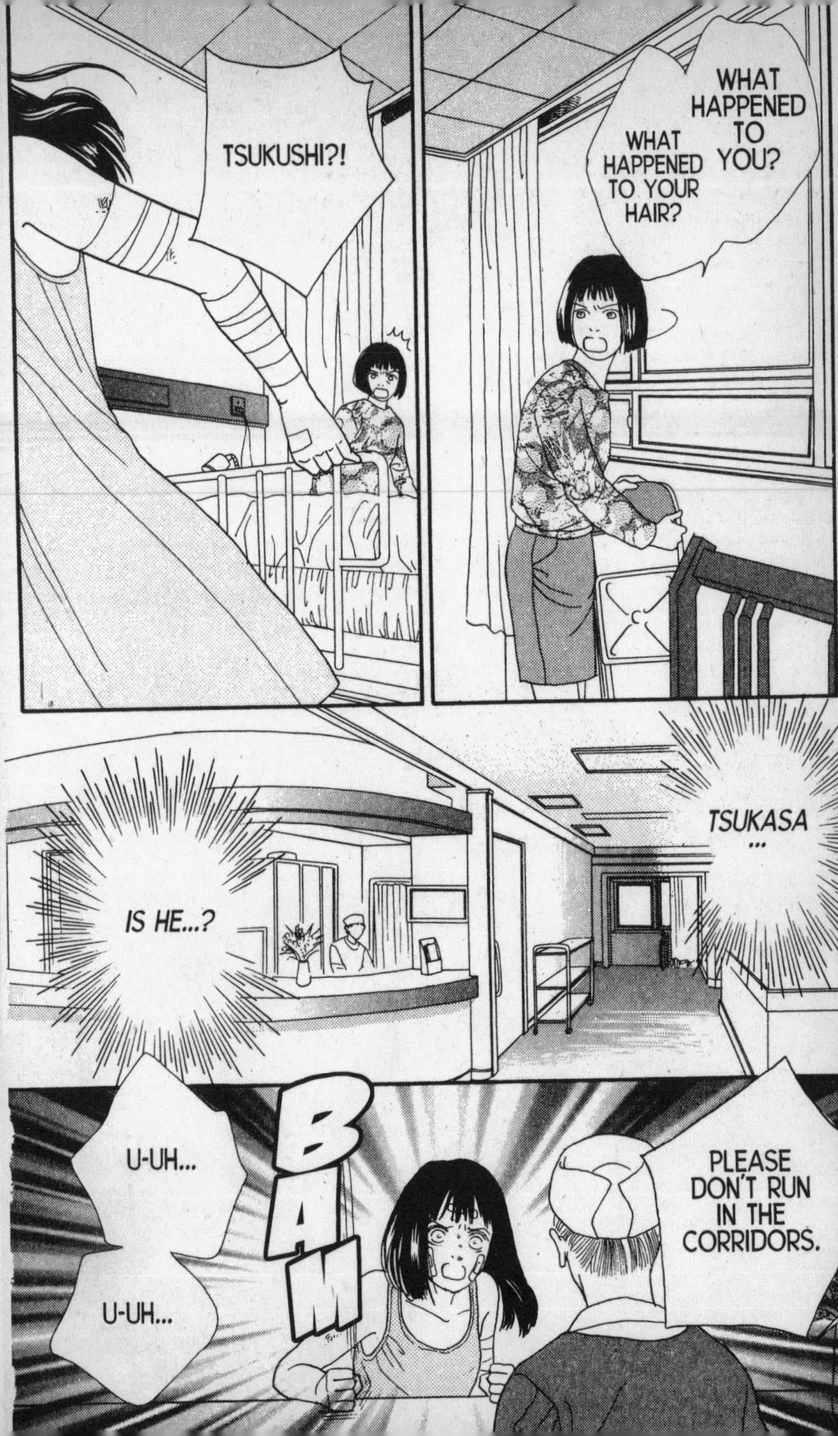
WHAT HAPPENED TO YOU?
WHAT HAPPENED TO YOUR HAIR?
TSUKUSHI?!
TSUKASA ...
IS HE...?
PLEASE DON'T RUN IN THE CORRIDORS.
BAM
U-UH...
U-UH...

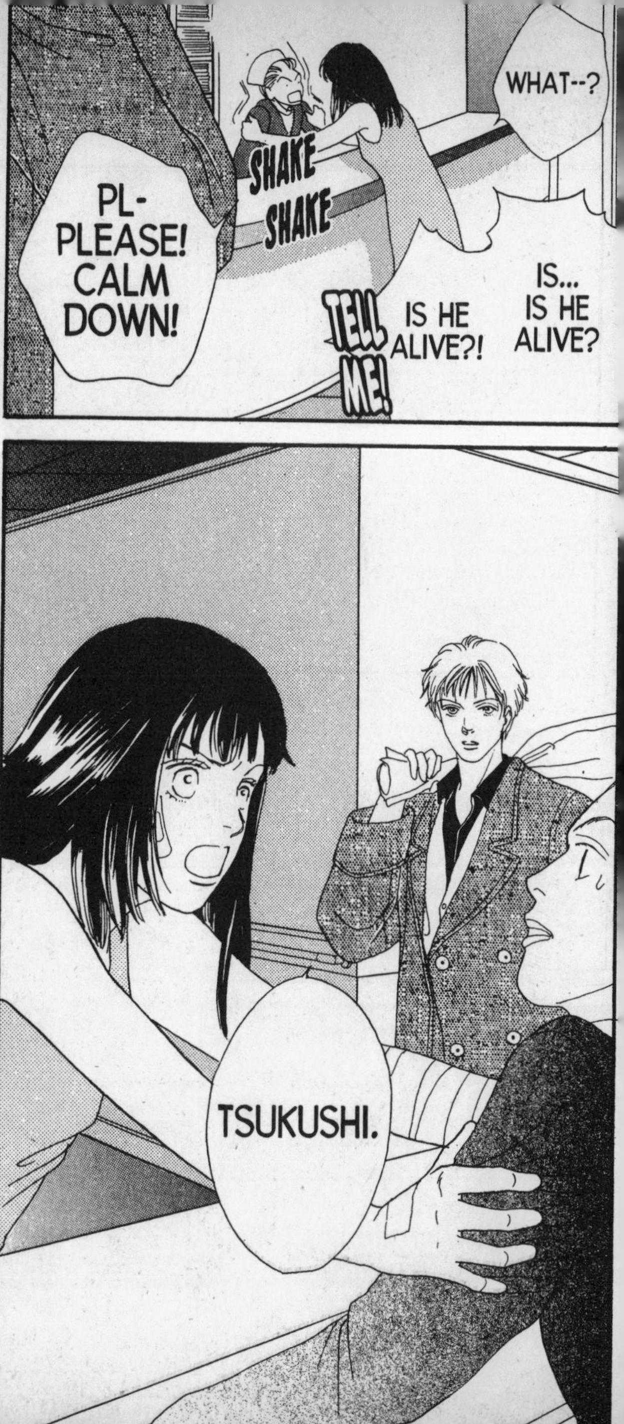
WHAT--?
IS... IS HE ALIVE?
IS HE ALIVE?!
TELL ME!
SHAKE
SHAKE
PL- PLEASE! CALM DOWN!
TSUKUSHI.

The other day, I made my first speech from a stage. It was the sneak preview of my anime!! There were five of us—Maki Mochida, Naoki Miyashita, Koji Yamamoto, and Kikuta Tomohiko, who sings the theme song.

I was so nervous. This kind of work seems exciting, but it's really not. I hardly ever find myself in front of large groups, and here I was, suddenly facing 400 people. I felt like Tsukushi must have in the Miss Teen Japan contest.

Face pale...

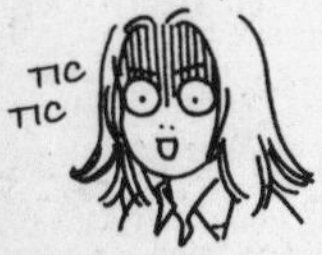
TIC
TIC

But the other four participants were all such nice people. They spoke up from time to time. It was a wonderful experience.

Thank you very much to all of you who came to see the film!

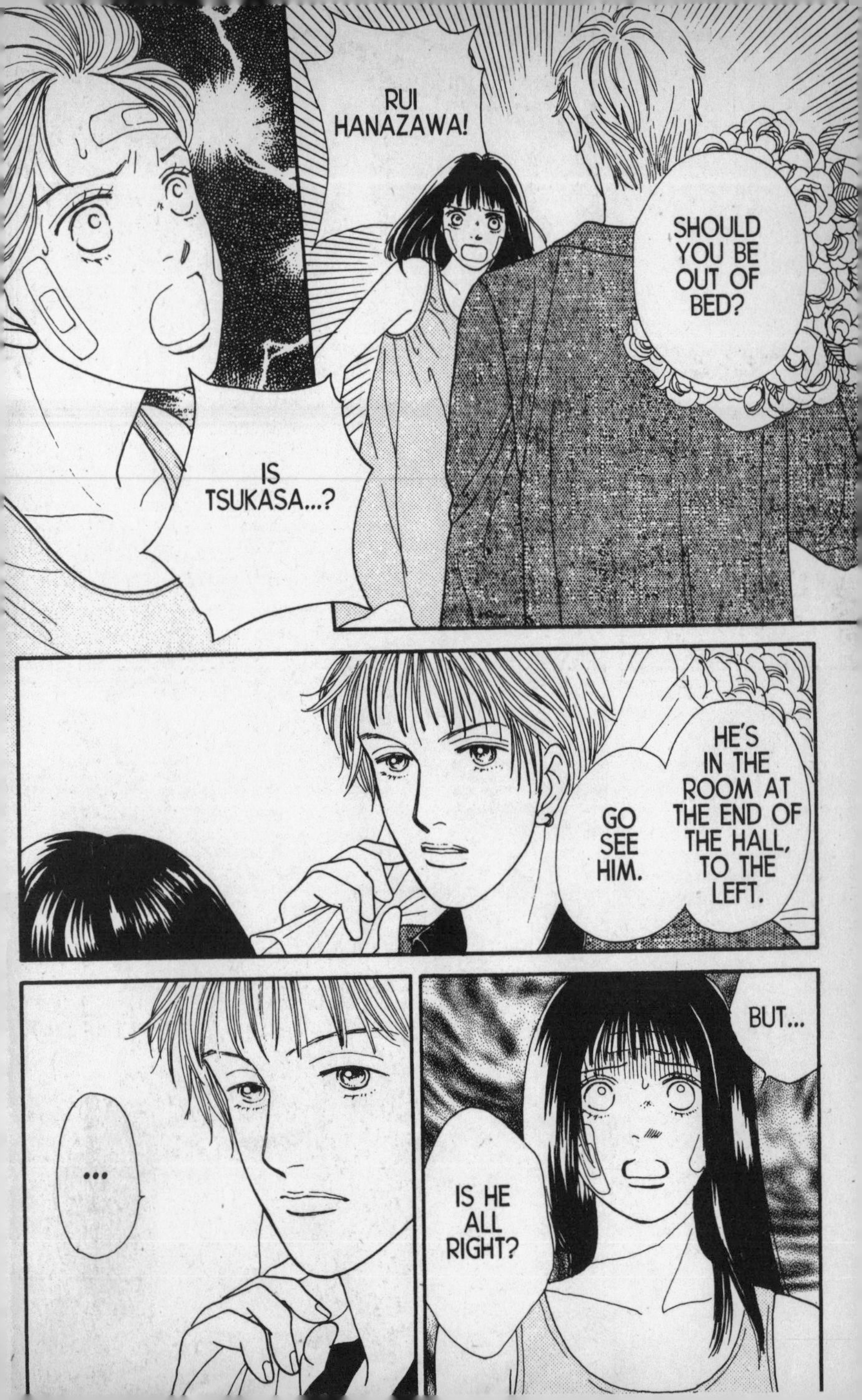
RUI HANAZAWA!
SHOULD YOU BE OUT OF BED?
IS TSUKASA...?
HE'S IN THE ROOM AT THE END OF THE HALL, TO THE LEFT.
GO SEE HIM.
BUT...
IS HE ALL RIGHT?
...

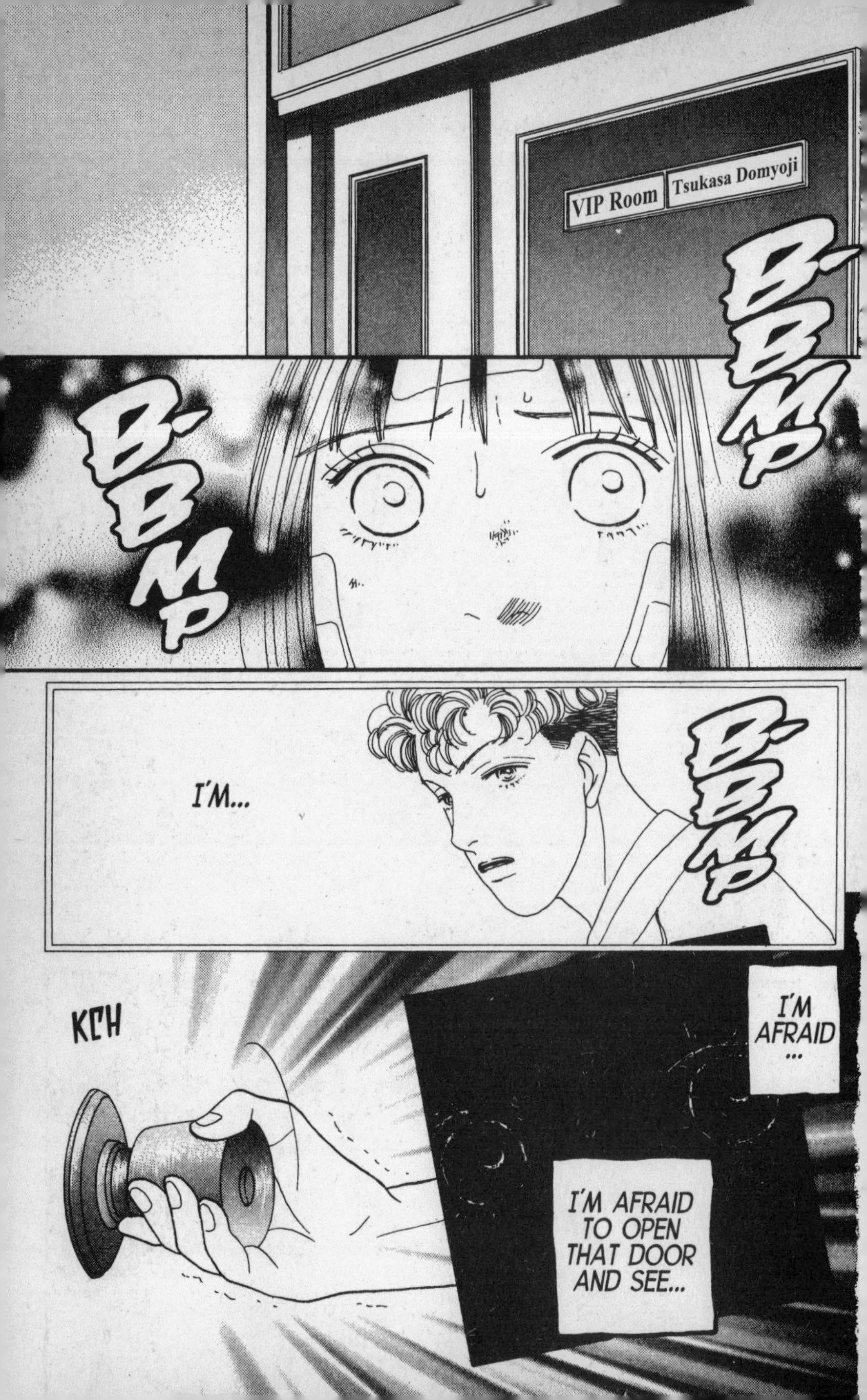

Tsukasa Domyoji
VIP Room
B-BMP
B-BMP
B-BMP
I'M...
I'M AFRAID...
I'M AFRAID TO OPEN THAT DOOR AND SEE...
KCH

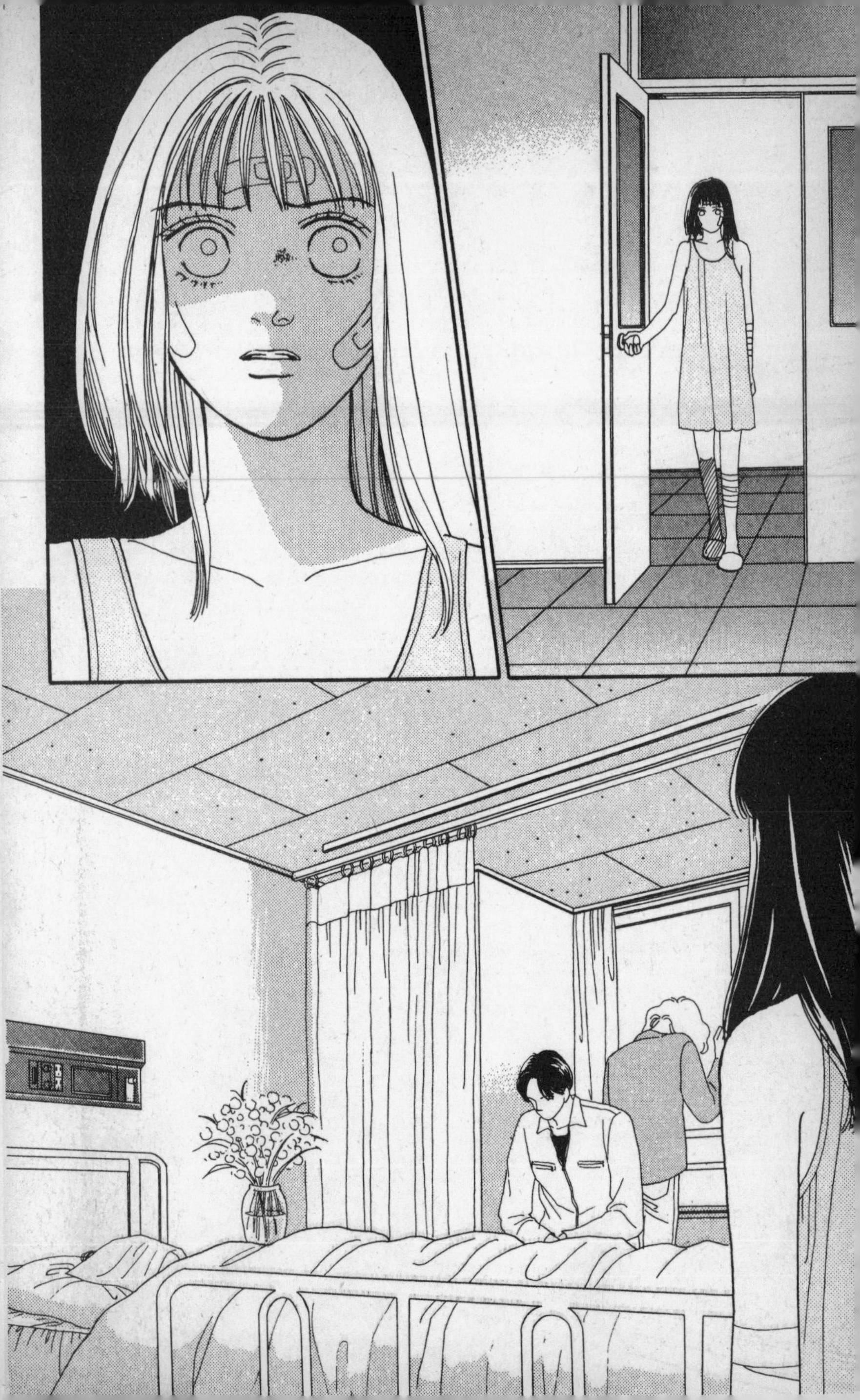

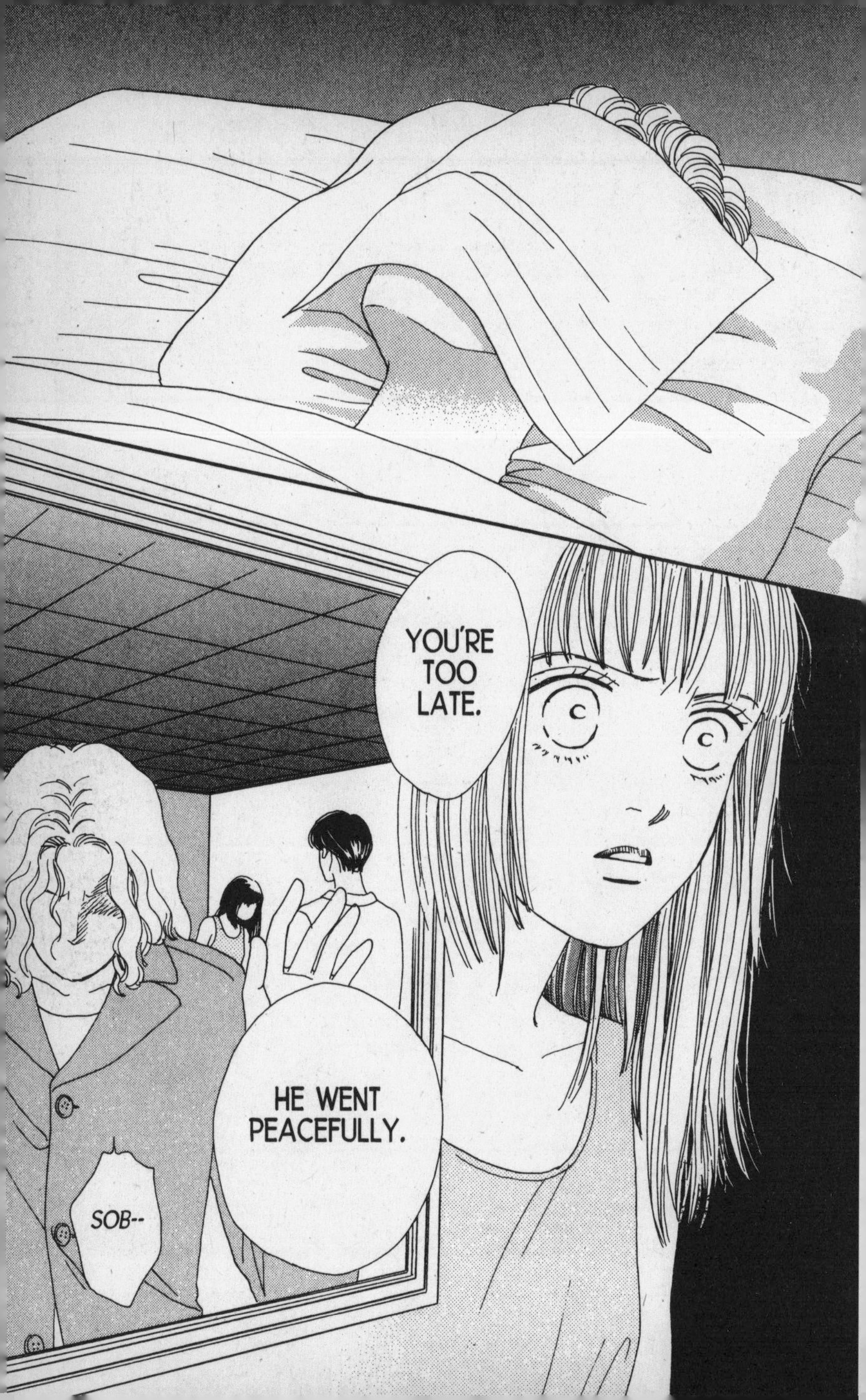
YOU'RE TOO LATE.
HE WENT PEACEFULLY.
SOB--

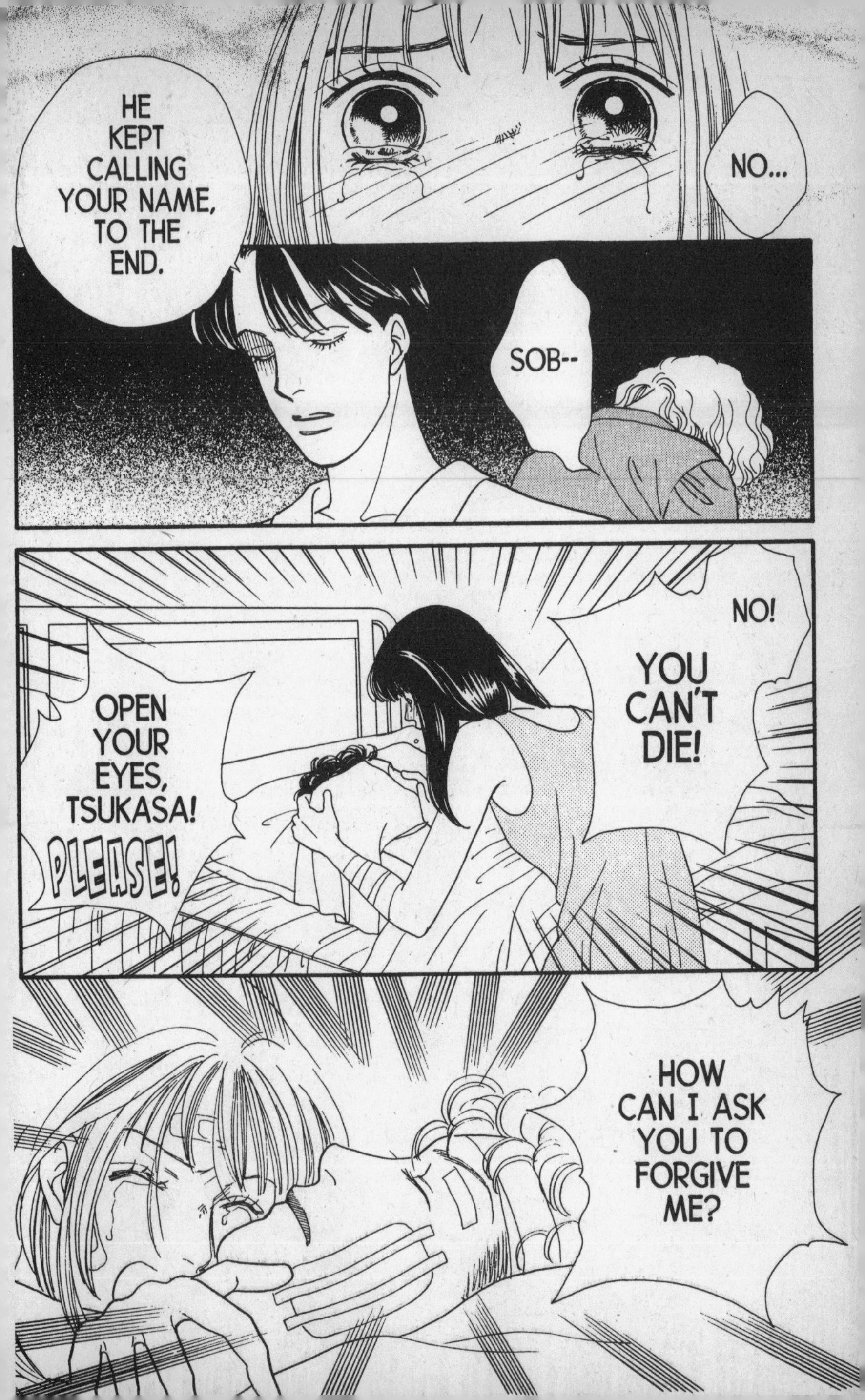
HE KEPT CALLING YOUR NAME, TO THE END.
NO...
SOB--
OPEN YOUR EYES, TSUKASA! PLEASE!
NO! YOU CAN'T DIE!
HOW CAN I ASK YOU TO FORGIVE ME?

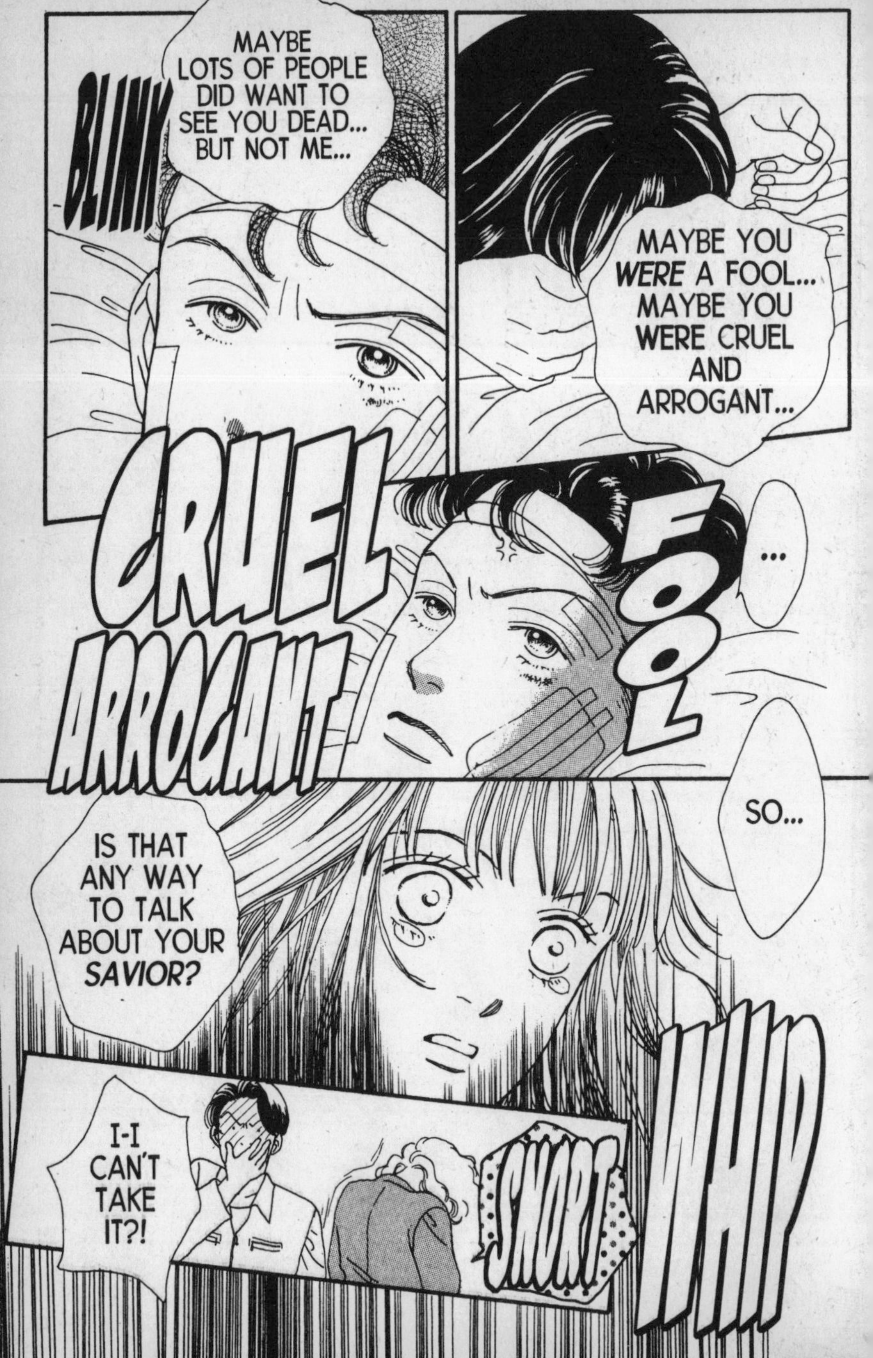
MAYBE YOU *WERE* A FOOL... MAYBE YOU WERE CRUEL AND ARROGANT...
BLINK
MAYBE LOTS OF PEOPLE DID WANT TO SEE YOU DEAD... BUT NOT ME...
...
FOOL
CRUEL
ARROGANT
SO...
WHIP
IS THAT ANY WAY TO TALK ABOUT YOUR *SAVIOR?*
SNORT
I-I CAN'T TAKE IT?!

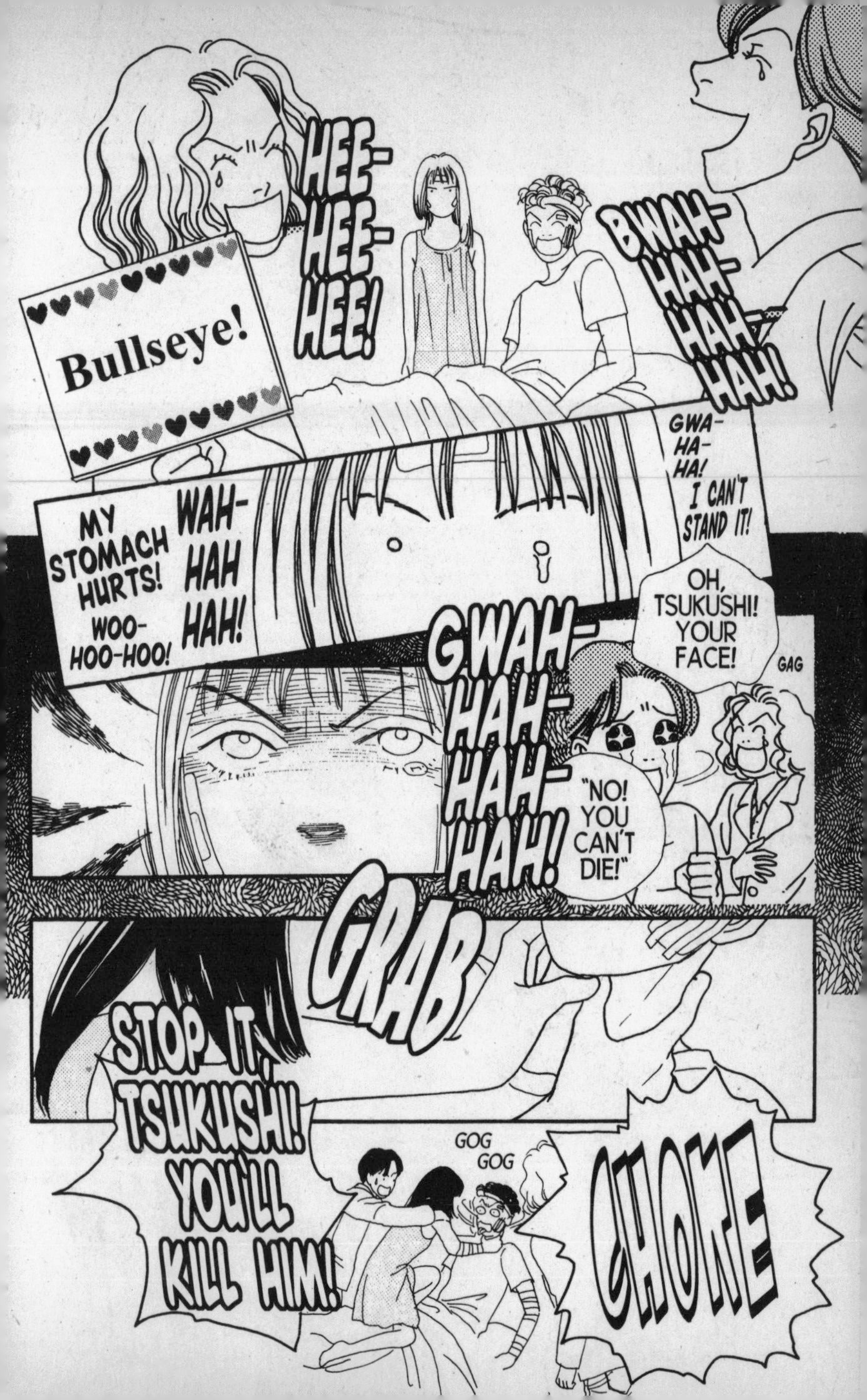
BWAH-HAH-HAH-HAH!
HEE-HEE-HEE!
Bullseye!
GWA-HA-HA! I CAN'T STAND IT!
WAH-HAH HAH HAH!
MY STOMACH HURTS!
WOO-HOO-HOO!
OH, TSUKUSHI! YOUR FACE!
GAG
GWAH-HAH-HAH-HAH!
"NO! YOU CAN'T DIE!"
GRAB
STOP IT, TSUKUSHI! YOU'LL KILL HIM!
CHOKE
GOG GOG

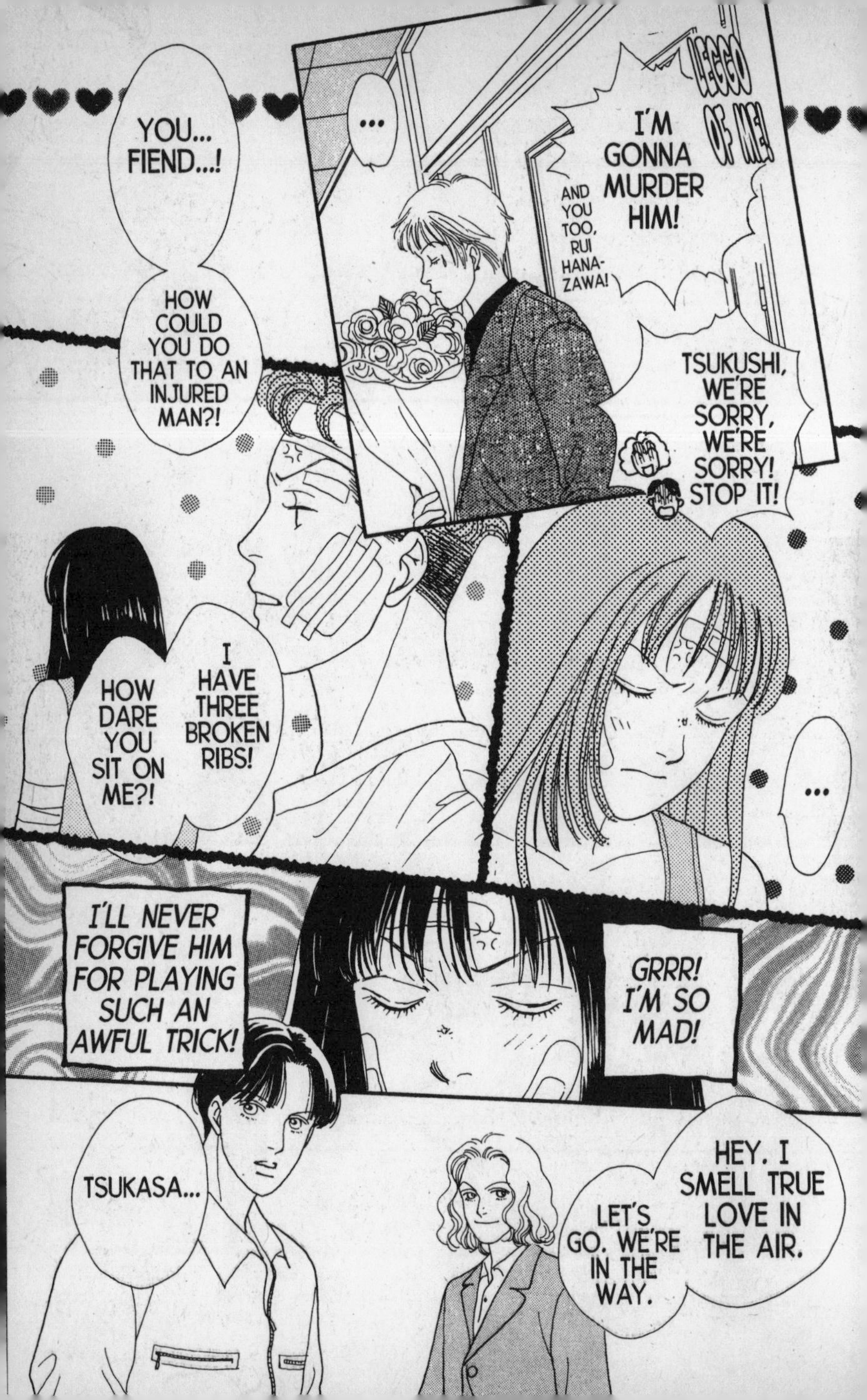
LEGGO OF ME!
I'M GONNA MURDER HIM!
AND YOU TOO, RUI HANAZAWA!
TSUKUSHI, WE'RE SORRY, WE'RE SORRY! STOP IT!
...
YOU... FIEND...!
HOW COULD YOU DO THAT TO AN INJURED MAN?!
...
I HAVE THREE BROKEN RIBS!
HOW DARE YOU SIT ON ME?!
GRRR! I'M SO MAD!
I'LL NEVER FORGIVE HIM FOR PLAYING SUCH AN AWFUL TRICK!
HEY. I SMELL TRUE LOVE IN THE AIR.
LET'S GO. WE'RE IN THE WAY.
TSUKASA...

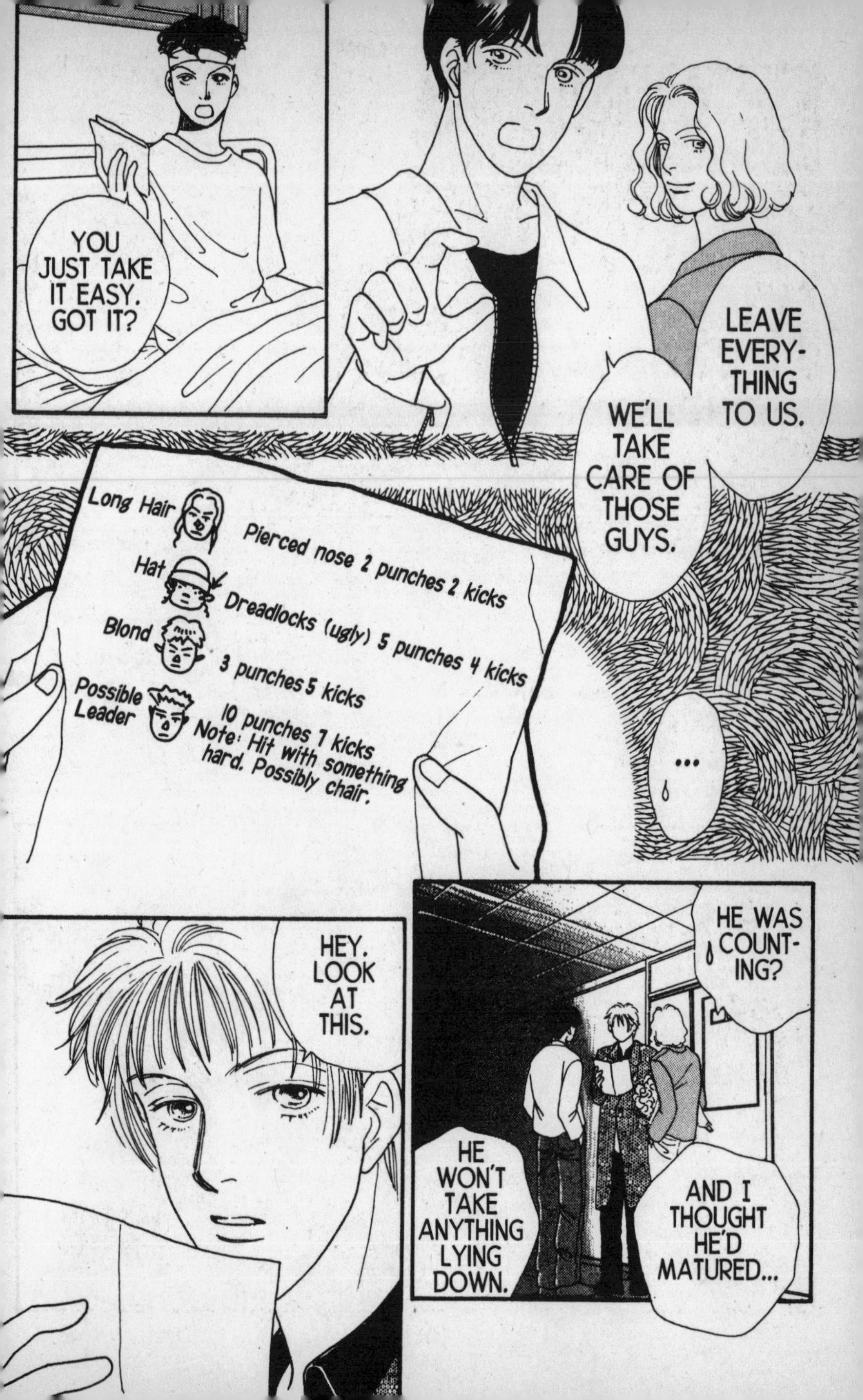
LEAVE EVERY-THING TO US.
WE'LL TAKE CARE OF THOSE GUYS.
YOU JUST TAKE IT EASY. GOT IT?
...
Long Hair
Pierced nose 2 punches 2 kicks
Hat
Dreadlocks (ugly) 5 punches 4 kicks
Blond
3 punches 5 kicks
Possible Leader
10 punches 7 kicks
Note: Hit with something hard. Possibly chair.
HE WAS COUNT-ING?
AND I THOUGHT HE'D MATURED...
HE WON'T TAKE ANYTHING LYING DOWN.
HEY. LOOK AT THIS.

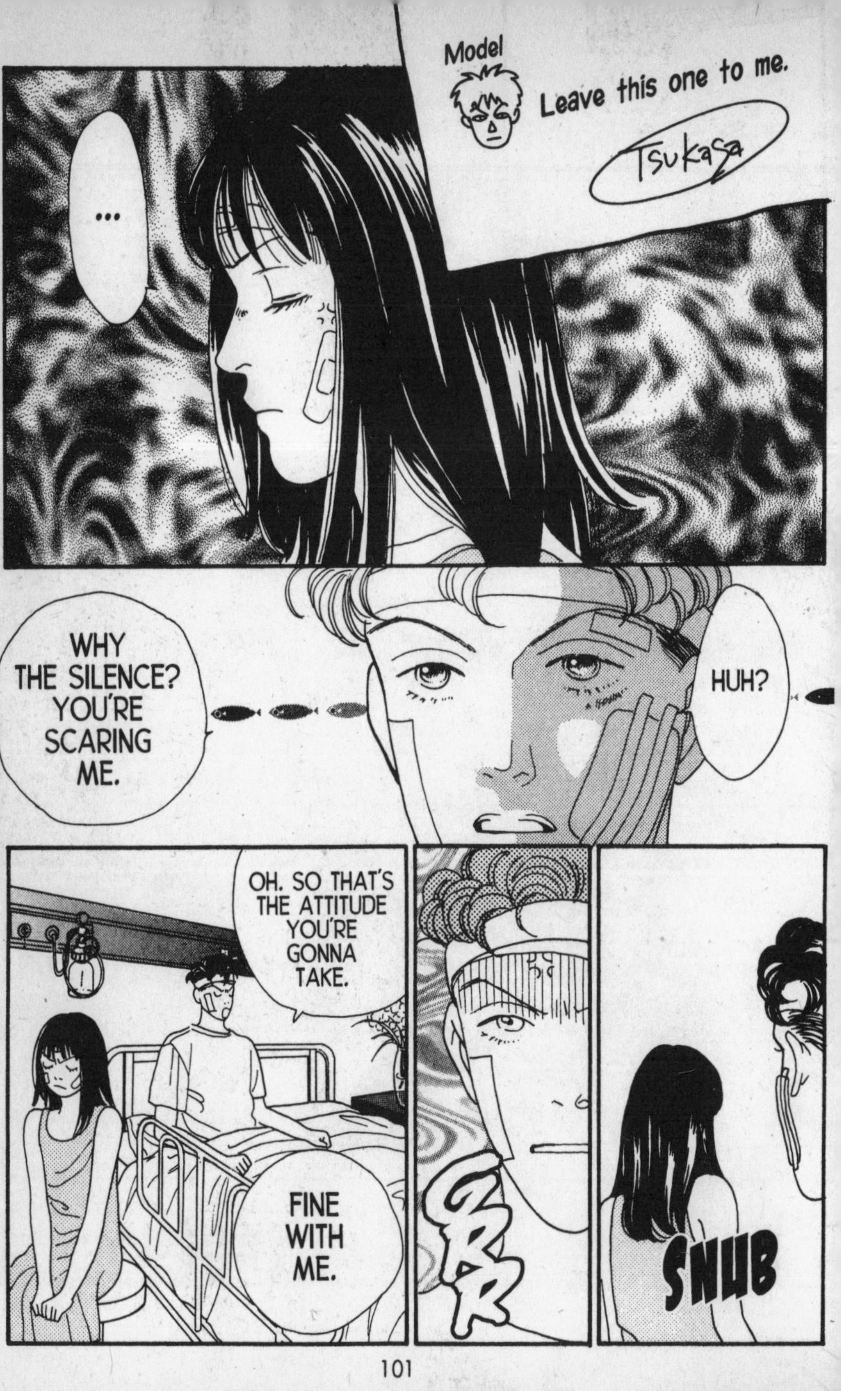
Model
Leave this one to me.
Tsukasa
...
HUH?
WHY THE SILENCE? YOU'RE SCARING ME.
SNUB
OH. SO THAT'S THE ATTITUDE YOU'RE GONNA TAKE.
FINE WITH ME.

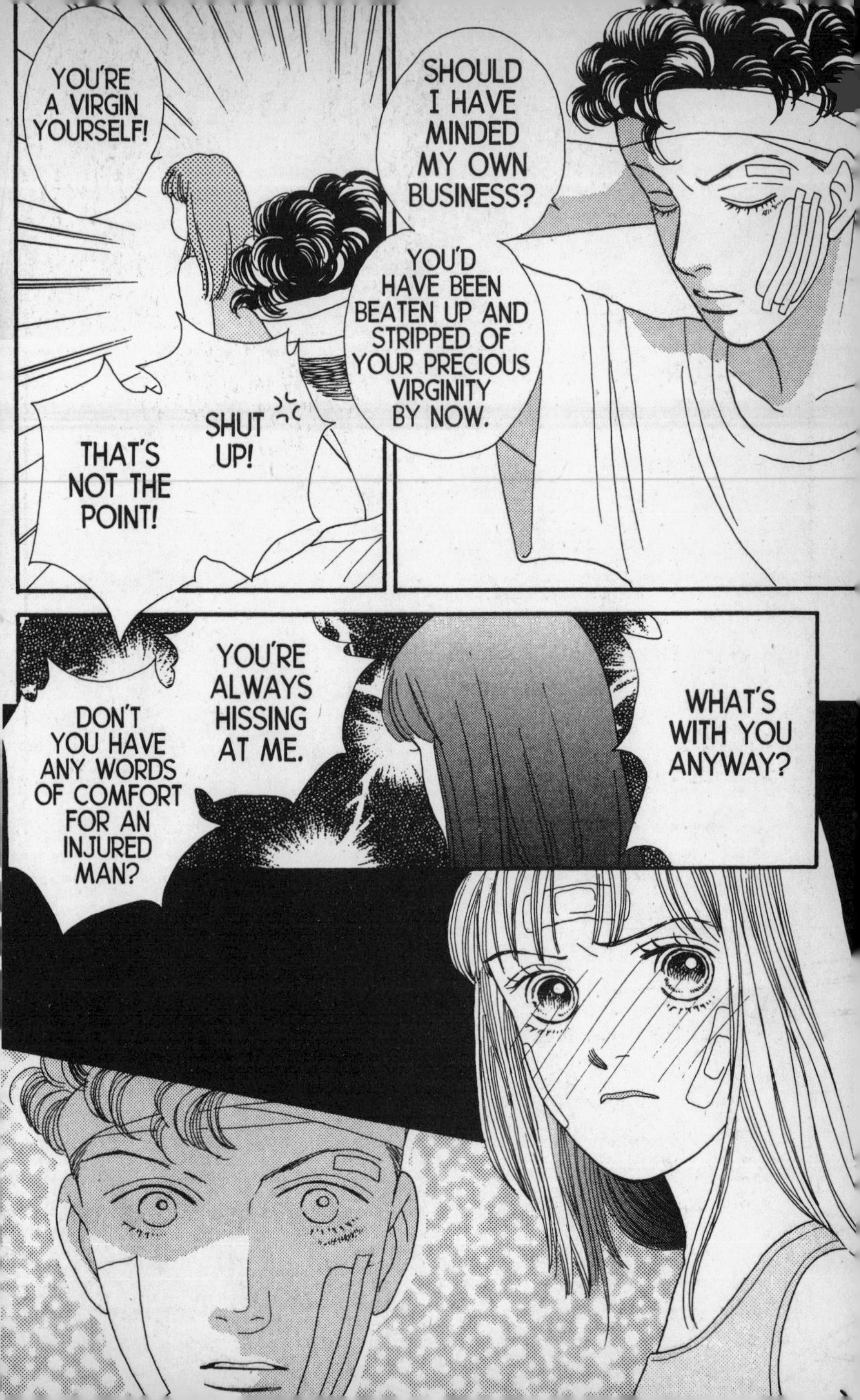
SHOULD I HAVE MINDED MY OWN BUSINESS?
YOU'D HAVE BEEN BEATEN UP AND STRIPPED OF YOUR PRECIOUS VIRGINITY BY NOW.
YOU'RE A VIRGIN YOURSELF!
SHUT UP!
THAT'S NOT THE POINT!
WHAT'S WITH YOU ANYWAY?
YOU'RE ALWAYS HISSING AT ME.
DON'T YOU HAVE ANY WORDS OF COMFORT FOR AN INJURED MAN?

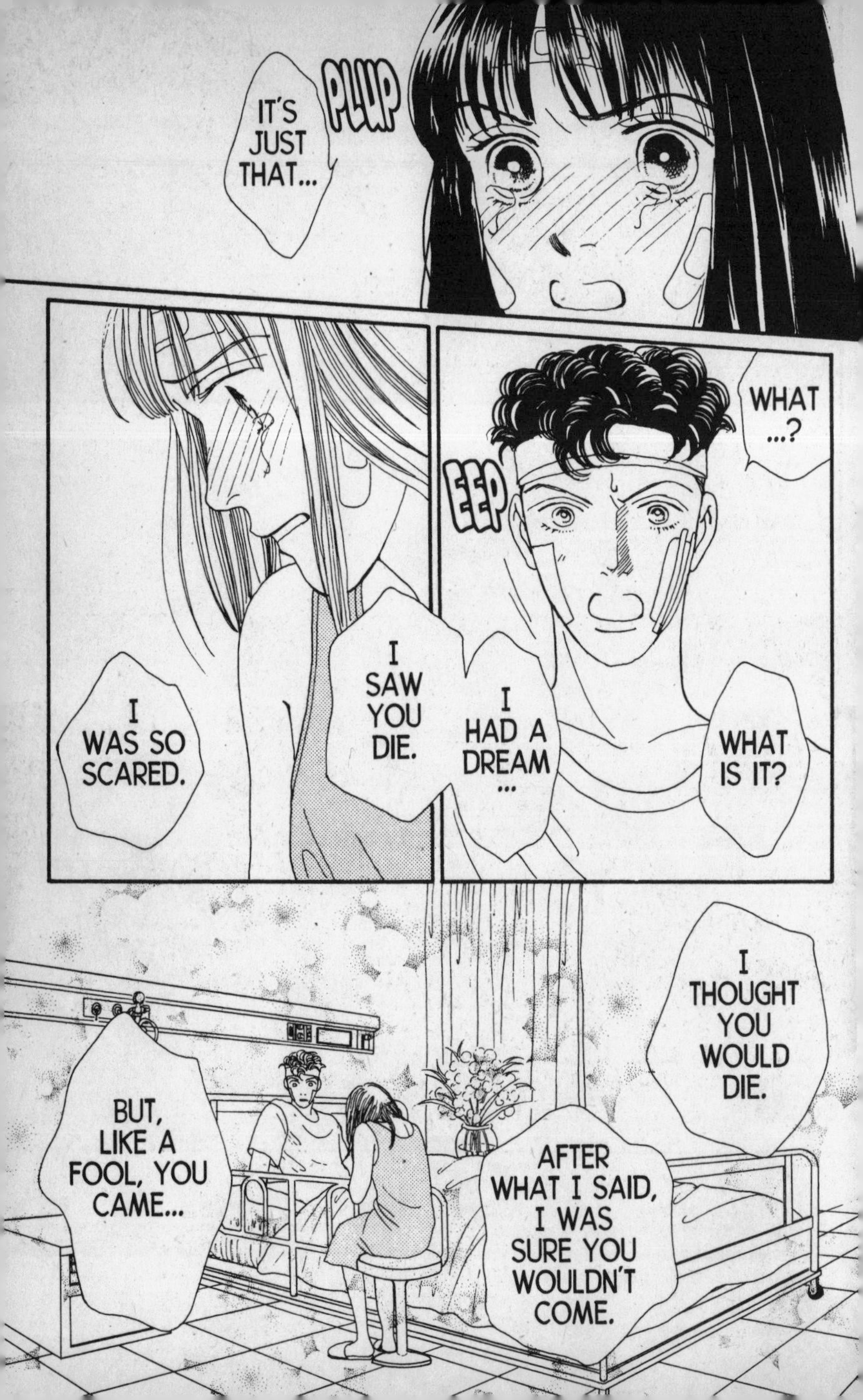
PLUP
IT'S JUST THAT...
WHAT ...?
EEP
WHAT IS IT?
I HAD A DREAM ...
I SAW YOU DIE.
I WAS SO SCARED.
I THOUGHT YOU WOULD DIE.
AFTER WHAT I SAID, I WAS SURE YOU WOULDN'T COME.
BUT, LIKE A FOOL, YOU CAME...

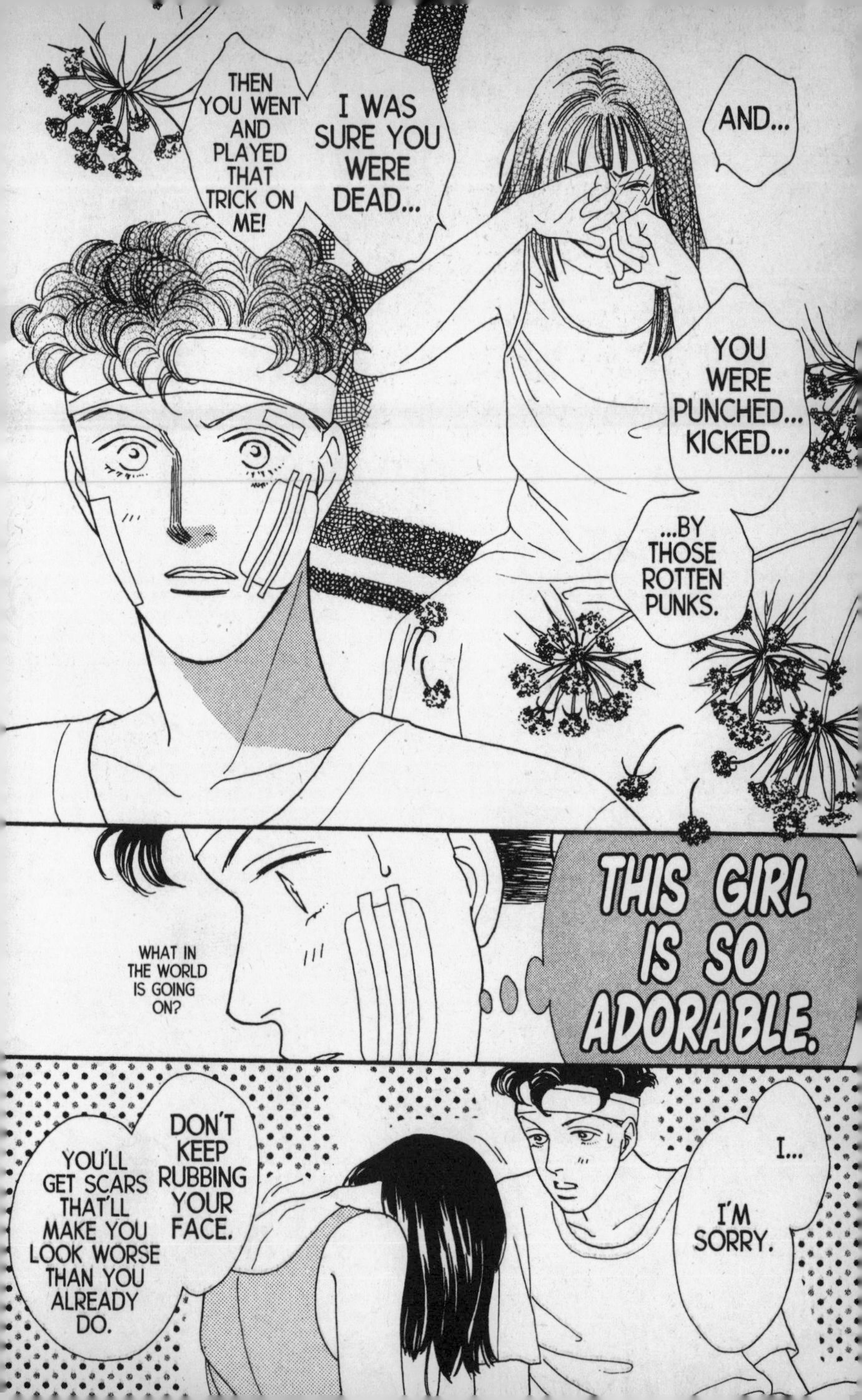
I WAS SURE YOU WERE DEAD...
THEN YOU WENT AND PLAYED THAT TRICK ON ME!
AND...
YOU WERE PUNCHED... KICKED...
...BY THOSE ROTTEN PUNKS.
THIS GIRL IS SO ADORABLE.
WHAT IN THE WORLD IS GOING ON?
I...
I'M SORRY.
DON'T KEEP RUBBING YOUR FACE.
YOU'LL GET SCARS THAT'LL MAKE YOU LOOK WORSE THAN YOU ALREADY DO.

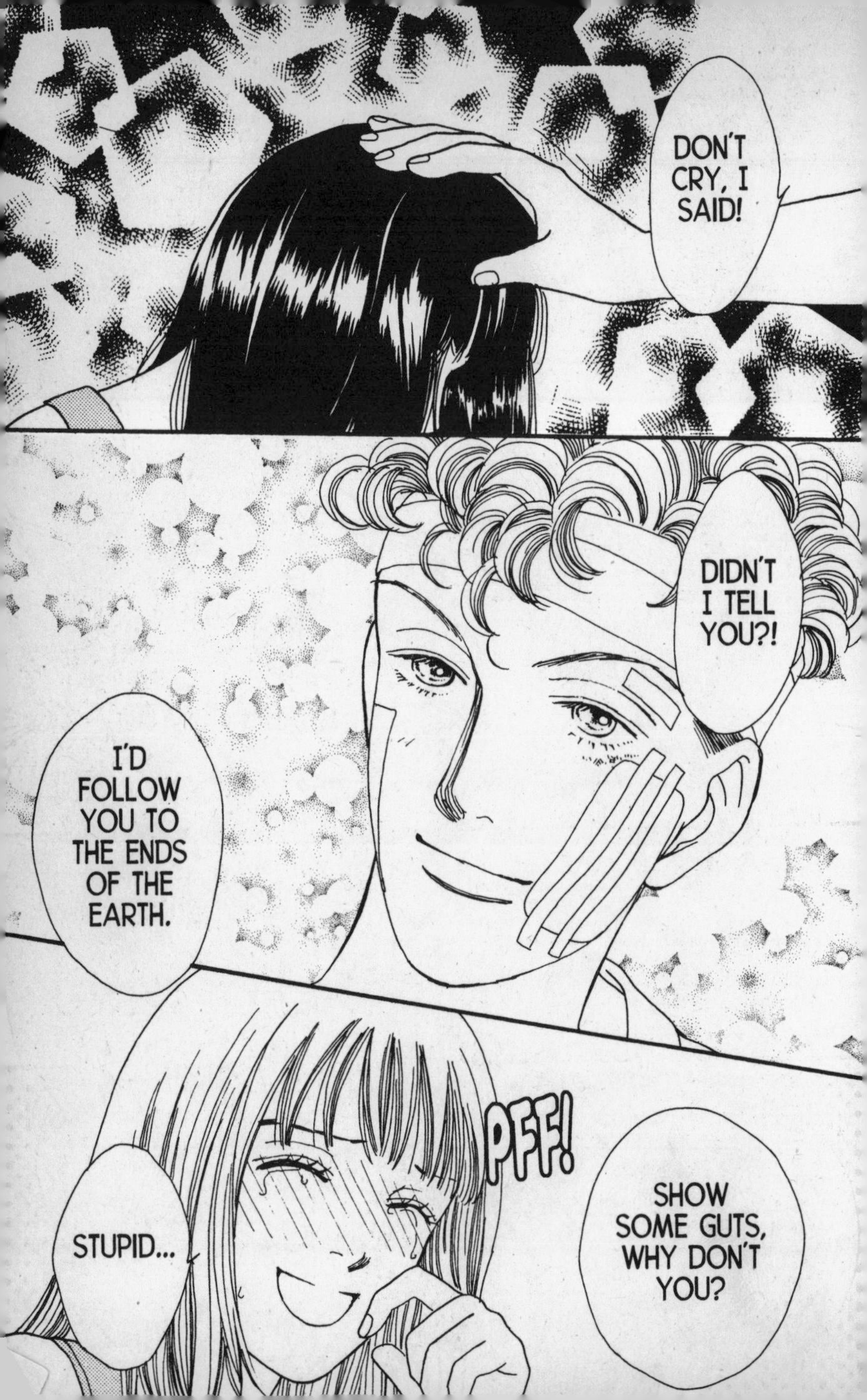
DON'T CRY, I SAID!
DIDN'T I TELL YOU?!
I'D FOLLOW YOU TO THE ENDS OF THE EARTH.
SHOW SOME GUTS, WHY DON'T YOU?
PFF!
STUPID...

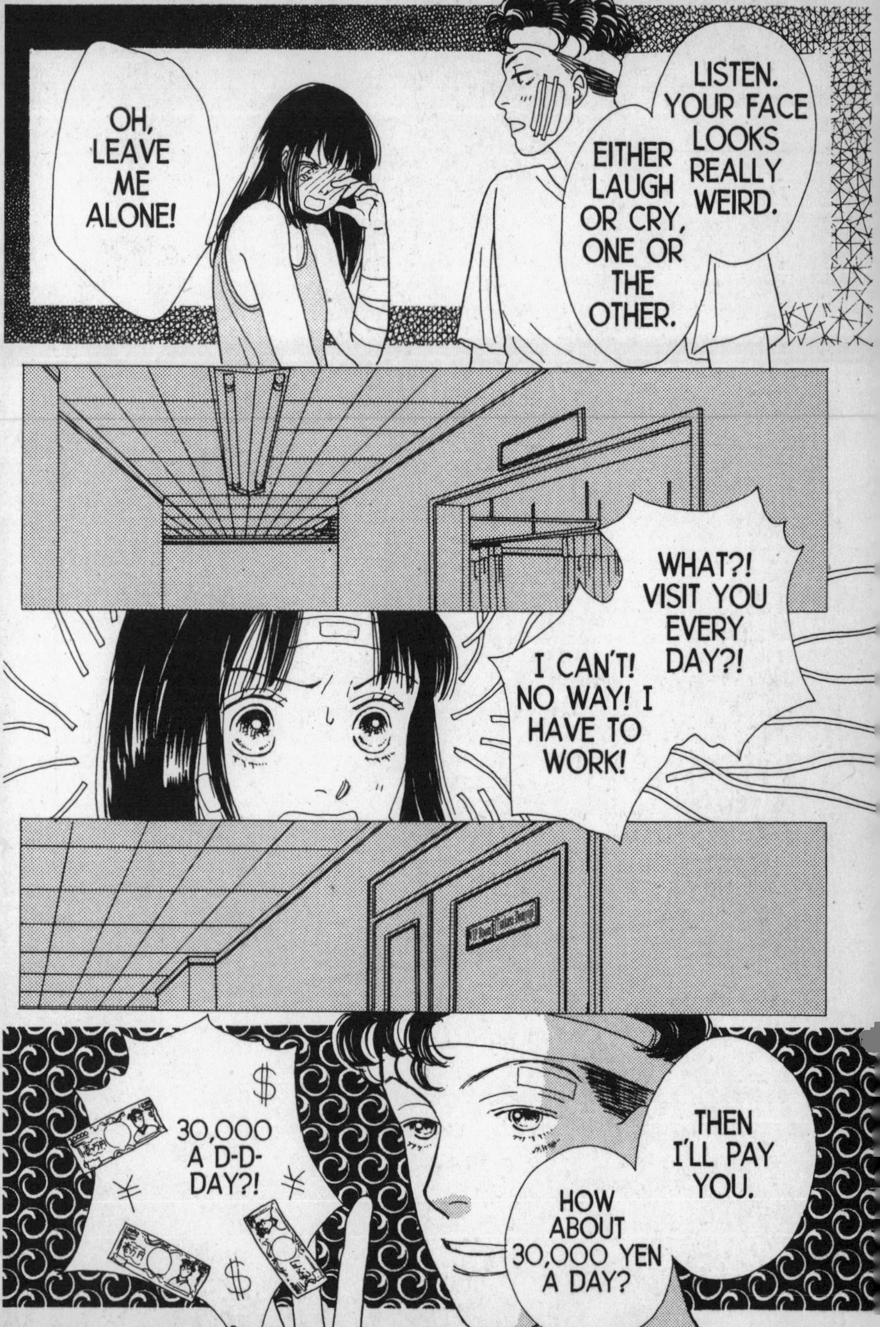
LISTEN. YOUR FACE LOOKS REALLY WEIRD.
EITHER LAUGH OR CRY, ONE OR THE OTHER.
OH, LEAVE ME ALONE!
WHAT?! VISIT YOU EVERY DAY?!
I CAN'T! NO WAY! I HAVE TO WORK!
THEN I'LL PAY YOU.
HOW ABOUT 30,000 YEN A DAY?
30,000 A D-D-DAY?!

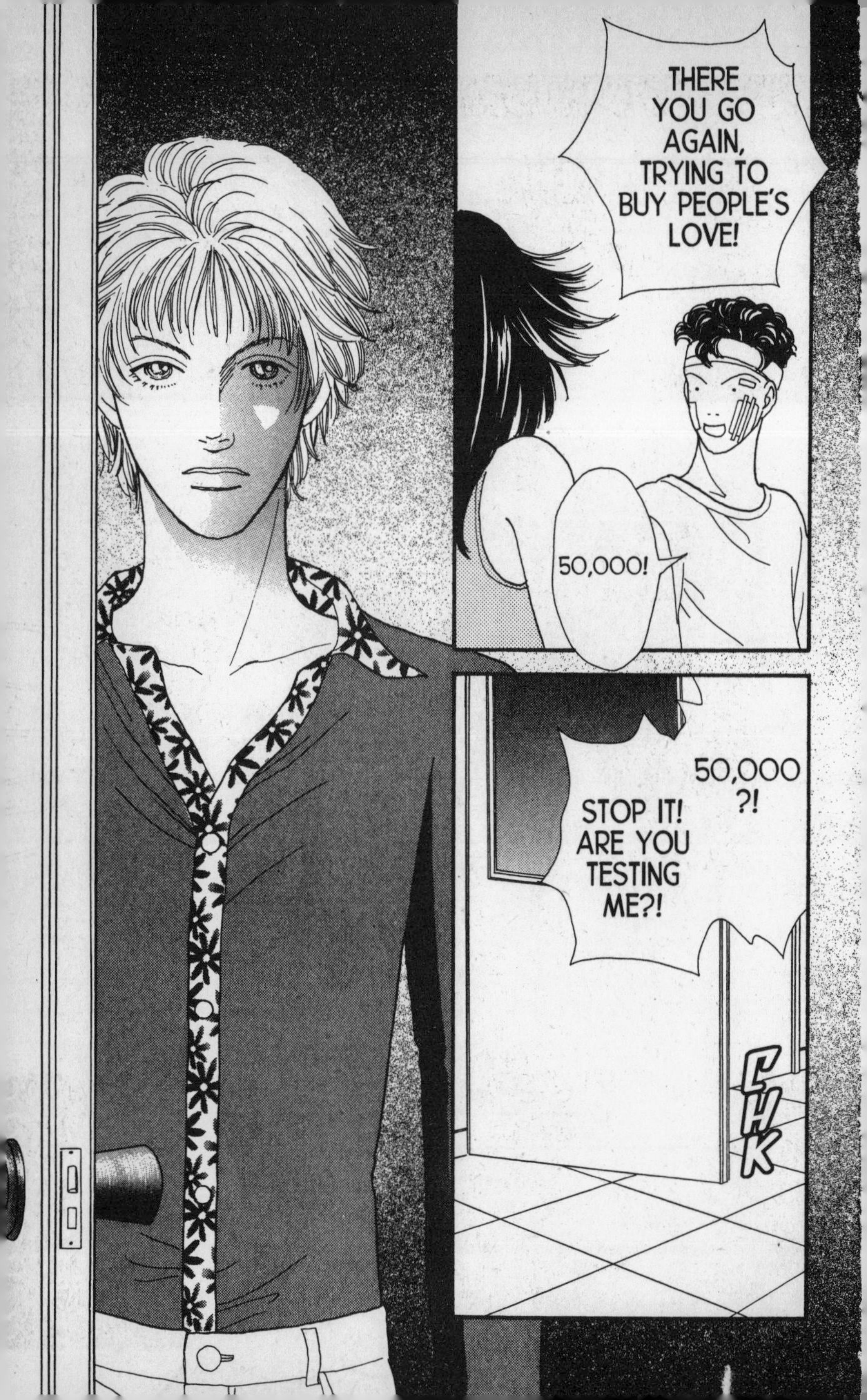
THERE YOU GO AGAIN, TRYING TO BUY PEOPLE'S LOVE!
50,000!
50,000 ?!
STOP IT! ARE YOU TESTING ME?!
CHK

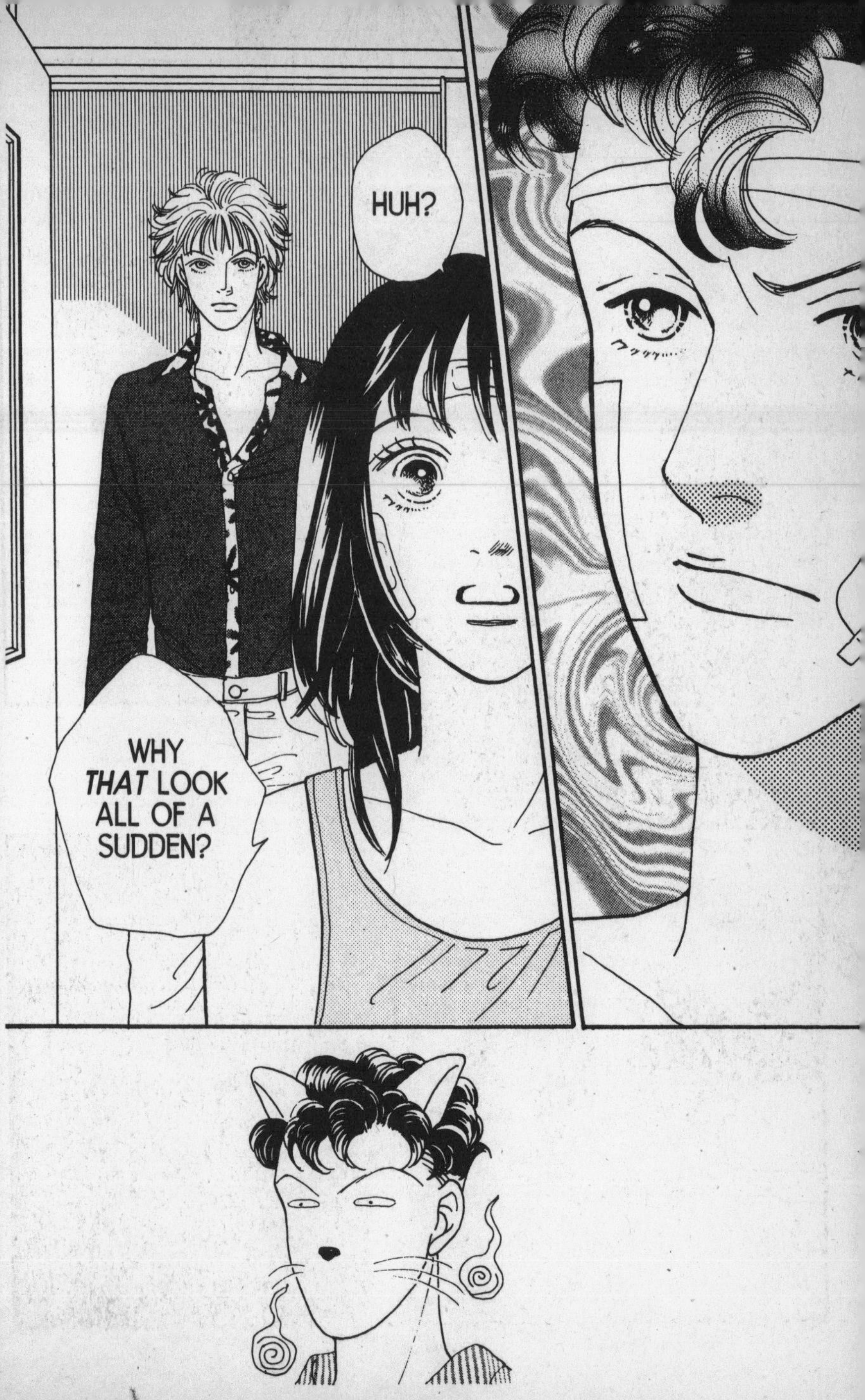
HUH?
WHY *THAT* LOOK ALL OF A SUDDEN?

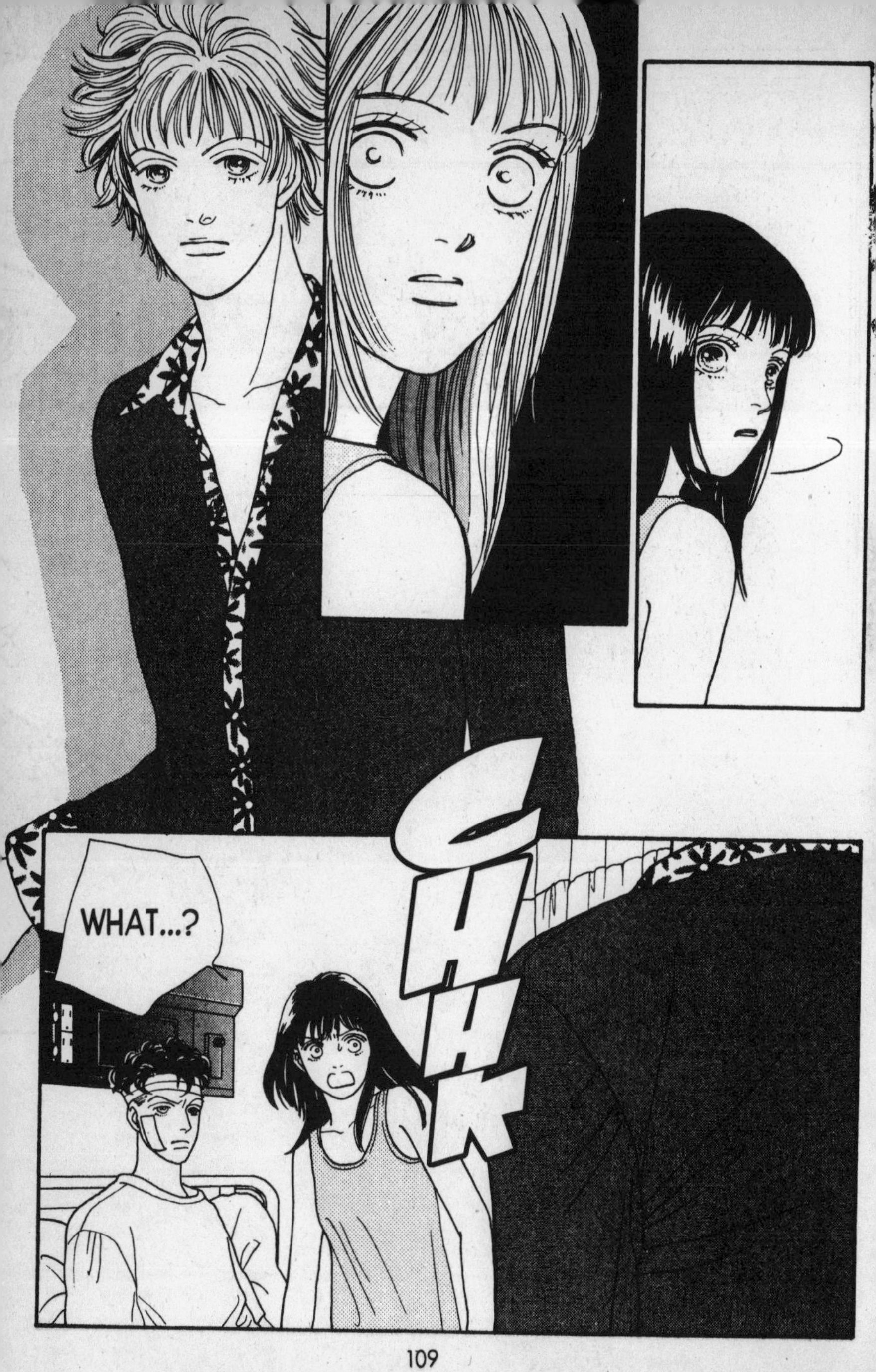
CHHK
WHAT...?

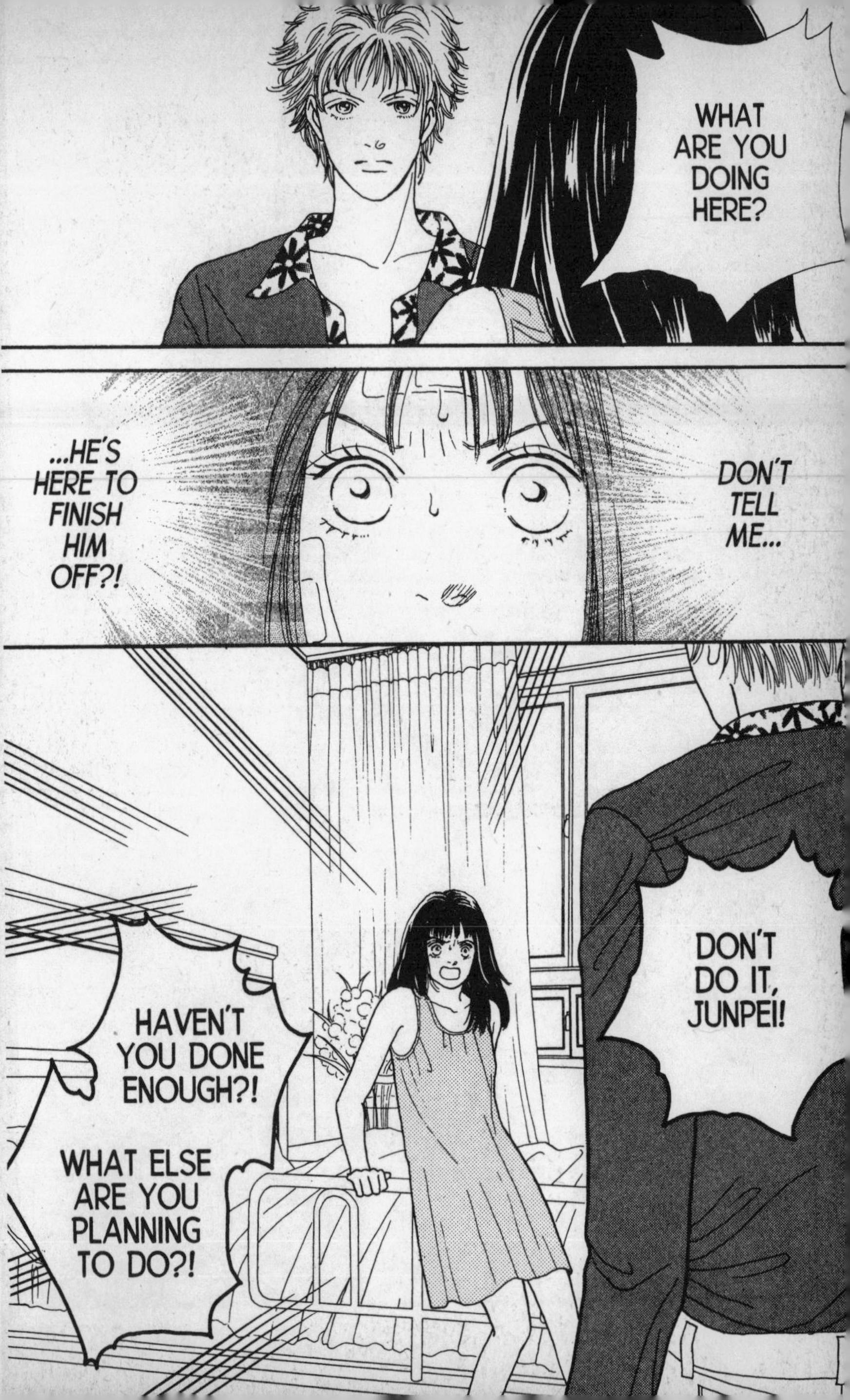
WHAT ARE YOU DOING HERE?
DON'T TELL ME...
...HE'S HERE TO FINISH HIM OFF?!
DON'T DO IT, JUNPEI!
HAVEN'T YOU DONE ENOUGH?!
WHAT ELSE ARE YOU PLANNING TO DO?!

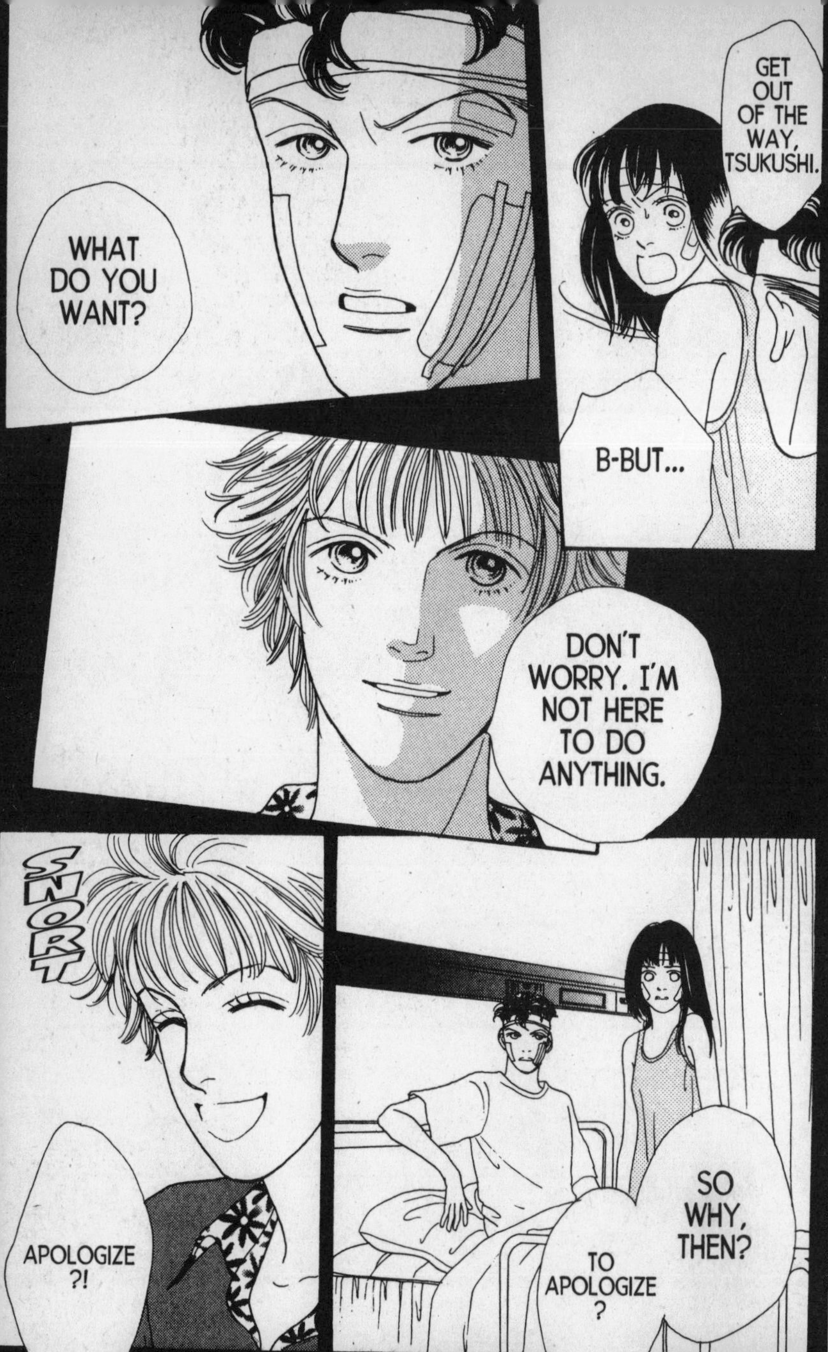
GET OUT OF THE WAY, TSUKUSHI.
B-BUT...
WHAT DO YOU WANT?
DON'T WORRY. I'M NOT HERE TO DO ANYTHING.
SO WHY, THEN?
TO APOLOGIZE?
SNORT
APOLOGIZE?!

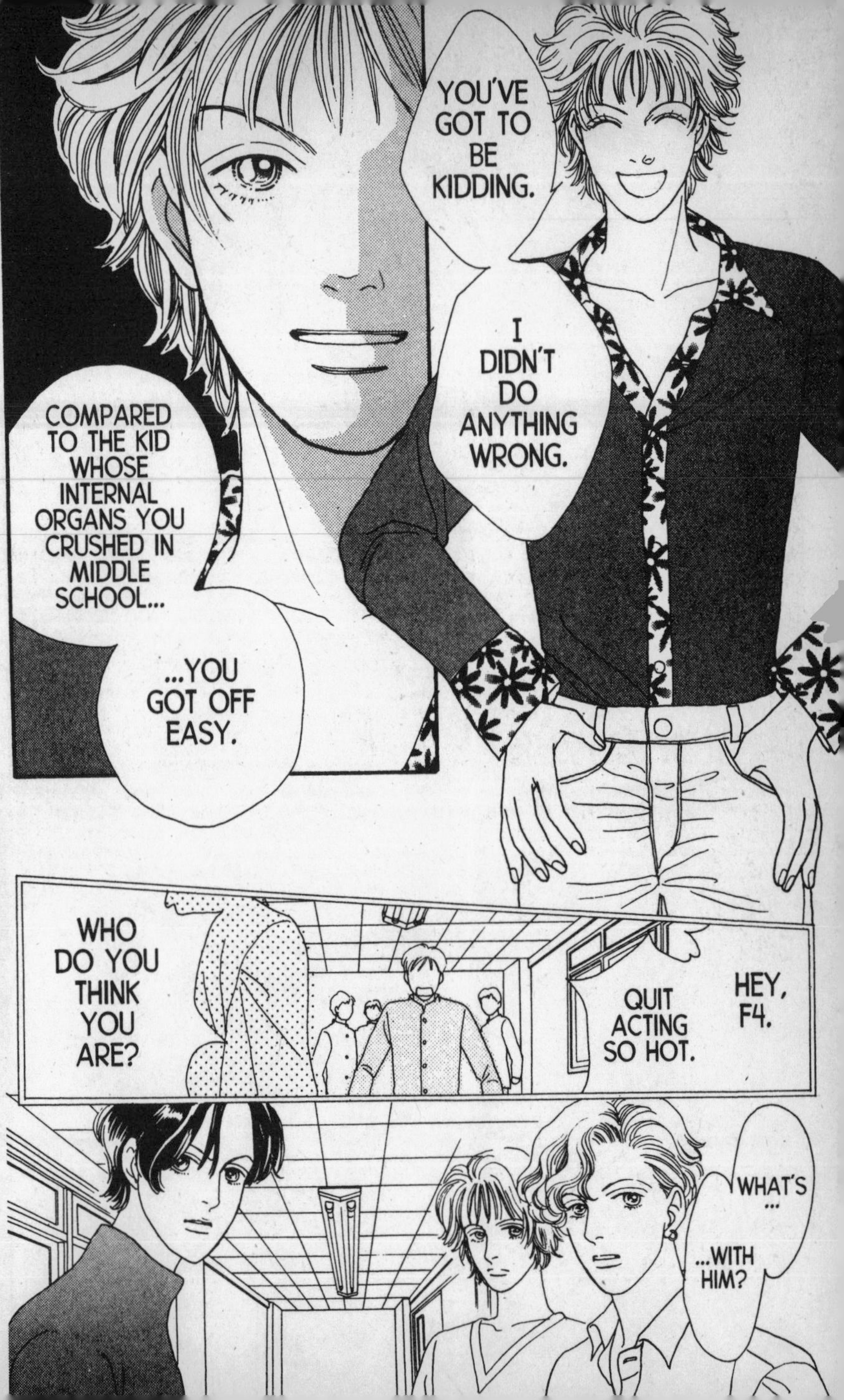
YOU'VE GOT TO BE KIDDING.
I DIDN'T DO ANYTHING WRONG.
COMPARED TO THE KID WHOSE INTERNAL ORGANS YOU CRUSHED IN MIDDLE SCHOOL...
...YOU GOT OFF EASY.
HEY, F4.
QUIT ACTING SO HOT.
WHO DO YOU THINK YOU ARE?
WHAT'S...
...WITH HIM?

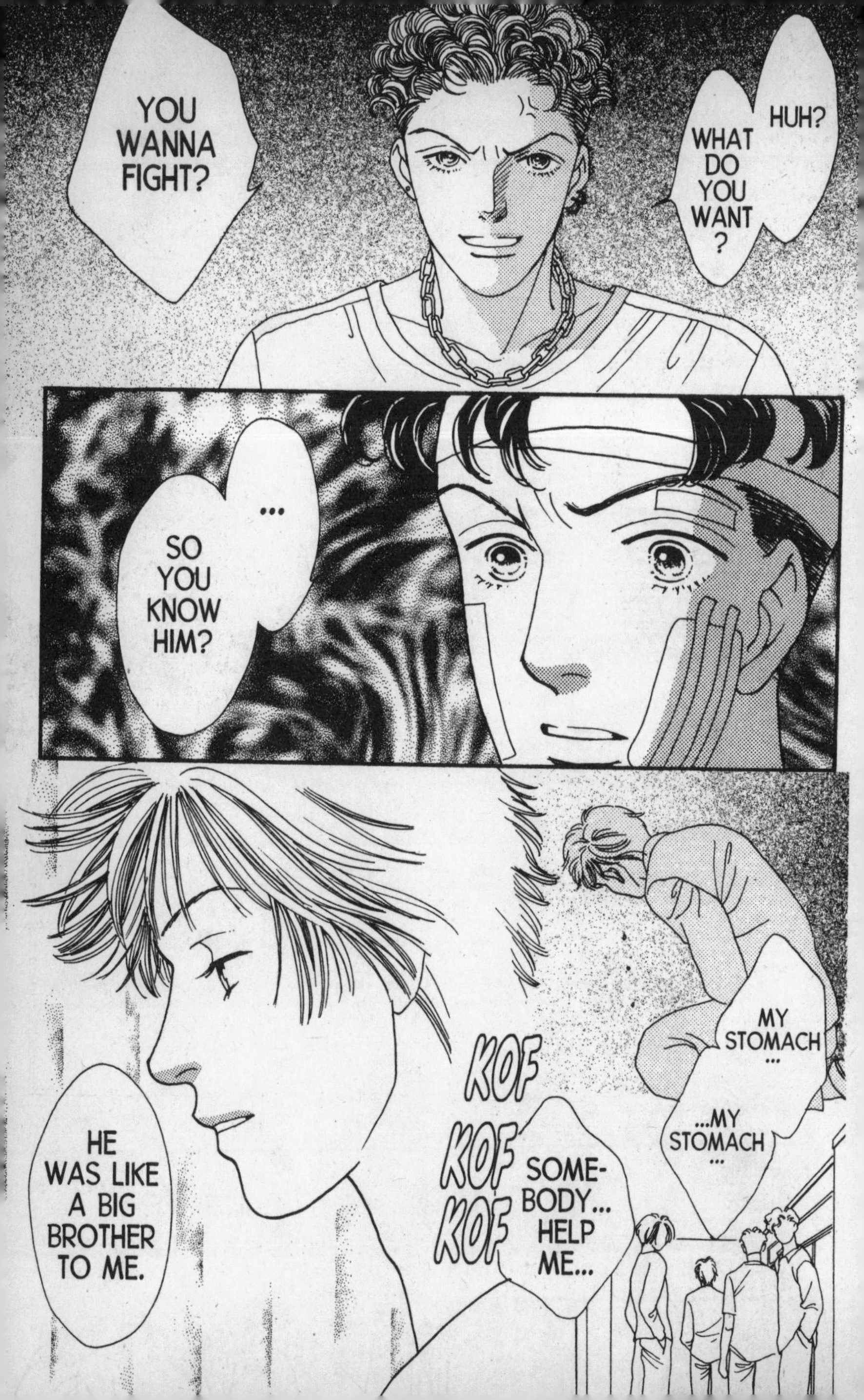
HUH? WHAT DO YOU WANT?
YOU WANNA FIGHT?
... SO YOU KNOW HIM?
MY STOMACH...
...MY STOMACH...
SOME-BODY... HELP ME...
KOF KOF KOF
HE WAS LIKE A BIG BROTHER TO ME.

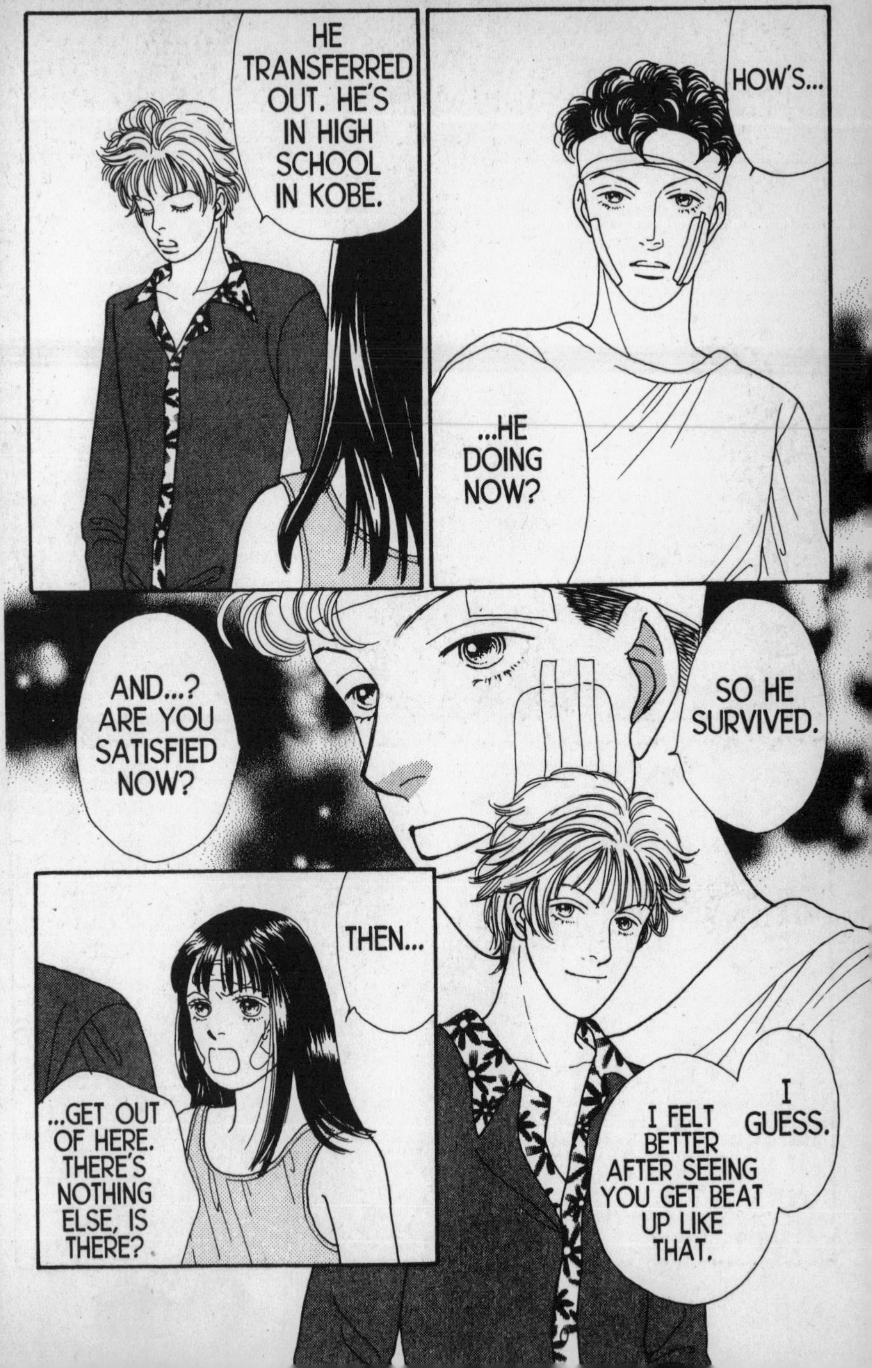
HOW'S...
...HE DOING NOW?
HE TRANSFERRED OUT. HE'S IN HIGH SCHOOL IN KOBE.
SO HE SURVIVED.
AND...? ARE YOU SATISFIED NOW?
I GUESS.
I FELT BETTER AFTER SEEING YOU GET BEAT UP LIKE THAT.
THEN...
...GET OUT OF HERE. THERE'S NOTHING ELSE, IS THERE?

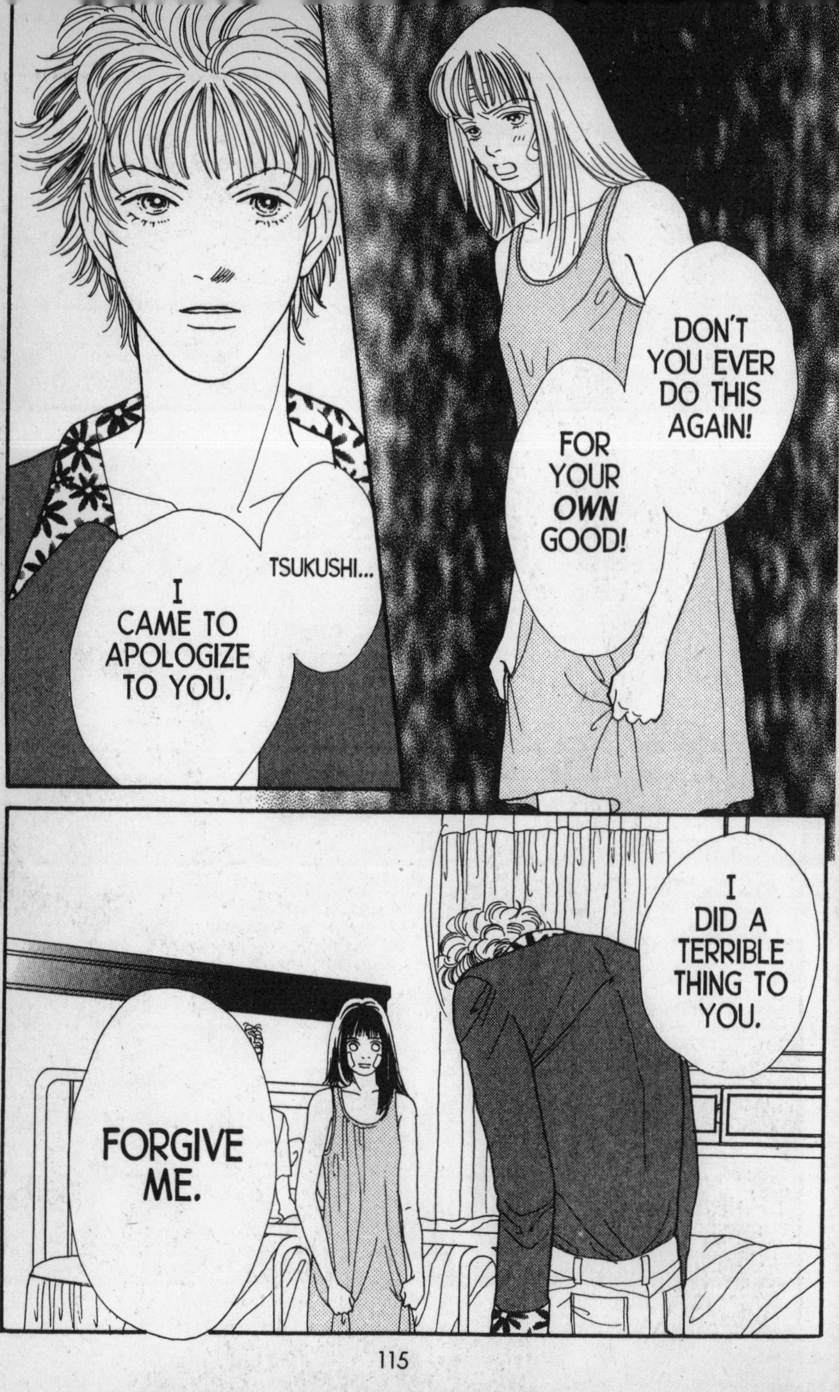
DON'T YOU EVER DO THIS AGAIN!
FOR YOUR *OWN* GOOD!
TSUKUSHI...
I CAME TO APOLOGIZE TO YOU.
I DID A TERRIBLE THING TO YOU.
FORGIVE ME.

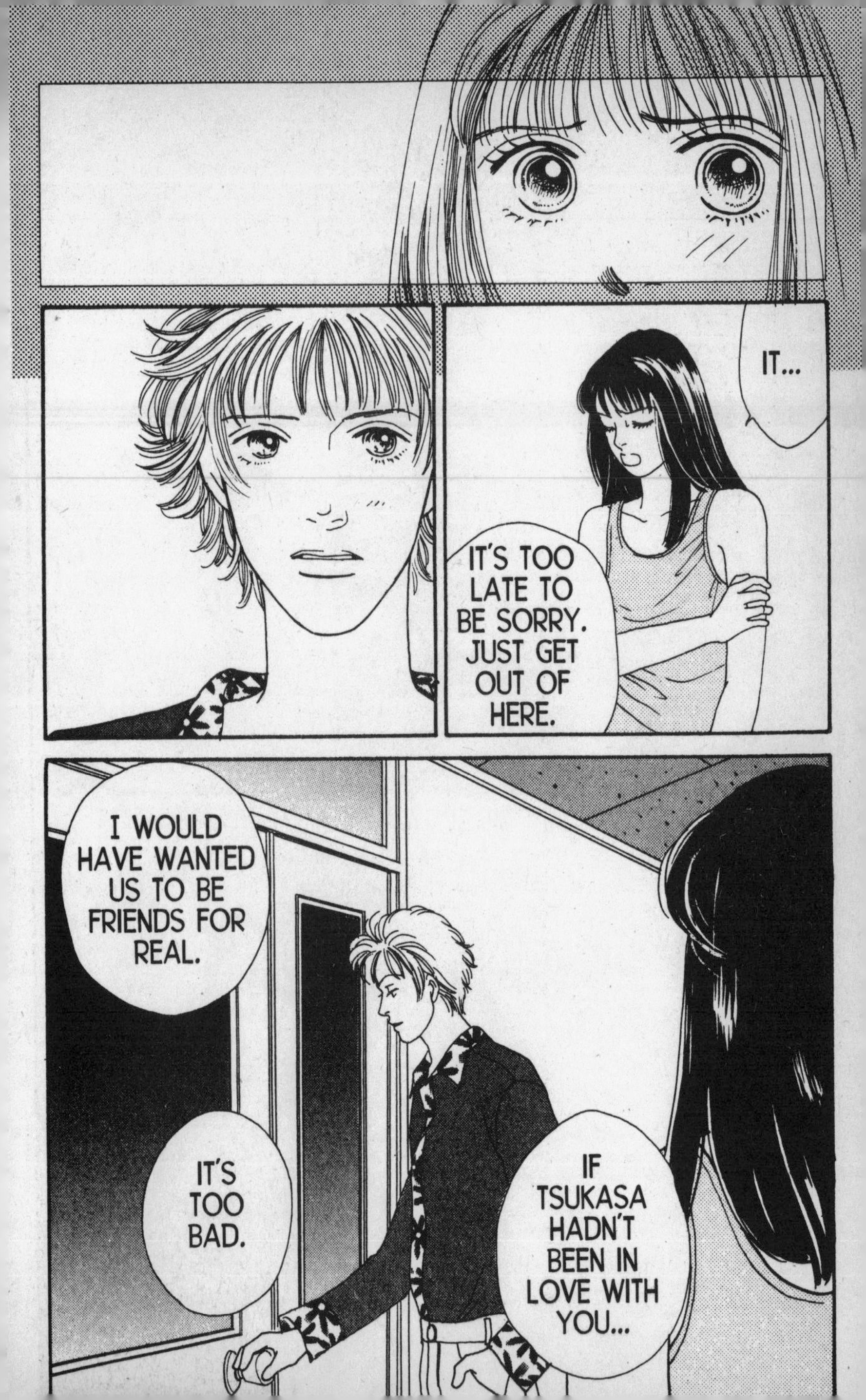
IT...
IT'S TOO LATE TO BE SORRY. JUST GET OUT OF HERE.
I WOULD HAVE WANTED US TO BE FRIENDS FOR REAL.
IT'S TOO BAD.
IF TSUKASA HADN'T BEEN IN LOVE WITH YOU...

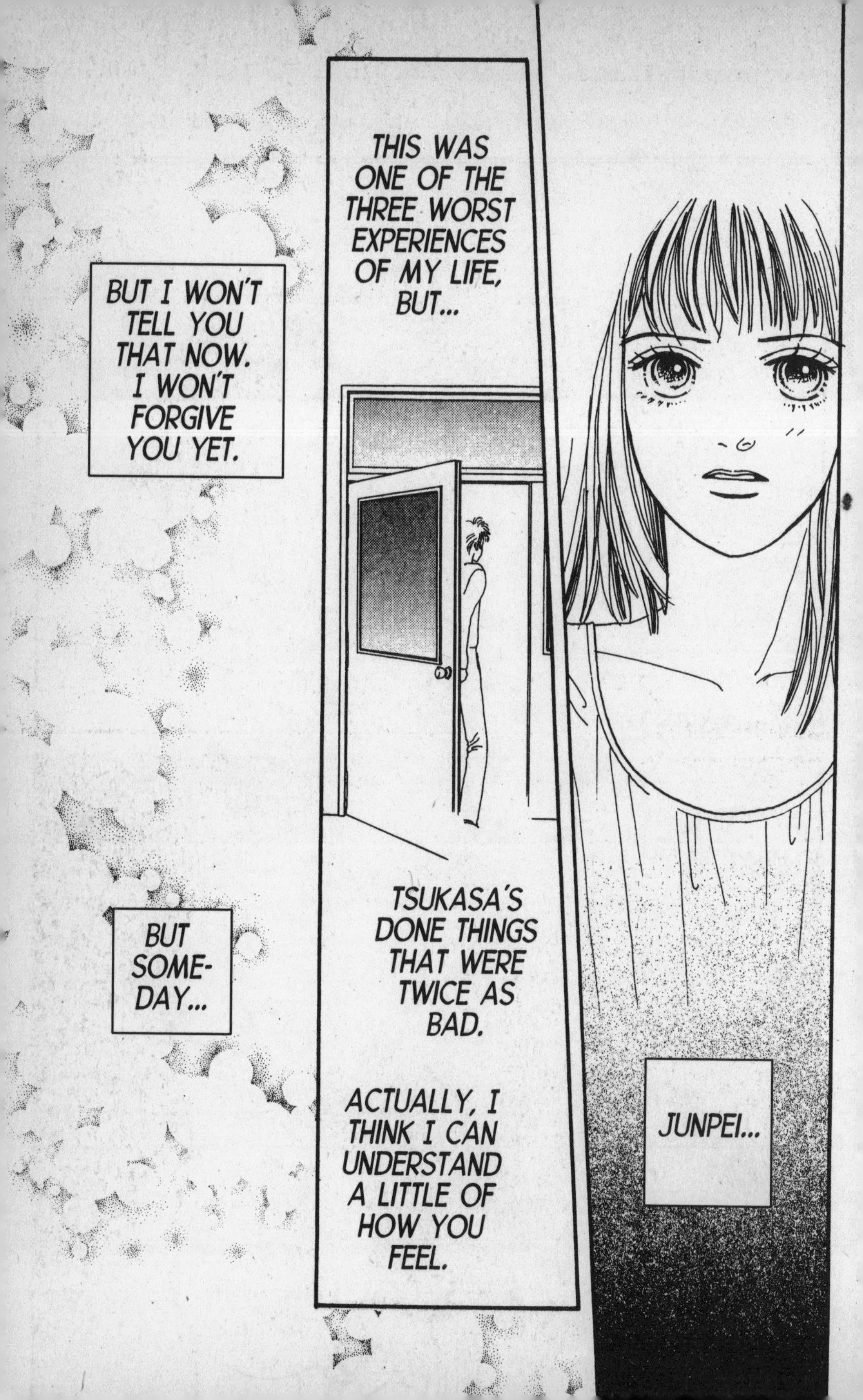

JUNPEI...
THIS WAS ONE OF THE THREE WORST EXPERIENCES OF MY LIFE, BUT...
TSUKASA'S DONE THINGS THAT WERE TWICE AS BAD.
ACTUALLY, I THINK I CAN UNDERSTAND A LITTLE OF HOW YOU FEEL.
BUT I WON'T TELL YOU THAT NOW. I WON'T FORGIVE YOU YET.
BUT SOME-DAY...

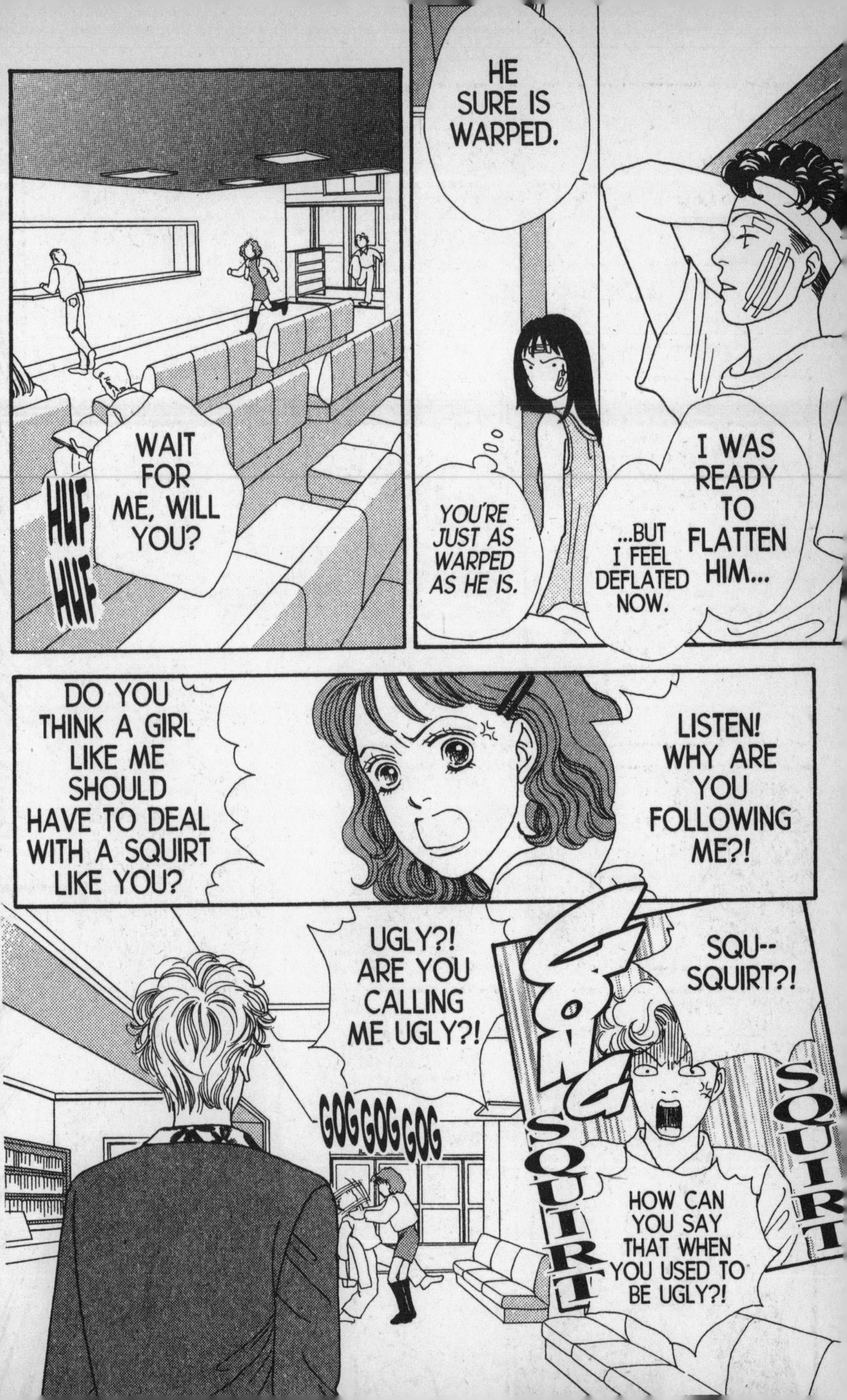
HE SURE IS WARPED.
I WAS READY TO FLATTEN HIM...
...BUT I FEEL DEFLATED NOW.
YOU'RE JUST AS WARPED AS HE IS.
WAIT FOR ME, WILL YOU?
HUF HUF
LISTEN! WHY ARE YOU FOLLOWING ME?!
DO YOU THINK A GIRL LIKE ME SHOULD HAVE TO DEAL WITH A SQUIRT LIKE YOU?
SQU-- SQUIRT?!
SQUIRT
SQUIRT
HOW CAN YOU SAY THAT WHEN YOU USED TO BE UGLY?!
UGLY?! ARE YOU CALLING ME UGLY?!
GOG GOG GOG

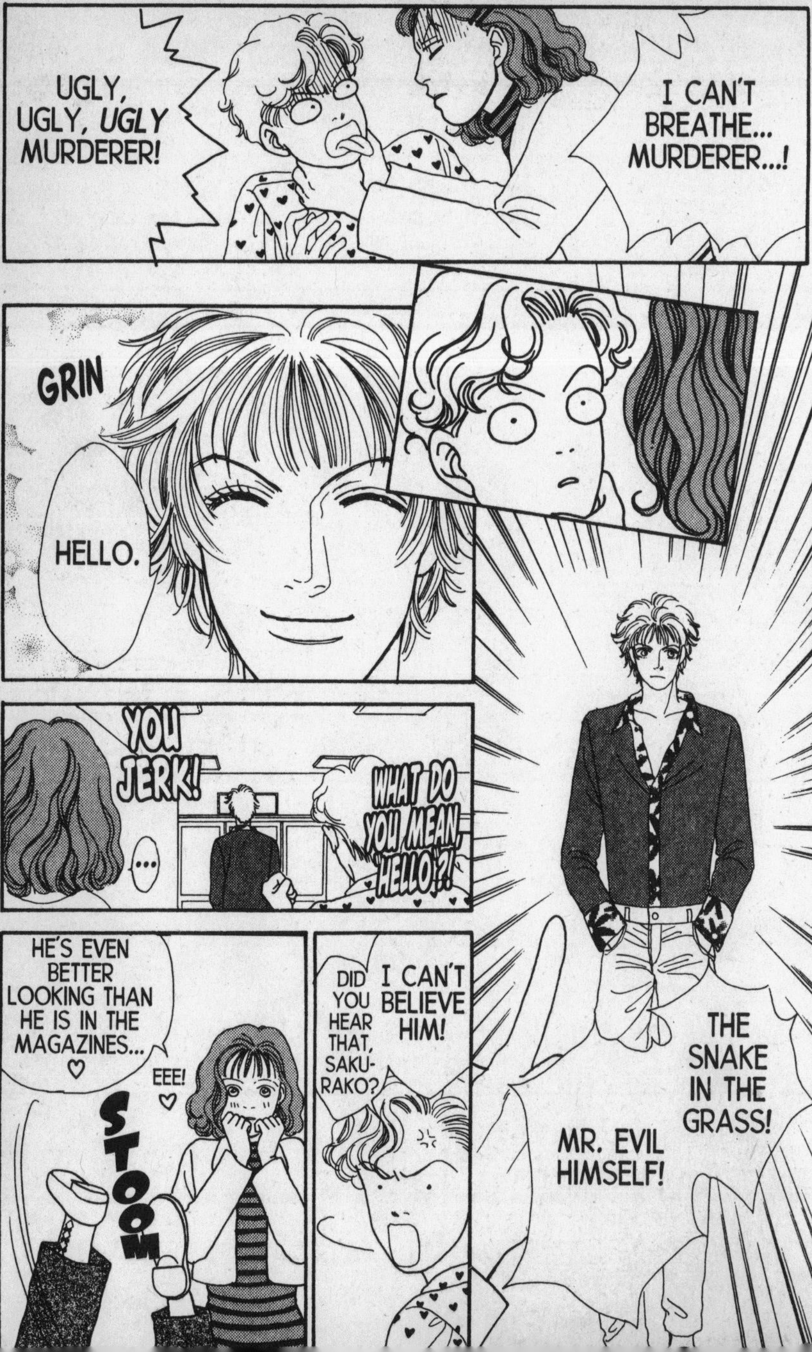
I CAN'T BREATHE... MURDERER...!
UGLY, UGLY, *UGLY* MURDERER!
THE SNAKE IN THE GRASS!
MR. EVIL HIMSELF!
GRIN
HELLO.
WHAT DO YOU MEAN, 'HELLO'?!
YOU JERK!
...
I CAN'T BELIEVE HIM!
DID YOU HEAR THAT, SAKURAKO?
HE'S EVEN BETTER LOOKING THAN HE IS IN THE MAGAZINES... ♡
EEE! ♡
STOOM

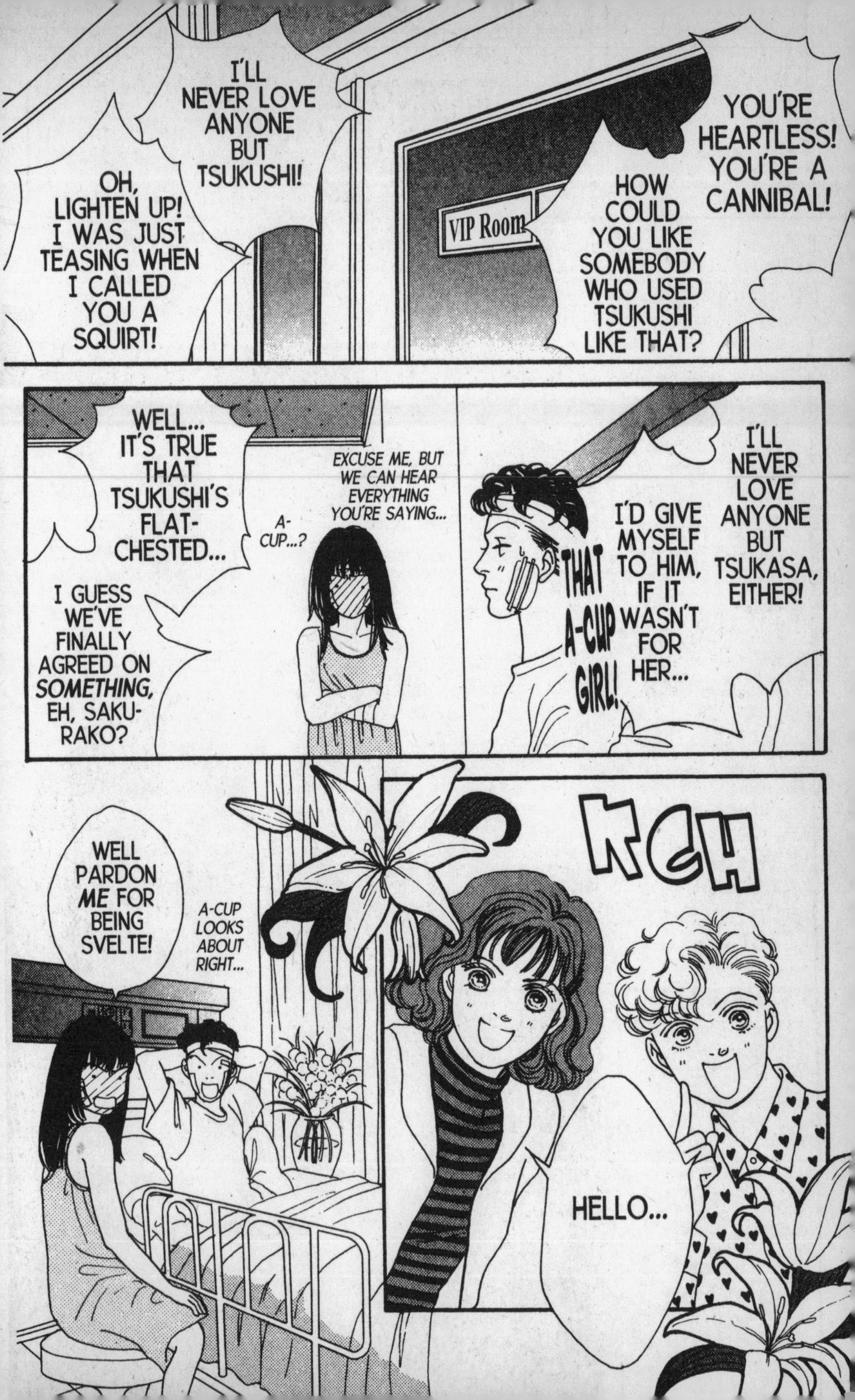
YOU'RE HEARTLESS! YOU'RE A CANNIBAL!
HOW COULD YOU LIKE SOMEBODY WHO USED TSUKUSHI LIKE THAT?
VIP Room
I'LL NEVER LOVE ANYONE BUT TSUKUSHI!
OH, LIGHTEN UP! I WAS JUST TEASING WHEN I CALLED YOU A SQUIRT!
I'LL NEVER LOVE ANYONE BUT TSUKASA, EITHER!
I'D GIVE MYSELF TO HIM, IF IT WASN'T FOR HER...
THAT A-CUP GIRL!
EXCUSE ME, BUT WE CAN HEAR EVERYTHING YOU'RE SAYING...
A-CUP...?
WELL... IT'S TRUE THAT TSUKUSHI'S FLAT-CHESTED...
I GUESS WE'VE FINALLY AGREED ON *SOMETHING*, EH, SAKURAKO?
KCH
HELLO...
A-CUP LOOKS ABOUT RIGHT...
WELL PARDON *ME* FOR BEING SVELTE!

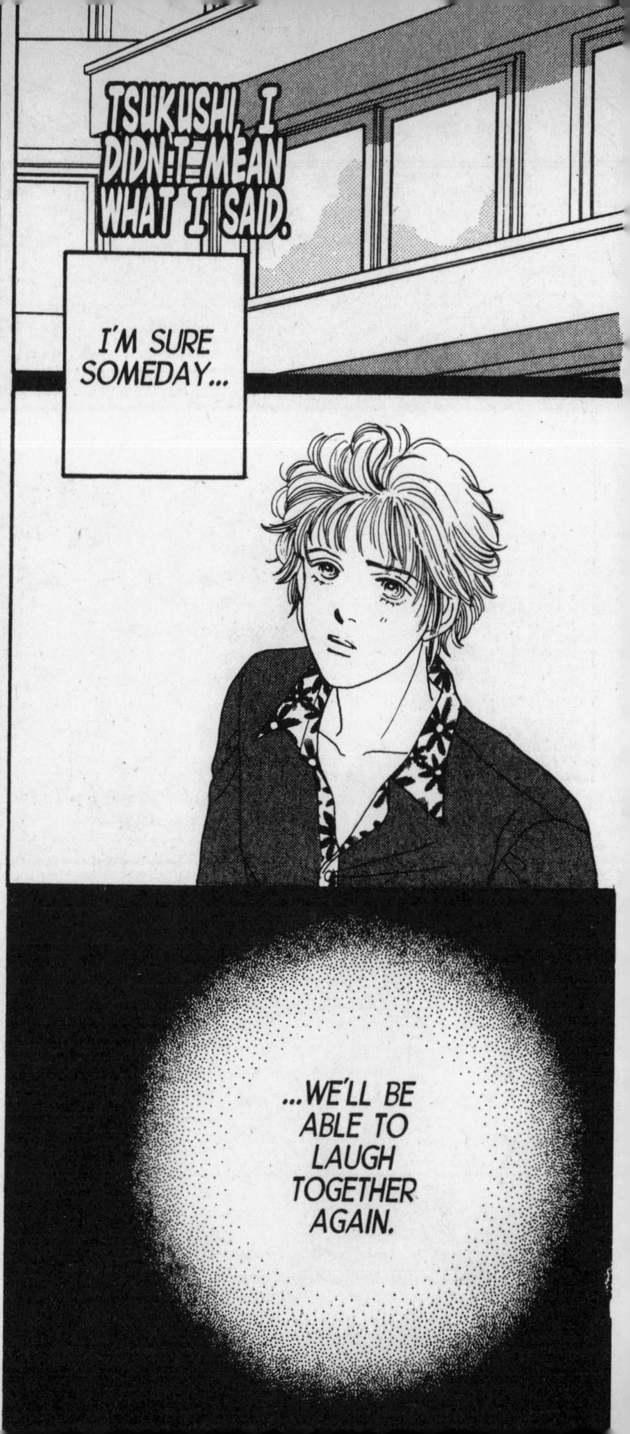
TSUKUSHI, I DIDN'T MEAN WHAT I SAID.
I'M SURE SOMEDAY...
...WE'LL BE ABLE TO LAUGH TOGETHER AGAIN.

Questions from My Readers!!

Q. How many volumes will there be all together?

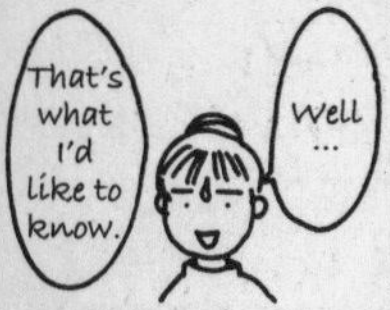
Well ...
That's what I'd like to know.

I received some letters telling me to hurry up and finish the story because they wanted to know how it ends.

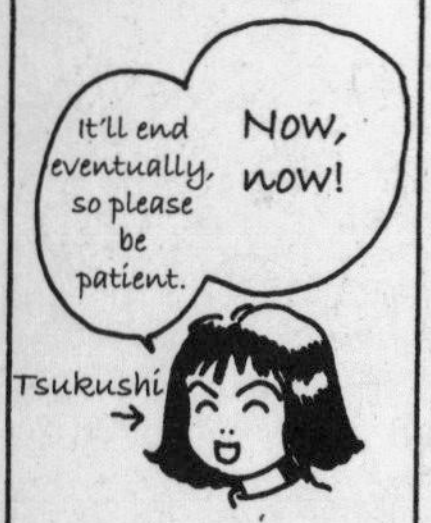
Now, now!
It'll end eventually, so please be patient.
Tsukushi

Q. Do you like men like Tsukasa?

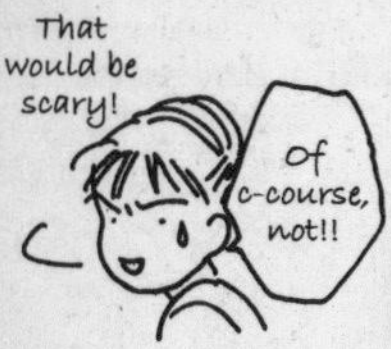
That would be scary!
Of c-course, not!!

Some cartoonists draw their hero as though he's their boyfriend, but I think I've been realistic about my characters.

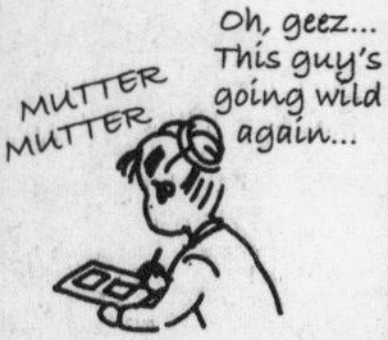
Oh, geez... This guy's going wild again...
MUTTER MUTTER

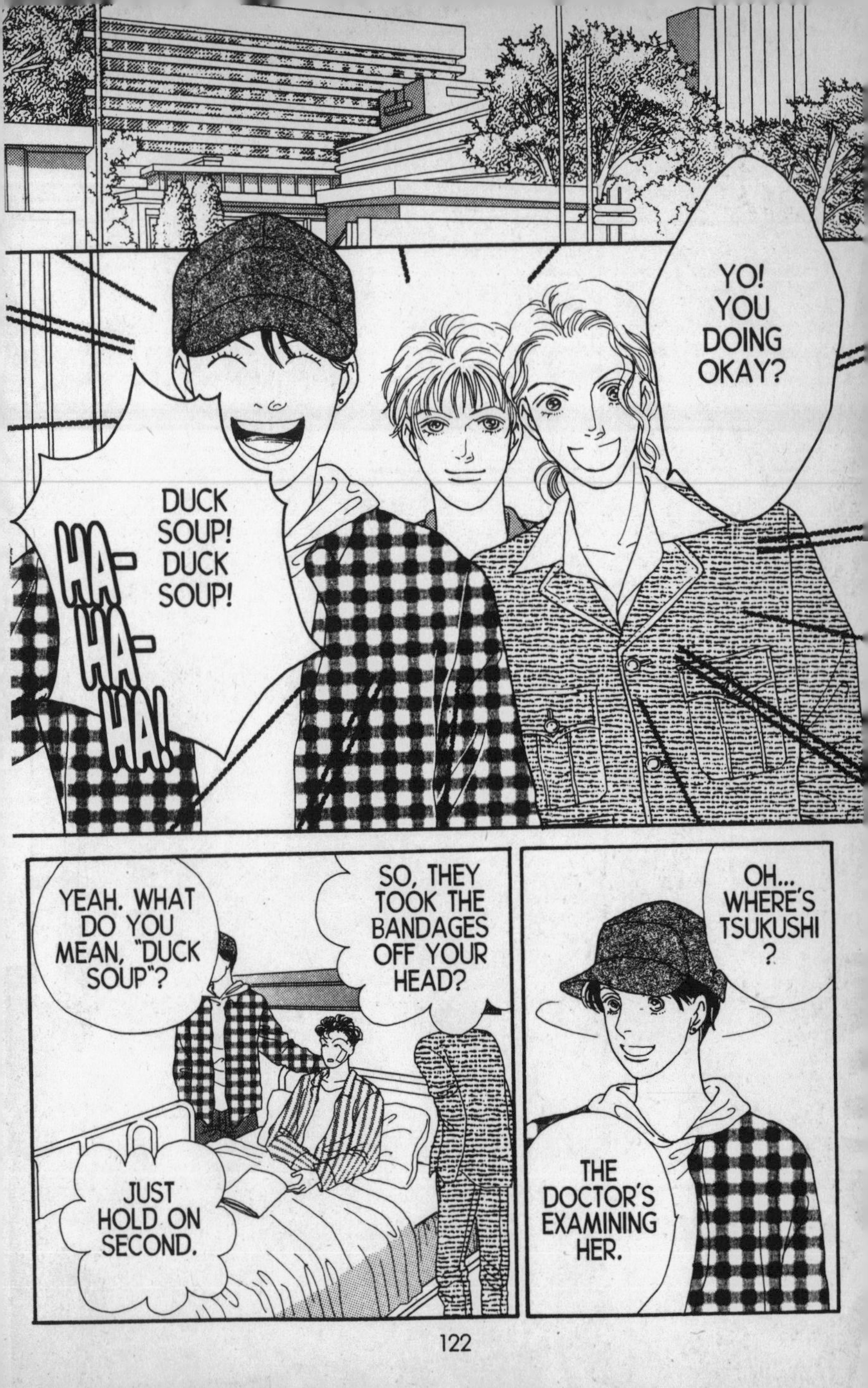
YO! YOU DOING OKAY?
DUCK SOUP! DUCK SOUP!
HA-HA-HA!
OH... WHERE'S TSUKUSHI?
THE DOCTOR'S EXAMINING HER.
SO, THEY TOOK THE BANDAGES OFF YOUR HEAD?
YEAH. WHAT DO YOU MEAN, "DUCK SOUP"?
JUST HOLD ON SECOND.

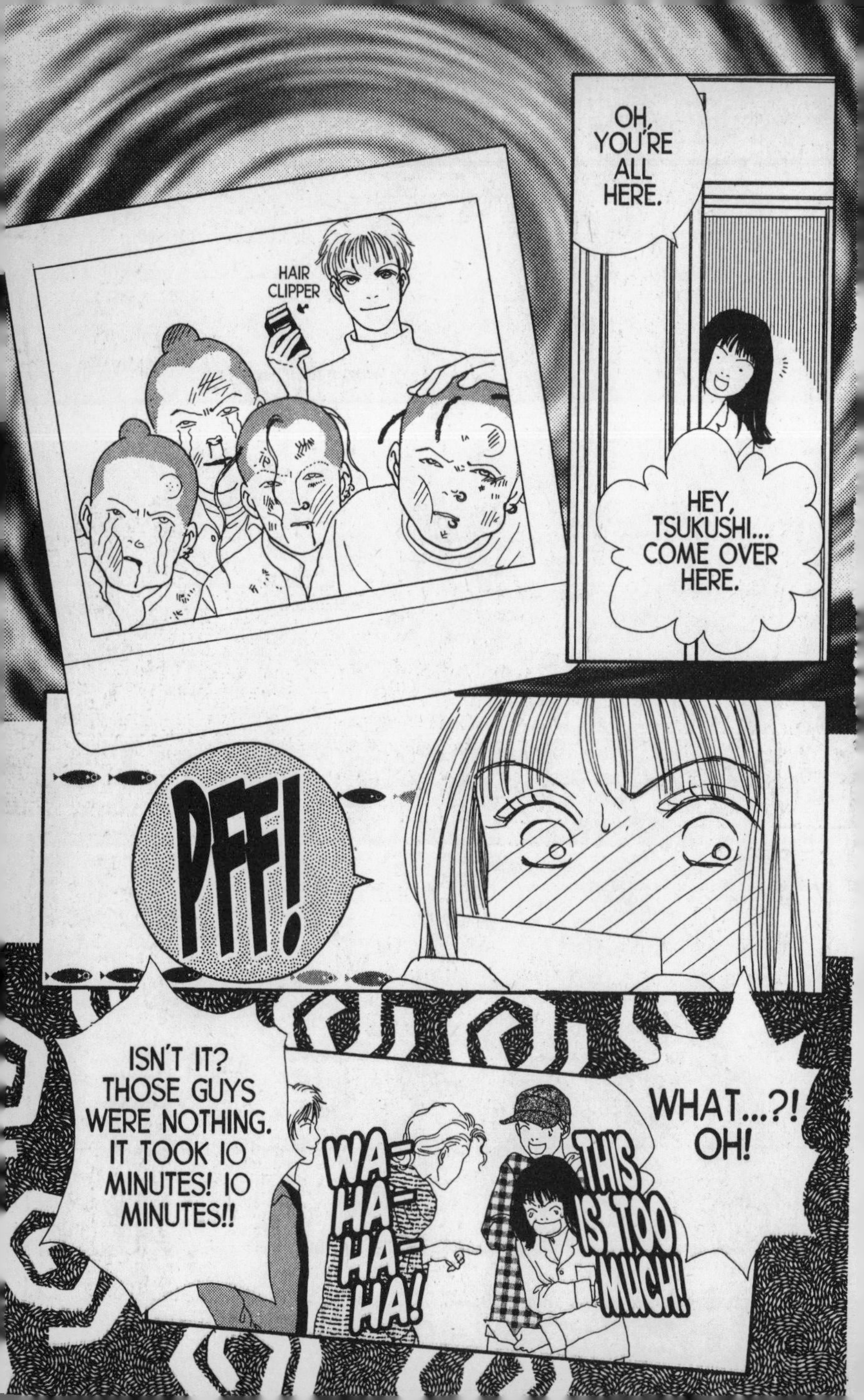
OH, YOU'RE ALL HERE.
HEY, TSUKUSHI... COME OVER HERE.
HAIR CLIPPER
PFF!
WHAT...?! OH!
THIS IS TOO MUCH!
WA-HA-HA-HA!
ISN'T IT? THOSE GUYS WERE NOTHING. IT TOOK 10 MINUTES! 10 MINUTES!!

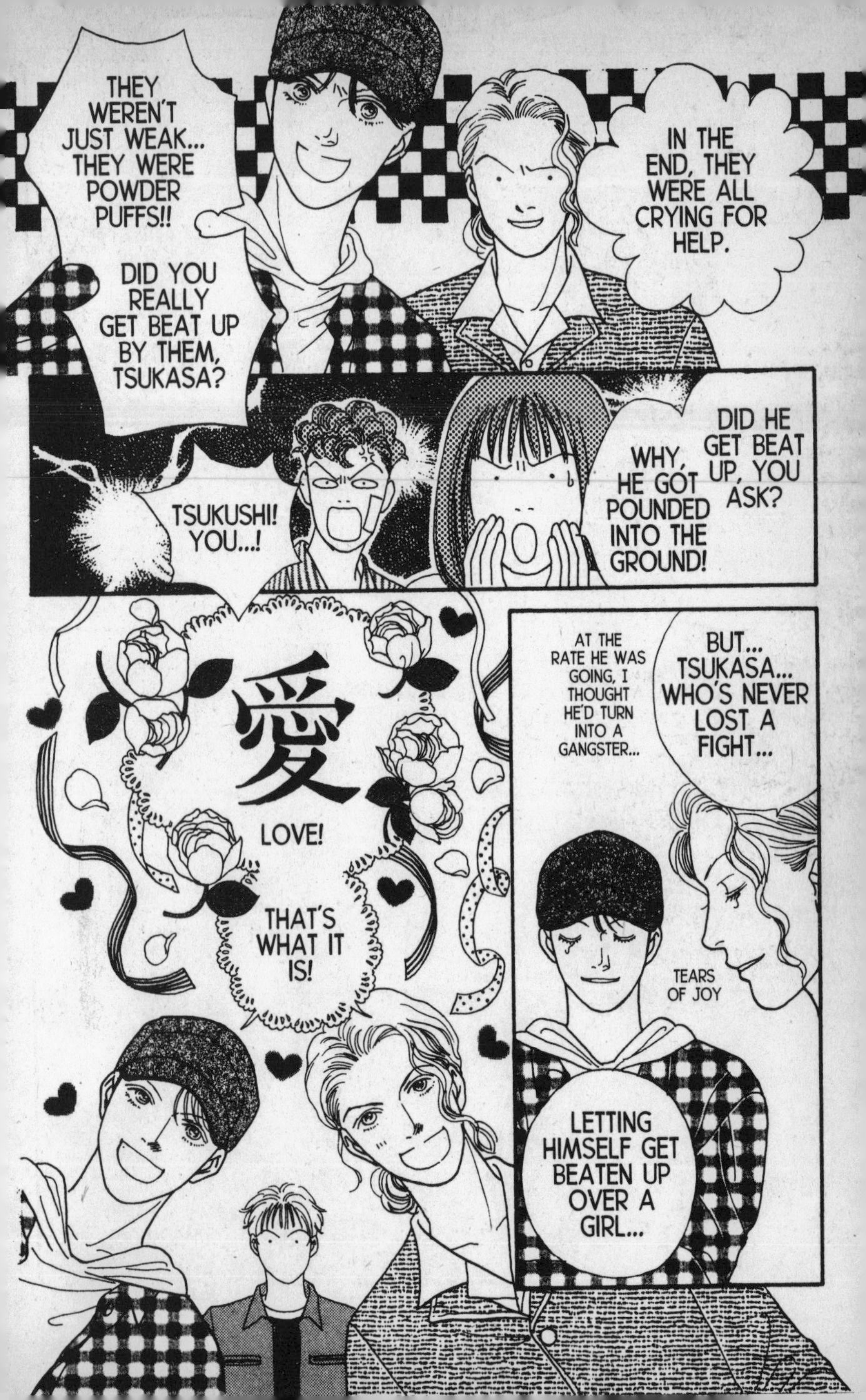
IN THE END, THEY WERE ALL CRYING FOR HELP.
THEY WEREN'T JUST WEAK... THEY WERE POWDER PUFFS!!
DID YOU REALLY GET BEAT UP BY THEM, TSUKASA?
DID HE GET BEAT UP, YOU ASK?
WHY, HE GOT POUNDED INTO THE GROUND!
TSUKUSHI! YOU...!
BUT... TSUKASA... WHO'S NEVER LOST A FIGHT...
AT THE RATE HE WAS GOING, I THOUGHT HE'D TURN INTO A GANGSTER...
TEARS OF JOY
LETTING HIMSELF GET BEATEN UP OVER A GIRL...
愛
LOVE!
THAT'S WHAT IT IS!

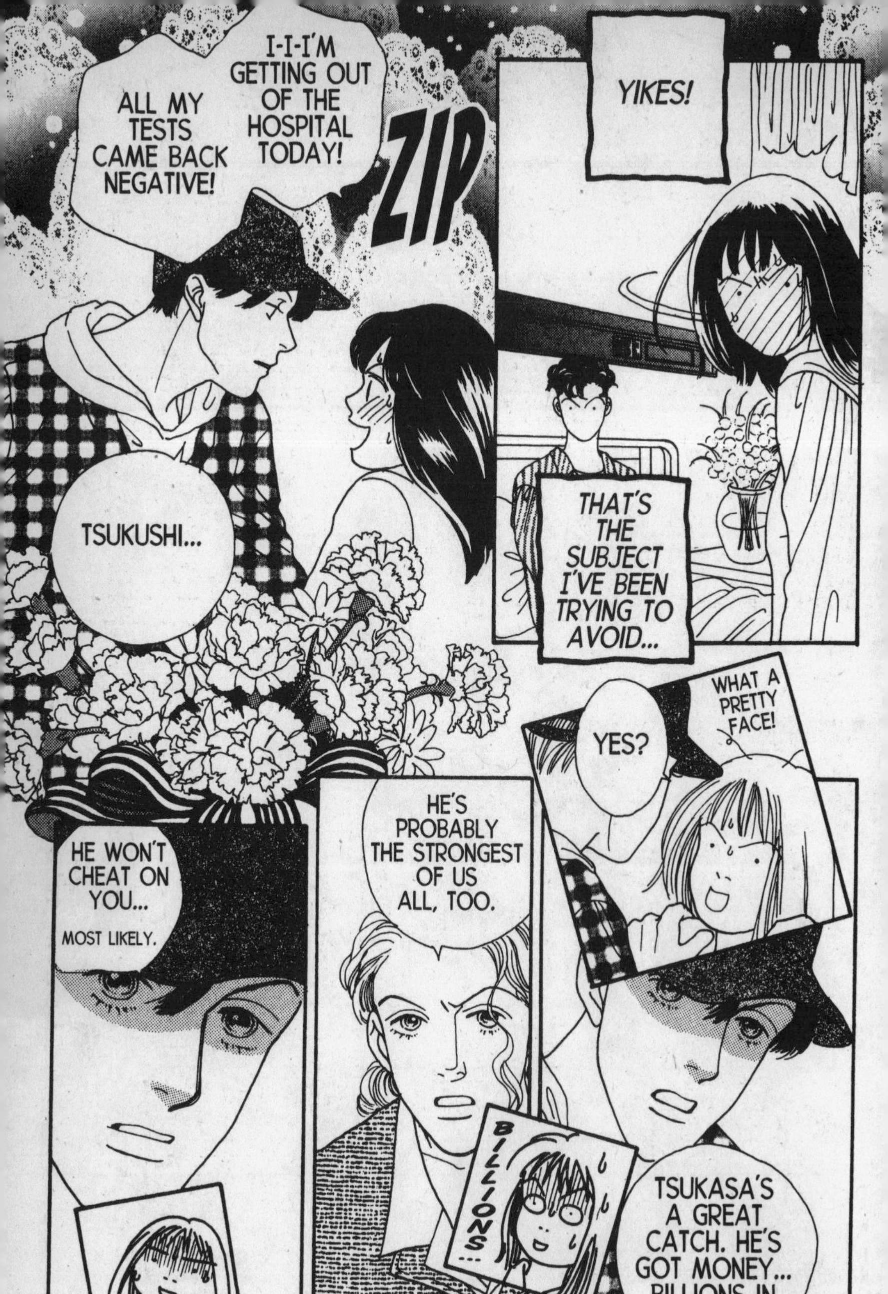
YIKES!
THAT'S THE SUBJECT I'VE BEEN TRYING TO AVOID...
I-I-I'M GETTING OUT OF THE HOSPITAL TODAY!
ALL MY TESTS CAME BACK NEGATIVE!
ZIP
TSUKUSHI...
WHAT A PRETTY FACE!
YES?
TSUKASA'S A GREAT CATCH. HE'S GOT MONEY... BILLIONS IN ASSETS.
HE'S PROBABLY THE STRONGEST OF US ALL, TOO.
BILLIONS...
HE WON'T CHEAT ON YOU...
MOST LIKELY.

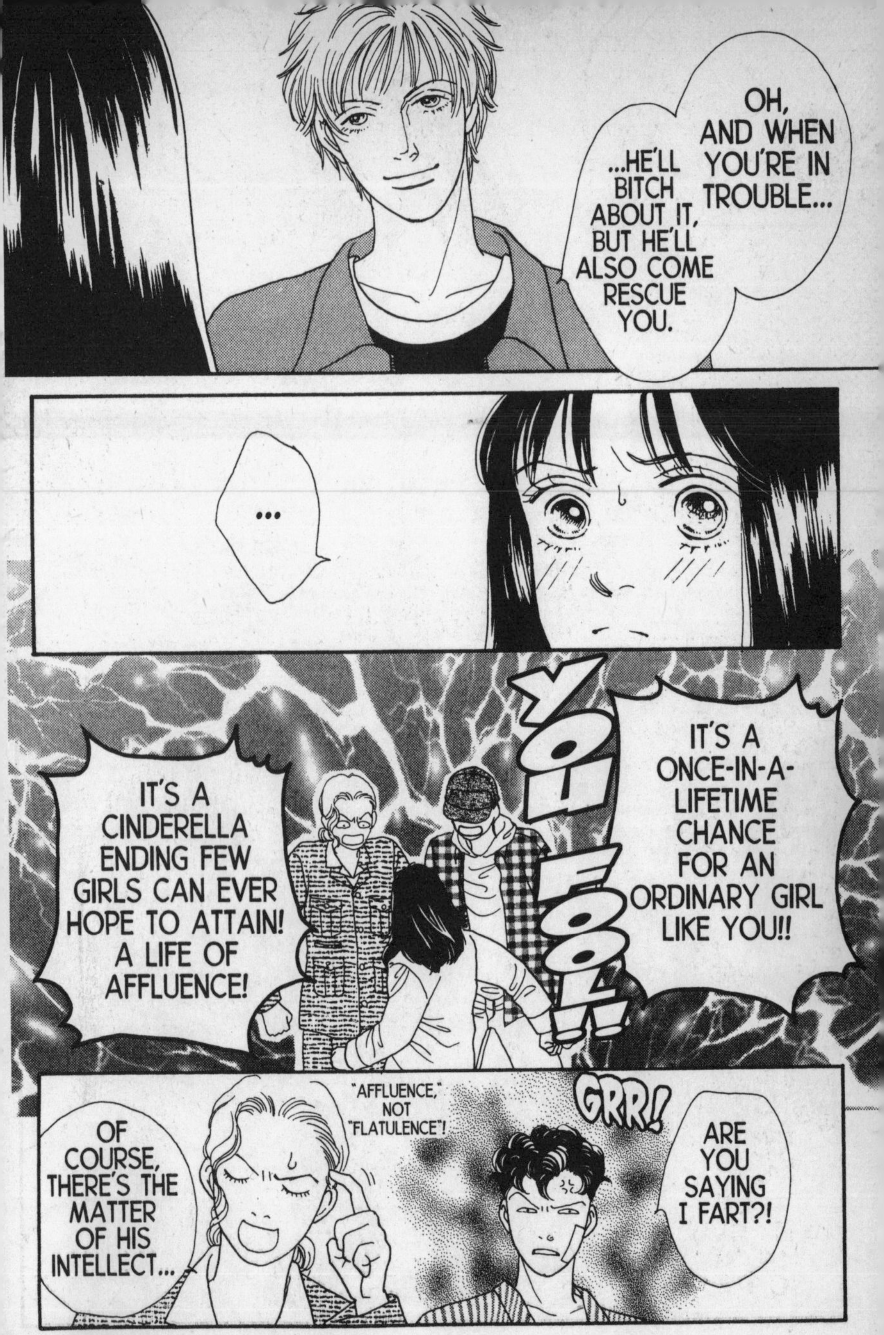
OH, AND WHEN YOU'RE IN TROUBLE...
...HE'LL BITCH ABOUT IT, BUT HE'LL ALSO COME RESCUE YOU.
...
IT'S A ONCE-IN-A-LIFETIME CHANCE FOR AN ORDINARY GIRL LIKE YOU!!
YOU FOOL!!
IT'S A CINDERELLA ENDING FEW GIRLS CAN EVER HOPE TO ATTAIN! A LIFE OF AFFLUENCE!
GRR!
ARE YOU SAYING I FART?!
"AFFLUENCE," NOT "FLATULENCE"!
OF COURSE, THERE'S THE MATTER OF HIS INTELLECT...

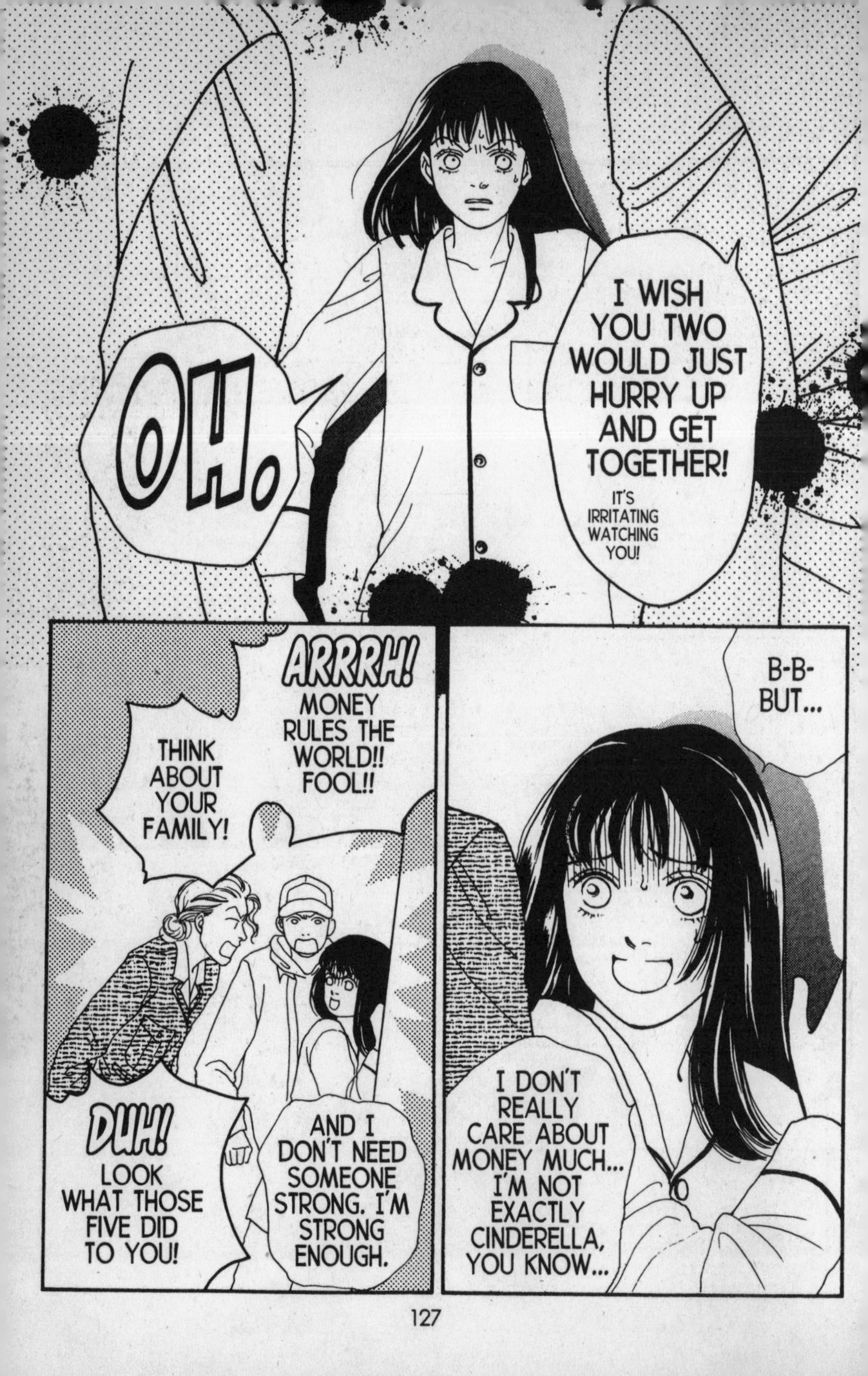
I WISH YOU TWO WOULD JUST HURRY UP AND GET TOGETHER!
IT'S IRRITATING WATCHING YOU!
OH.
B-B-BUT...
I DON'T REALLY CARE ABOUT MONEY MUCH... I'M NOT EXACTLY CINDERELLA, YOU KNOW...
ARRRH! MONEY RULES THE WORLD!! FOOL!!
THINK ABOUT YOUR FAMILY!
AND I DON'T NEED SOMEONE STRONG. I'M STRONG ENOUGH.
DUH! LOOK WHAT THOSE FIVE DID TO YOU!

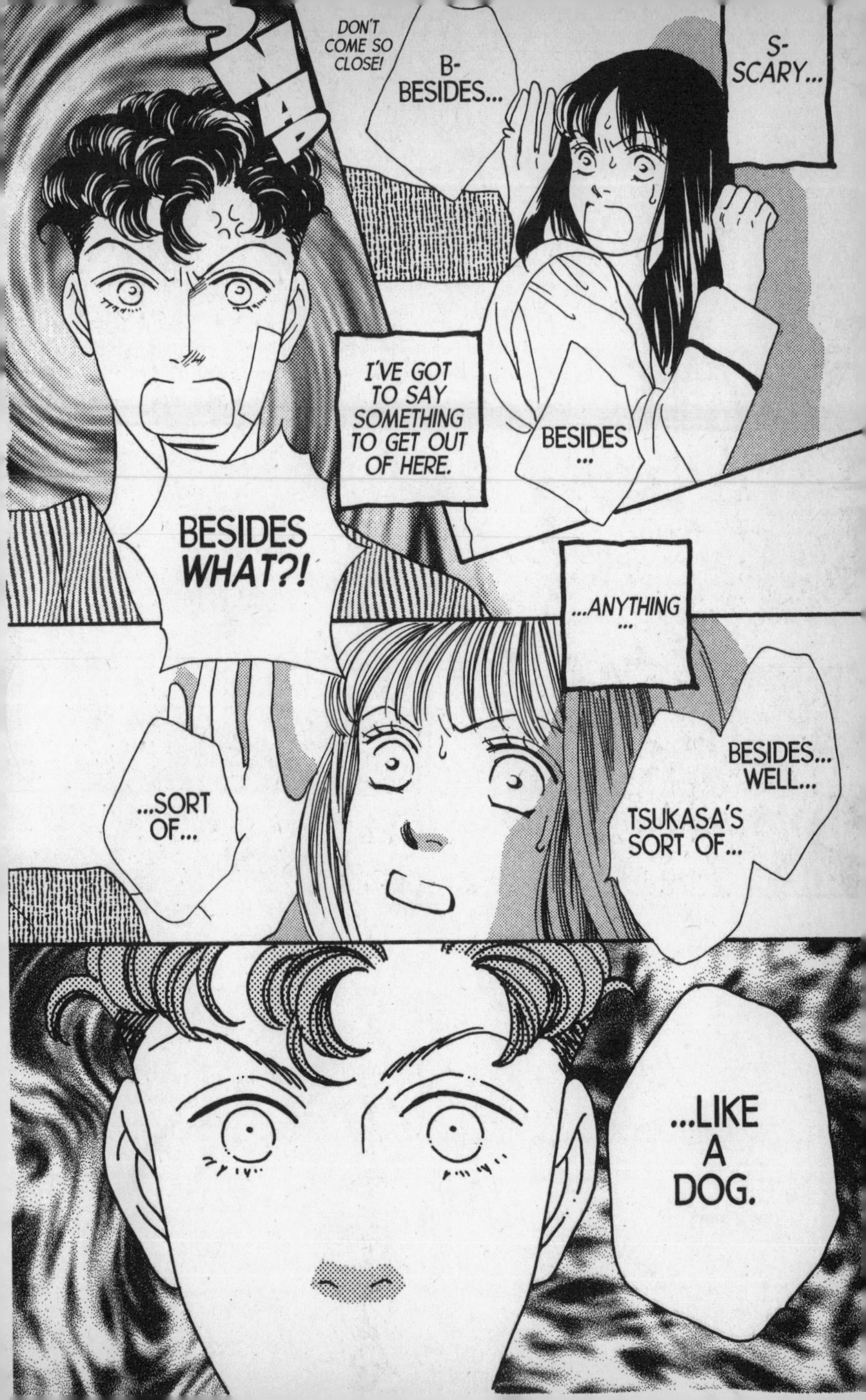
S-SCARY...
B-BESIDES...
DON'T COME SO CLOSE!
I'VE GOT TO SAY SOMETHING TO GET OUT OF HERE.
BESIDES ...
SNAP
BESIDES WHAT?!
...ANYTHING ...
BESIDES... WELL...
TSUKASA'S SORT OF...
...SORT OF...
...LIKE A DOG.

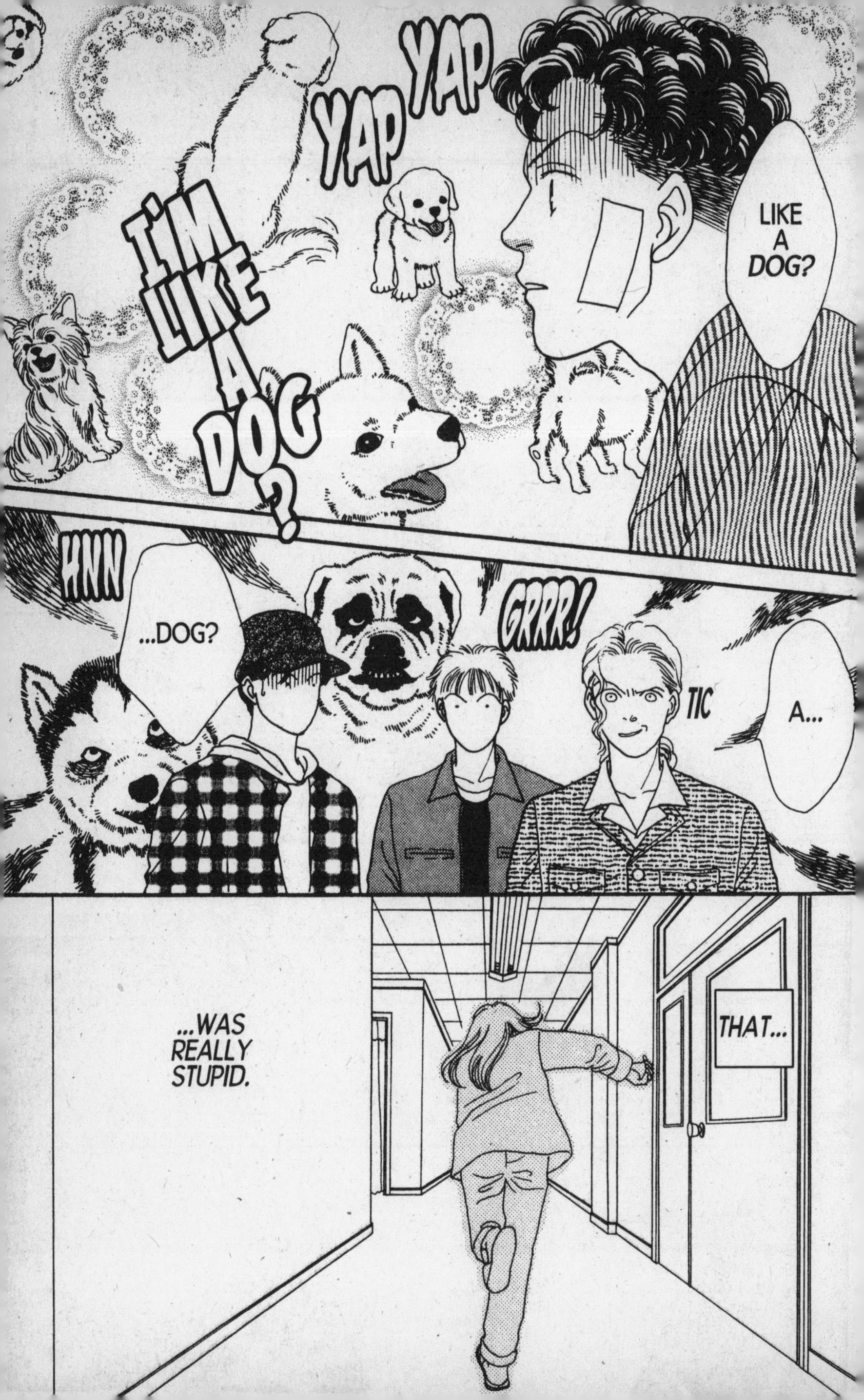
LIKE A DOG?
YAP YAP
I'M LIKE A DOG?
A...
TIC
GRRR!
...DOG?
HNN
THAT...
...WAS REALLY STUPID.

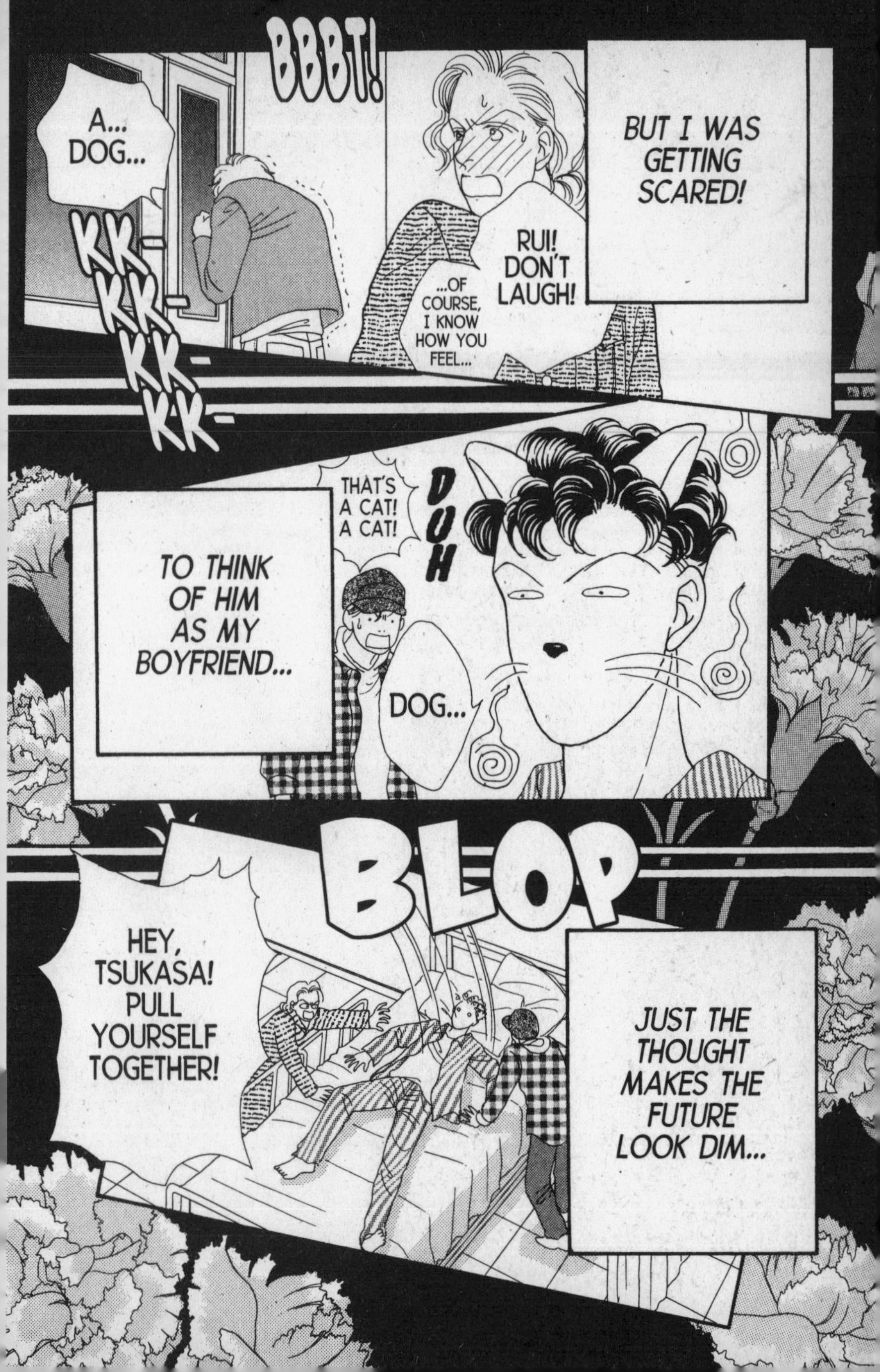

BUT I WAS GETTING SCARED!
BBBT!
RUI! DON'T LAUGH!
...OF COURSE, I KNOW HOW YOU FEEL...
A... DOG...
KK-KK-KK-KK-
DUH
THAT'S A CAT! A CAT!
DOG...
TO THINK OF HIM AS MY BOYFRIEND...
JUST THE THOUGHT MAKES THE FUTURE LOOK DIM...
BLOP
HEY, TSUKASA! PULL YOURSELF TOGETHER!

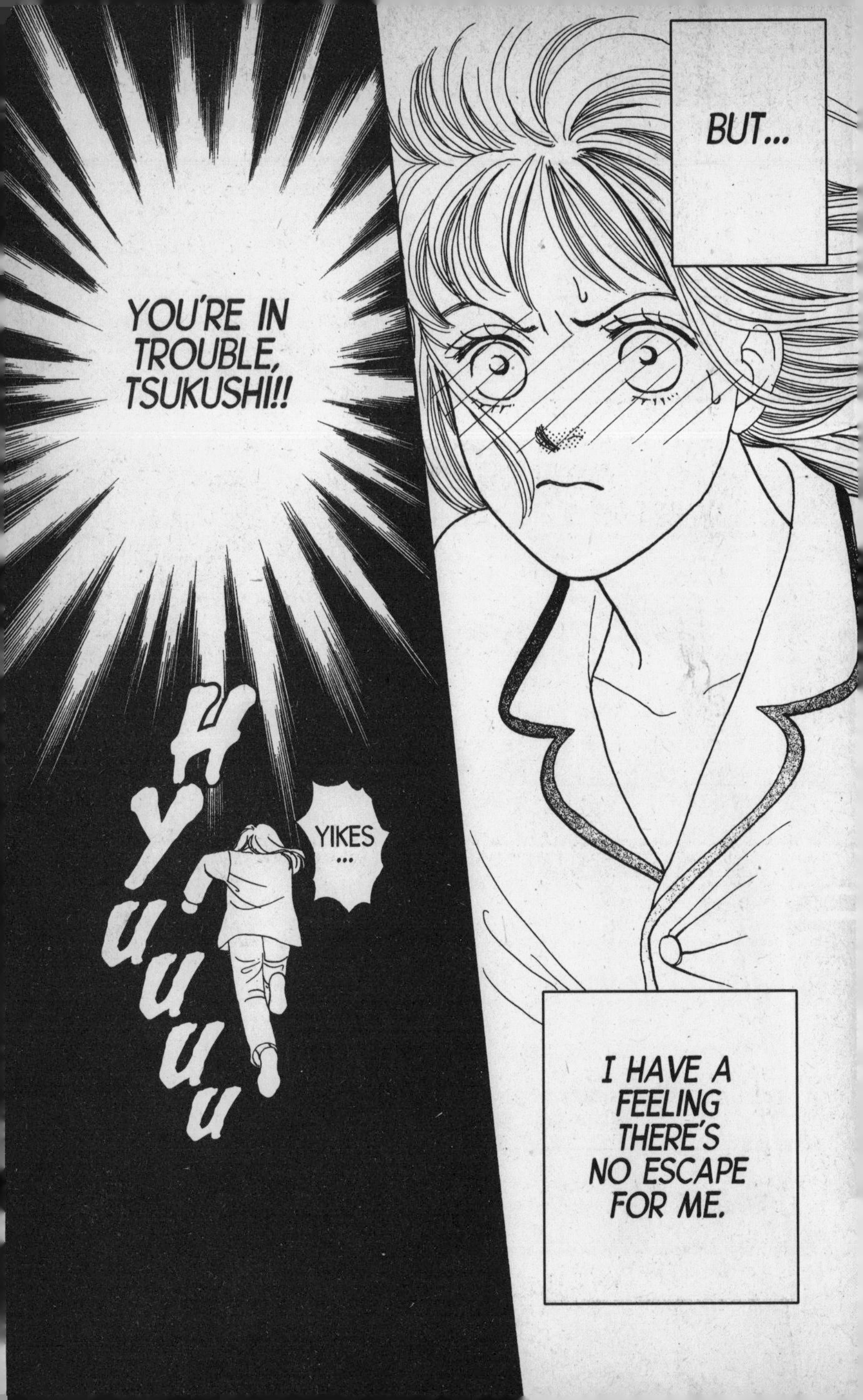
BUT...
I HAVE A FEELING THERE'S NO ESCAPE FOR ME.
YOU'RE IN TROUBLE, TSUKUSHI!!
HYUUUUU
YIKES...

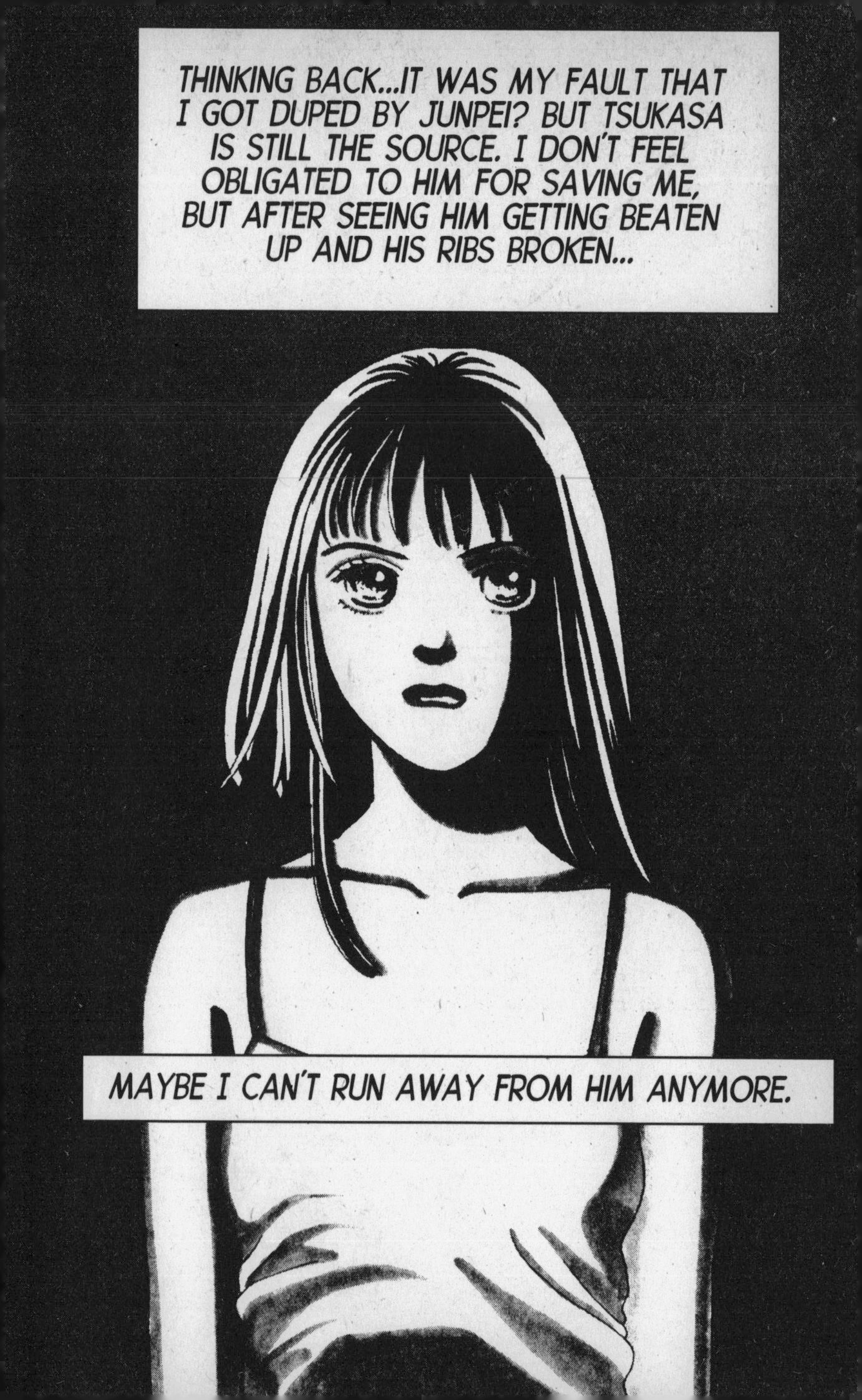
THINKING BACK...IT WAS MY FAULT THAT I GOT DUPED BY JUNPEI? BUT TSUKASA IS STILL THE SOURCE. I DON'T FEEL OBLIGATED TO HIM FOR SAVING ME, BUT AFTER SEEING HIM GETTING BEATEN UP AND HIS RIBS BROKEN...
MAYBE I CAN'T RUN AWAY FROM HIM ANYMORE.

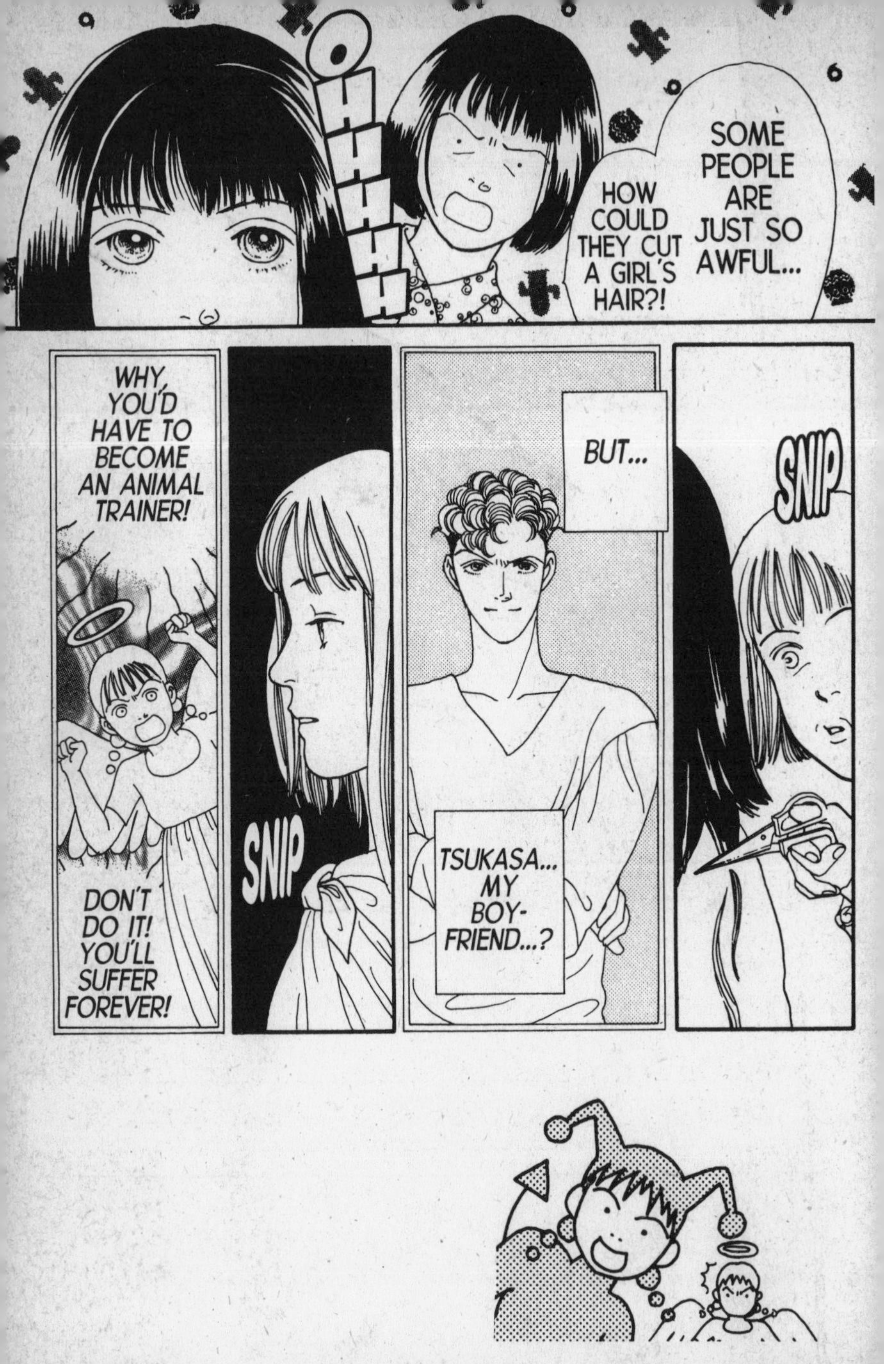
SOME PEOPLE ARE JUST SO AWFUL...
HOW COULD THEY CUT A GIRL'S HAIR?!
OHHHHH
SNIP
BUT...
TSUKASA... MY BOY-FRIEND...?
SNIP
WHY, YOU'D HAVE TO BECOME AN ANIMAL TRAINER!
DON'T DO IT! YOU'LL SUFFER FOREVER!

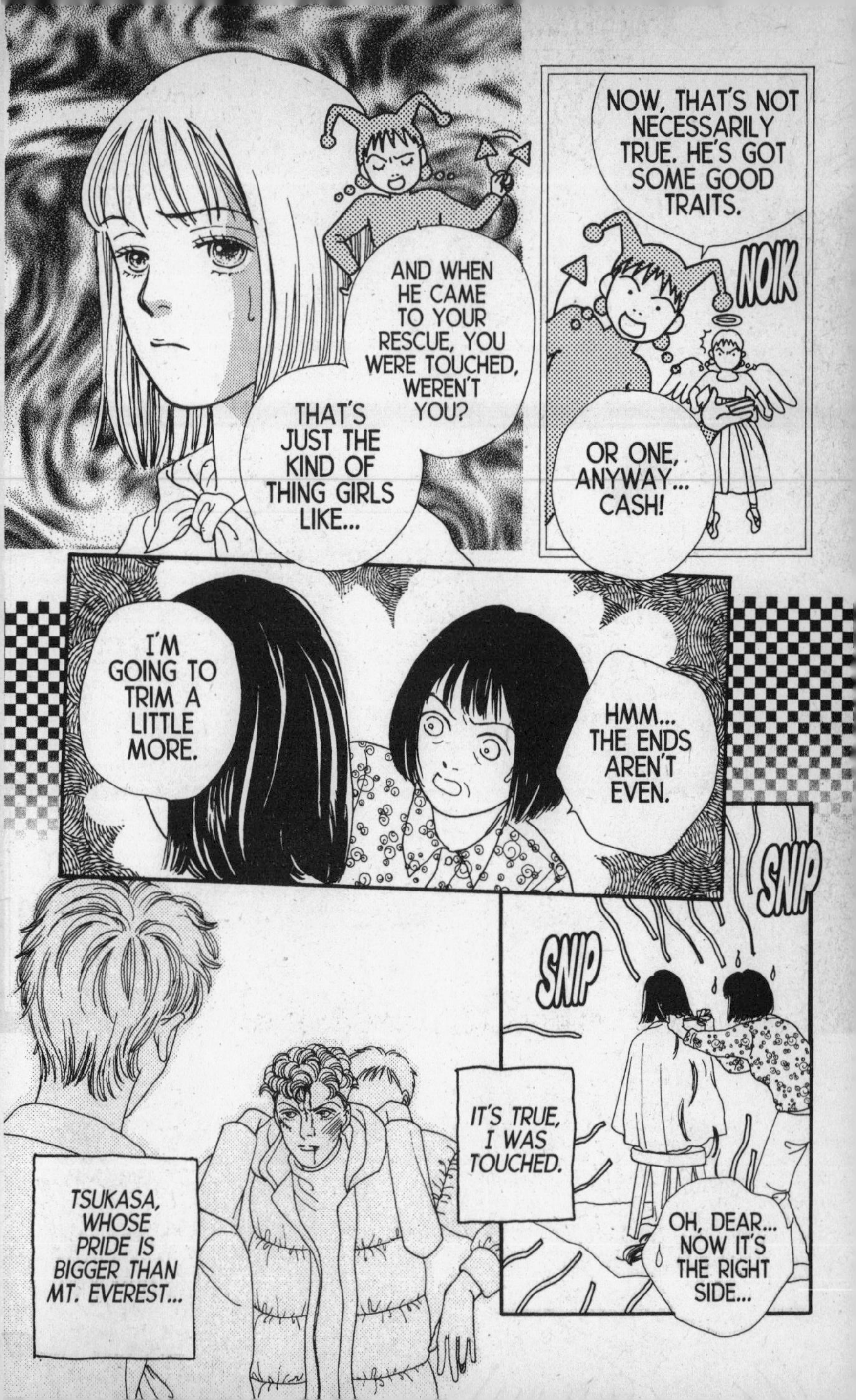
NOW, THAT'S NOT NECESSARILY TRUE. HE'S GOT SOME GOOD TRAITS.
NOIK
OR ONE, ANYWAY... CASH!
AND WHEN HE CAME TO YOUR RESCUE, YOU WERE TOUCHED, WEREN'T YOU?
THAT'S JUST THE KIND OF THING GIRLS LIKE...
HMM... THE ENDS AREN'T EVEN.
I'M GOING TO TRIM A LITTLE MORE.
SNIP
SNIP
OH, DEAR... NOW IT'S THE RIGHT SIDE...
IT'S TRUE, I WAS TOUCHED.
TSUKASA, WHOSE PRIDE IS BIGGER THAN MT. EVEREST...

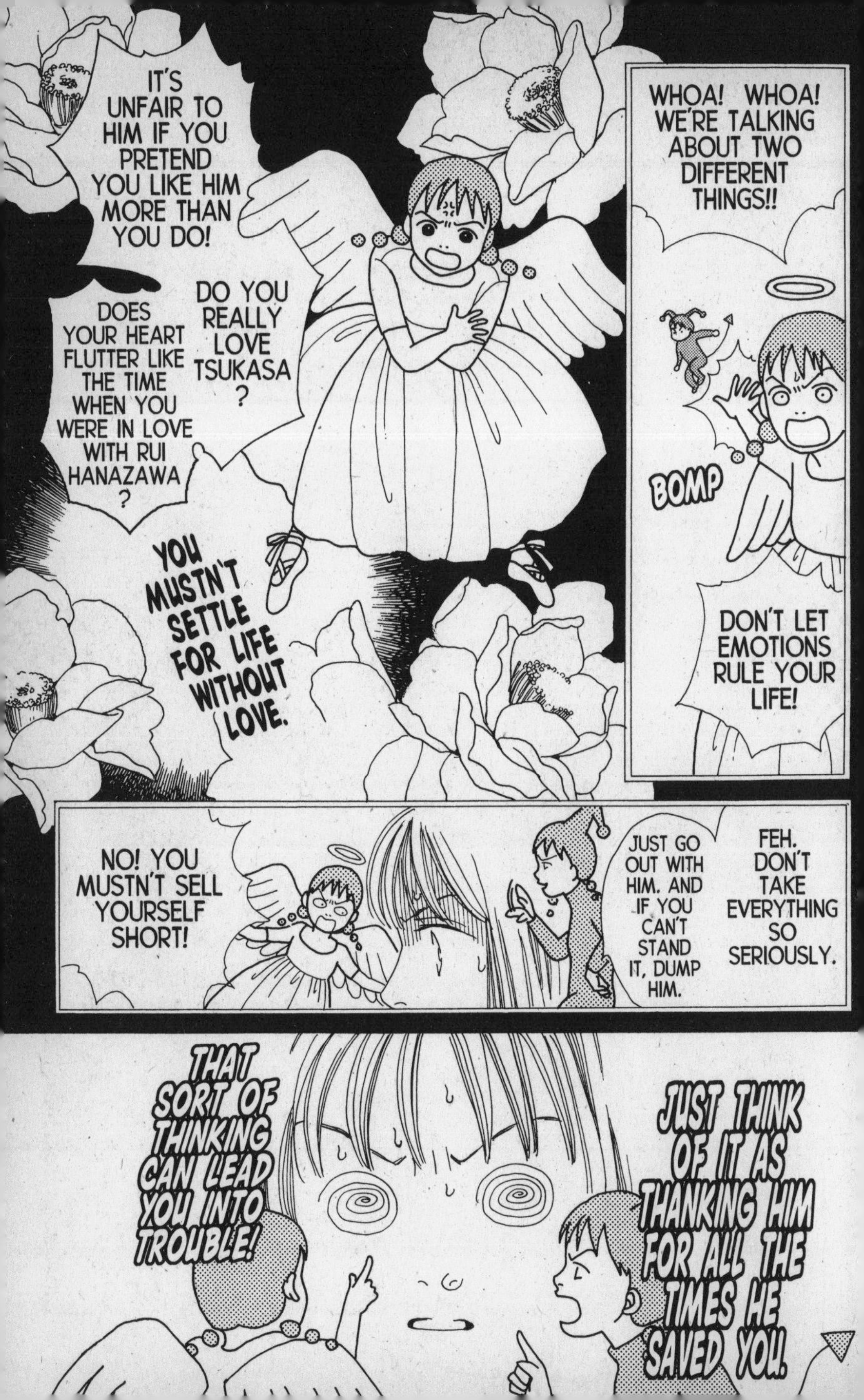

WHOA! WHOA! WE'RE TALKING ABOUT TWO DIFFERENT THINGS!!
BOMP
DON'T LET EMOTIONS RULE YOUR LIFE!
IT'S UNFAIR TO HIM IF YOU PRETEND YOU LIKE HIM MORE THAN YOU DO!
DO YOU REALLY LOVE TSUKASA?
DOES YOUR HEART FLUTTER LIKE THE TIME WHEN YOU WERE IN LOVE WITH RUI HANAZAWA?
YOU MUSTN'T SETTLE FOR LIFE WITHOUT LOVE.
FEH. DON'T TAKE EVERYTHING SO SERIOUSLY.
JUST GO OUT WITH HIM. AND IF YOU CAN'T STAND IT, DUMP HIM.
NO! YOU MUSTN'T SELL YOURSELF SHORT!
JUST THINK OF IT AS THANKING HIM FOR ALL THE TIMES HE SAVED YOU.
THAT SORT OF THINKING CAN LEAD YOU INTO TROUBLE!

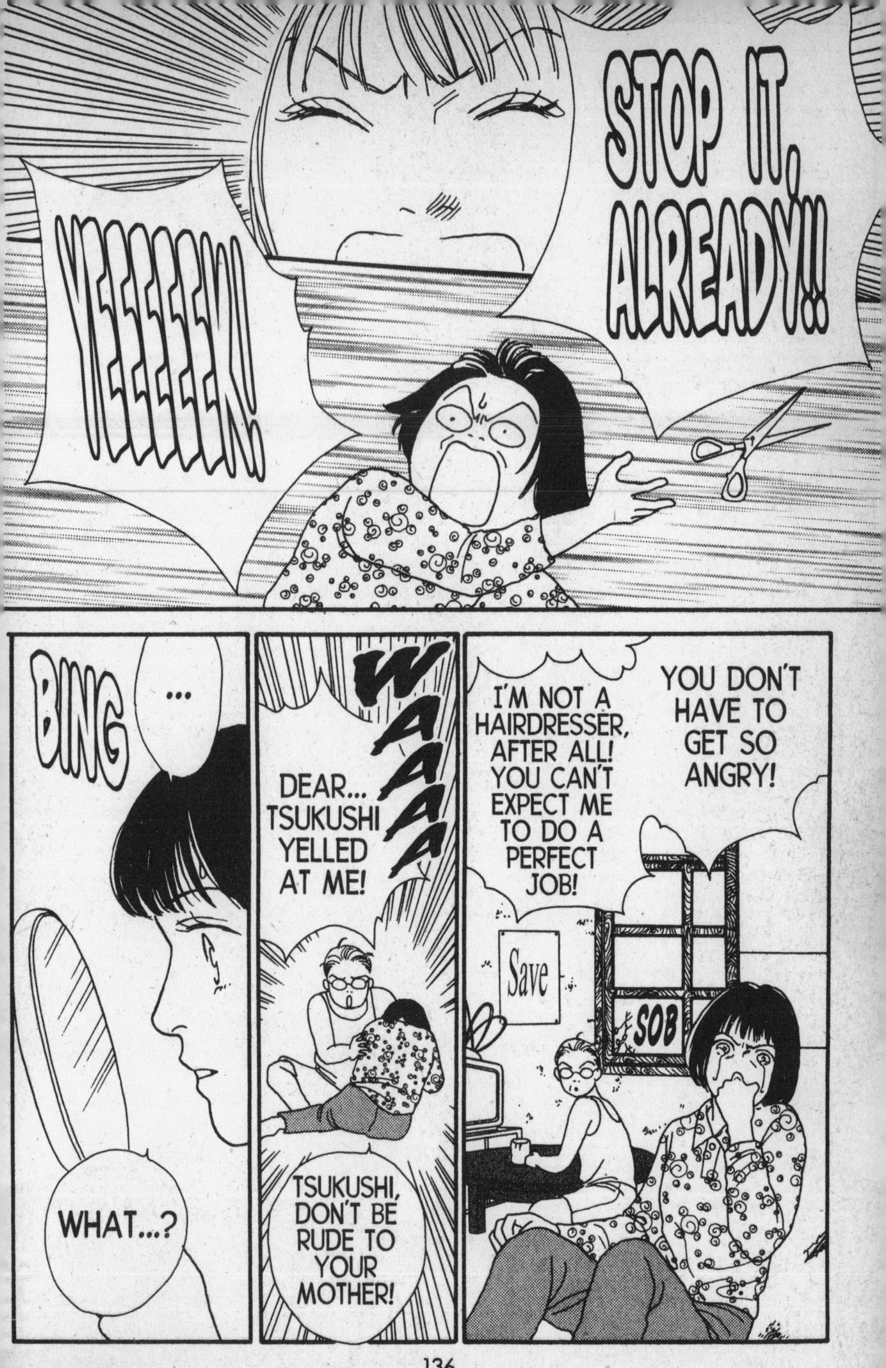
STOP IT, ALREADY!!
YEEEEEK!
YOU DON'T HAVE TO GET SO ANGRY!
I'M NOT A HAIRDRESSER, AFTER ALL! YOU CAN'T EXPECT ME TO DO A PERFECT JOB!
Save
SOB
WAAAA
DEAR... TSUKUSHI YELLED AT ME!
TSUKUSHI, DON'T BE RUDE TO YOUR MOTHER!
BING
...
WHAT...?

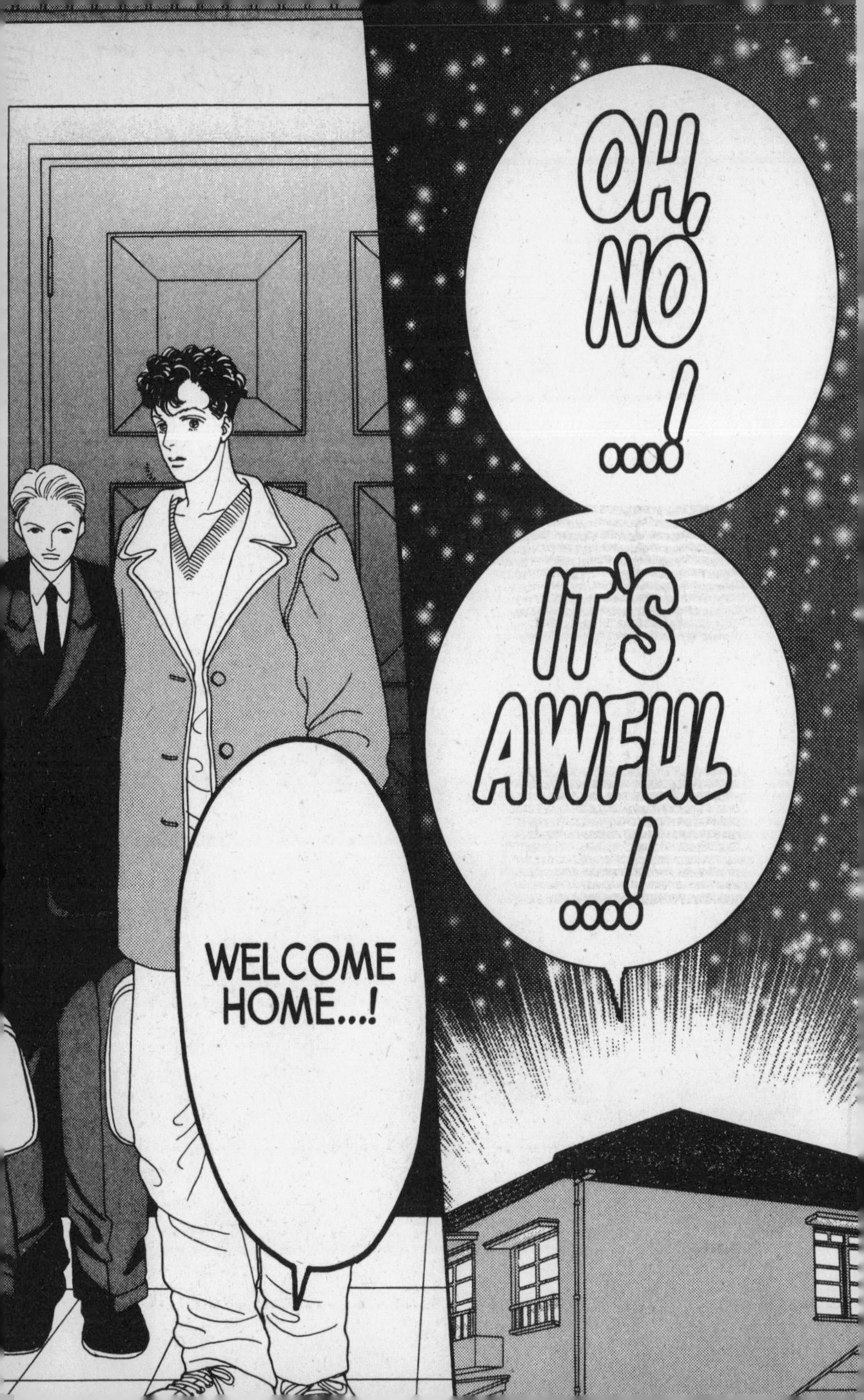
OH, NO ....!
IT'S AWFUL ....!
WELCOME HOME...!

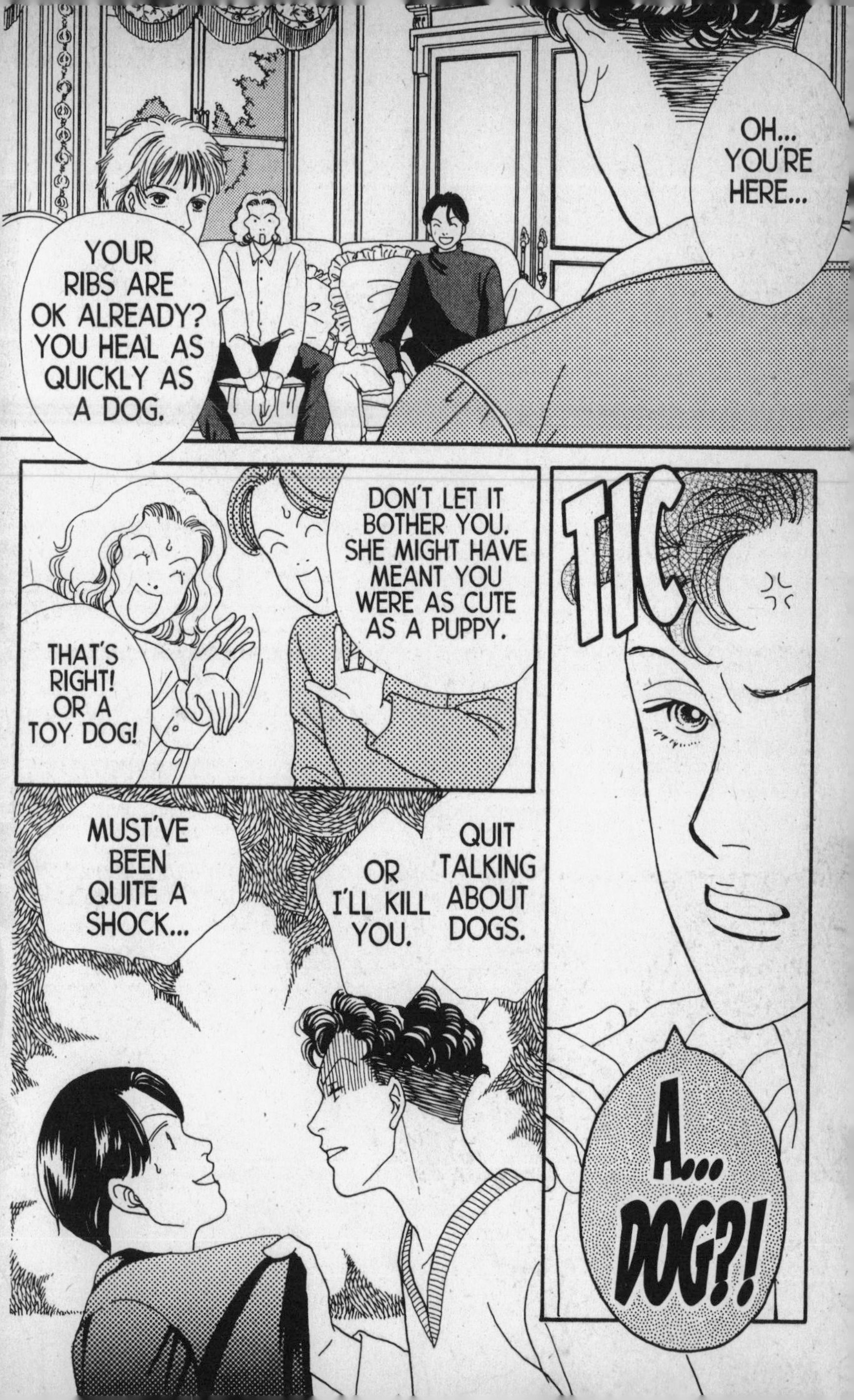
OH... YOU'RE HERE...
YOUR RIBS ARE OK ALREADY? YOU HEAL AS QUICKLY AS A DOG.
TIC
A... DOG?!
DON'T LET IT BOTHER YOU. SHE MIGHT HAVE MEANT YOU WERE AS CUTE AS A PUPPY.
THAT'S RIGHT! OR A TOY DOG!
QUIT TALKING ABOUT DOGS.
OR I'LL KILL YOU.
MUST'VE BEEN QUITE A SHOCK...

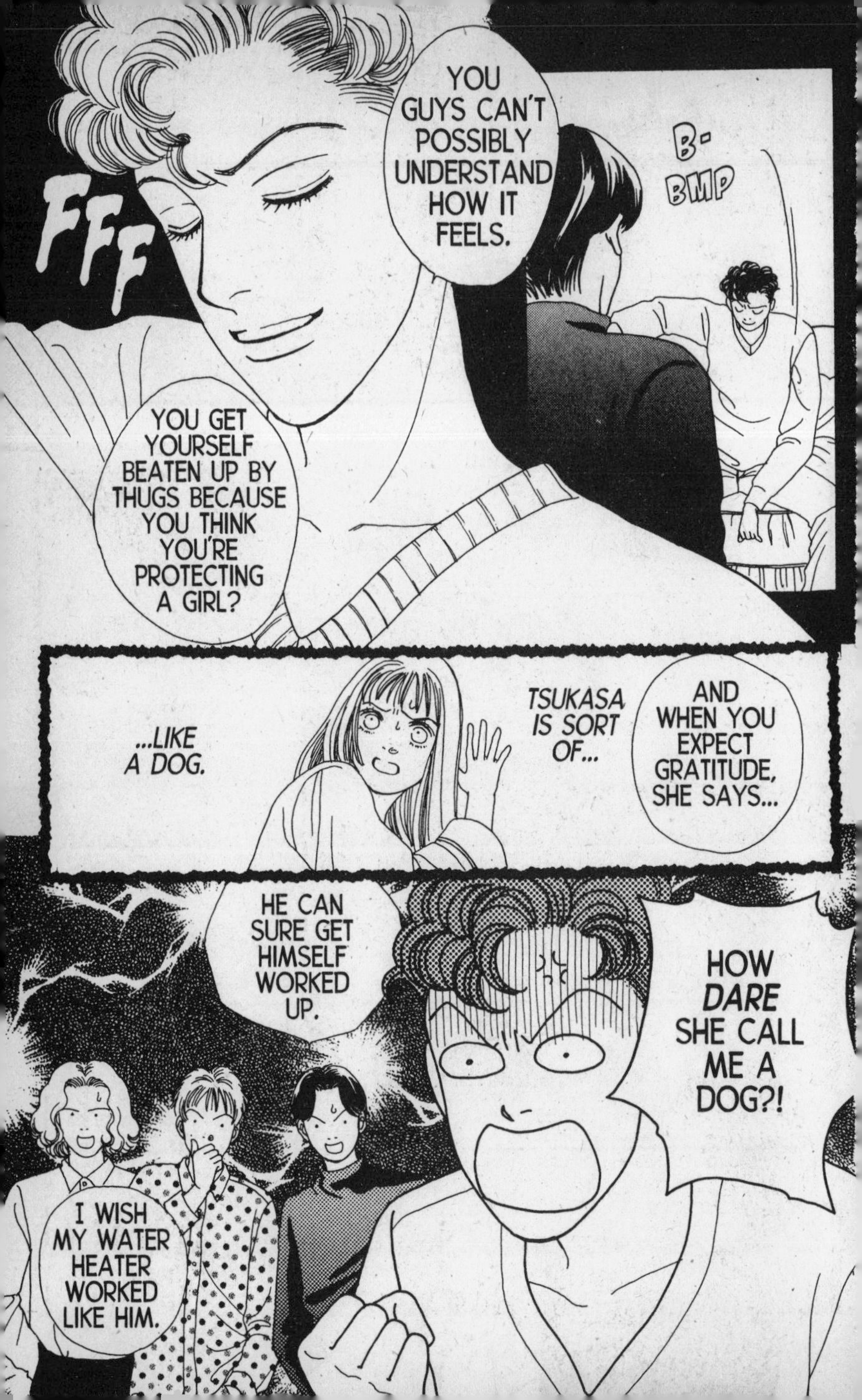
YOU GUYS CAN'T POSSIBLY UNDERSTAND HOW IT FEELS.
B-BMP
FFF
YOU GET YOURSELF BEATEN UP BY THUGS BECAUSE YOU THINK YOU'RE PROTECTING A GIRL?
AND WHEN YOU EXPECT GRATITUDE, SHE SAYS...
TSUKASA IS SORT OF...
...LIKE A DOG.
HOW *DARE* SHE CALL ME A DOG?!
HE CAN SURE GET HIMSELF WORKED UP.
I WISH MY WATER HEATER WORKED LIKE HIM.

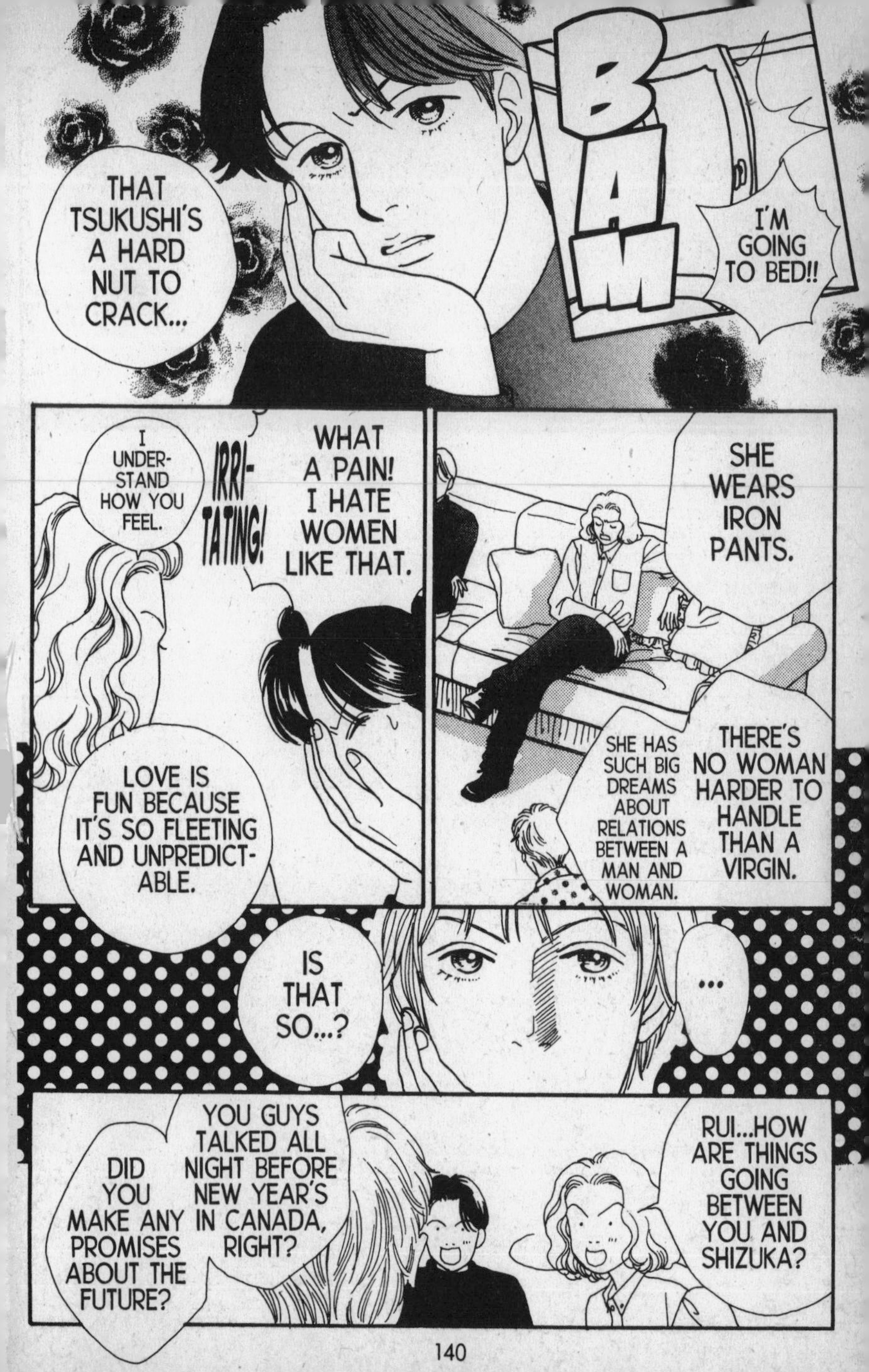
BAM
I'M GOING TO BED!!
THAT TSUKUSHI'S A HARD NUT TO CRACK...
SHE WEARS IRON PANTS.
THERE'S NO WOMAN HARDER TO HANDLE THAN A VIRGIN.
SHE HAS SUCH BIG DREAMS ABOUT RELATIONS BETWEEN A MAN AND WOMAN.
WHAT A PAIN! I HATE WOMEN LIKE THAT.
IRRI-TATING!
I UNDER-STAND HOW YOU FEEL.
LOVE IS FUN BECAUSE IT'S SO FLEETING AND UNPREDICT-ABLE.
...
IS THAT SO...?
RUI...HOW ARE THINGS GOING BETWEEN YOU AND SHIZUKA?
YOU GUYS TALKED ALL NIGHT BEFORE NEW YEAR'S IN CANADA, RIGHT?
DID YOU MAKE ANY PROMISES ABOUT THE FUTURE?

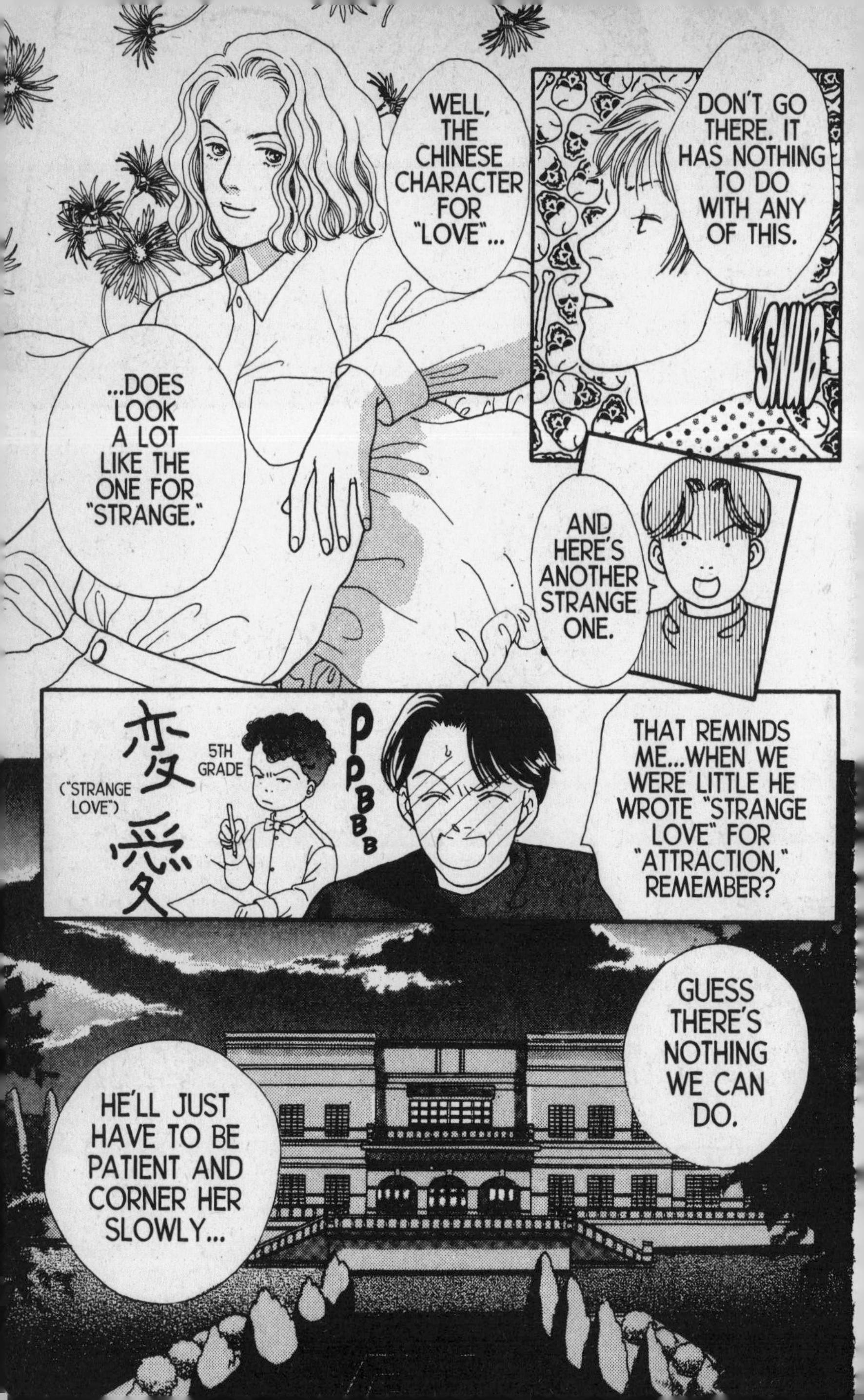
WELL, THE CHINESE CHARACTER FOR "LOVE"...
...DOES LOOK A LOT LIKE THE ONE FOR "STRANGE."
DON'T GO THERE. IT HAS NOTHING TO DO WITH ANY OF THIS.
AND HERE'S ANOTHER STRANGE ONE.
THAT REMINDS ME...WHEN WE WERE LITTLE HE WROTE "STRANGE LOVE" FOR "ATTRACTION," REMEMBER?
PPBBB
5TH GRADE
変愛
("STRANGE LOVE")
GUESS THERE'S NOTHING WE CAN DO.
HE'LL JUST HAVE TO BE PATIENT AND CORNER HER SLOWLY...

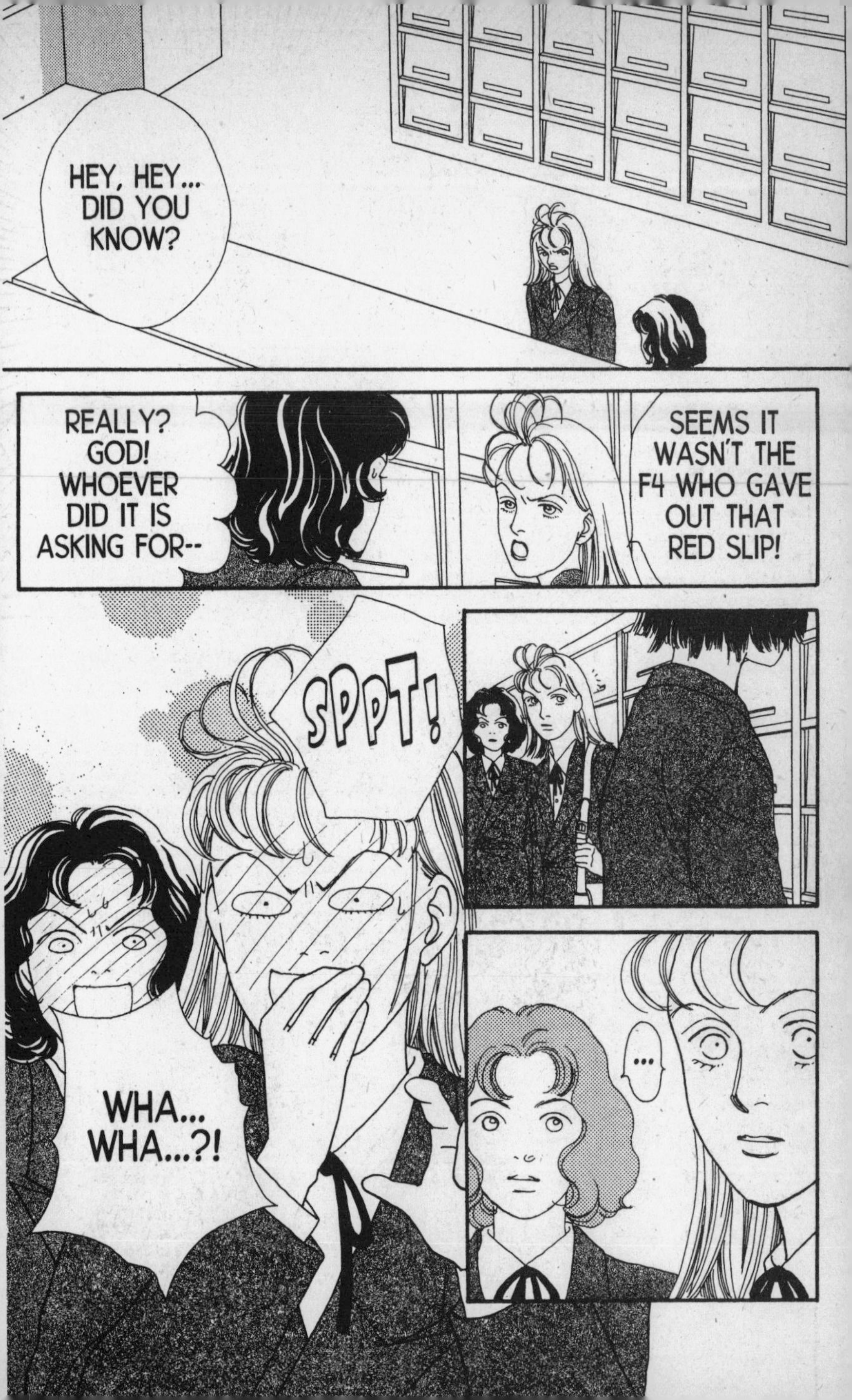
HEY, HEY... DID YOU KNOW?
SEEMS IT WASN'T THE F4 WHO GAVE OUT THAT RED SLIP!
REALLY? GOD! WHOEVER DID IT IS ASKING FOR--
...
SPPT!
WHA... WHA...?!

MORE QUESTIONS!!

Q. Were you ever a cartoonist's assistant?

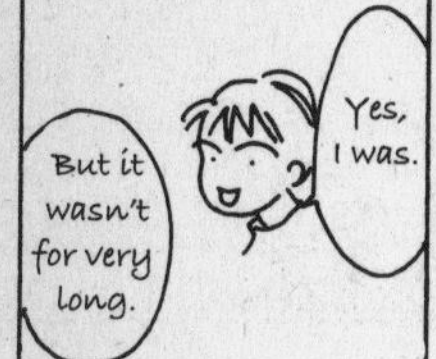
Yes, I was.
But it wasn't for very long.

All of the cartoonists I worked with were really famous. (But I usually spent just a day or two with them.) I'd just debuted and couldn't do much of anything, but they all let me work, without a sign of displeasure. When I look back now, I get cold sweats. I dirtied up some manuscripts... Yikes! Working as an assistant was a great experience. My cartoonist friends and I sometimes help each other out. After working around 30 hours without sleeping, we get this natural high and someone starts laughing.

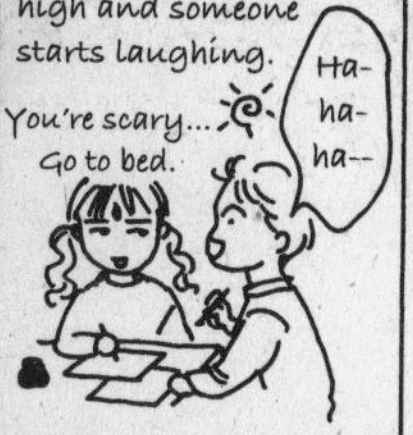
Ha-ha-ha--
You're scary... Go to bed.

It brings back fond memories. I can't work 30 hours straight without sleeping anymore. How wonderful to be young!

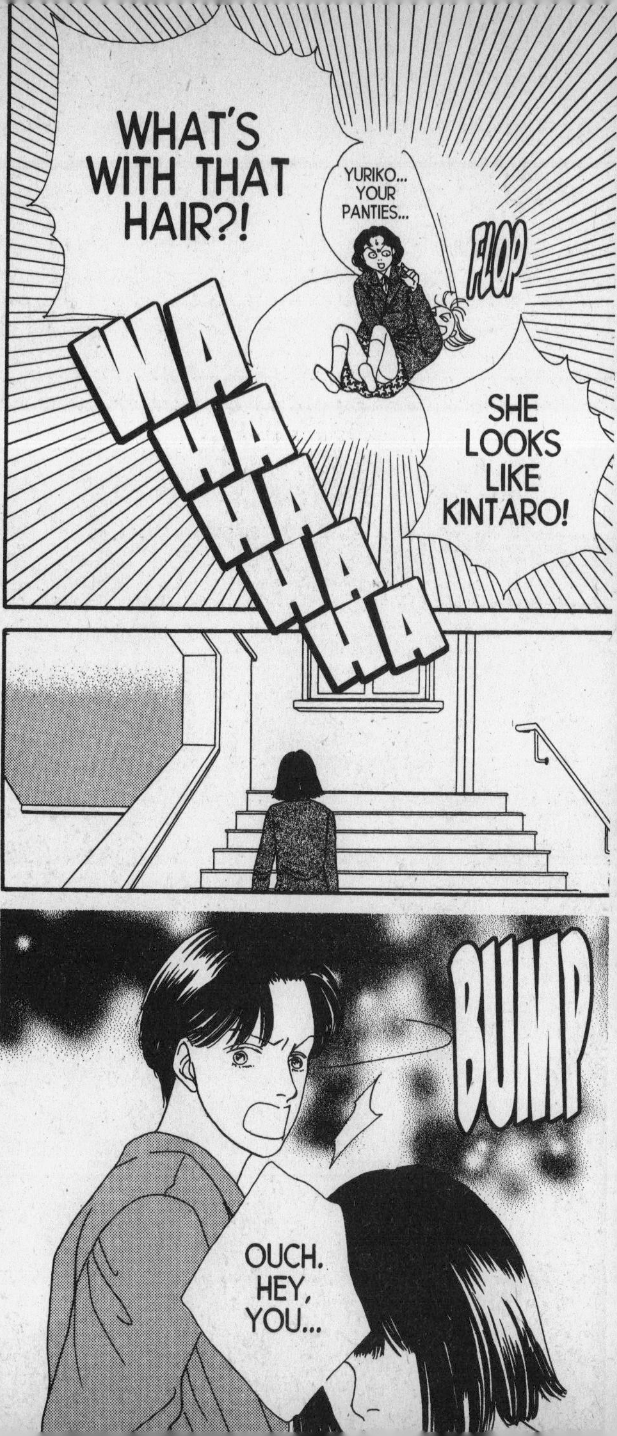
WHAT'S WITH THAT HAIR?!
YURIKO... YOUR PANTIES...
FLOP
WA HA HA HA HA HA
SHE LOOKS LIKE KINTARO!
BUMP
OUCH. HEY, YOU...

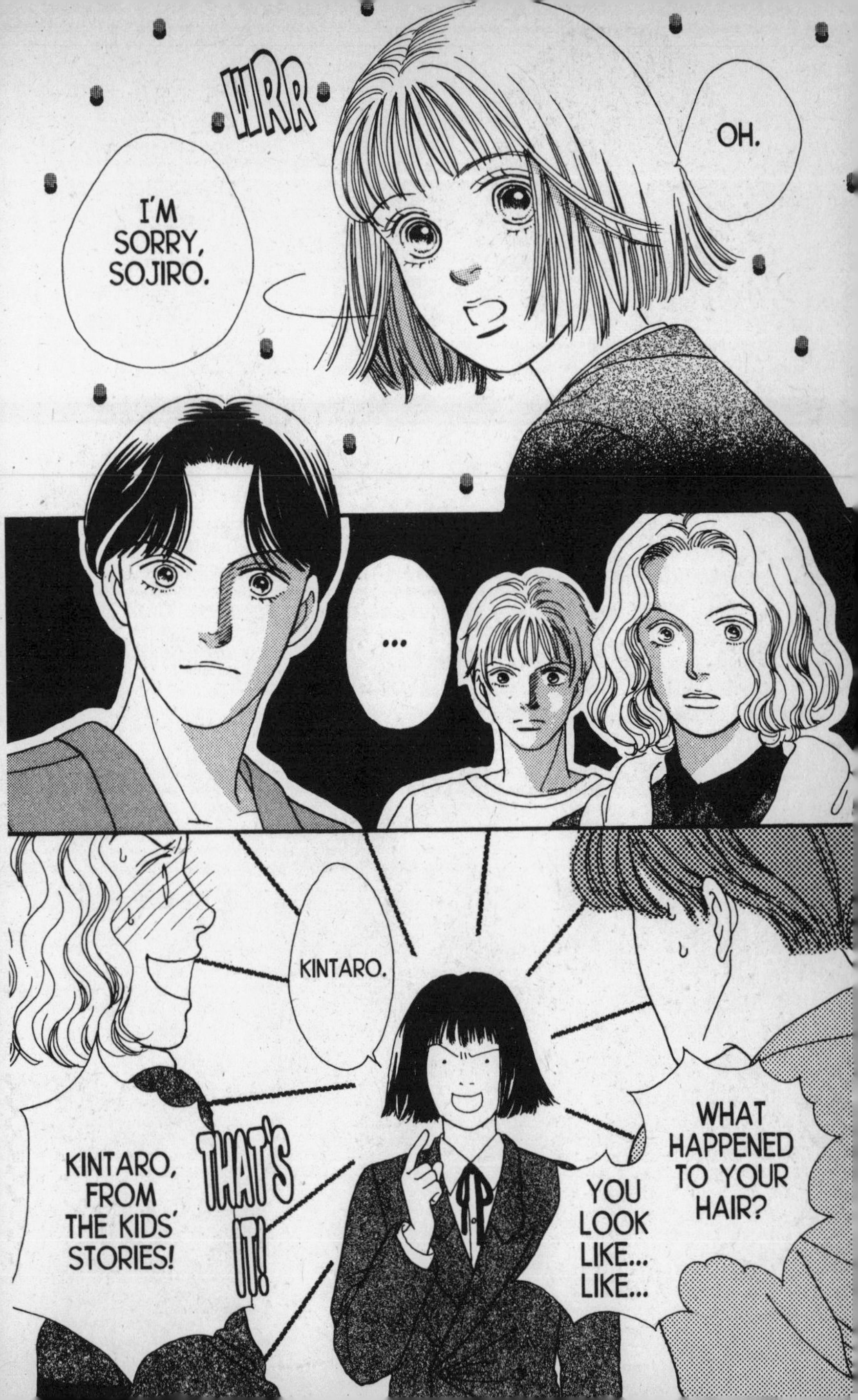
OH.
WRR
I'M SORRY, SOJIRO.
...
WHAT HAPPENED TO YOUR HAIR?
YOU LOOK LIKE... LIKE...
KINTARO.
THAT'S IT!
KINTARO, FROM THE KIDS' STORIES!

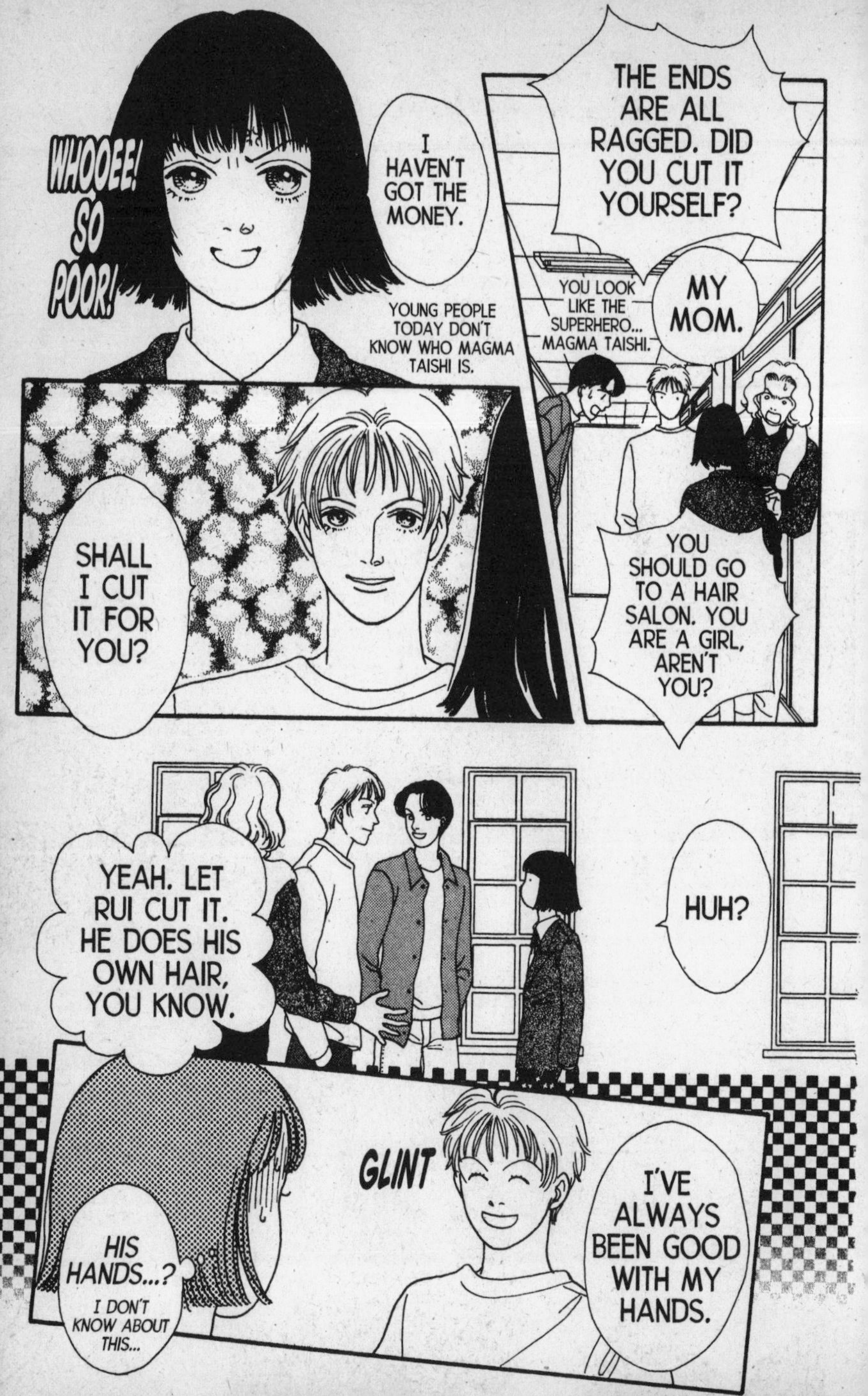
THE ENDS ARE ALL RAGGED. DID YOU CUT IT YOURSELF?
MY MOM.
YOU LOOK LIKE THE SUPERHERO... MAGMA TAISHI.
YOU SHOULD GO TO A HAIR SALON. YOU ARE A GIRL, AREN'T YOU?
I HAVEN'T GOT THE MONEY.
YOUNG PEOPLE TODAY DON'T KNOW WHO MAGMA TAISHI IS.
WHOOEE! SO POOR!
SHALL I CUT IT FOR YOU?
HUH?
YEAH. LET RUI CUT IT. HE DOES HIS OWN HAIR, YOU KNOW.
I'VE ALWAYS BEEN GOOD WITH MY HANDS.
GLINT
HIS HANDS...?
I DON'T KNOW ABOUT THIS...

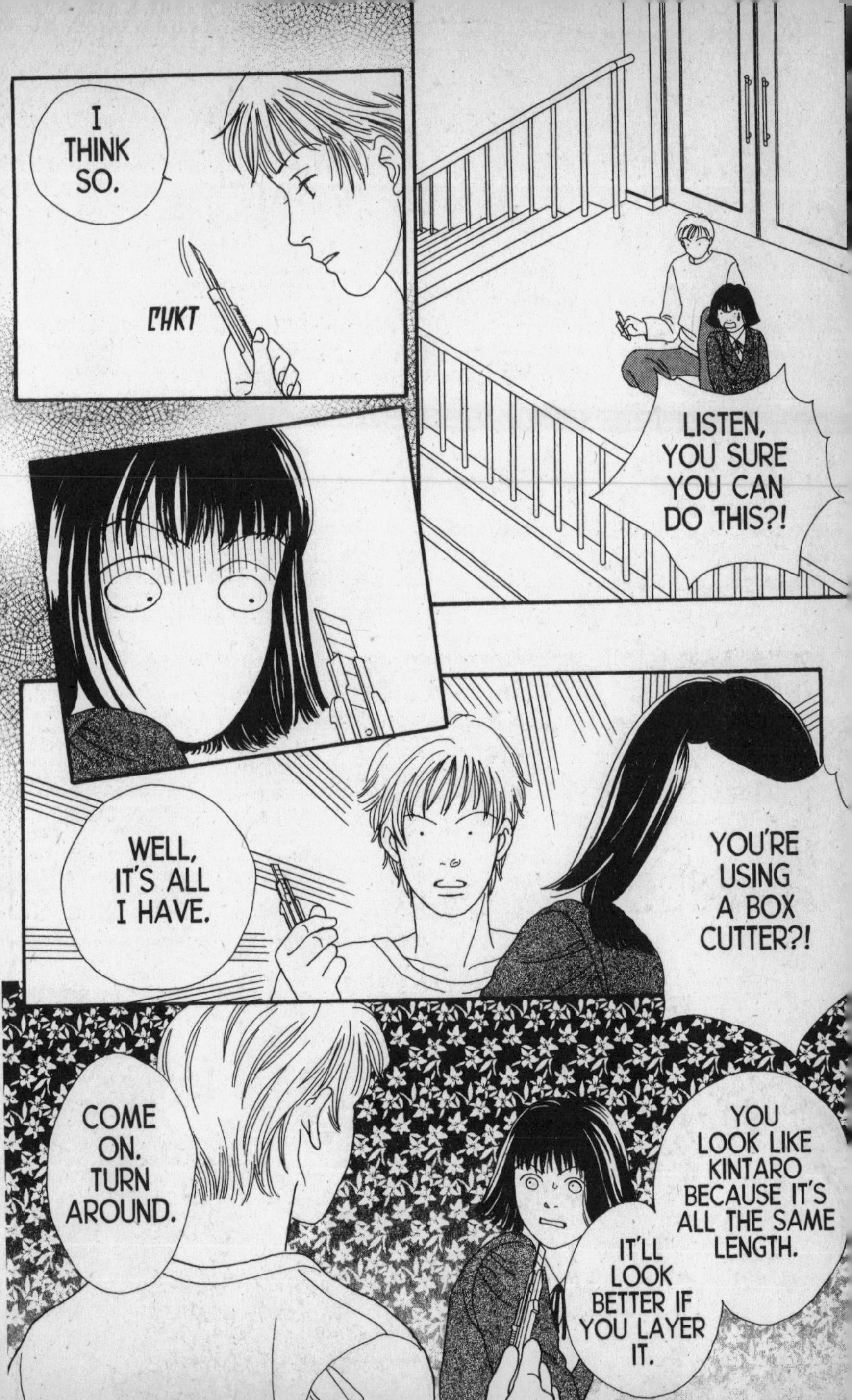

LISTEN, YOU SURE YOU CAN DO THIS?!
I THINK SO.
CHKT
YOU'RE USING A BOX CUTTER?!
WELL, IT'S ALL I HAVE.
YOU LOOK LIKE KINTARO BECAUSE IT'S ALL THE SAME LENGTH.
IT'LL LOOK BETTER IF YOU LAYER IT.
COME ON. TURN AROUND.

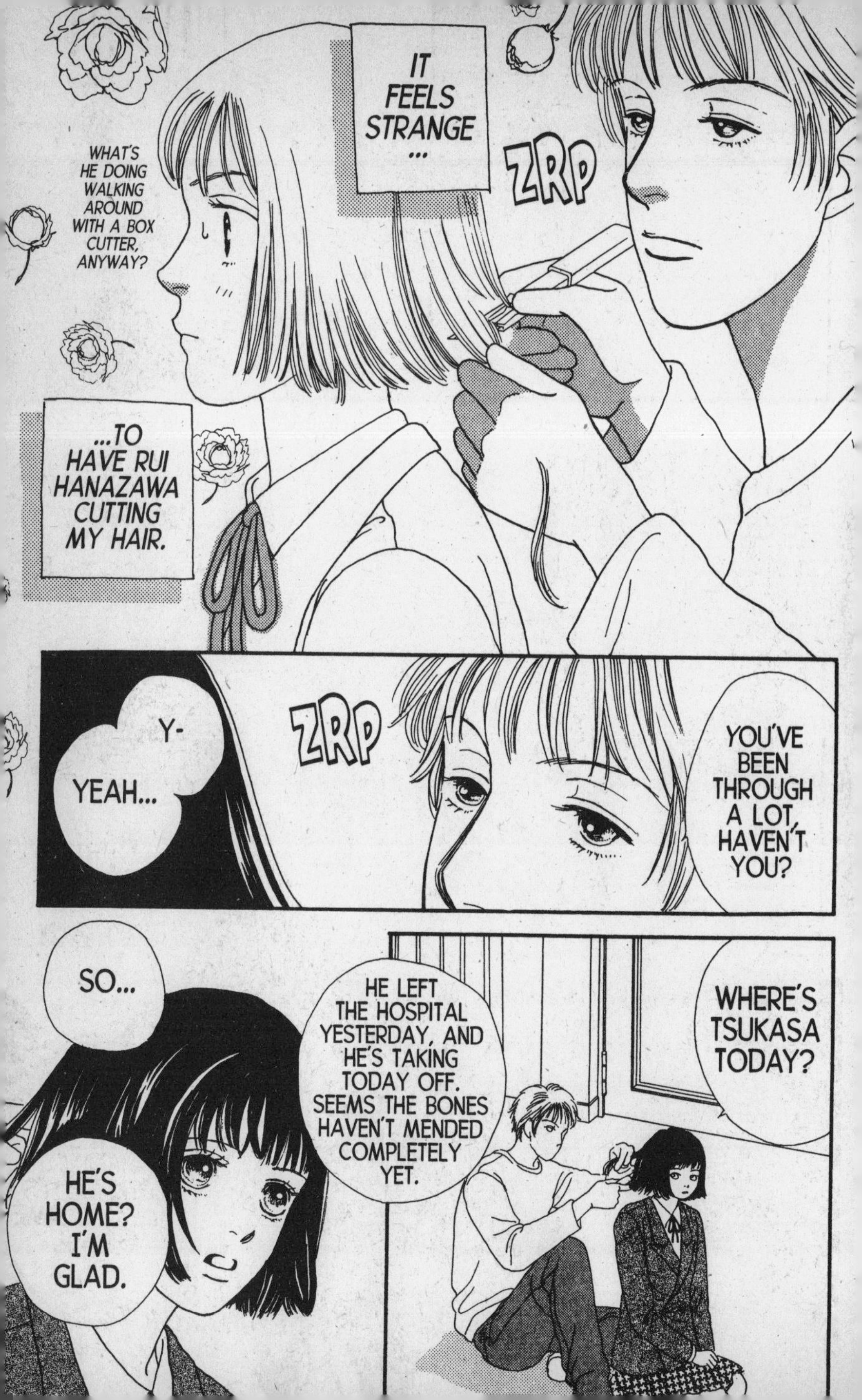
IT FEELS STRANGE ...
ZRP
WHAT'S HE DOING WALKING AROUND WITH A BOX CUTTER, ANYWAY?
...TO HAVE RUI HANAZAWA CUTTING MY HAIR.
YOU'VE BEEN THROUGH A LOT, HAVEN'T YOU?
ZRP
Y- YEAH...
WHERE'S TSUKASA TODAY?
HE LEFT THE HOSPITAL YESTERDAY, AND HE'S TAKING TODAY OFF. SEEMS THE BONES HAVEN'T MENDED COMPLETELY YET.
SO...
HE'S HOME? I'M GLAD.

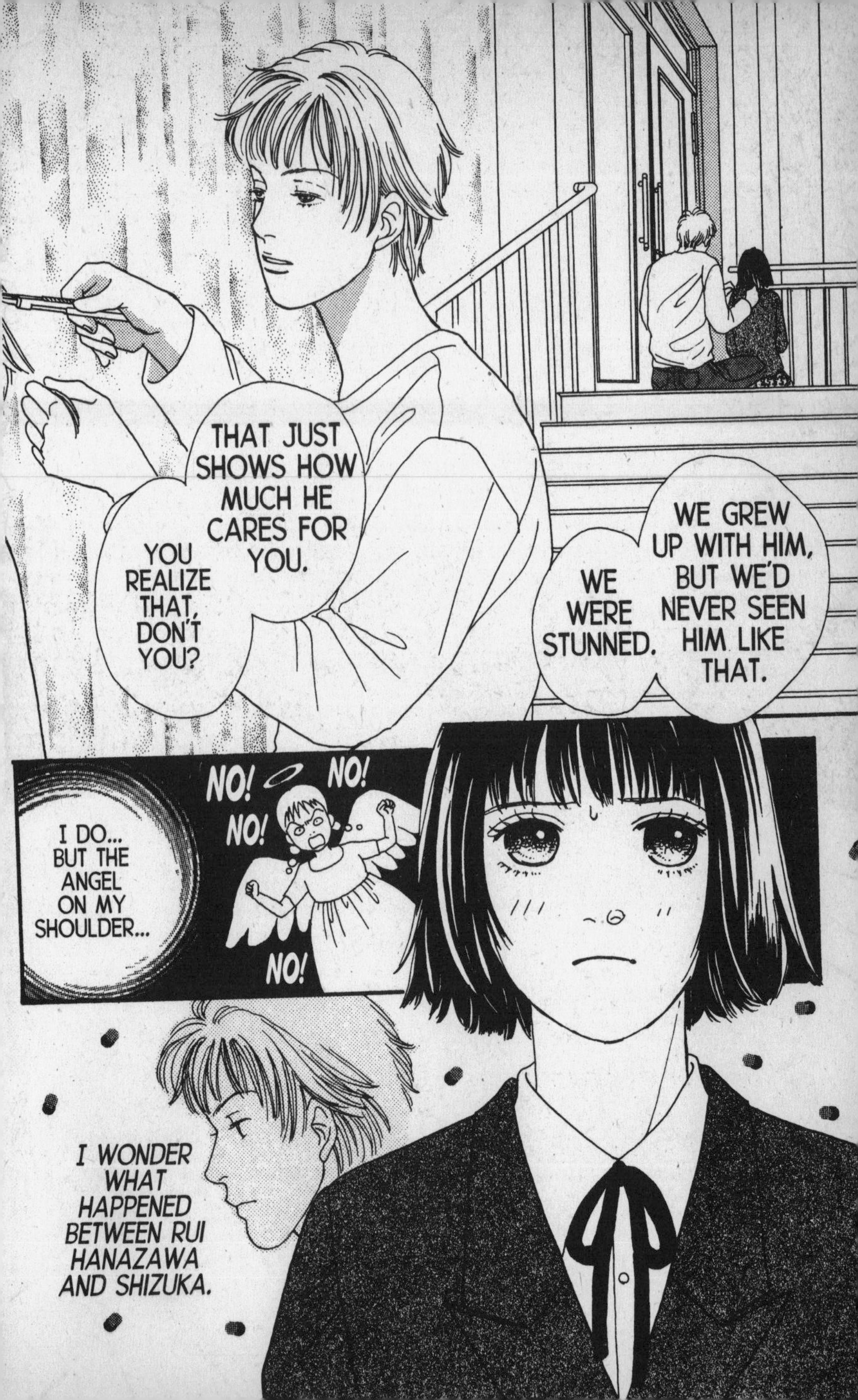
WE GREW UP WITH HIM, BUT WE'D NEVER SEEN HIM LIKE THAT.
WE WERE STUNNED.
THAT JUST SHOWS HOW MUCH HE CARES FOR YOU.
YOU REALIZE THAT, DON'T YOU?
NO! NO!
NO!
NO!
I DO... BUT THE ANGEL ON MY SHOULDER...
I WONDER WHAT HAPPENED BETWEEN RUI HANAZAWA AND SHIZUKA.

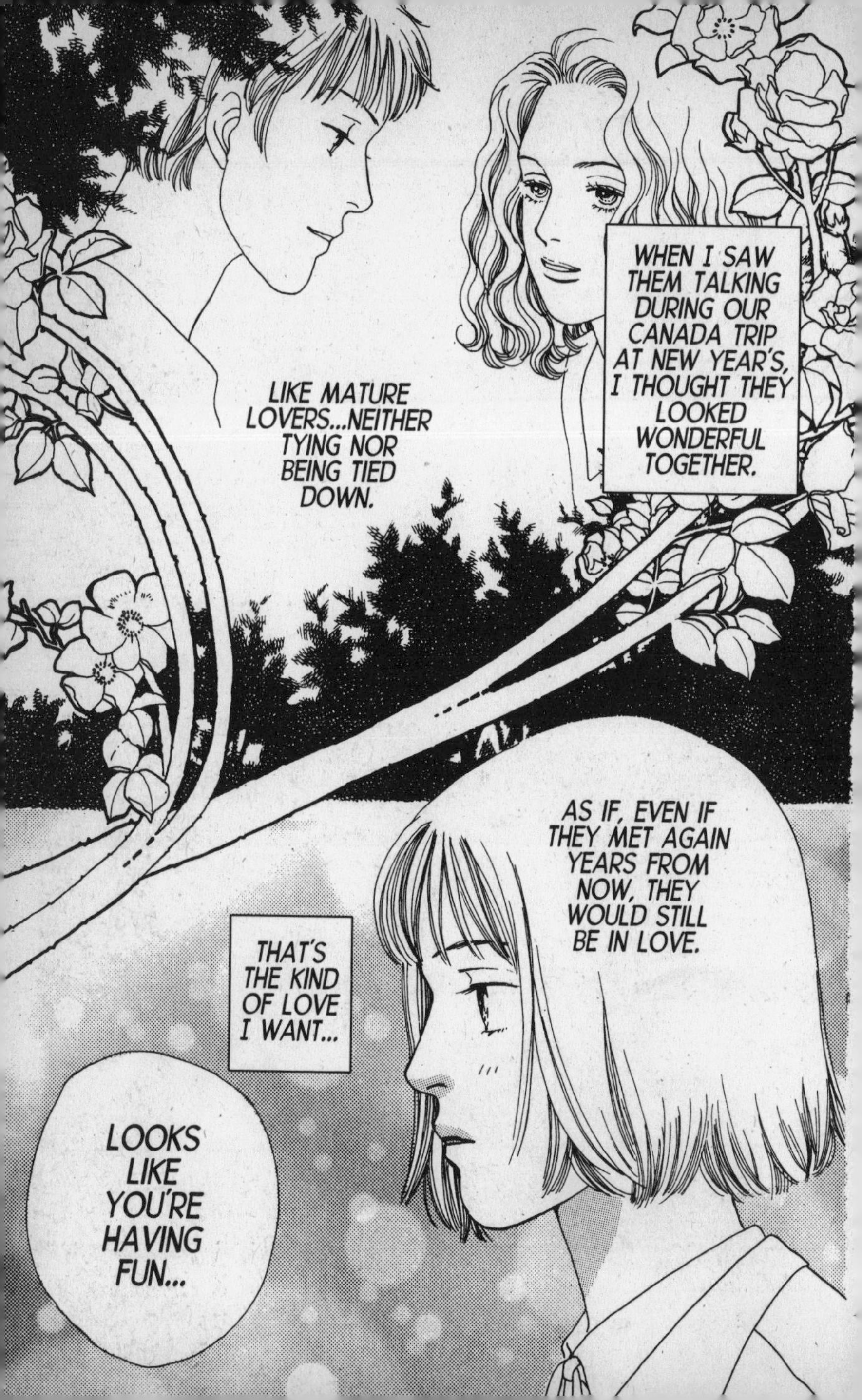
WHEN I SAW THEM TALKING DURING OUR CANADA TRIP AT NEW YEAR'S, I THOUGHT THEY LOOKED WONDERFUL TOGETHER.
LIKE MATURE LOVERS...NEITHER TYING NOR BEING TIED DOWN.
AS IF, EVEN IF THEY MET AGAIN YEARS FROM NOW, THEY WOULD STILL BE IN LOVE.
THAT'S THE KIND OF LOVE I WANT...
LOOKS LIKE YOU'RE HAVING FUN...

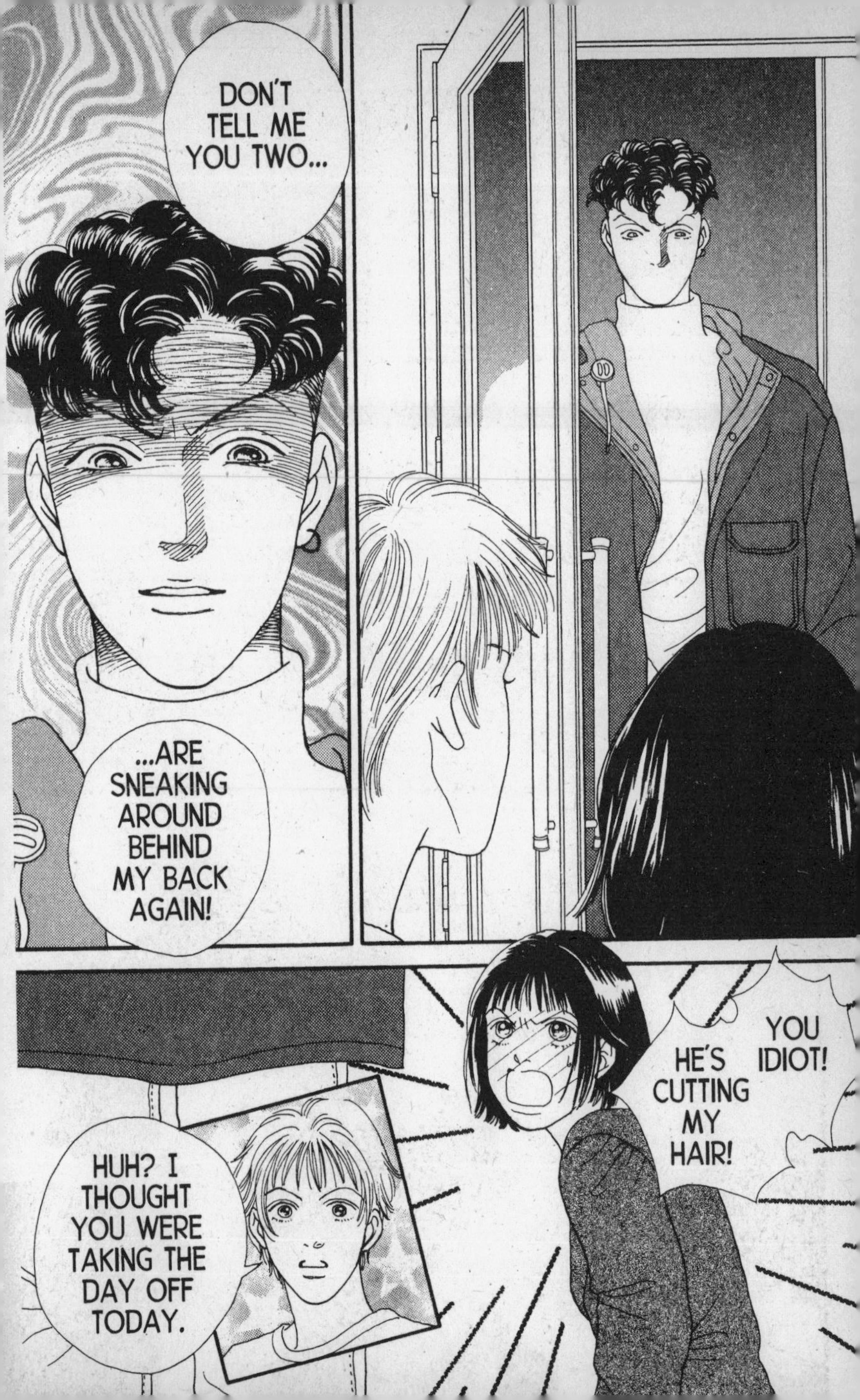
DON'T TELL ME YOU TWO...
...ARE SNEAKING AROUND BEHIND MY BACK AGAIN!
YOU IDIOT!
HE'S CUTTING MY HAIR!
HUH? I THOUGHT YOU WERE TAKING THE DAY OFF TODAY.

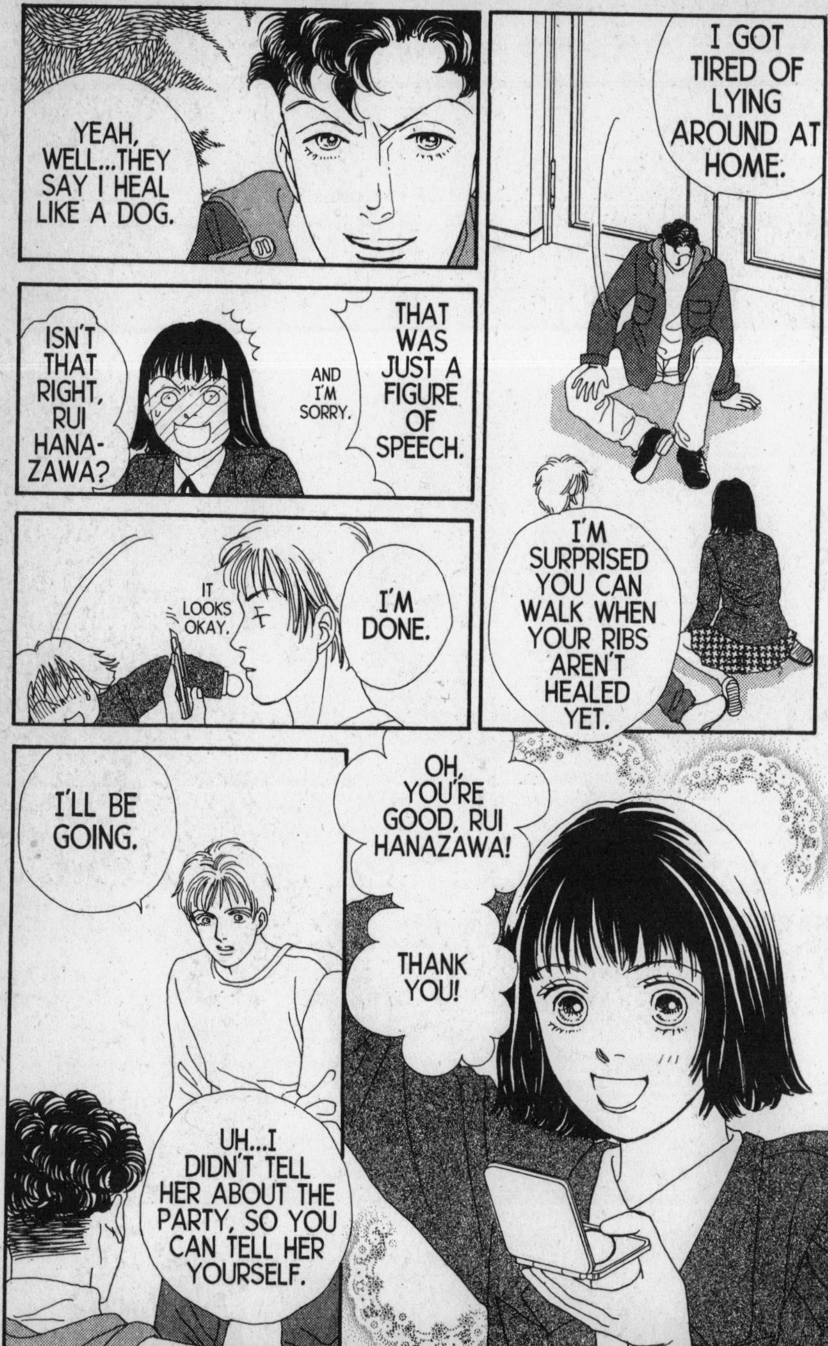

I GOT TIRED OF LYING AROUND AT HOME.
I'M SURPRISED YOU CAN WALK WHEN YOUR RIBS AREN'T HEALED YET.
YEAH, WELL...THEY SAY I HEAL LIKE A DOG.
THAT WAS JUST A FIGURE OF SPEECH.
AND I'M SORRY.
ISN'T THAT RIGHT, RUI HANA-ZAWA?
I'M DONE.
IT LOOKS OKAY.
OH, YOU'RE GOOD, RUI HANAZAWA!
THANK YOU!
I'LL BE GOING.
UH...I DIDN'T TELL HER ABOUT THE PARTY, SO YOU CAN TELL HER YOURSELF.

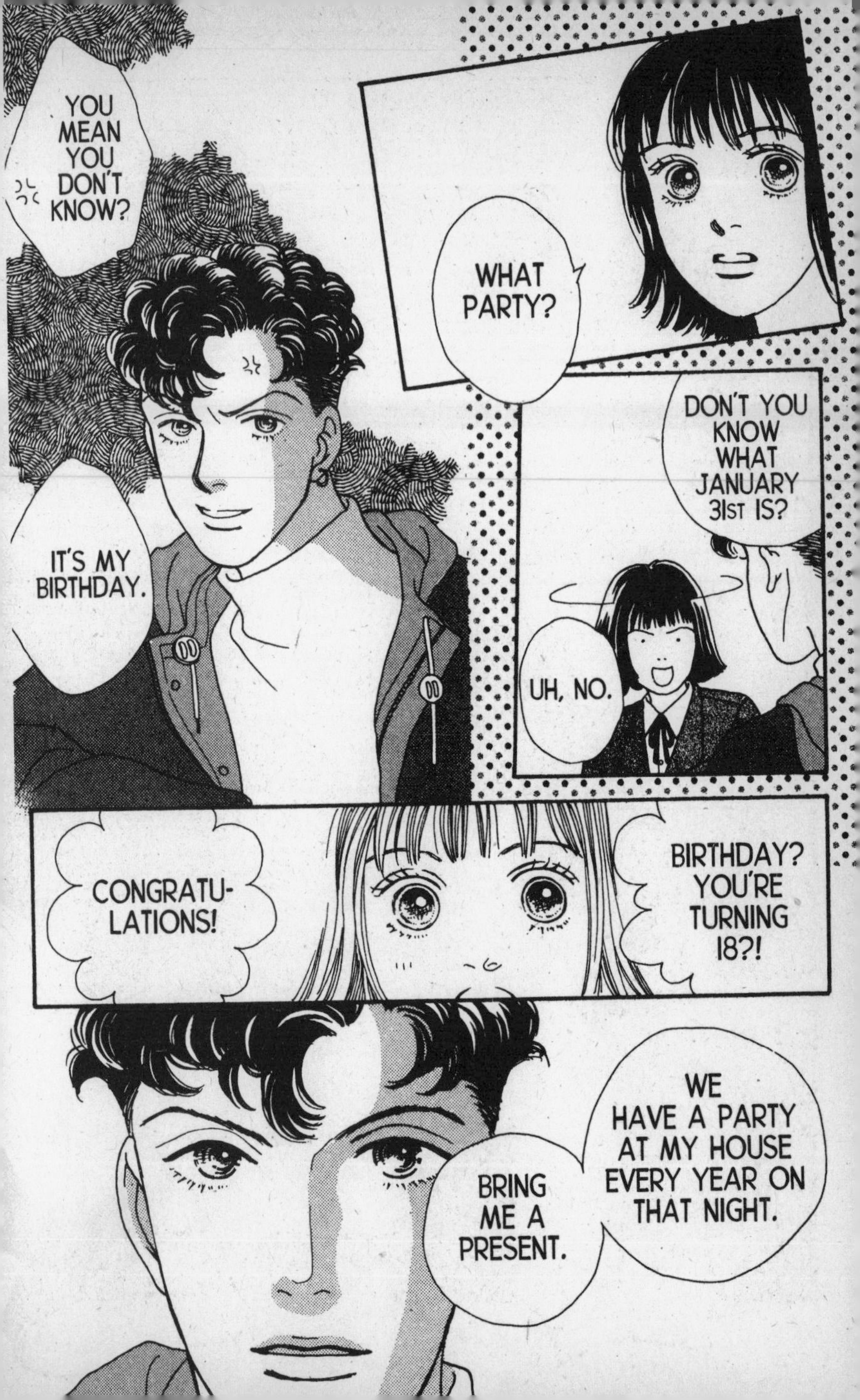
WHAT PARTY?
DON'T YOU KNOW WHAT JANUARY 31ST IS?
UH, NO.
YOU MEAN YOU DON'T KNOW?
IT'S MY BIRTHDAY.
BIRTHDAY? YOU'RE TURNING 18?!
CONGRATU-LATIONS!
WE HAVE A PARTY AT MY HOUSE EVERY YEAR ON THAT NIGHT.
BRING ME A PRESENT.

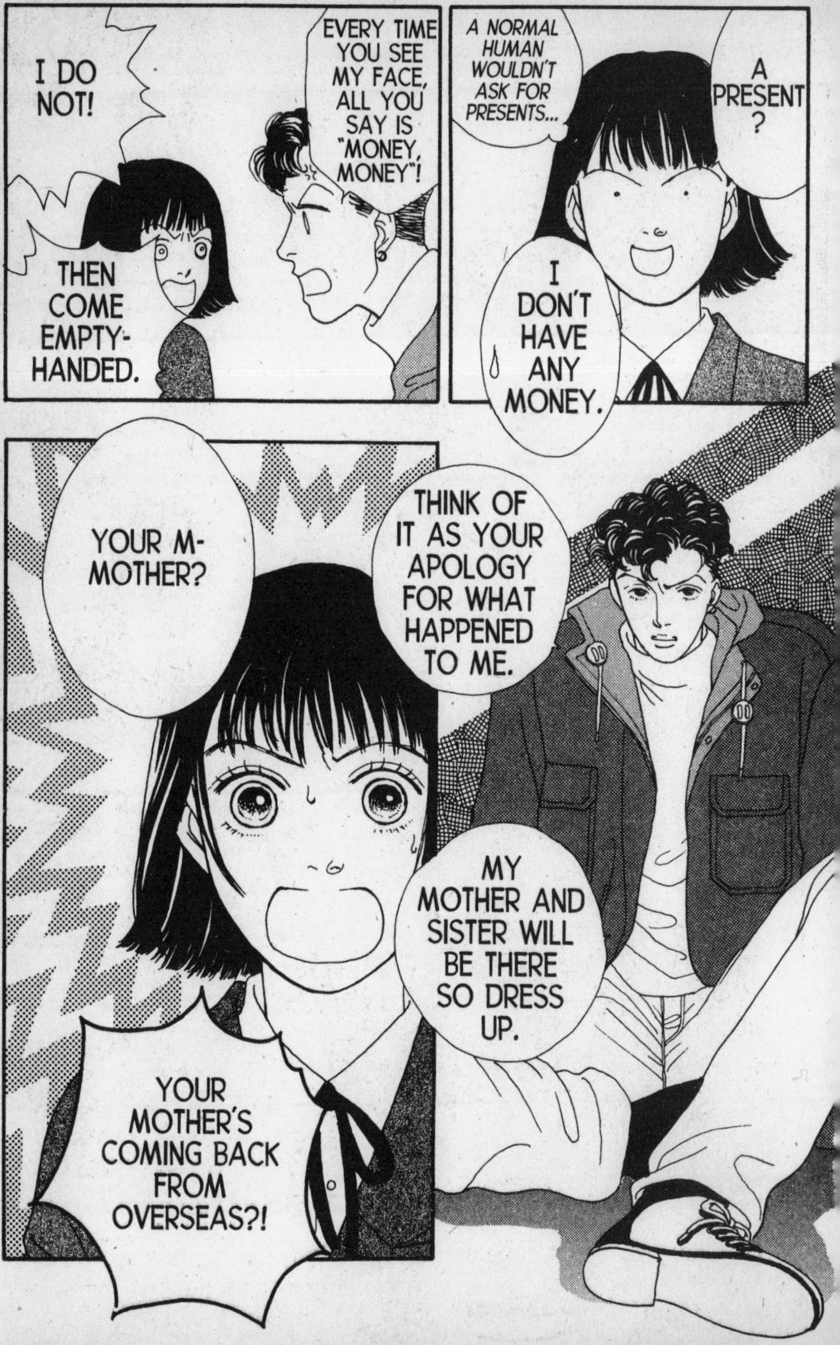
A PRESENT?
A NORMAL HUMAN WOULDN'T ASK FOR PRESENTS...
I DON'T HAVE ANY MONEY.
EVERY TIME YOU SEE MY FACE, ALL YOU SAY IS "MONEY, MONEY"!
I DO NOT!
THEN COME EMPTY-HANDED.
THINK OF IT AS YOUR APOLOGY FOR WHAT HAPPENED TO ME.
MY MOTHER AND SISTER WILL BE THERE SO DRESS UP.
YOUR M-MOTHER?
YOUR MOTHER'S COMING BACK FROM OVERSEAS?!

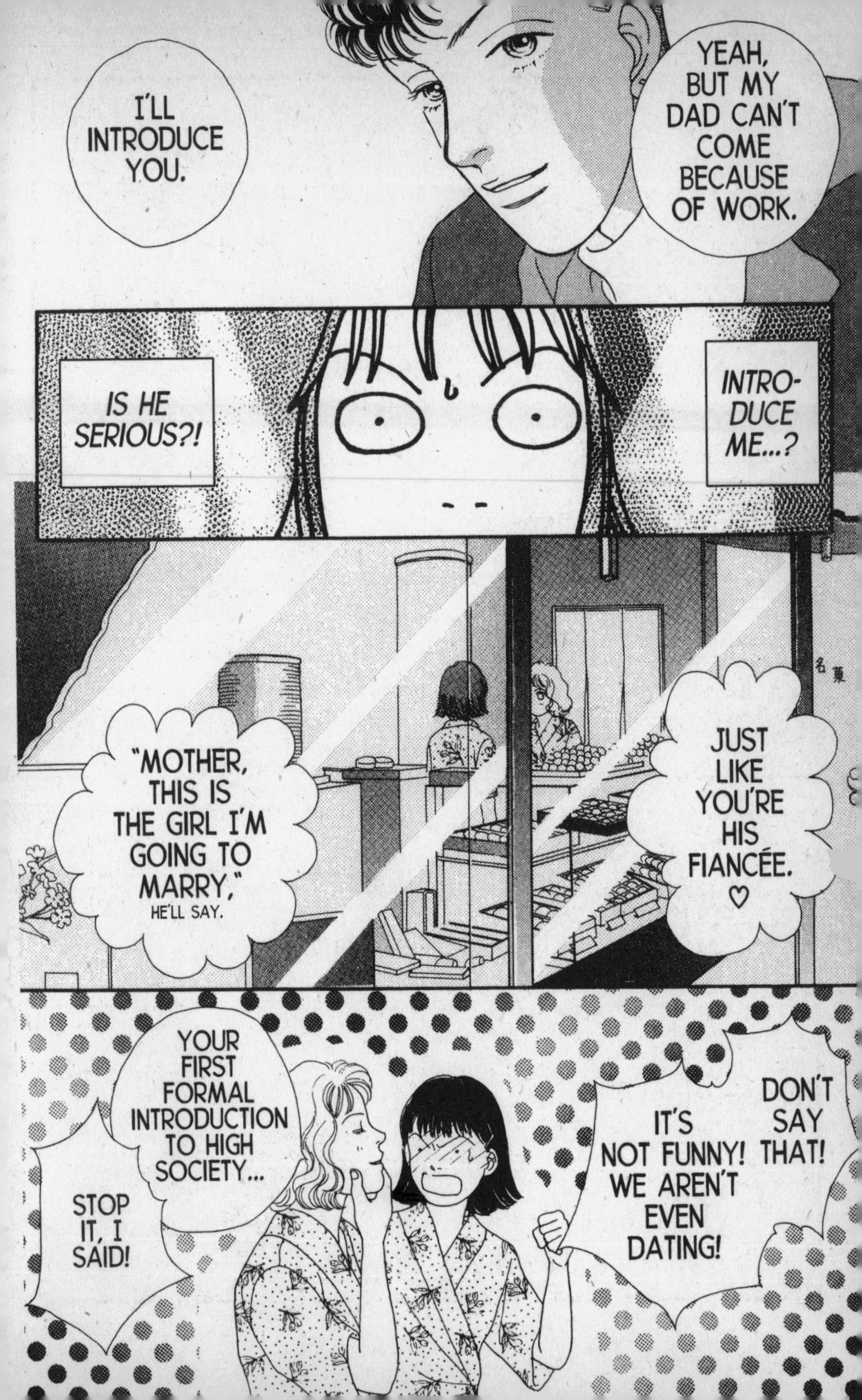
YEAH, BUT MY DAD CAN'T COME BECAUSE OF WORK.
I'LL INTRODUCE YOU.
INTRO-DUCE ME...?
IS HE SERIOUS?!
JUST LIKE YOU'RE HIS FIANCÉE. ♡
"MOTHER, THIS IS THE GIRL I'M GOING TO MARRY," HE'LL SAY.
DON'T SAY THAT!
IT'S NOT FUNNY! WE AREN'T EVEN DATING!
YOUR FIRST FORMAL INTRODUCTION TO HIGH SOCIETY...
STOP IT, I SAID!

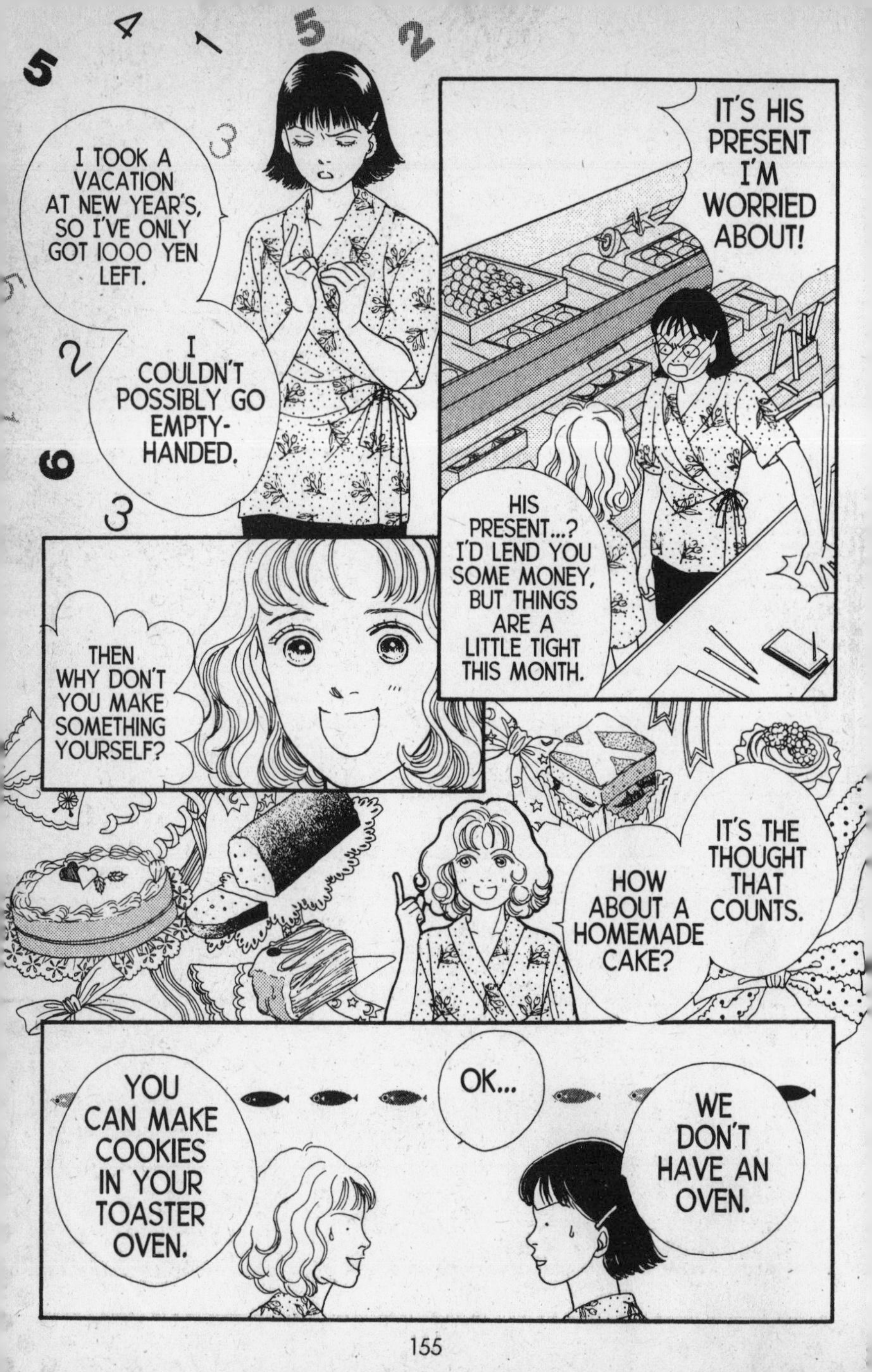
IT'S HIS PRESENT I'M WORRIED ABOUT!
HIS PRESENT...? I'D LEND YOU SOME MONEY, BUT THINGS ARE A LITTLE TIGHT THIS MONTH.
I TOOK A VACATION AT NEW YEAR'S, SO I'VE ONLY GOT 1000 YEN LEFT.
I COULDN'T POSSIBLY GO EMPTY-HANDED.
THEN WHY DON'T YOU MAKE SOMETHING YOURSELF?
IT'S THE THOUGHT THAT COUNTS.
HOW ABOUT A HOMEMADE CAKE?
WE DON'T HAVE AN OVEN.
OK...
YOU CAN MAKE COOKIES IN YOUR TOASTER OVEN.

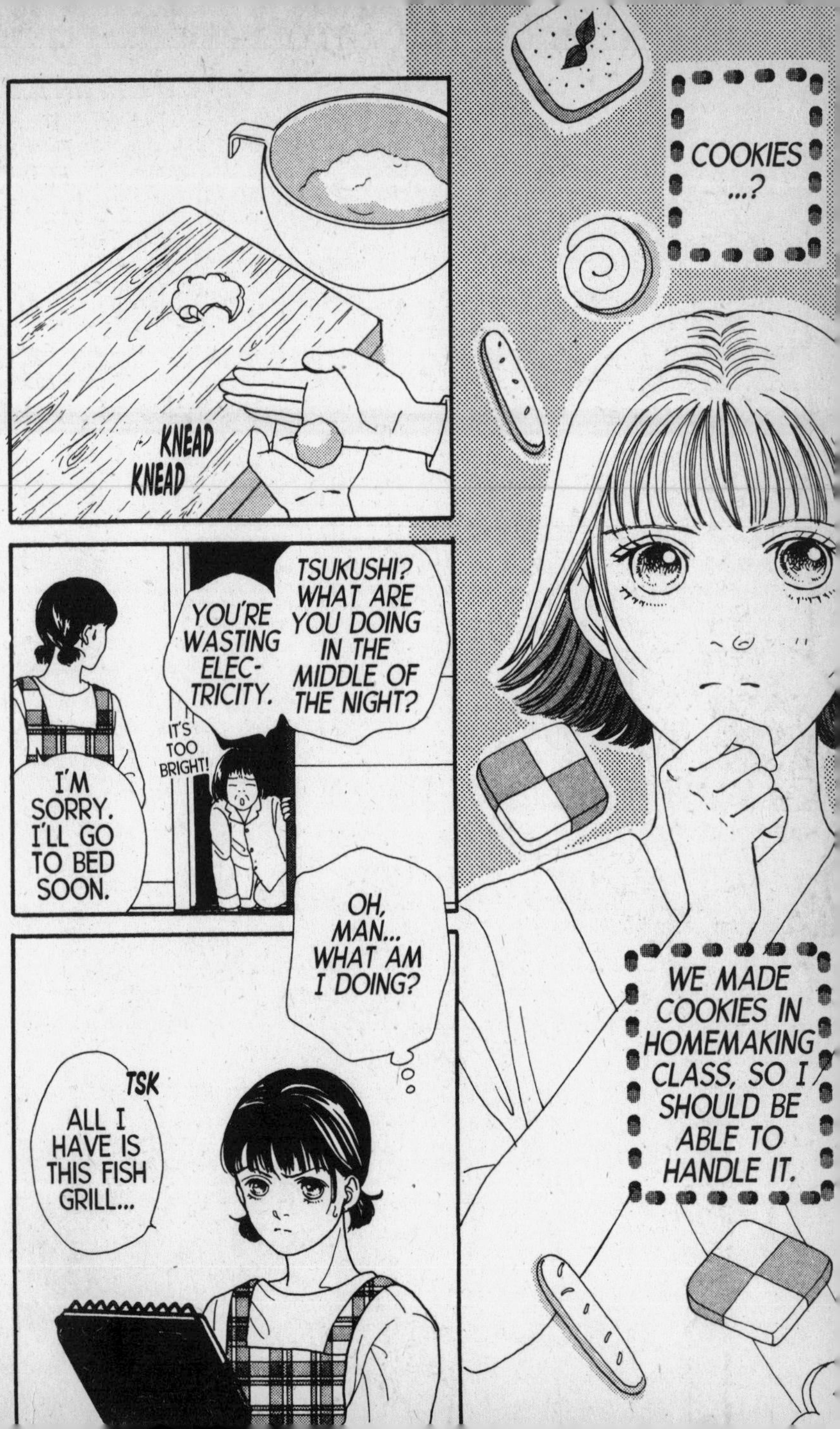
COOKIES ...?
WE MADE COOKIES IN HOMEMAKING CLASS, SO I SHOULD BE ABLE TO HANDLE IT.
KNEAD KNEAD
TSUKUSHI? WHAT ARE YOU DOING IN THE MIDDLE OF THE NIGHT?
YOU'RE WASTING ELEC-TRICITY.
IT'S TOO BRIGHT!
I'M SORRY. I'LL GO TO BED SOON.
OH, MAN... WHAT AM I DOING?
TSK
ALL I HAVE IS THIS FISH GRILL...

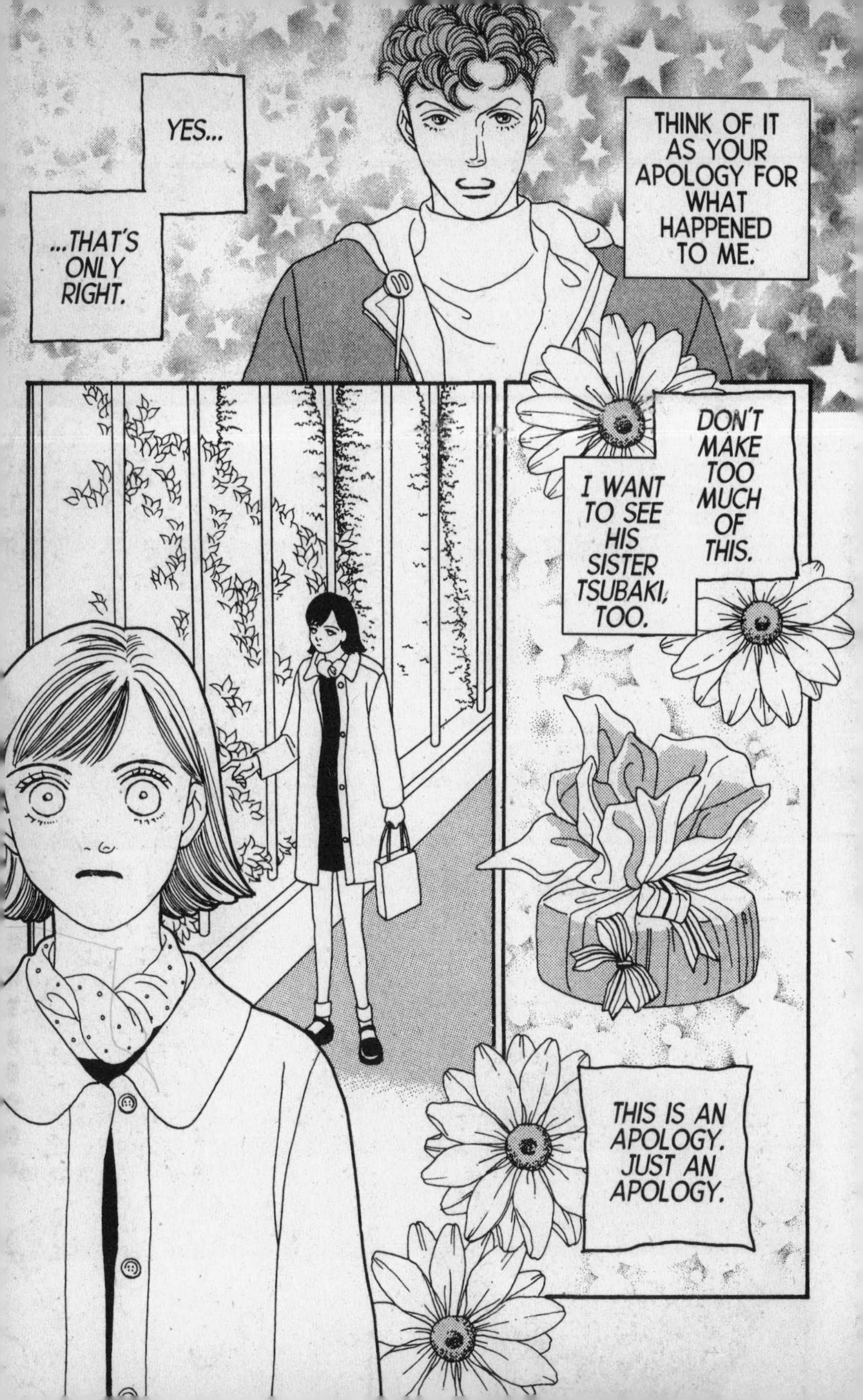
THINK OF IT AS YOUR APOLOGY FOR WHAT HAPPENED TO ME.
YES...
...THAT'S ONLY RIGHT.
DON'T MAKE TOO MUCH OF THIS.
I WANT TO SEE HIS SISTER TSUBAKI, TOO.
THIS IS AN APOLOGY. JUST AN APOLOGY.

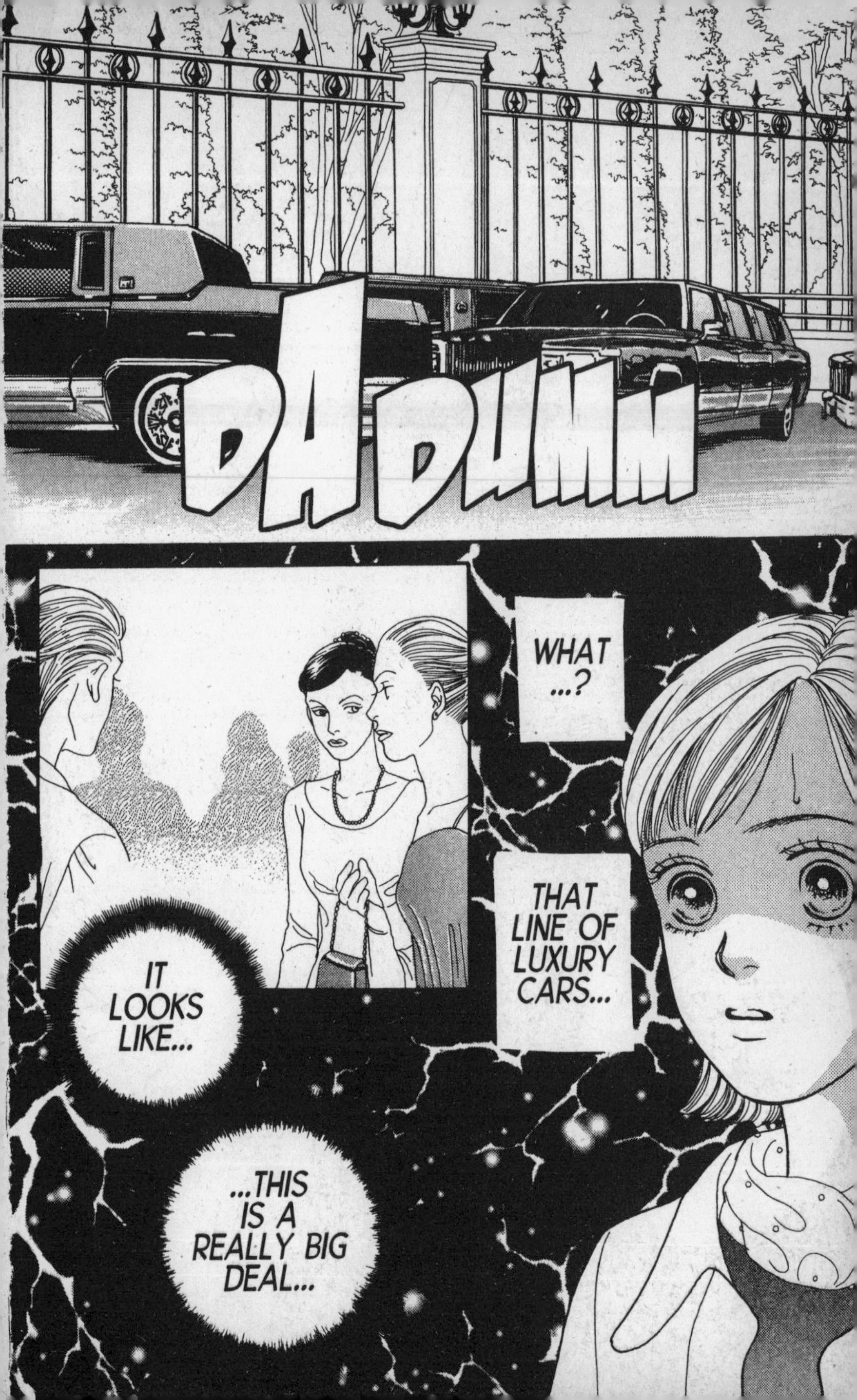
DA DUMM
WHAT ...?
THAT LINE OF LUXURY CARS...
IT LOOKS LIKE...
...THIS IS A REALLY BIG DEAL...

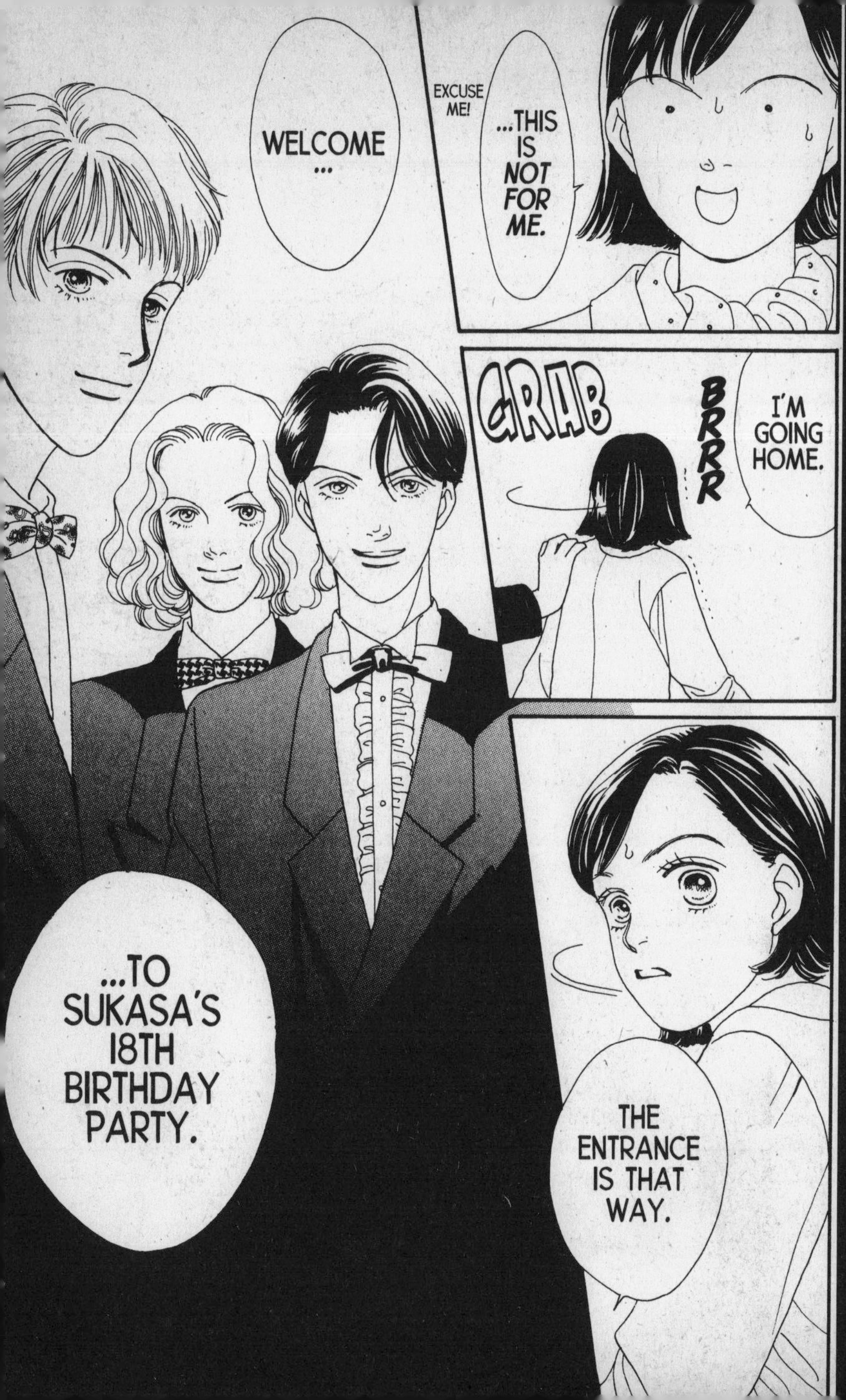
EXCUSE ME!
...THIS IS NOT FOR ME.
I'M GOING HOME.
BRRR
GRAB
THE ENTRANCE IS THAT WAY.
WELCOME...
...TO SUKASA'S 18TH BIRTHDAY PARTY.

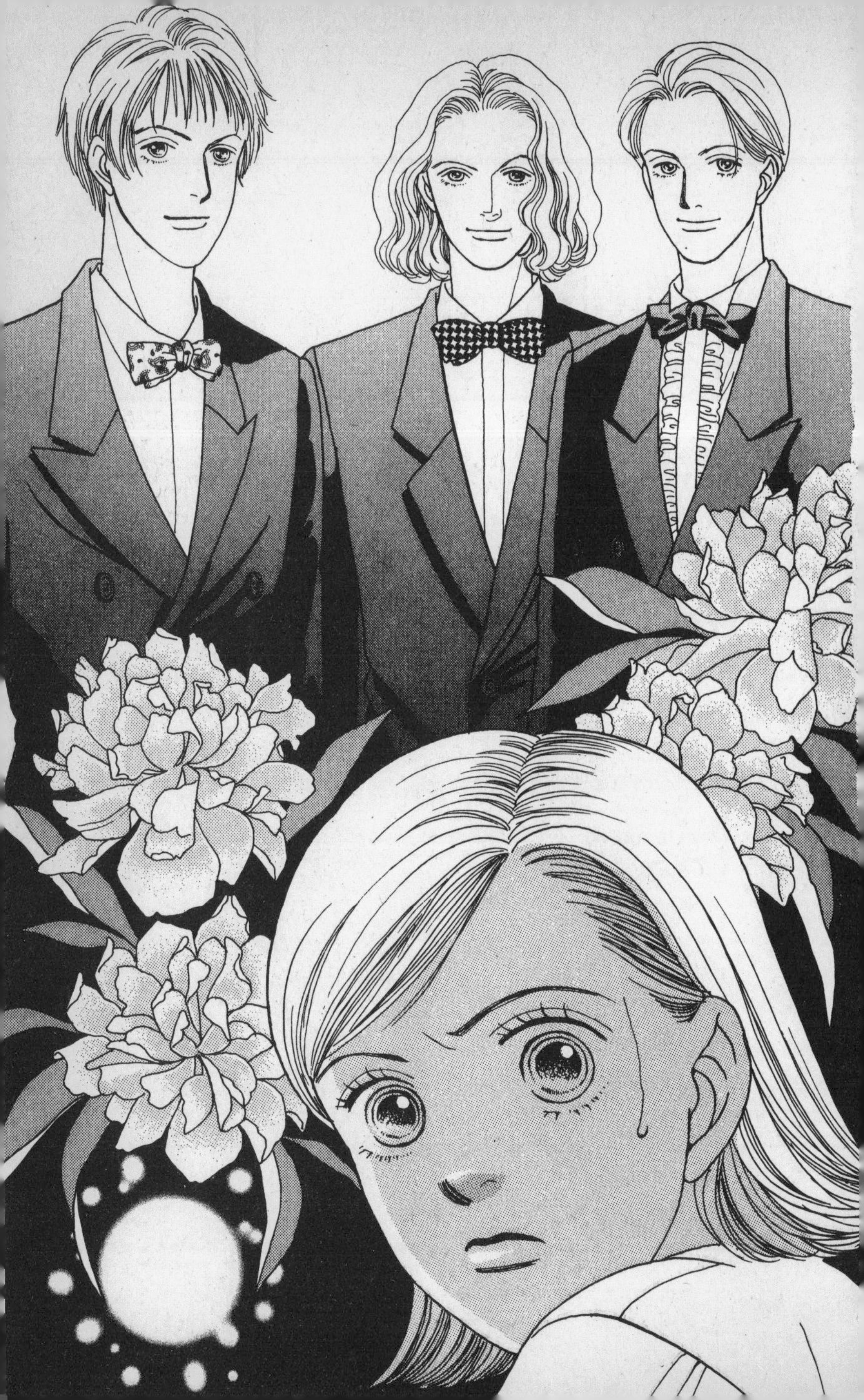

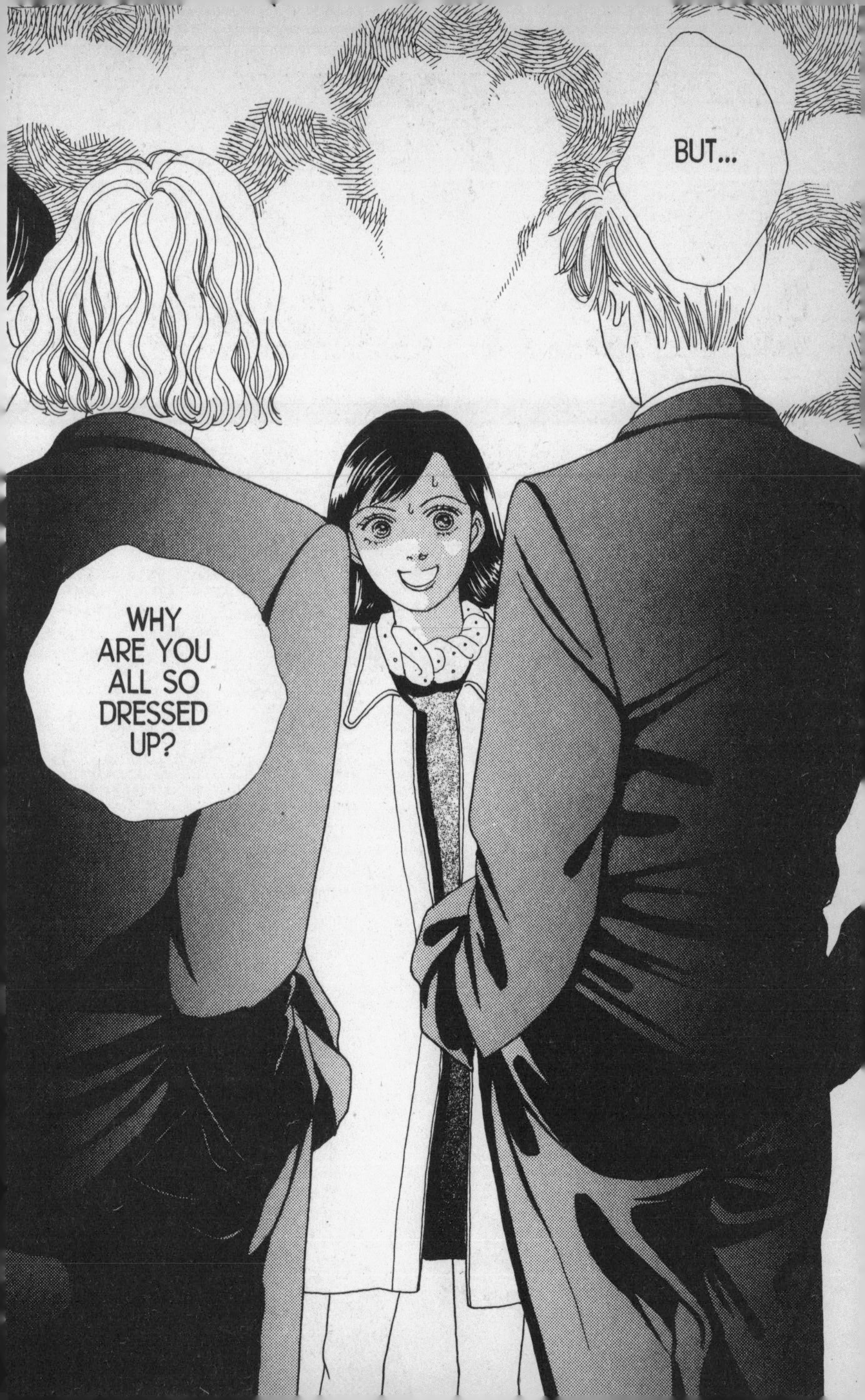
BUT...
WHY ARE YOU ALL SO DRESSED UP?

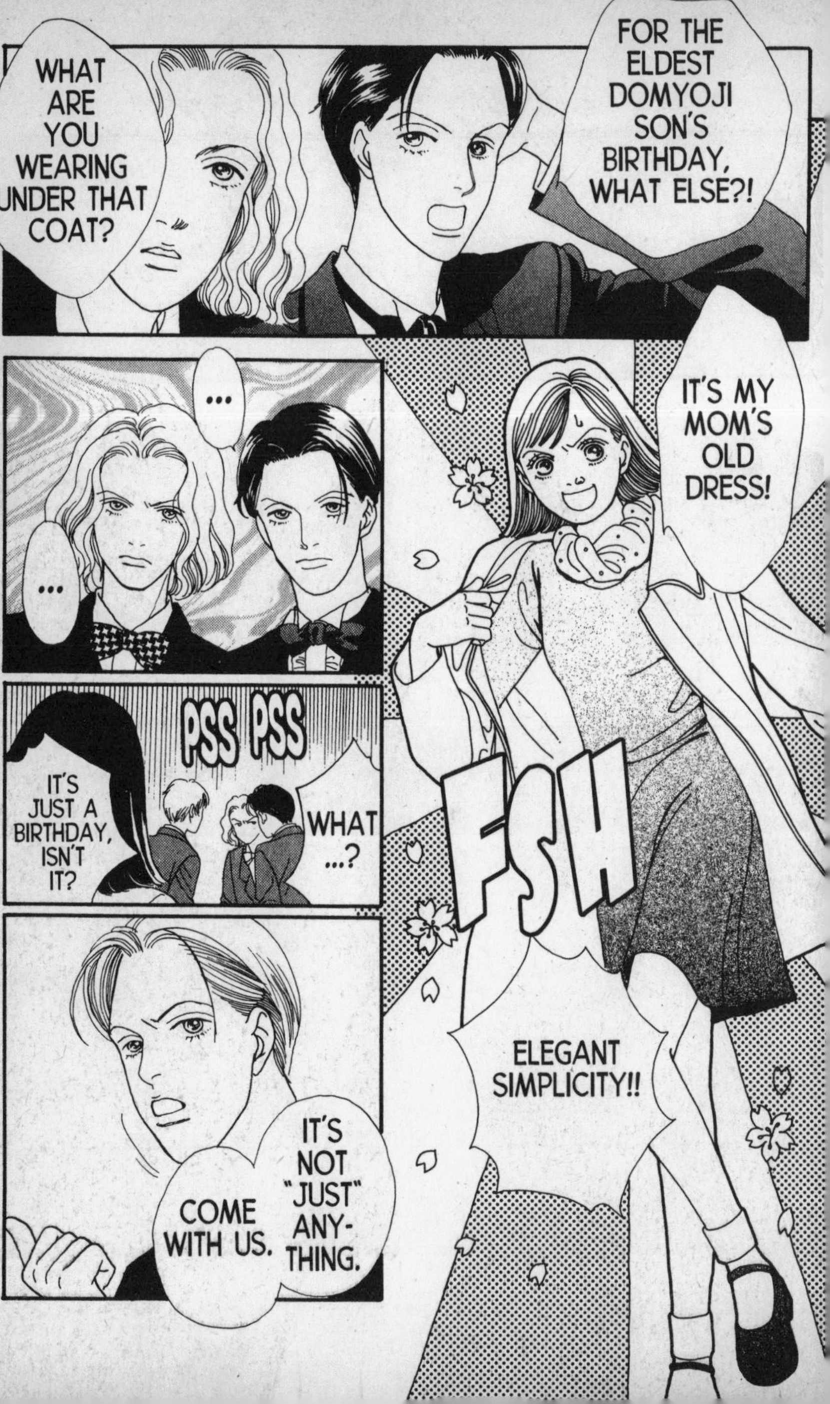
FOR THE ELDEST DOMYOJI SON'S BIRTHDAY, WHAT ELSE?!
WHAT ARE YOU WEARING UNDER THAT COAT?
IT'S MY MOM'S OLD DRESS!
FSH
ELEGANT SIMPLICITY!!
...
...
PSS PSS
WHAT ...?
IT'S JUST A BIRTHDAY, ISN'T IT?
IT'S NOT "JUST" ANY-THING.
COME WITH US.

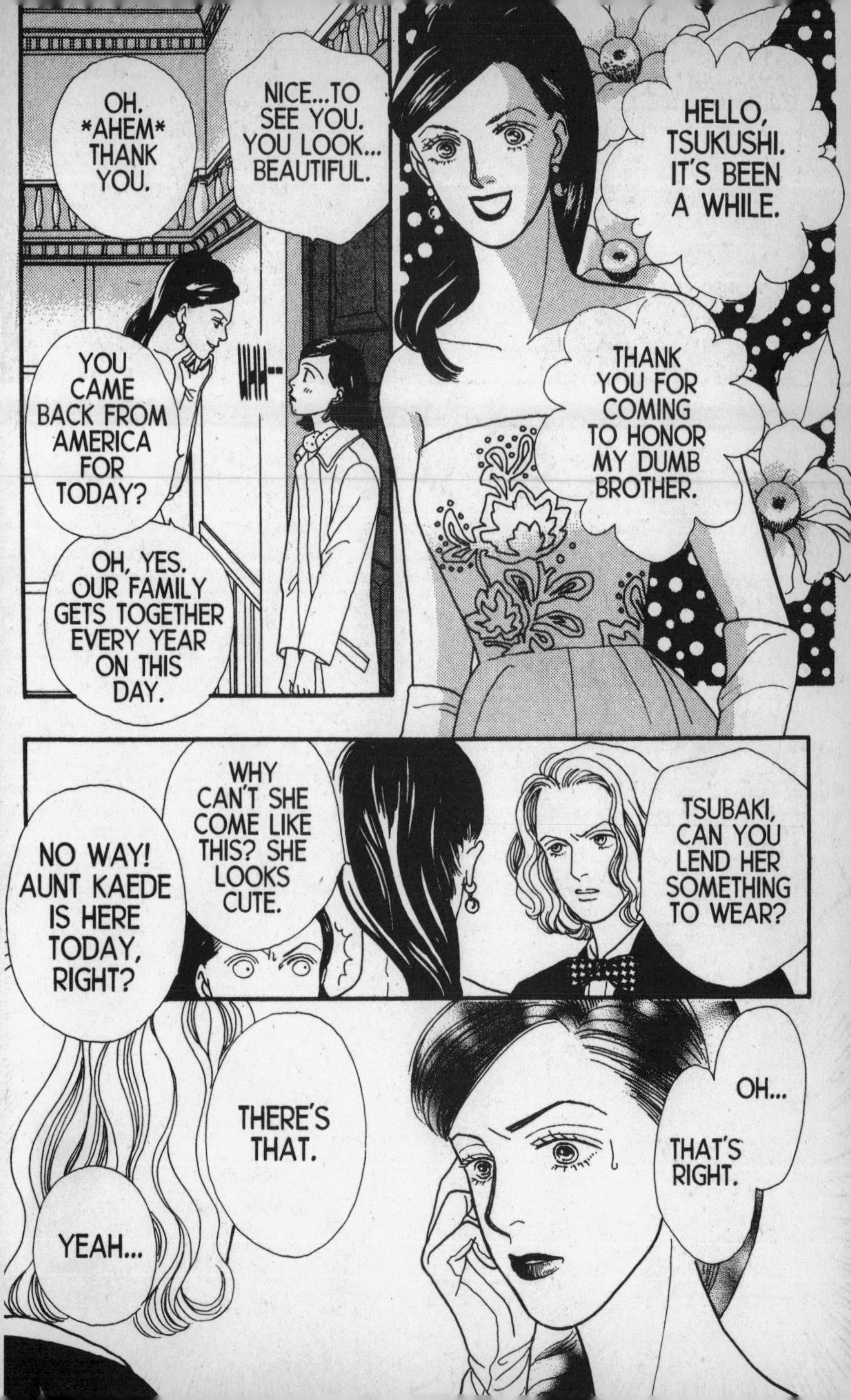
HELLO, TSUKUSHI. IT'S BEEN A WHILE.
THANK YOU FOR COMING TO HONOR MY DUMB BROTHER.
NICE...TO SEE YOU. YOU LOOK... BEAUTIFUL.
OH. *AHEM* THANK YOU.
UHH--
YOU CAME BACK FROM AMERICA FOR TODAY?
OH, YES. OUR FAMILY GETS TOGETHER EVERY YEAR ON THIS DAY.
TSUBAKI, CAN YOU LEND HER SOMETHING TO WEAR?
WHY CAN'T SHE COME LIKE THIS? SHE LOOKS CUTE.
NO WAY! AUNT KAEDE IS HERE TODAY, RIGHT?
OH... THAT'S RIGHT.
THERE'S THAT.
YEAH...

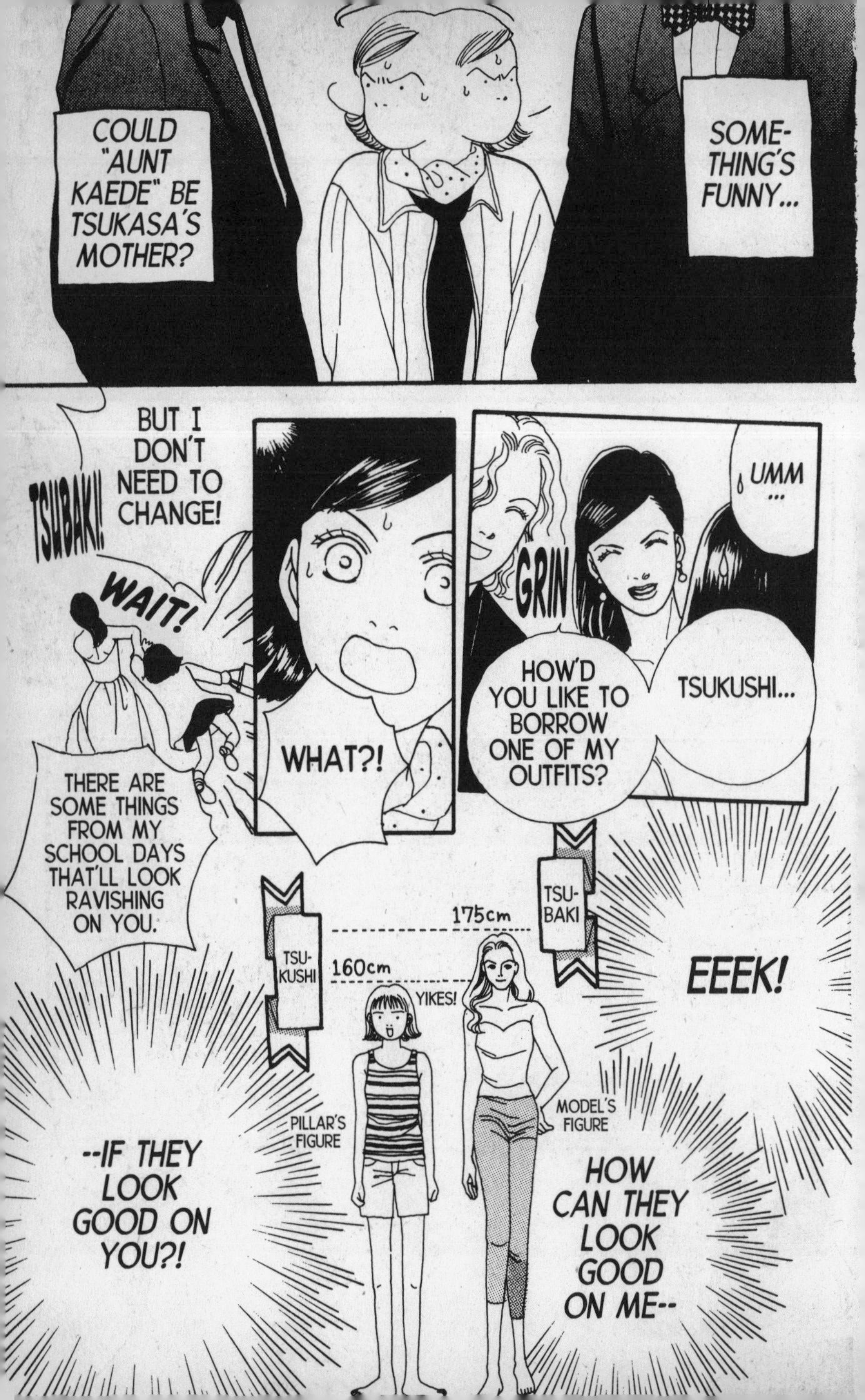
SOMETHING'S FUNNY...
COULD "AUNT KAEDE" BE TSUKASA'S MOTHER?
UMM ...
GRIN
TSUKUSHI...
HOW'D YOU LIKE TO BORROW ONE OF MY OUTFITS?
WHAT?!
BUT I DON'T NEED TO CHANGE!
TSUBAKI!!
WAIT!
THERE ARE SOME THINGS FROM MY SCHOOL DAYS THAT'LL LOOK RAVISHING ON YOU.
TSUBAKI
175cm
TSUKUSHI
160cm
EEEK!
YIKES!
MODEL'S FIGURE
PILLAR'S FIGURE
HOW CAN THEY LOOK GOOD ON ME--
--IF THEY LOOK GOOD ON YOU?!

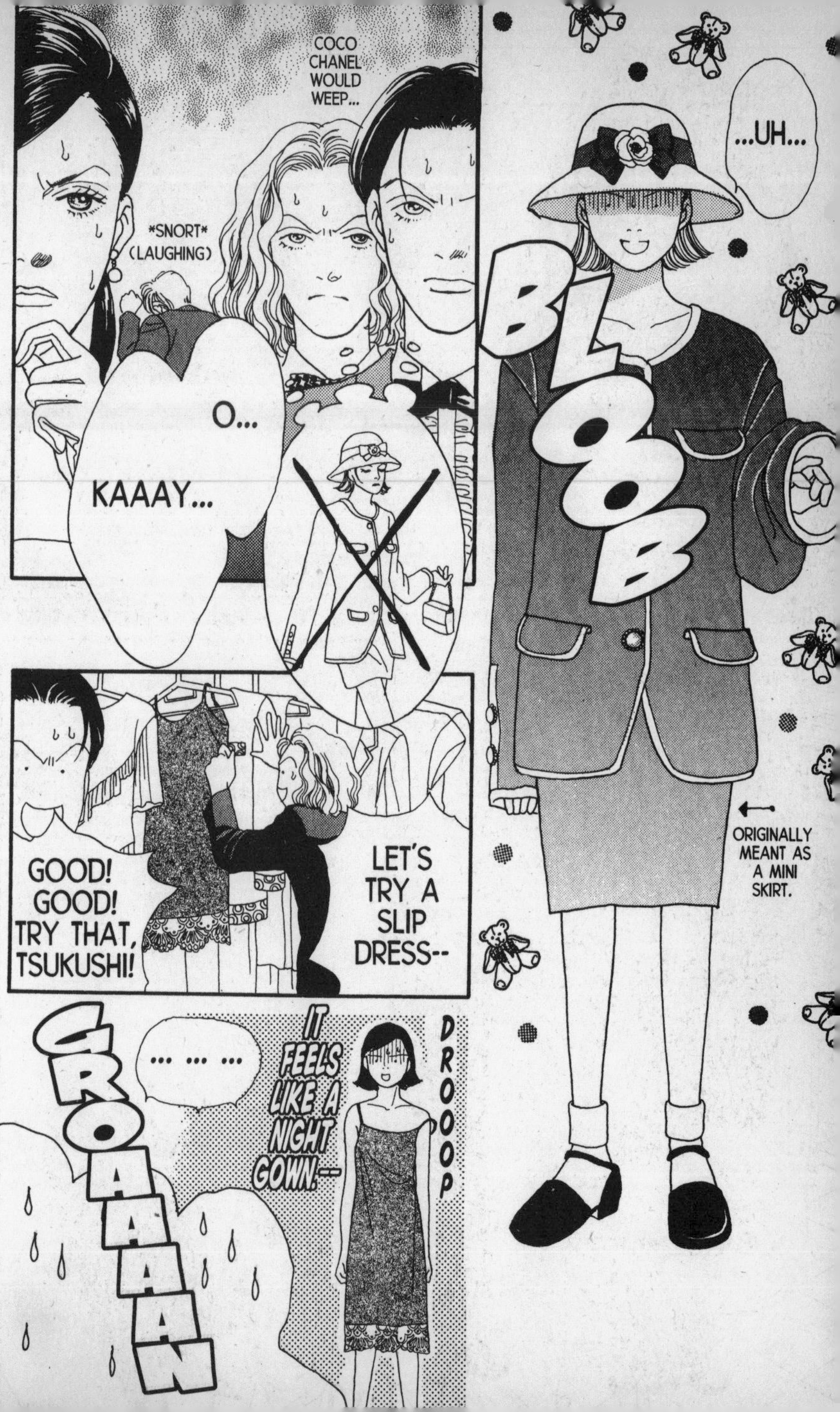
...UH...
BLOOB
ORIGINALLY MEANT AS A MINI SKIRT.
COCO CHANEL WOULD WEEP...
SNORT (LAUGHING)
O... KAAAY...
LET'S TRY A SLIP DRESS--
GOOD! GOOD! TRY THAT, TSUKUSHI!
DROOOOP
IT FEELS LIKE A NIGHT GOWN.--
... ...
GROAAAAN

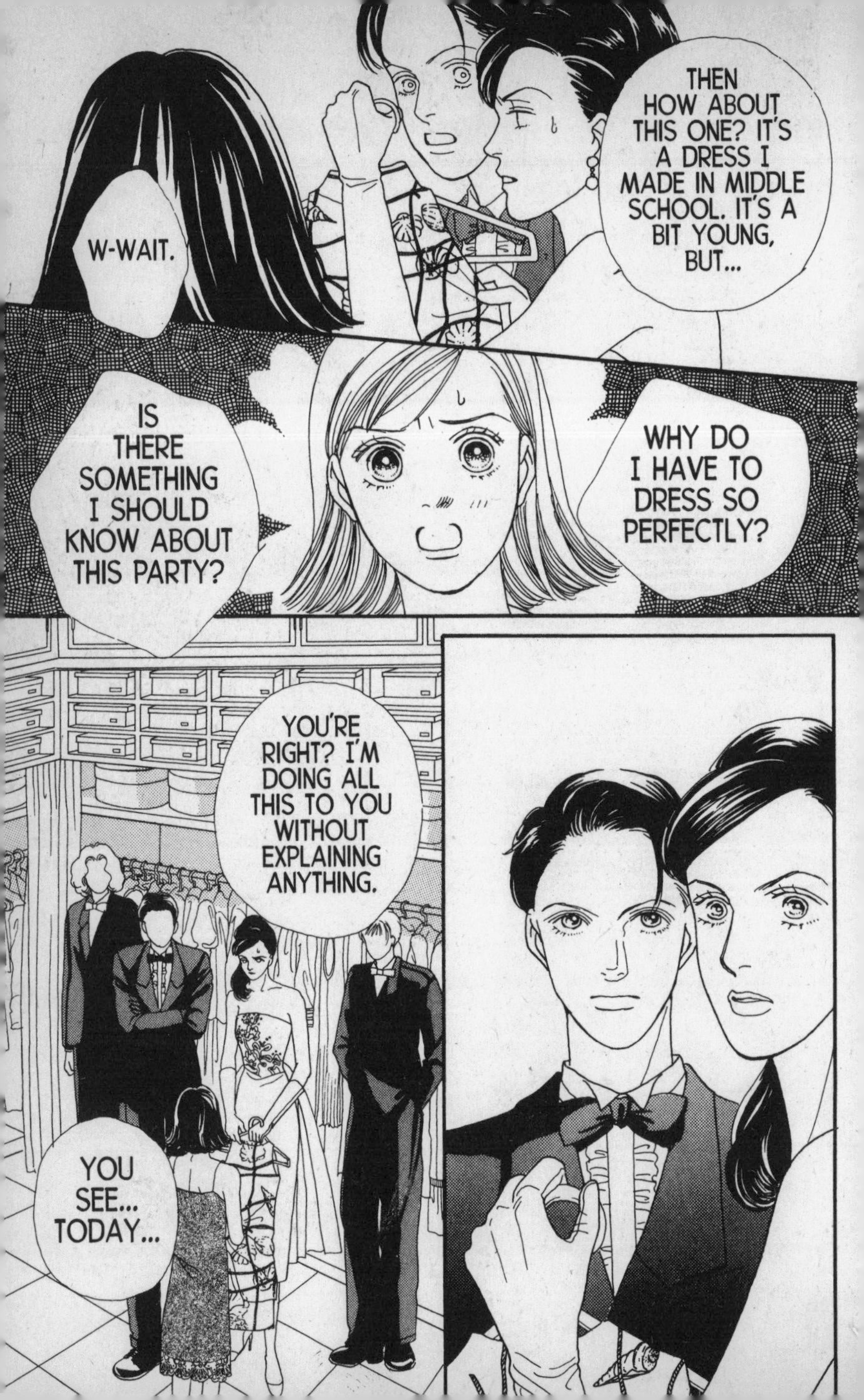
THEN HOW ABOUT THIS ONE? IT'S A DRESS I MADE IN MIDDLE SCHOOL. IT'S A BIT YOUNG, BUT...
W-WAIT.
WHY DO I HAVE TO DRESS SO PERFECTLY?
IS THERE SOMETHING I SHOULD KNOW ABOUT THIS PARTY?
YOU'RE RIGHT? I'M DOING ALL THIS TO YOU WITHOUT EXPLAINING ANYTHING.
YOU SEE... TODAY...

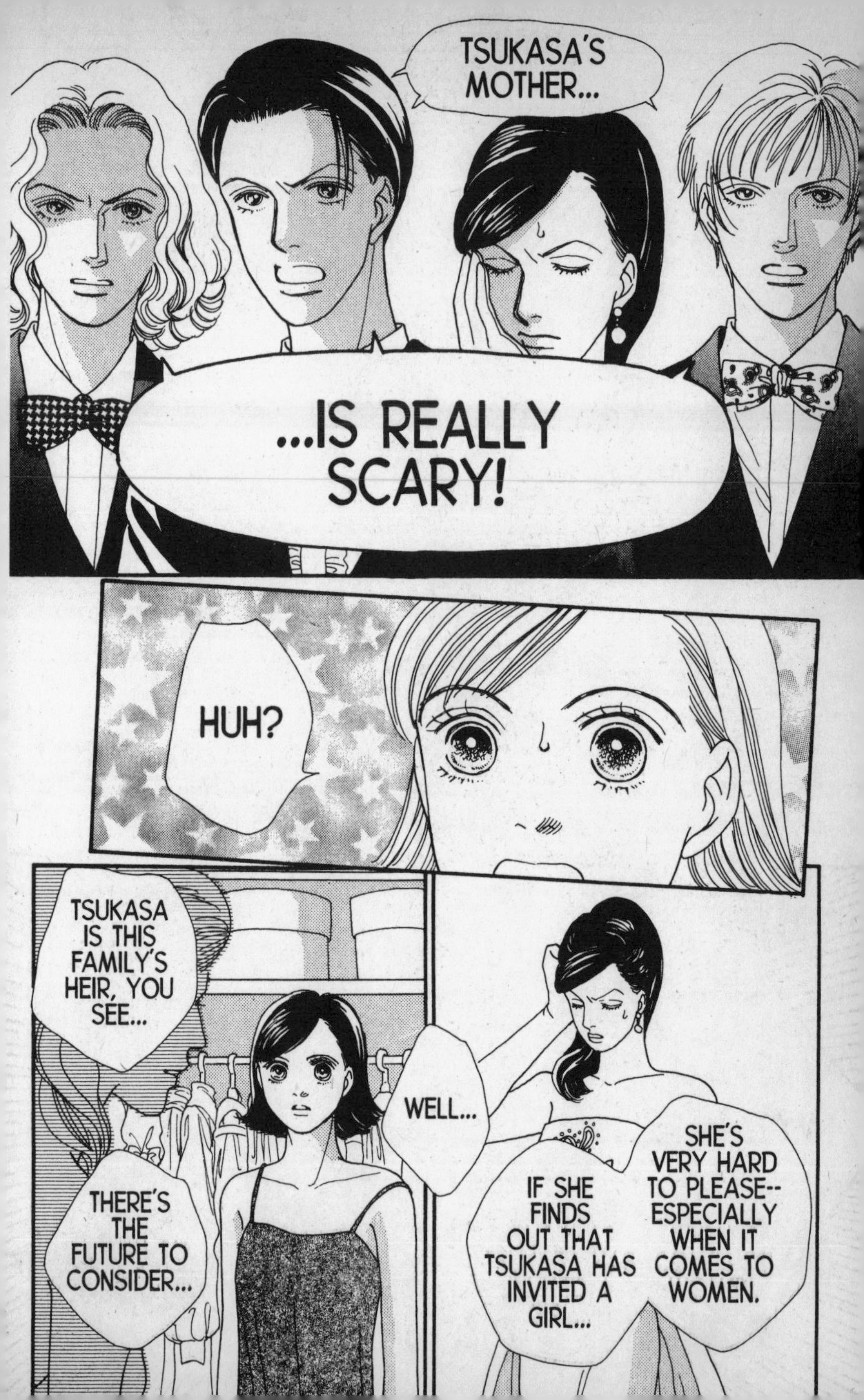
TSUKASA'S MOTHER...
...IS REALLY SCARY!
HUH?
WELL...
SHE'S VERY HARD TO PLEASE-- ESPECIALLY WHEN IT COMES TO WOMEN.
IF SHE FINDS OUT THAT TSUKASA HAS INVITED A GIRL...
TSUKASA IS THIS FAMILY'S HEIR, YOU SEE...
THERE'S THE FUTURE TO CONSIDER...

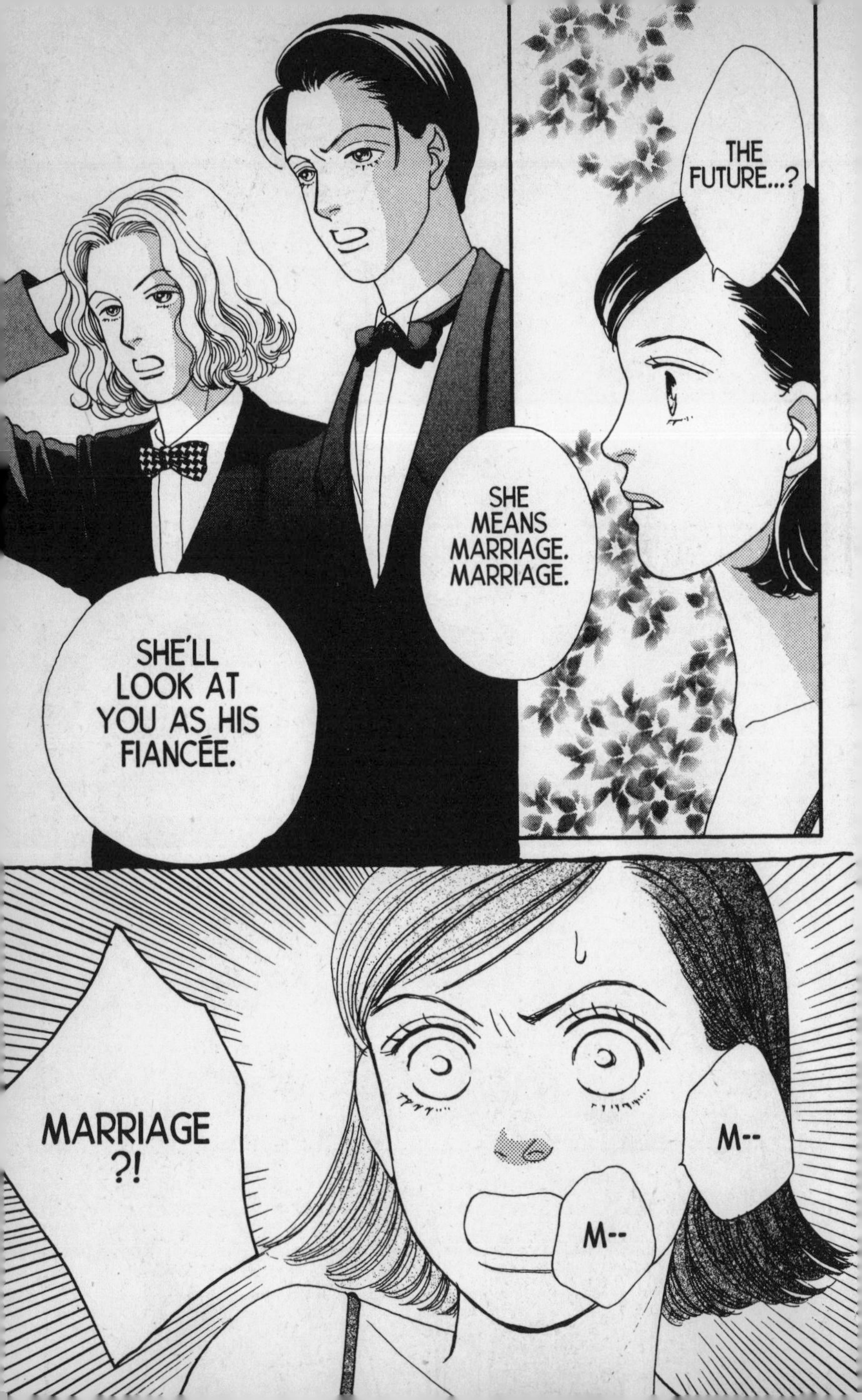
THE FUTURE...?
SHE MEANS MARRIAGE. MARRIAGE.
SHE'LL LOOK AT YOU AS HIS FIANCÉE.
M--
M--
MARRIAGE ?!

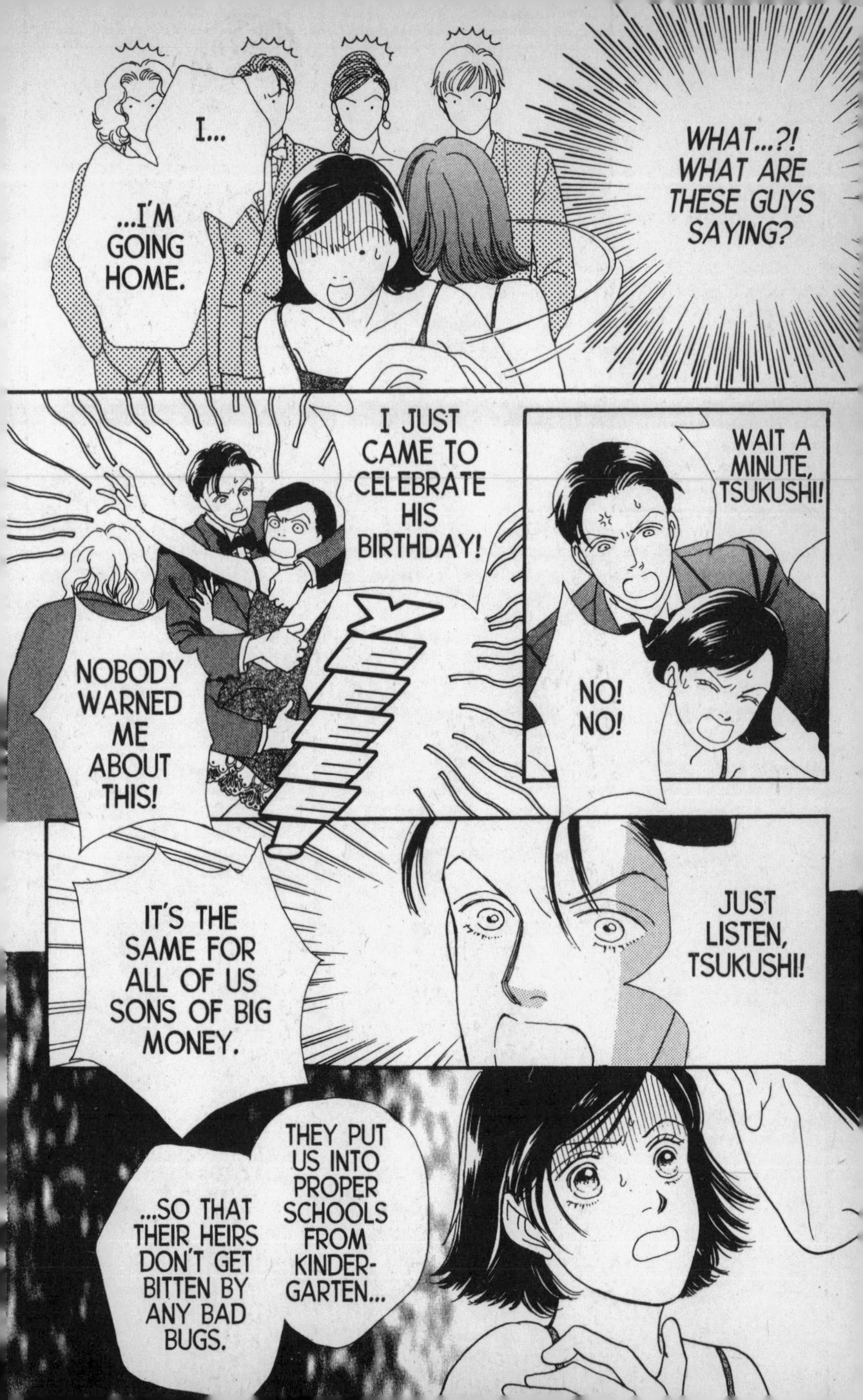
WHAT...?! WHAT ARE THESE GUYS SAYING?
I...
...I'M GOING HOME.
WAIT A MINUTE, TSUKUSHI!
NO! NO!
I JUST CAME TO CELEBRATE HIS BIRTHDAY!
NOBODY WARNED ME ABOUT THIS!
JUST LISTEN, TSUKUSHI!
IT'S THE SAME FOR ALL OF US SONS OF BIG MONEY.
THEY PUT US INTO PROPER SCHOOLS FROM KINDER-GARTEN...
...SO THAT THEIR HEIRS DON'T GET BITTEN BY ANY BAD BUGS.

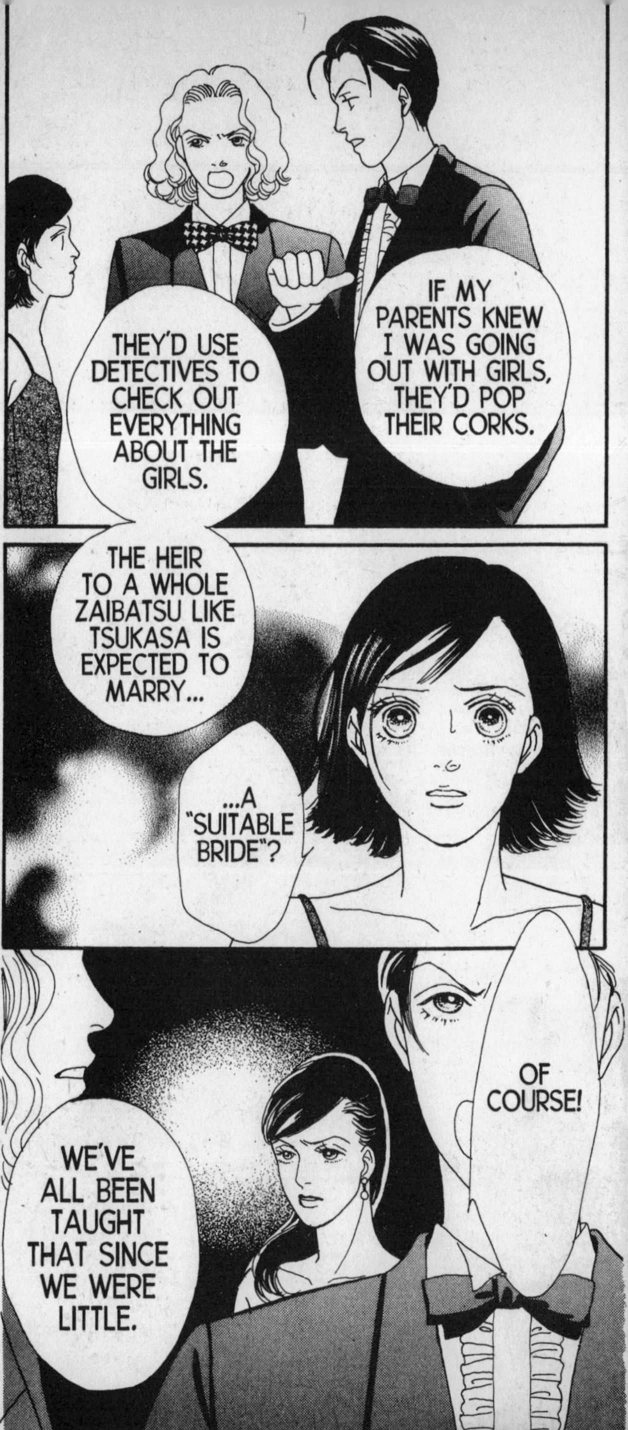
IF MY PARENTS KNEW I WAS GOING OUT WITH GIRLS, THEY'D POP THEIR CORKS.
THEY'D USE DETECTIVES TO CHECK OUT EVERYTHING ABOUT THE GIRLS.
THE HEIR TO A WHOLE ZAIBATSU LIKE TSUKASA IS EXPECTED TO MARRY...
...A "SUITABLE BRIDE"?
OF COURSE!
WE'VE ALL BEEN TAUGHT THAT SINCE WE WERE LITTLE.

And now...
This is the last quarter-page for Vol. 15.

Actually, I'll be traveling to Spain next week. But I have so much work to do before I leave that it's making me dizzy. Right now, as I'm writing this, it is 6:30 in the morning. Not that I woke up early...I'll be going to bed soon! I'll tell you about my Spain trip in Vol. 16!!

Of course, I'll probably sit there doing nothing.

Well, thanks for reading my book!!

See you next volume!

Yoko Kamio

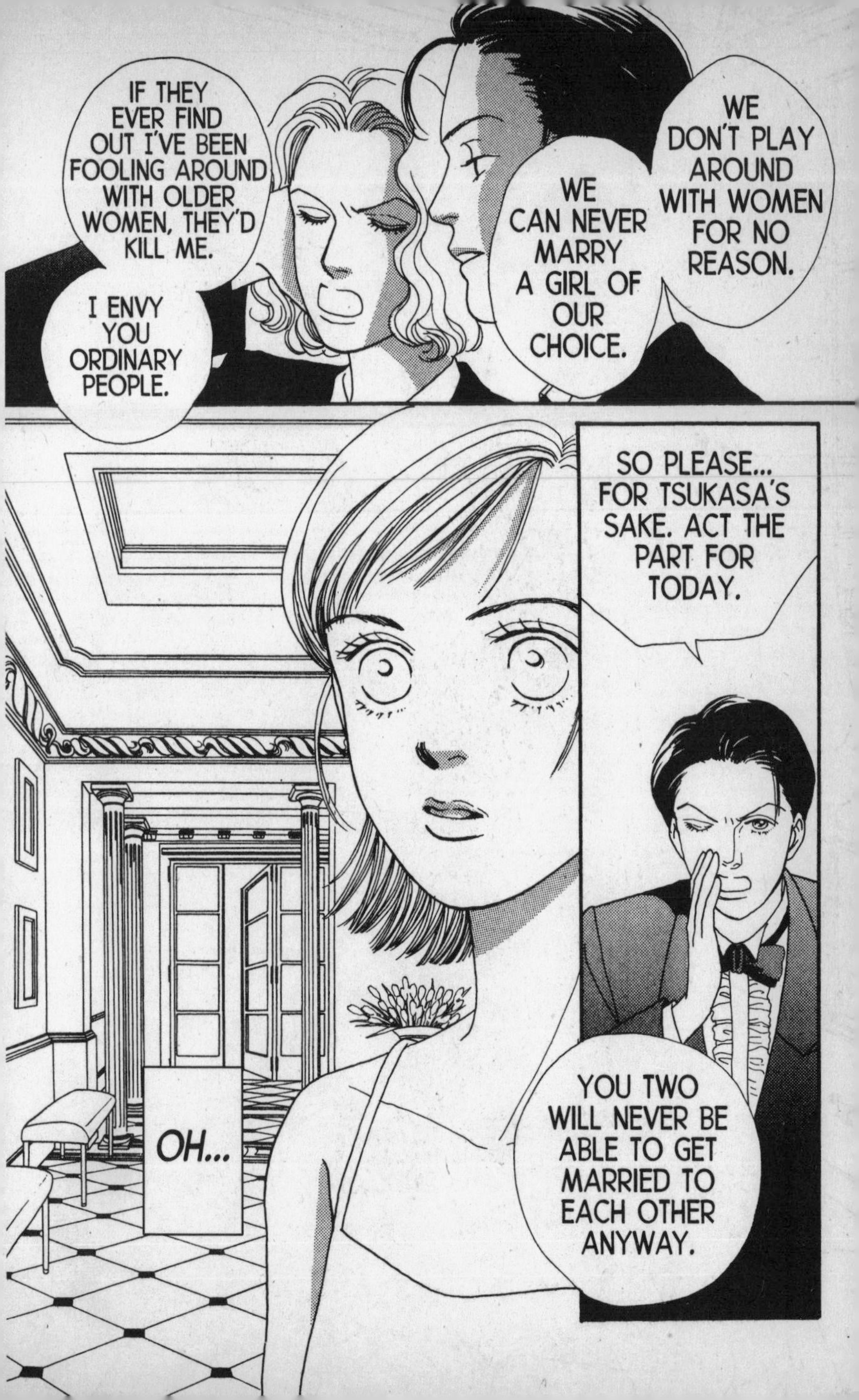
WE DON'T PLAY AROUND WITH WOMEN FOR NO REASON.
WE CAN NEVER MARRY A GIRL OF OUR CHOICE.
IF THEY EVER FIND OUT I'VE BEEN FOOLING AROUND WITH OLDER WOMEN, THEY'D KILL ME.
I ENVY YOU ORDINARY PEOPLE.
SO PLEASE... FOR TSUKASA'S SAKE. ACT THE PART FOR TODAY.
YOU TWO WILL NEVER BE ABLE TO GET MARRIED TO EACH OTHER ANYWAY.
OH...

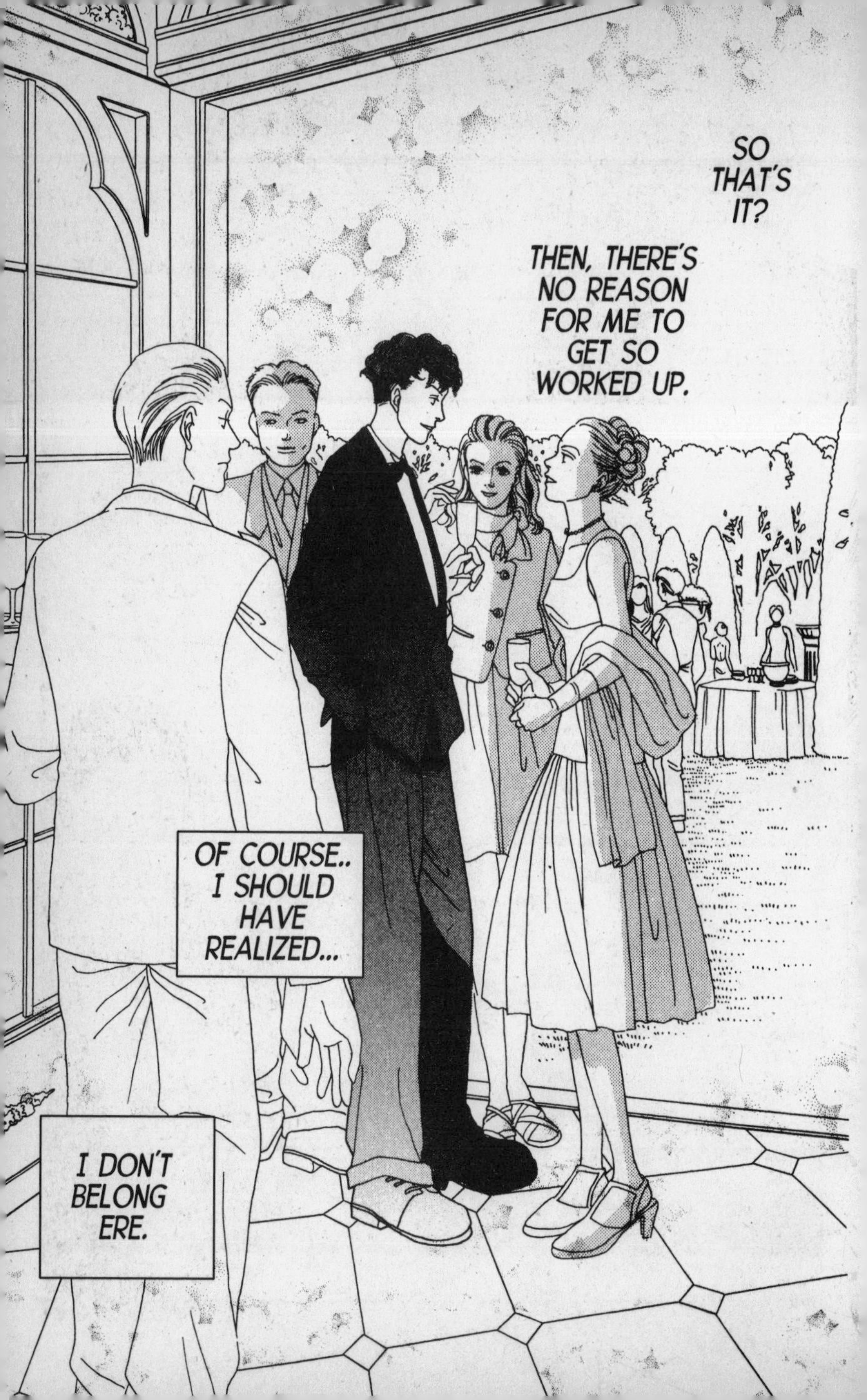
SO THAT'S IT?
THEN, THERE'S NO REASON FOR ME TO GET SO WORKED UP.
OF COURSE.. I SHOULD HAVE REALIZED...
I DON'T BELONG ERE.

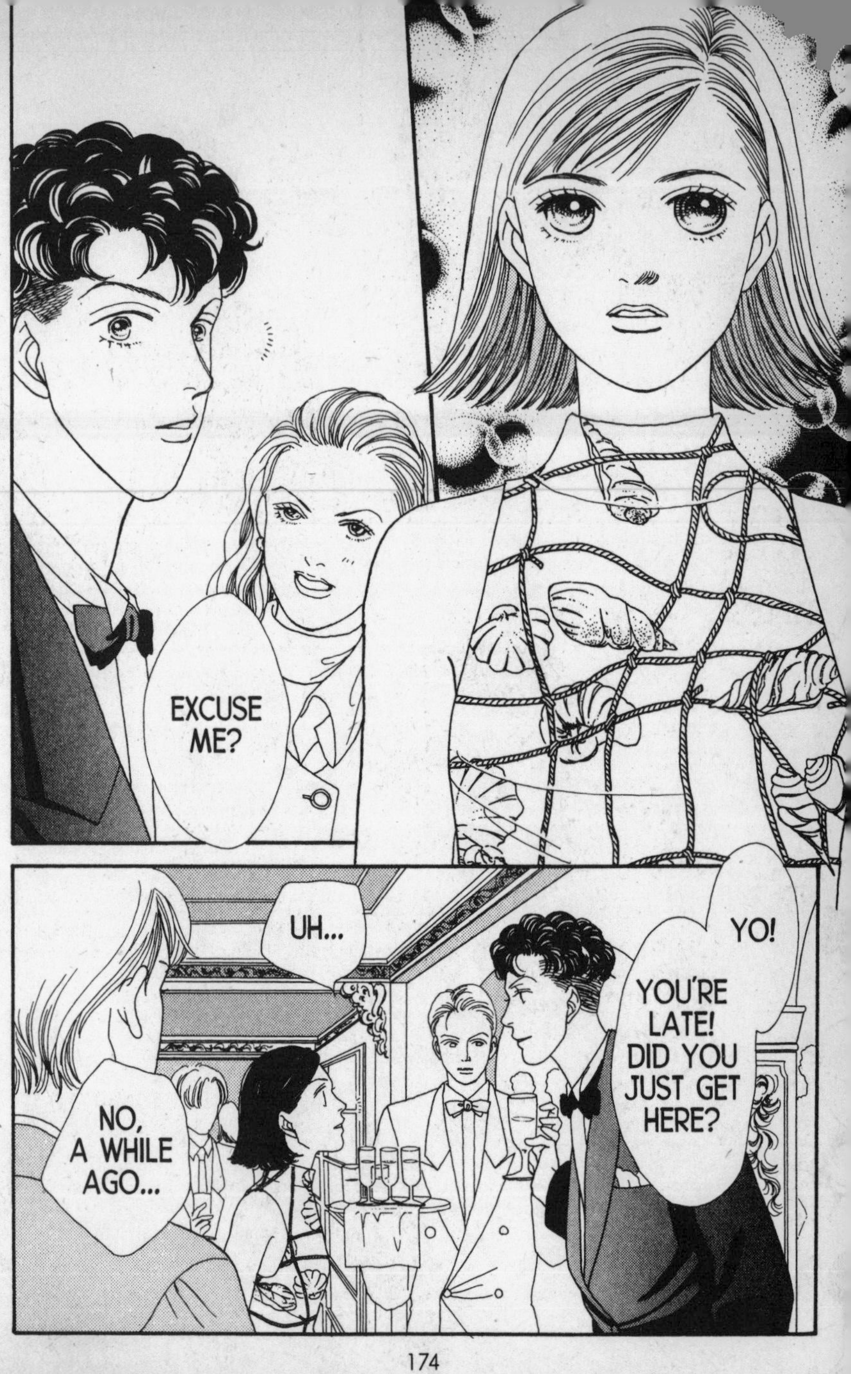
EXCUSE ME?
YO!
YOU'RE LATE! DID YOU JUST GET HERE?
UH...
NO, A WHILE AGO...

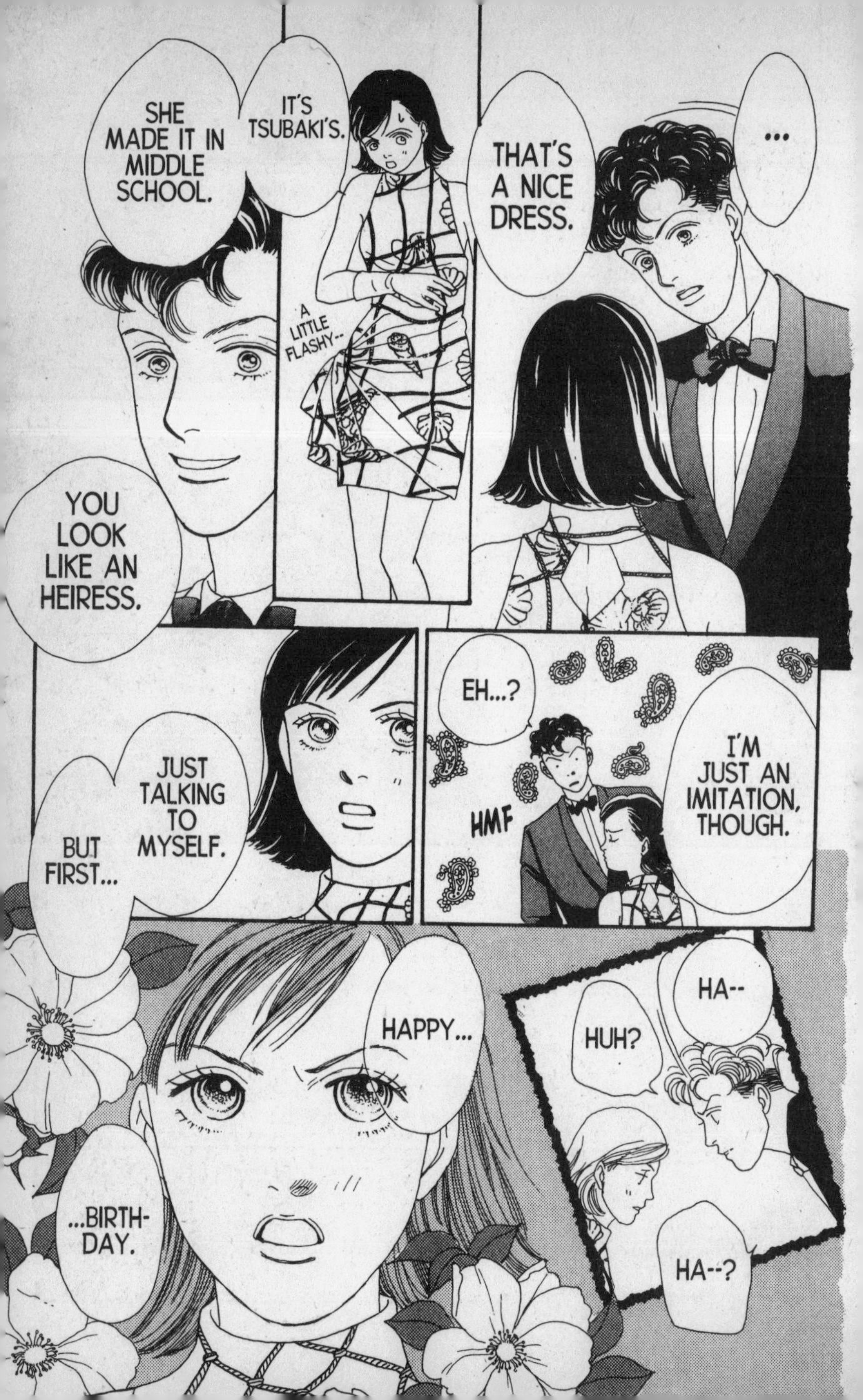
...
THAT'S A NICE DRESS.
IT'S TSUBAKI'S.
A LITTLE FLASHY--
SHE MADE IT IN MIDDLE SCHOOL.
YOU LOOK LIKE AN HEIRESS.
I'M JUST AN IMITATION, THOUGH.
EH...?
HMF
JUST TALKING TO MYSELF.
BUT FIRST...
HA--
HUH?
HA--?
HAPPY...
...BIRTH-DAY.

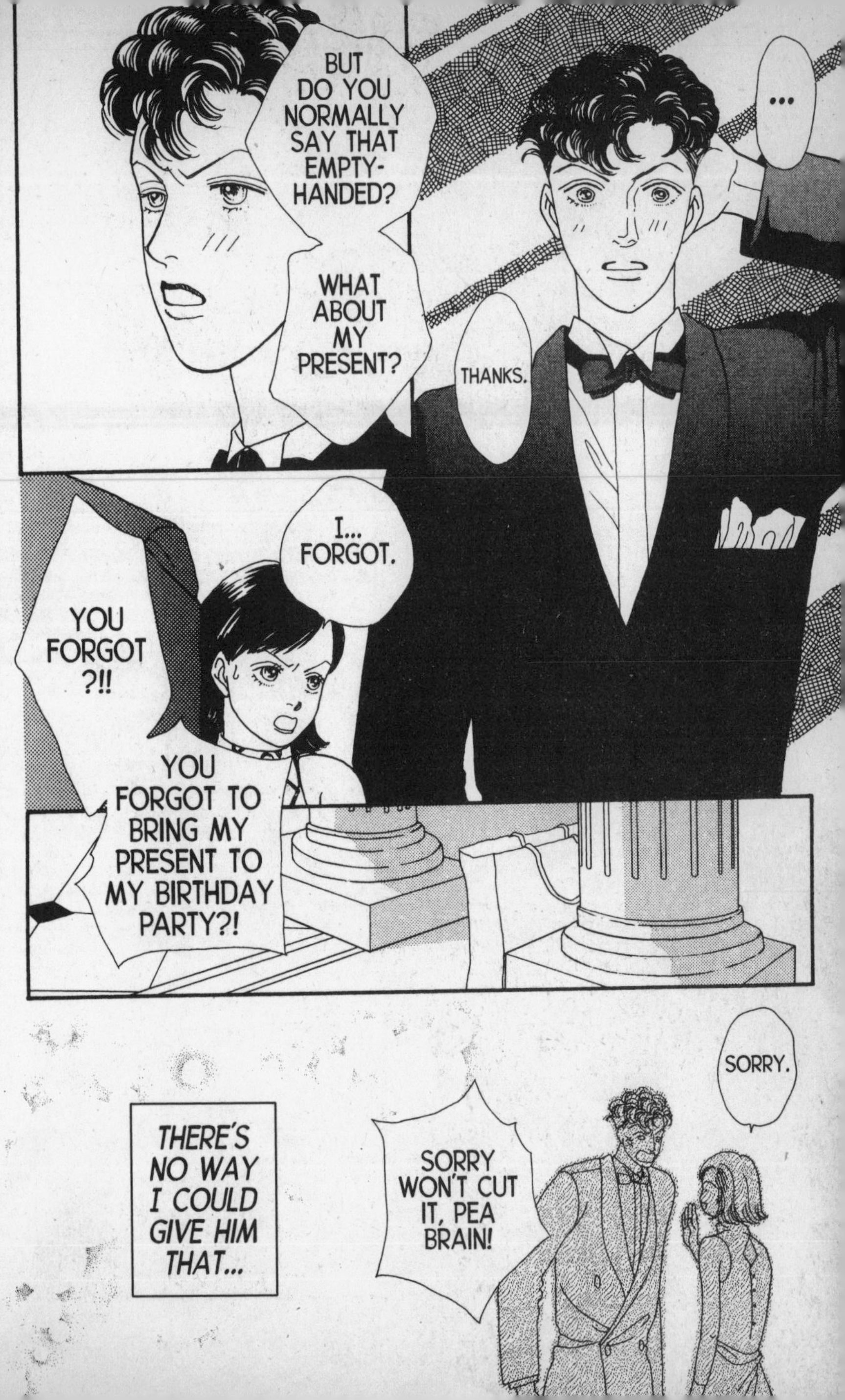
...
THANKS.
BUT DO YOU NORMALLY SAY THAT EMPTY-HANDED?
WHAT ABOUT MY PRESENT?
I... FORGOT.
YOU FORGOT ?!!
YOU FORGOT TO BRING MY PRESENT TO MY BIRTHDAY PARTY?!
SORRY.
SORRY WON'T CUT IT, PEA BRAIN!
THERE'S NO WAY I COULD GIVE HIM THAT...

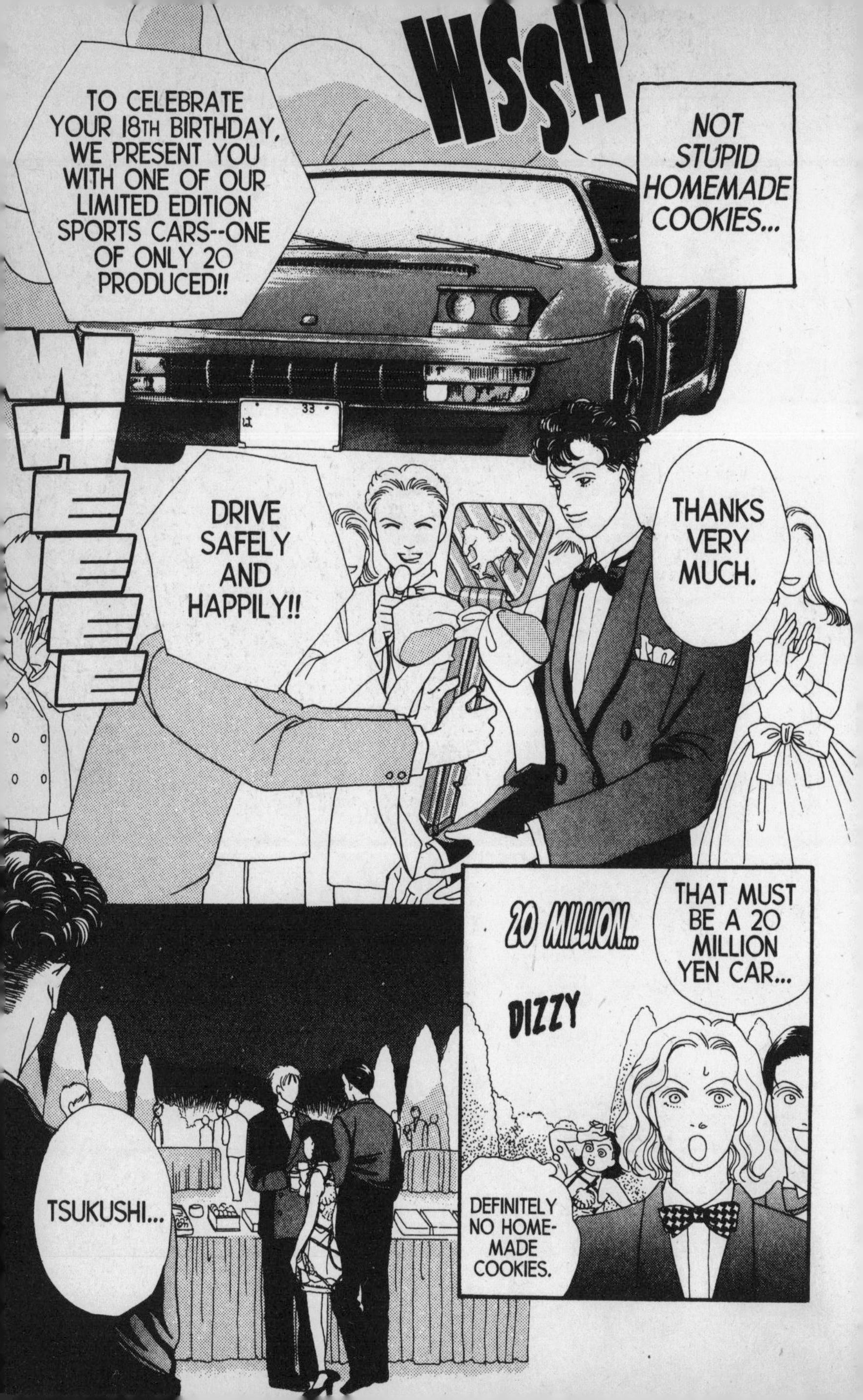
WSSH
NOT STUPID HOMEMADE COOKIES...
TO CELEBRATE YOUR 18TH BIRTHDAY, WE PRESENT YOU WITH ONE OF OUR LIMITED EDITION SPORTS CARS--ONE OF ONLY 20 PRODUCED!!
WHEEEEE
DRIVE SAFELY AND HAPPILY!!
THANKS VERY MUCH.
THAT MUST BE A 20 MILLION YEN CAR...
20 MILLION...
DIZZY
DEFINITELY NO HOME-MADE COOKIES.
TSUKUSHI...

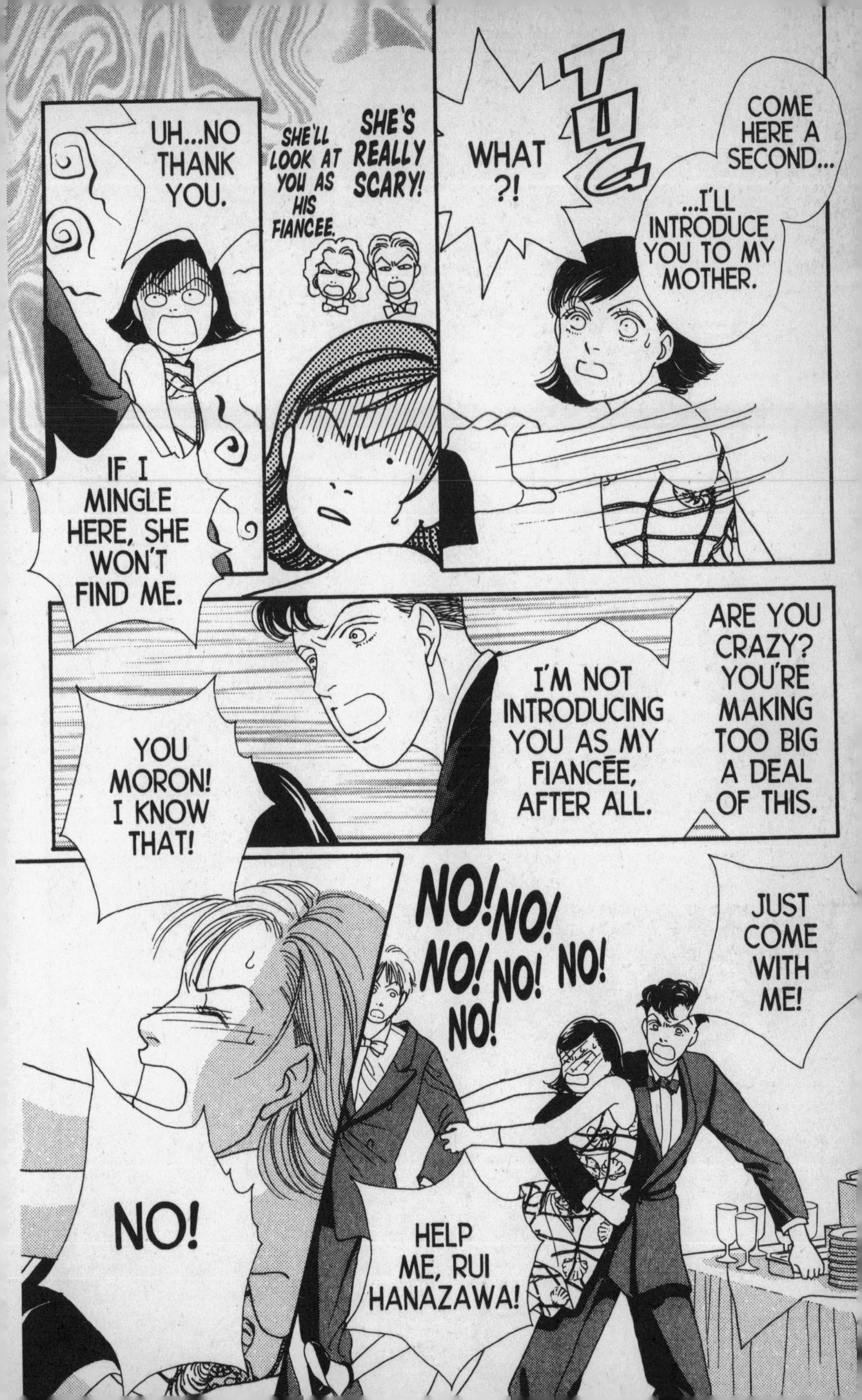
COME HERE A SECOND...
...I'LL INTRODUCE YOU TO MY MOTHER.
TUG
WHAT ?!
SHE'S REALLY SCARY!
SHE'LL LOOK AT YOU AS HIS FIANCEE.
UH...NO THANK YOU.
IF I MINGLE HERE, SHE WON'T FIND ME.
ARE YOU CRAZY? YOU'RE MAKING TOO BIG A DEAL OF THIS.
I'M NOT INTRODUCING YOU AS MY FIANCÉE, AFTER ALL.
YOU MORON! I KNOW THAT!
JUST COME WITH ME!
NO! NO! NO! NO! NO! NO!
HELP ME, RUI HANAZAWA!
NO!

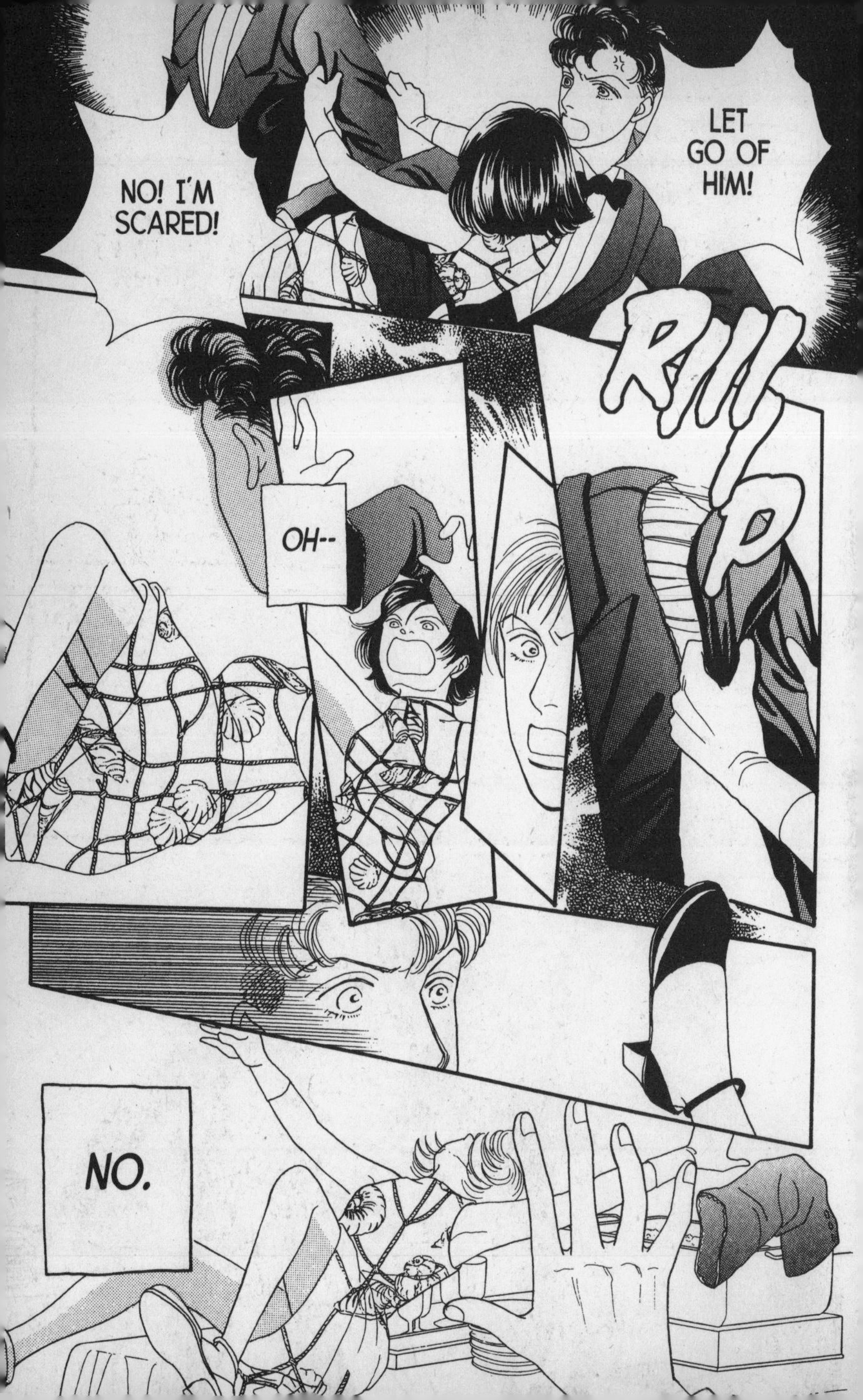
LET GO OF HIM!
NO! I'M SCARED!
RIIIP
OH--
NO.

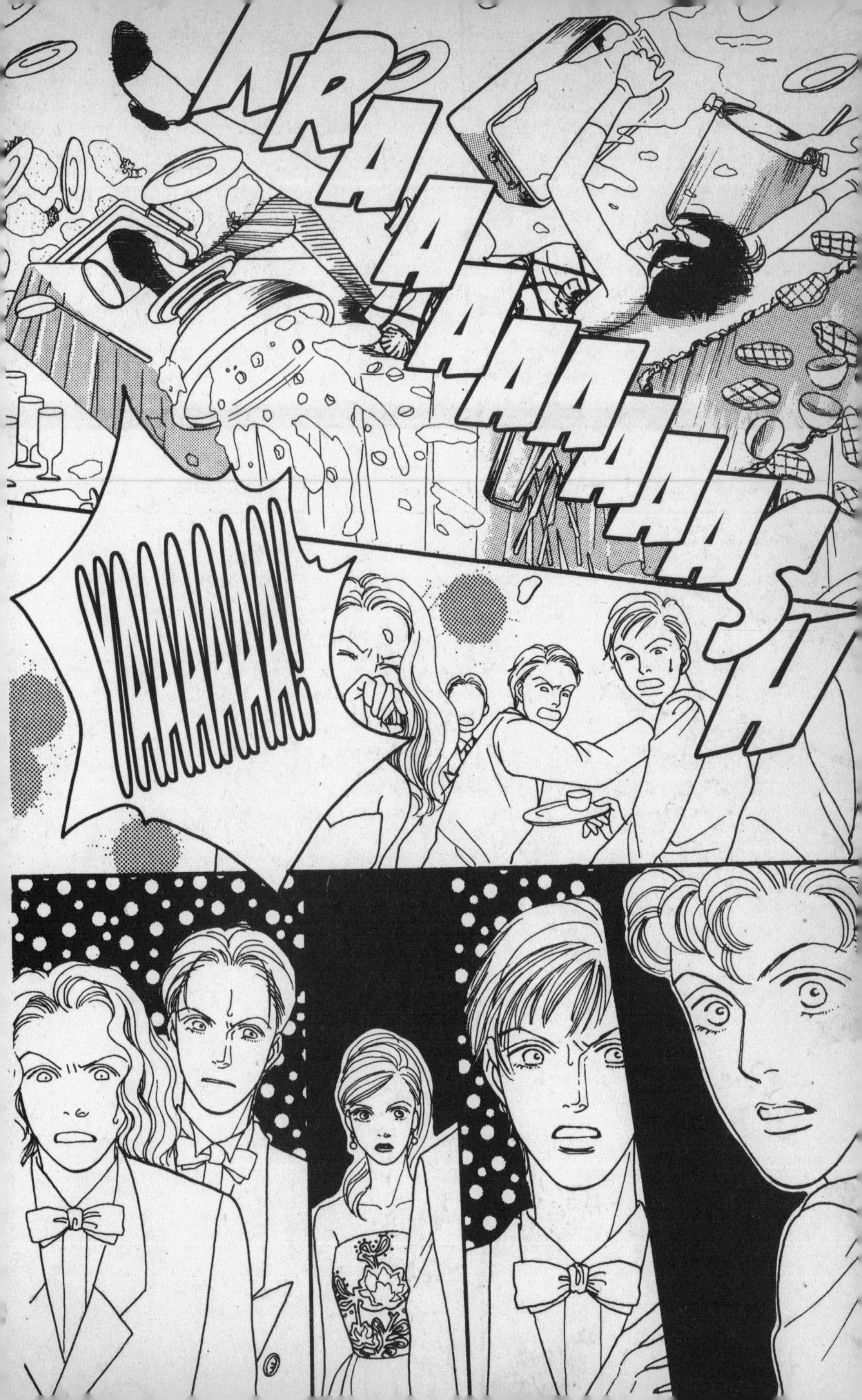
WRAAAAAAAAASH
YAAAAAAA!!

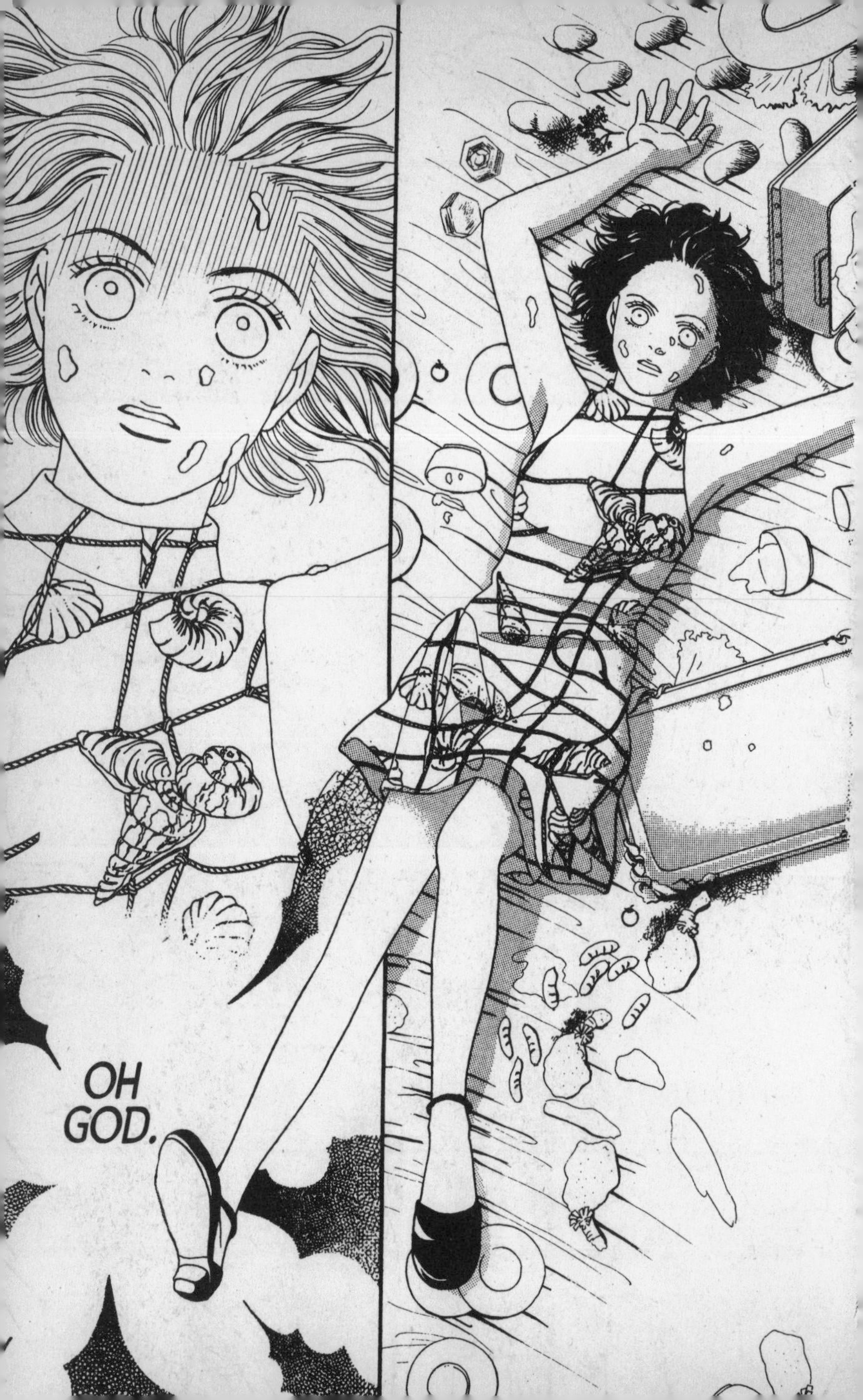
OH GOD.

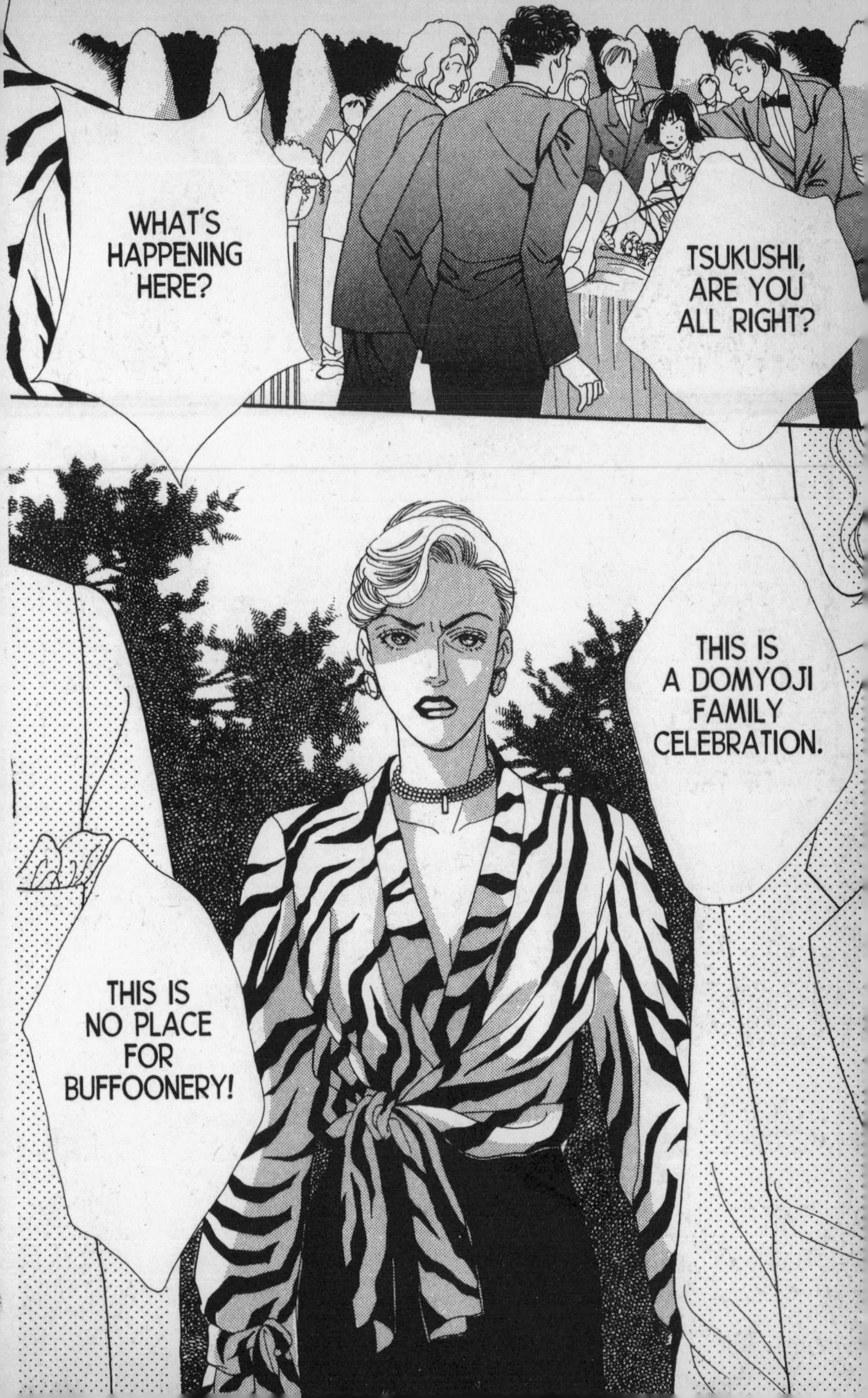
TSUKUSHI, ARE YOU ALL RIGHT?
WHAT'S HAPPENING HERE?
THIS IS A DOMYOJI FAMILY CELEBRATION.
THIS IS NO PLACE FOR BUFFOONERY!

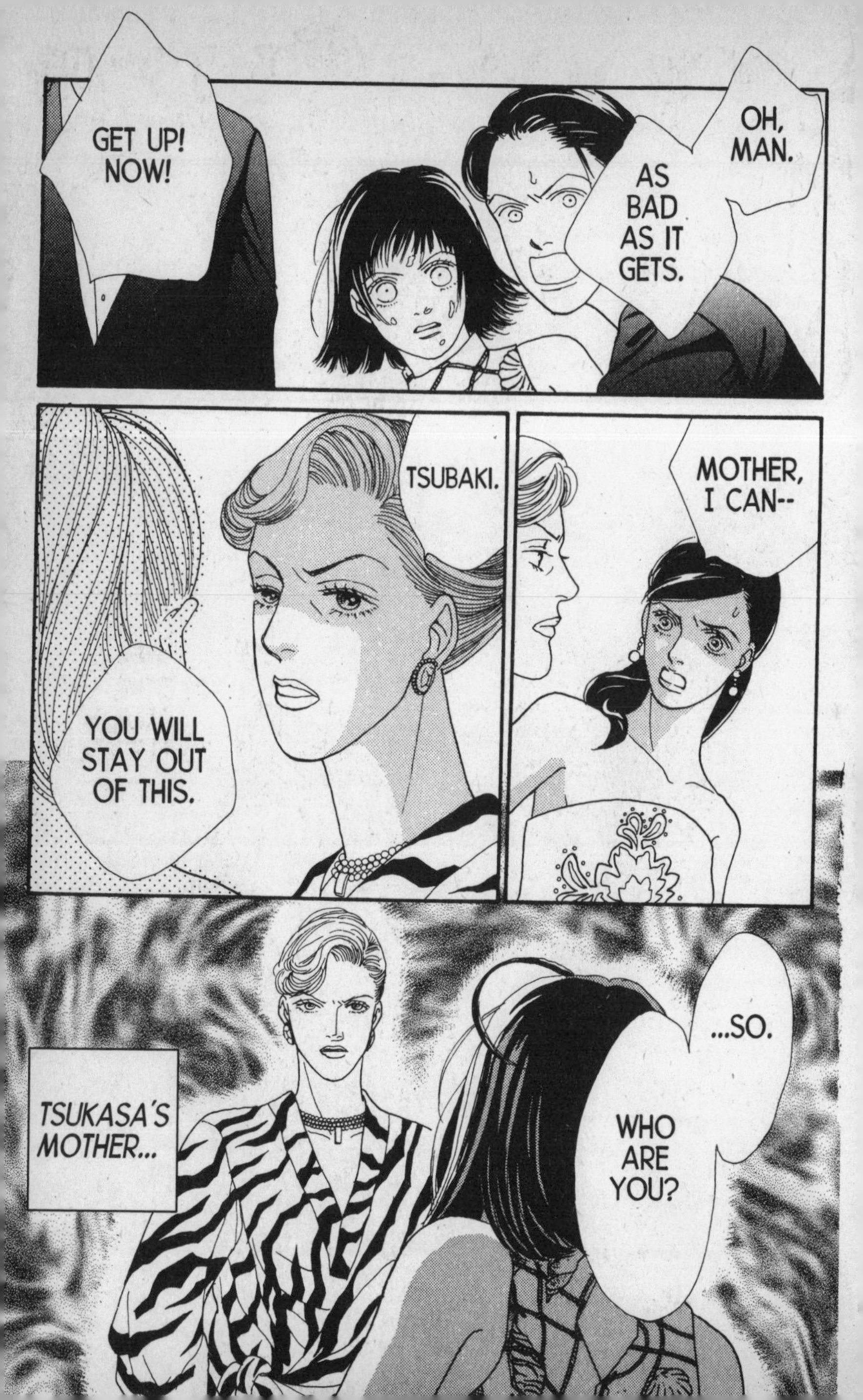
OH, MAN.
AS BAD AS IT GETS.
GET UP! NOW!
MOTHER, I CAN--
TSUBAKI.
YOU WILL STAY OUT OF THIS.
...SO.
WHO ARE YOU?
TSUKASA'S MOTHER...

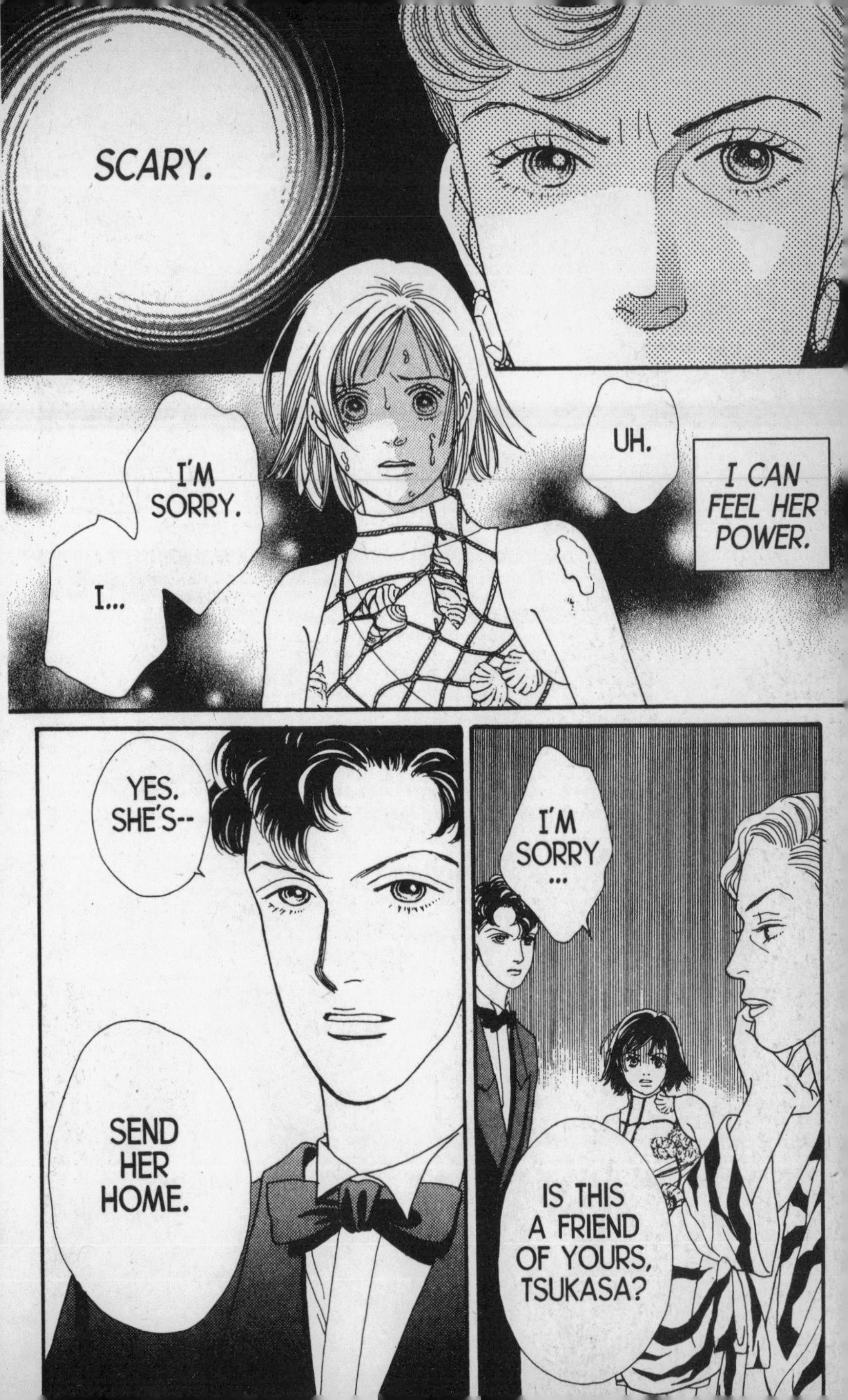
SCARY.
I CAN FEEL HER POWER.
UH.
I'M SORRY.
I...
I'M SORRY ...
IS THIS A FRIEND OF YOURS, TSUKASA?
YES. SHE'S--
SEND HER HOME.

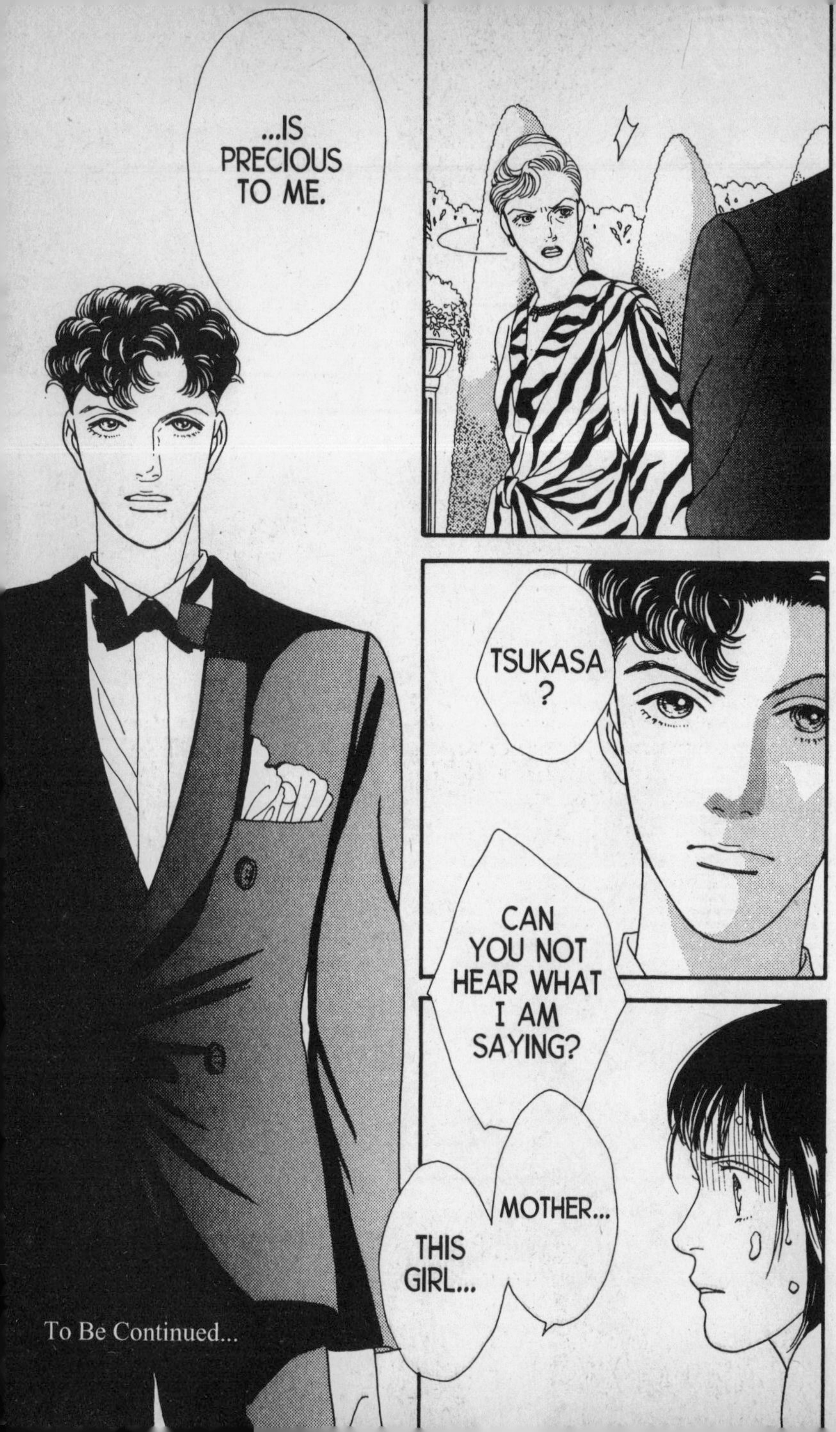
TSUKASA?
CAN YOU NOT HEAR WHAT I AM SAYING?
MOTHER...
THIS GIRL...
...IS PRECIOUS TO ME.
To Be Continued...

If you enjoyed this volume of

BOYS over FLOWERS™

Hana Yori Dango

then here's some more manga you might be interested in.

©1991 Yumi TAMURA/ Shogakukan Inc.

BASARA

Yumi Tamura's *BASARA* is a post-apocalyptic fantasy/adventure series that was one of the most popular shôjo manga of the '90s in Japan. *BASARA* takes place in a very different setting than *BOYS OVER FLOWERS*, but it is similar at its core. They both feature a strong female fighting against an oppressive group. This is the story of how a young girl becomes "the child of destiny," seeking revenge for her dead twin brother. *BASARA* is heavier on the action and lighter on the humor than *BOYS OVER FLOWERS*.

©1992 Yuu WATASE/ Shogakukan Inc.

FUSHIGI YÛGI

In Yuu Watase's *FUSHIGI YÛGI* we follow the young girl, Miaka Yuki, as she gets pulled into the world of the book, The Universe of the Four Gods. Within this book is a fictional, ancient Chinese world. In this world she becomes the priestess of the god Suzaku and must find all seven of her Celestial-Warrior protectors. This story is filled with romance and action, with a dash of humor.

©1997 Yuu WATASE/ Shogakukan Inc.

CERES: CELESTIAL LEGEND

Also by Yuu Watase, *CERES: CELESTIAL LEGEND* is somewhat darker than *FUSHIGI YÛGI*. Sixteen-year-old Aya Mikage's body houses a legendary power, and her family is determined to kill her in order to suppress it.

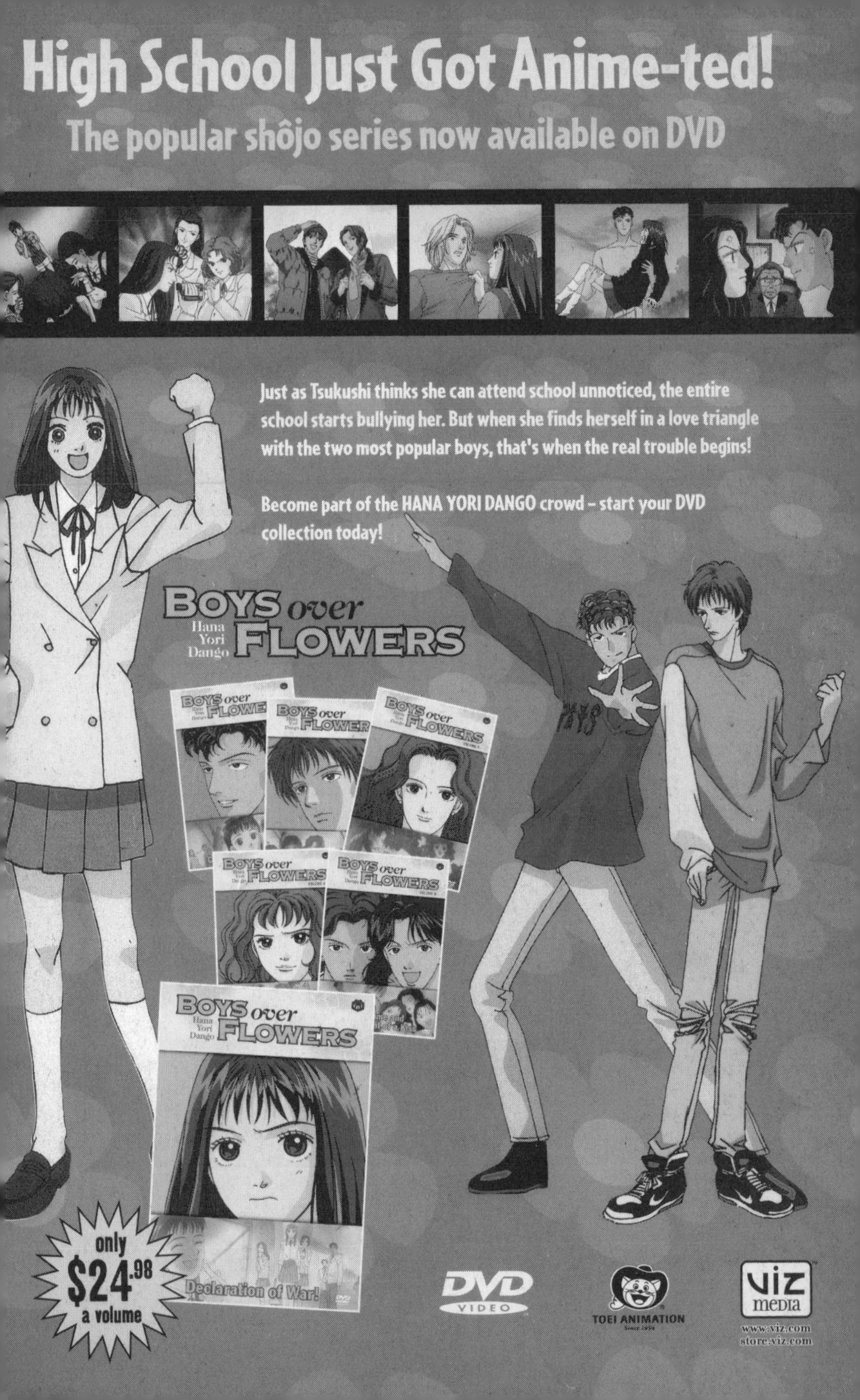
High School Just Got Anime-ted!
The popular shôjo series now available on DVD
Just as Tsukushi thinks she can attend school unnoticed, the entire school starts bullying her. But when she finds herself in a love triangle with the two most popular boys, that's when the real trouble begins!
Become part of the HANA YORI DANGO crowd – start your DVD collection today!
BOYS over FLOWERS
Hana Yori Dango
Declaration of War!
only $24.98 a volume
DVD VIDEO
TOEI ANIMATION
viz media
www.viz.com
store.viz.com

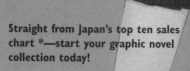

LOVE SHOJO? LET US KNOW!

☐ Please do NOT send me information about VIZ Media products, news and events, special offers, or other information.

☐ Please do NOT send me information from VIZ' trusted business partners.

Name: _____

Address: _____

City: _____ **State:** _____ **Zip:** _____

E-mail: _____

☐ **Male** ☐ **Female**   **Date of Birth** (mm/dd/yyyy): ___ / ___ / _____   (Under 13? Parental consent required)

What race/ethnicity do you consider yourself? (check all that apply)

☐ White/Caucasian   ☐ Black/African American   ☐ Hispanic/Latino

☐ Asian/Pacific Islander   ☐ Native American/Alaskan Native   ☐ Other: _____

What VIZ shojo title(s) did you purchase? (indicate title(s) purchased)

_____

What other shojo titles from other publishers do you own? _____

_____

Reason for purchase: (check all that apply)

☐ Special offer   ☐ Favorite title / author / artist / genre

☐ Gift   ☐ Recommendation   ☐ Collection

☐ Read excerpt in VIZ manga sampler   ☐ Other _____

Where did you make your purchase? (please check one)

☐ Comic store   ☐ Bookstore   ☐ Mass/Grocery Store

☐ Newsstand   ☐ Video/Video Game Store

☐ Online (site:_____)   ☐ Other _____

How many shojo titles have you purchased i

(please check one from each column)

SHOJO MANGA

- [ ] None
- [ ] 1 – 4
- [ ] 5 – 10
- [ ] 11+

VIZ SHOJO

- [ ] None
- [ ] 1 – 4
- [ ] 5 – 10

What do you like most about sh

- [ ] Romance
- [ ] Comedy
- [ ] Other ______

Do you purchase every volume of your favorite shojo series?

- [ ] Yes! Gotta have 'em as my own
- [ ] No. Please explain: ______

Who are your favorite shojo authors / artists? ______

What shojo titles would like you translated and sold in English? ______

THANK YOU! Please send the completed form to:

NJW Research
ATTN: VIZ Media Shojo Survey
42 Catharine Street
Poughkeepsie, NY 12601

Your privacy is very important to us. All information provided will be used for internal purposes only and will not be sold or otherwise divulged.